Phenomenology in an
African Context

SUNY series, Philosophy and Race

Robert Bernasconi and T. Denean Sharpley-Whiting, editors

Phenomenology in an African Context

Contributions and Challenges

Edited by

ABRAHAM OLIVIER, M. JOHN LAMOLA,
AND JUSTIN SANDS

SUNY
PRESS

Published by State University of New York Press, Albany

For information, contact State University of New York Press, Albany, NY
www.sunypress.edu

Library of Congress Cataloging-in-Publication Data

Names: Olivier, Abraham, editor. | Lamola, Malesela John, editor. | Sands, Justin, editor.
Title: Phenomenology in an African context : contributions and challenges / edited by Abraham Olivier, M. John Lamola, and Justin Sands.
Description: Albany, NY : State University of New York Press, [2023] | Series: SUNY series, philosophy and race | Includes bibliographical references and index.
Identifiers: LCCN 2022060816 | ISBN 9781438494876 (hardcover : alk. paper) | ISBN 9781438494883 (ebook) | ISBN 9781438494869 (pbk. : alk. paper)
Subjects: LCSH: Phenomenology. | Philosophy—Africa.
Classification: LCC B829.5 .P473 2023 | DDC 199/.6—dc23/eng/20230628
LC record available at https://lccn.loc.gov/2022060816

10 9 8 7 6 5 4 3 2 1

Contents

Part 3
Art, Culture, Language, Politics, and Liberation

Introduction

ABRAHAM OLIVIER, M. JOHN LAMOLA,
AND JUSTIN SANDS

The contributions to this anthology show in various ways how the African context challenges phenomenology to self-apply its classic method of suspension, that is, to put itself in brackets and self-reflect radically upon the methodological assumptions its proponents make. Such self-reflection makes a difference to the way phenomenology is practiced. Our contributions show in diverse ways how the African context poses challenges that give rise to a difference in practicing phenomenology. These challenges bring to the fore a different, critical African phenomenology of its own, one that expounds the lived experience of those who are marginalized especially because they are black Africans and considered "different." In their respective contributions to this anthology, the authors reflect on what Mabogo More calls a "phenomenology of difference" and Lewis Gordon speaks of as "critical" phenomenology.

The designation "African phenomenology" invites questions about its specific theoretical scope, methodology, and themes compared to related philosophical traditions, in particular Africana and Western (European or Anglo-American) phenomenology, and the larger discursive terrain of African and Africana philosophy, decolonization, and the global movement of phenomenology. African phenomenology, per se, as could be differentiated from *Africana phenomenology* as a species of African diasporic philosophy, has never sought to self-define as a unique methodology of doing philosophy on the African continent. Neither does it have a school of self-proclaimed advocates who have ever sought to sell the phenomenological method as some efficacious way of resolving Africa's philosophical challenges or celebrating her achievements. However, a panoramic analysis of the practice of philosophy in Africa will discern and find abundant traces of both implicit and explicit utilization of the phenomenological method in the variety of endeavors undertaken by African philosophers in making sense of the mysteries and contradictions of Africa of the past and the present. The collection of essays in this anthology is both a testament to this practice and, at the same time, a performative demonstration of such an African phenomenology.

The phenomenological method, with its various theoretical approaches to studying the seminal structures of consciousness from the lived perspective of the first person, has been a cornerstone in the thought of many prominent African philosophers. These include, for example, Paulin Hountondji, Tsenay Serequeberhan, D. A. Masolo, Achille Mbembe, Mabogo More, Noel Chabani Manganyi, Mogobe Ramose, M. John Lamola, Rozena Maart, and proponents of Africana philosophy such as Lucius Outlaw, Paget Henry, George Yancy, Linda Martin Alcoff, and Lewis Gordon. This anthology is fortunate to present the latest works of some of these thinkers.

As evidenced by the seminal works of W. E. B. Du Bois, Léopold Sédar Senghor, and Frantz Fanon, the theoretical focus on the critical analysis of the lived experience of slavery and the prevalent workings of colonialism, with its intersectional modalities of exclusion in race, gender, nationality, culture, class, and religion, has permeated the writings of many African philosophers. This includes African philosophers from the analytical tradition such as Kwasi Wiredu and Kwame Gyekye, and Africana philosophers such as Paul Taylor, Charles Mill, and Naomi Zack. This does not imply that all African and Africana philosophers are phenomenologists. It means rather that, in the main, African and Africana philosophers bear a common phenomenological concern, namely a profound quest for the unveiling of all the nuances of the black African experience.

The three sections of this introduction give an overview of contributions on the scope, methodology, and selected themes of this anthology. Section 1 outlines issues of origin, methodology, and scope; section 2 sketches contributions on the themes of consciousness, identity, existence, and embodiment; and section 3 offers summaries of contributions on themes of art, culture, language, politics, and liberation.

Issues of Origin, Scope, and Methodology

Section 1 of this anthology contains contributions to the origin, scope, and methodology of African phenomenology. This includes Olivier's and Gordon's programmatic overview of the relation between Western, Africana, and African phenomenology. That is followed by Hountondji's autobiographical and counterfactual reflections on "Why Husserl in Africa" and Eldridge's and Schryver's discussions of the work of Hountondji. One can fairly designate Hountondji as the father of African phenomenology. Therefore, we have decided to grant a significant part of section 1 to Hountondji's work, in particular to his influential critical adoption of Husserl's writings. Now to a sketch of the contributions.

In "African Phenomenology—What Is That?" Abraham Olivier introduces the term "African phenomenology" in distinction to Western (European or Anglo-American) and Africana phenomenology. On the one hand, he shows that African phenomenologists often make use of Western phenomenologists in their thinking. This includes, for instance, references of Hountondji to Husserl, More to Sartre, Serequeberhan to Heidegger, and Mbembe to Merleau-Ponty. These are all contributors to this anthology and on their own terms can be considered grounding proponents of African phenomenology. This does not mean, on the other hand, that Africans are not original on their own terms. Olivier consequently identifies four distinctive approaches characterizing African phenomenology. They include critical transcendental phenomenology, existential phenomenology, hermeneutical phenomenology, and a postphenomenological approach. These approaches show both commonalities and distinctions between phenomenologists inside and outside the African context.

In "Some Reflections from Africana Phenomenology on African Phenomenology," Lewis Gordon focuses on his argument of "ontological suspension." He argues that putting to the side ontological claims facilitates a relationship to reality and meaning that affords addressing challenges to the legitimacy of reason as posed by Africana or African diasporic philosophy and is, thus, of relevance to contemporary African phenomenology, which also faces rising critical concerns from the project of decolonizing thought. African phenomenology accordingly relates to phenomenology as articulated by European thinkers such as Husserl, Dilthey, Stein, Sartre, and Merleau-Ponty not as the latter standing as robust universality in relation to which the former is a particularity, but instead as particularities of something greater than themselves. The result is a phenomenological bracketing of European claims on the universality of reason toward developing a shift in the geography of reason. African phenomenology is part of the project of shifting the geography of reason, of unshackling the chains of colonial/neocolonial chauvinism through the realization that all thinking is a human affair and that human beings think everywhere. Gordon argues that such suspension requires decisions and in the process of making decisions, one learns not least to be creative and to invent new ways of thinking. In this sense, African phenomenology poses a radical critical challenge to bracket and rethink phenomenology itself.

In "Why Husserl in Africa?" Paulin Hountondji as it were puts himself in brackets and poses the self-critical question as to why he was so strongly impressed by Husserl's doctrine during the very first years of his studying philosophy and in some of his writings. Hountondji points out that he has no problem acknowledging that his critique of ethno-philosophy was based among other demands on the idea of philosophy defended by Husserl especially in his (Husserl's) *Philosophy as Rigorous Science*. Hountondji had already made this clear in his book *The Struggle for Meaning*. In this chapter, he offers some more autobiographical reflections on his encounters with Husserl's work. This includes an exposition of the beginnings of his studies in France that led to working on Husserl, his encounter with other thinkers such as Louis Althusser and Alioune Diop, his ethnocritique, and his critical adoption of Husserl's view of what he calls the struggle for meaning. He concludes by giving a brief discussion of his critical adoption of Husserl's phenomenology and the struggle for meaning.

In "Hountondji and Husserl: Subjectivity, Responsibility, and Phenomenology in the Critique of Ethnophilosophy," Patrick Eldridge undertakes a reconstruction and critical evaluation of Hountondji's critique of ethnophilosophy as a phenomenological project. It is an attempt to show that Hountondji did not so much abandon his work in phenomenology as drastically refashion it. His aim is to provide a synoptic reading of Hountondji and Husserl, demonstrating how phenomenology organically unites the seemingly disparate impulses of Hountondji's work: the elaboration of a philosophical theory of objective knowledge, the critique of theoretical extraversion in Africa, and the call for a sociological theory of collective representations. This demonstration consists in drawing out answers to four interrelated questions posed to Hountondji: For what is the philosophizing subject responsible? Who is the responsible, philosophizing subject? To whom is the philosophizing subject responsible? In light of its responsibilities, what then must the subject do? Eldridge argues that the answers to these questions make manifest the task that Hountondji sets for the African philosopher: to combat the destructive intellectual legacies of colonization by reinvigorating the thoughts and practices of their community by their own radical commitment to truth.

In "Philosophical Universality in Crisis: Hountondji's Interruption of Husserlian Phenomenology," Carmen De Schryver argues that decolonial criticism is by and large dominated by a "disenchantment" with the universalist aspirations of European philosophy, regarding these as manifestation of the historical elision of colonized forms of thought. Some decolonial thinkers question this anti-universalist turn and argue that the unsettling of European epistemic privilege opens up the possibility of a discourse that is *truly* universalist. Her chapter contributes to the decolonial reclamation of the universal by taking up the question of universality as it unfolds in the African phenomenological tradition. She does so by considering the work of Paulin Hountondji, focusing on his relation to Edmund Husserl in order to think through the extent to which Husserlian phenomenology remains inflected by Eurocentrism and thus results in "false universalities." She argues that the end of Hountondji's critique is not to dismiss as simply Eurocentric Husserl's hopes for a universal science. To the contrary: it is to explore, for the first time, the possibility of critically reappropriating the universalist aims of phenomenology for decolonial thought. De Schryver concludes that Hountondji offers us a radical vision of universalism that requires us to rethink the very method and scope of phenomenology itself.

Consciousness, Identity, Existence, and Embodiment

Section 2 of the anthology comprises chapters on the themes of consciousness, identity, existence, and embodiment by Mabogo More, M. John Lamola, Keolebogile Mbebe and Thabang Dladla, Rianna Oelofsen, and Ada Agada.

In "Chabani Manganyi: The Lived Experience of Difference," Mabogo More argues that Black scholars such as W. E. B. Du Bois, Frantz Fanon, George Yancy, Naomi Zack, Lewis Gordon, Paget Henry, Linda Martin Alcoff, Aimé Césaire, Steve Biko, and more importantly for his purpose, Noel Chabani Manganyi and many others, have conceptualized their existence phenomenologically and existentially by attempting to disclose or reveal what in Fanon's words is "the lived experience of Blackness" from concealment in the space of the human. He consequently agrees with Manganyi that Black philosophers share that they are each in their own ways forced to be existential phenomenologists. Black phenomenologists, he writes, share a deep understanding of the relationship between Blackness, ontology, and racism. Heidegger and most European phenomenologists could not, or would not, envision this relationship because of their Eurocentric perspective of Being and *Dasein*. More thus designates and endorses Manganyi's project as a fundamental stripping away of what conceals this difference. It is in this sense a phenomenology of difference and diversity.

In "A Post-Sartrean Reflection on Being Black in the World: Reading Steve Biko through Slavoj Žižek," M. John Lamola analyzes what he calls the "ontological condition of the Black African within her protracted colonial milieu." He finds the postcolonial African as a being with a "quixotic ontology." He argues that Black Africans are, on the one hand, subjects who are susceptible to doubting their humanity to the extent that their humanity is questioned and denied by others. This state of being "black in the world" is one that is, on the other hand, forever "yearning for freedom for self-actualization." Lamola explores the paradoxical state of experiencing the negativity surrounding being black, which "perversely endures as a threatened-but-defiant self-affirming existence." He starts by explaining his use of Sartre, Hegel, and Žižek as a framework to develop his argument. This is followed by linking Biko's analysis of the Black human condition with Abraham Olivier's subversive use of Heidegger to analyze life in South African townships as a being deprived of its possibility to *be*. He then applies his reading of Hegel and Žižek to his analysis of the consciousness of the denied potential of Black Being. Finally, he links Archibald Mafeje's notion of "Africanity as combative ontology" as a strategy, more precisely as "absolute recoil" against the denied potential of Black Being.

In "Blackness as a Conundrum for Phenomenology" Keolebogile Mbebe and Thabang Dladla offer reflections on how Blackness presents a conundrum for phenomenology not only as a condition about which to theorize but also as a position from which one may theorize. Following a recapitulation of the liberatory essence of African/Black philosophy, Mbebe and Dladla elaborate their central claim, that Blackness imposes an alternative phenomenology to Western phenomenology by giving a point of view from those who do not die but end, as can be explicated from the notion of social death. They develop this claim by expanding on the notion of violence as used by Orlando Patterson and adopted by the Afropessimist school. Afropessimists view the effects of the historical episode of slavery, for instance, as resulting in intractable social death. Mbembe and Dladla use the concept of gratuitous violence encapsulated in the phenomenon of social death as employed by Afropessimism for their analysis of Blackness as a position of *nonbeing* from which one may theorize.

In "Merleau-Ponty, Embodied Subjectivity, and (White) Women Dancing," Rianna Oelofsen argues that given the role that "white supremacy" plays in Africa, an analysis of the phenomenon of whiteness is relevant. More specifically, her contribution adds an investigation into the embodiment of white womanhood. She investigates white womanhood as a way of being-in-the-world, which she considers at once a result and support of the structures of white supremacy. Using Merleau-Ponty's concept of embodied subjectivity, she argues that prescriptions under white supremacy and patriarchy subordinates women to a particular bodily comportment and spatiality of "feminine whiteness." She examines the example of dancing to demonstrate how "white womanness" can be understood as inhabiting the world in a whitely feminine way assuming "white feminine" values and priorities. Furthermore, she argues that the construction of the subjectivity of "white womanness" relies on social structures and a whitely discourse of structural gestures in a society, which systematically deny and undermine the recognition of the black "other" as equal. Consequently, "whiteliness" (white supremacy) can be (and is) present even where individual agents do not have the conscious intentions to harm, or diminish the "other."

In "The Experience of Community and the Meaningful Life," Ada Agada discusses the traditional African conception of community and relates the experience of community with the idea of a meaningful life. His ultimate goal is to show that a communal approach to human life helps combat pessimism. He argues that pessimism arises from the knowledge of the fact of evil in the world, the certainty of death, uncertainty about the existence of an omniscient and omnipotent God, and the destabilizing impact these factors have on any illusion of coherence in the structure of a typical human life. He argues that while pessimism about human existence is well founded, the experience of community enhances practical living by blunting the edge of pessimism through increasing the moments of meaning that an individual can ever find in her solitary state.

The communal experience takes into full account the impossibility of the human being attaining her apotheosis. Nevertheless, communal experience affirms that this being is fit for consolation and should legitimately enjoy the moments of meaning guaranteed to it as a passion useful to the community of human beings.

Art, Culture, Language, Politics, and Liberation

Section 3 of the anthology deals with culture, politics, and liberation and includes contributions from Achille Mbembe, Schalk Gerber, Tsenay Serequeberhan, Alena Rettová, Uchenna Okeja, and Justin Sands.

In "Savage Objects: On the Restitution of Alienated Meaning," Achille Mbembe builds upon previous work. This chapter establishes a nexus between subjects dehumanized by colonialism and the objects of their creative cultural self-expression in the possession of Europeans. The essay explicates different "gazes" with regard to African cultural artifacts and art collections. A first is the "missionary gaze," which subjected African art objects to satanic, demonic artifacts that testified to the paganism and immorality of Africans. Then there is the "ethnographical gaze," which expounds how African art served to mediate a particular self-awareness of a Europe that was battling to understand its new subjecthood as the dominator of the world. Finally he identifies the "epistemic gaze" concerning the plunder of Africa's cultural objects, which has had a profound effect on the misappropriation of Africa's self-knowledge. Mbembe points out that, currently, the question being asked is whether Europe should restitute these objects. He contends that the phenomenological issue of the meaning of their presence in Europe, and what they signify in European consciousness, is not radically interrogated, nor has a metric of what Africa lost in them been established. Consequently, Mbembe makes a case for recentering the debate on the repatriation and restitution of African ancient artifacts from European museums around the historical, philosophical, anthropological, and political stakes of the act of restitution.

In "On the Phenomenology of a Shared World in Achille Mbembe," Schalk Gerber situates Achille Mbembe's contribution to African phenomenology among its commentators and critics. It retraces Mbembe's thinking together with that of Jean-Luc Nancy and Frantz Fanon. Gerber argues that Mbembe's contribution to African phenomenology is in the move to rethink the *relation* of our being-in-the-world not as opposed to but as *with* others. This allows a case to be made for our shared existence in one world. Such relational thinking underscores the "being-in-common" that we share as opposed to a common being that we do not all share and that leads some to be reduced to the "nonbeing of the African subject under slavery, colonialization, and apartheid." Gerber thus argues that Mbembe's thinking opens onto the question of the reparation of human dignity as the making meaning *with* others (through our *Mitsein*), as opposed to the subjugation to fixed meanings imposed from elsewhere for the sake of political and economic exploitation. Gerber concludes that Mbembe's contribution concerns a reflection on the African lived experience of *both* the struggle against subjugation as well as the lived experience of moments of reparation, which is indicated, for instance, with the notion of Afropolitanism.

In "The Voice of African Philosophy," Tsenay Serequeberhan is concerned with exploring the possibilities for philosophy in the present postcolonial African situation. He argues for an African philosophical perspective centered on exploring the reflective heritage of the African liberation struggle. The focus of Serequeberhan's contribution is thus to critically examine core or key elements of this discourse. In this, his "aim is to explore the possible beyond the demise of colonialism, in the hope of catching-sight-of a truly postcolonial future." His contribution is a concise articulation of the hermeneutical orientation within the contemporary discourse of African philosophy. But more than this he considers "the voice of African philosophy" to be the self-imposed vocalization of the philosophic response of "our being to the call of our freedom: our humanness" in the wake of a postcolonial future. As he puts it: "It is the reflexive-reflective counterpart to the practical efforts—that is, political, cultural, economic—in the Diaspora and on the Continent, focused on compelling the Occident to see itself in the horrors of its own making. In this *seeing*, and the boomerang counterglance of all the rest of *us*, it is possible, as Fanon stated not too long ago, 'to put afoot a new humanity.' "

In "Communal Space, Communal Temporality: Kwasi Wiredu and Henri Bergson in Dialogue," Justin Sands presents an argument for how African cosmologies and concepts of personhood can engage the West through core phenomenological issues. His chapter is an initial dialogue between Kwasi Wiredu and Henri Bergson, where he proposes that Wiredu's notion of a self that only becomes a person through community holds a sense of temporality that can be revealed through Bergsonian *duration*. Likewise, Bergson's understanding of the interpenetrability between time and space brings Wiredu's sense of becoming a person into a phenomenological register, giving it a sense of time-consciousness and hermeneutics. Through this, Sands proposes that Wiredu's sense of Akan metaphysics—and its rejection of natural/supernatural and immanent/transcendent distinctions—brings Bergson's concept of the interrelation between memory, world, and the self into a cultural-political register, thereby bringing out the political-cultural aspect of his work. Through critical dialogues such as this, Sands argues that African phenomenology presents not just strident challenges to the colonial-laden issues within phenomenology but also new pathways for inquiry and understanding.

In "Artifacts of the Emotion and Existence in Unjust Structures," Uchenna Okeja takes "artifacts of emotion" to refer to the creative expressions that the dispossessed and people at the fringes of society rely on to survive the harsh conditions they must live with daily. Such expressions, so Okeja argues, are "invoked with reference to the tenacity of the hard done by to live normal lives, despite cruel and unforgiving circumstances created by unjust structures." He states as the aim of his contribution to show how artifacts of the emotion constitute a concept that enables us to grapple with questions about meaning in life for the people who live under unjust social and political structures. The concept of "artifacts of the emotion" he contends is specifically suitable for this task because it captures a unique but shared circumstance of what he calls the "unmitigated suffering and disadvantage" of the dispossessed, humiliated, and marginalized. The core of his argument is that, for one who must live daily with the disastrous effects of the intense negotiation of unmitigated suffering and disadvantage, emotional artifacts become a creative art of survival, a meaning-giving activity that helps to recapture the significance of their agency.

In "Experience and Text: Toward an African-Language Phenomenology," Alena Rettová takes works of Paulin Hountondji as a point of departure to illustrate two phenomenological orientations, a text-focused and an experience-focused one. She poses the question as to how they come together. Rettová's contribution interrogates the textual nature of the expression of experience and identifies two key aspects of this textuality: language and genre. As for language, she insists on the need to consider the specificity of a language in the philosophical expression and demonstrates the impact of specific language qualities on thought. This leads her to a statement of the importance of relating African philosophy to African-language texts. She then goes on to consider genre as the way language is assembled in a text. She argues that it is through genre that language is anchored to a cultural and historical context. This suggests that genre is a key parameter that unfolds a variety of Afrophone texts for philosophy. Rettová's contribution concludes by raising the question of the need of the African-language textual expression of experience. She insists on such texts being the foundation of an African-language phenomenology.

Conclusion

We hope to demonstrate through the contributions to this anthology how in the African context phenomenology is challenged to put itself in brackets and self-reflect radically upon the methodological assumptions its proponents make. Consequently, our contributions showcase in diverse ways how the African context poses challenges that give rise to a difference in practicing phenomenology. Indeed, through addressing these challenges a different, critical African phenomenology of its own comes to the fore. This is a phenomenology that self-reflects from the perspective of the crises of the constitutive effect of unjust postcolonial structures and disenabling lived conditions on the genesis of consciousness. Contributions to African phenomenology can be seen ultimately as an attempt to face the challenge of critical self-reflection that this crisis brings to the fore.

Part 1

Origin, Methodology, and Scope

1

African Phenomenology—What Is That?

ABRAHAM OLIVIER

Introduction

In his essay "Chabani Manganyi: The Lived Experience of Difference" Mabogo More writes:

> Phenomenology and existentialism among African people in South Africa have a long history, which unfortunately has not been explicitly thematized or philosophically engaged. Recently, a lot of work has been done on Steve Biko as an Africana existentialist philosopher.[1] Unfortunately, very little, if at all, attention has been directed to the entire Black existential-phenomenology tradition in this country, a poeticist tradition fashioned and sustained in the great literary production of South Africans, which took the form of what Paget Henry describes as "the imagistic phenomenology" of consciousness. (More 2023, 00)[2]

It seems fair to say that what More writes about phenomenology in South Africa goes for phenomenology in Africa in general. Technically, the term "African phenomenology" has low currency in the sense that it is not used widely, or "thematized" explicitly, or introduced systematically. It is not that phenomenology has not been practiced in the African context. Some of its main proponents include Paulin Hountondji, Tsenay Serequeberhan, D. A. Masolo, Achille Mbembe, Mabogo More, Noel Chabani Manganyi, Mogobe Ramose, M. John Lamola, Michael Cloete, and Rozena Maart. However, as More indicates, there is not yet any comprehensive systematic introduction to or philosophical engagement with African phenomenology as compared to its adjacent field, Africana phenomenology,[3] or for that matter Western (European or Anglo-American) phenomenology.[4]

The aim of this chapter is to address this lacuna by attempting to give a brief systematic introduction to African phenomenology in distinction to Africana and Western phenomenology. Upfront I want to make a personal disclaimer. Given the focus of African phenomenology on problems of the lived experience of black people under colonial and postcolonial conditions of oppression in the African context, and the fact that I am a white male, structurally privileged by the very same conditions, makes my attempt to contribute to this field problematic from the outset. It seems the least I could do—if not keeping silent—is to submit my own contribution to phenomenological self-critique and question my own positionality. Thus, I cannot and do not claim to introduce African phenomenology as if I can speak for black Africans. Rather, I seek to introduce the phenomenology of black African scholars themselves. My point of departure is that the best way to explore African phenomenology is to examine the assumptions and approaches of its contributors and bring their work to the fore.

Section 1 starts with a discussion of the relation between African, Africana, and Western phenomenology. Section 2 first explores some methodological assumptions and distinctive features of African phenomenology and then sets out to outline for further exploration four approaches in African phenomenology. They include critical transcendental phenomenology, existential phenomenology, hermeneutic phenomenology, and postphenomenology.

African, Africana, and Western Phenomenology

As I said, "African phenomenology" has not yet seen any introductory works coining the term as is the case with Africana phenomenology or Western traditions of phenomenology. A typical way to introduce a field of study is to delineate its contours in comparison to its cognate fields as Paget Henry does in his introduction to Africana phenomenology (Henry

2006). This prompts the question as to how exactly African phenomenology is related to Africana phenomenology and Western phenomenology. These relations are complex to say the least and, given the brevity of space, I can only attempt to give an outline of some of their assumptions and contours. The danger is to grossly simplify, distort, or glibly touch upon what needs careful dissection. However, following Paget Henry's example, I think it is necessary to make distinctions between Africana, African, and Western phenomenologies in order to at least address the inevitable question: What exactly is African phenomenology and what distinguishes it from other phenomenologies? Modest as my claim is to just outline, I am aware that my answer may be wanting if not simply defective. This is then why I make extensive use of existing introductions of Africana phenomenology such as Henry's, Gordon's, and Outlaw's to model on.

I begin with Paget Henry's comparison of definitions of what he designates as classic "European phenomenology" and Africana phenomenology, which I use for an attempt to outline the methodological contours of African phenomenology. Henry writes: "By phenomenology, I mean the discursive practice through which self-reflective descriptions of the constituting activities of consciousness are produced after the 'natural attitude' of everyday life has been bracketed by some ego-displacing technique. An Africana phenomenology would thus be the self-reflective descriptions of the constituting activities of the consciousness of Africana peoples, after the natural attitudes of Africana egos have been displaced by de-centering techniques practiced in these cultures" (Henry 2006, 1). Henry uses basic aspects of Husserl's classic method of phenomenology to work out a definition of Africana phenomenology that one can deploy well to delineate the contours of African phenomenology. In Henry's terms then, one may speak of African phenomenology as a self-reflective description of the constituting activities of the consciousness of specifically black peoples on the African continent, after the natural attitudes of African subjects (egos) have been "displaced by de-centering techniques practiced in these cultures." One may immediately want to know why the use of the term "de-centering" here. Have not Black African subjects rather been "displaced" by all kinds of "de-centering techniques" when their countries were invaded by colonizers who took center stage in Africa? Why and how should African phenomenology still want to "de-center" displaced black African subjects?

Henry seems to deploy the technique of "de-centering" in a very specific way to cover this concern. One could distinguish the following two aspects in his use of the technique.

The first aspect refers to the classic phenomenological aspect of bracketing, which Husserl refers to with the Greek term *epochē*. This involves the suspension of the "natural attitude" of the subject (the ego) to take things for granted as a given, that is, as an objective world, replete with a variety of material entities with particular properties and causal relations. Consequently, the subject that practices phenomenology "de-centers" itself by subjecting the activities of its own consciousness to self-reflection. Such self-reflection inquires how things, objects, other subjects, and itself appear in the subject's own experience, thus in what ways and in which context they are given to consciousness. The idea is that through such bracketing the constituting activities of consciousness can come to the fore and become available to description. African and Africana phenomenology seem to share this methodological approach of de-centering qua self-bracketing with classic European phenomenology.

The second aspect of the "de-centering" technique of phenomenology seems to mark a decisive difference between classic Western phenomenology on the one hand and African and Africana phenomenology on the other. In Husserl's classic transcendental approach, the focus is on the reasoning capacities of consciousness that humans are purported to share universally, independent of their particular cultural heritage or social, political, and economic conditions. In African and Africana phenomenology it seems rather different in that social, cultural, economic, and political factors are considered to be a central part of the constitutive activities of consciousness. This difference is what the de-centering technique of phenomenology seems to bring to the fore. Consider, for instance, Du Bois's notion of *double consciousness* in the opening passage of the first chapter of *The Souls of Black Folks*, titled "Of Our Spiritual Strivings." Du Bois writes: "It is a peculiar sensation, this double-consciousness, this sense of always looking at one's self through the eyes of others, of measuring one's soul by the tape of a world that looks on in amused contempt and pity. One ever feels his twoness,—an American, a Negro; two souls, two thoughts, two unreconciled strivings; two warring ideals in one dark body, whose dogged strength alone keeps it from being torn asunder" (Du Bois 1969, chap. 1). Du Bois offers a poignant description of the formative effect of racialization or "negrification" on the "the souls of black folks," that is, on the (self-)consciousness of Americans of African descent. As Henry succinctly puts it, "DuBoisian double consciousness is a phenomenological account of the self-consciousness of these African subjects whose 'We' had been shattered and challenged by this process of negrification"

(Henry 2006, 7). The experience of the institutionalization of the racial distance between whites and blacks in the United States thus contested the self-consciousness of "the pre-colonial collective identities of the Akan, Hausa, Yoruba, Fon and other African ethnic groups" (Henry 2006, 6–7). The result is, as Du Bois puts it, a feeling of twoness, feeling one is "an American, a Negro; two souls," two consciousnesses.

In a similar way Fanon uses the term "sociogeny" to describe the shaping effect of racial conditions on the formation of the activities of consciousness in *Black Skins, White Masks* (Fanon 1967, 4). By sociogeny Fanon means roughly that which is created or constructed by the social world. The social world as a peopled space is for Fanon, as Gordon puts it, "an achievement of intersubjectivity" (Gordon 2008a). Fanon's concept of sociogeny seems to correspond with Husserl's notion of intersubjective genesis in his later work *Cartesian Meditations* (Fourth and Fifth Meditations) in its basic sense that consciousness, and its sense-giving capacity of concept formation, is developed through social interaction (intersubjectivity). However, unlike Husserl, Fanon puts particular emphasis on a critical analysis of the destructive experiential effect of racist social interaction that fails mutual recognition. One can say Fanon's concept of sociogeny thus brings to the fore the reversed, destructive, effect of what Husserl later takes to be the intersubjective genesis of consciousness.

A last example is Steve Biko's use of the term *Black consciousness* to describe the formative effect of the racialized society of apartheid on the consciousness of persons and peoples. Here is one of his uncompromising depictions of its destructive effect in *I Write What I Like*: "All in all the black man has become a shell, a shadow of man, completely defeated, drowning in his own misery, a slave, an ox bearing the yoke of oppression with sheepish timidity. This *is* the first truth, bitter as it may seem, that we have to acknowledge before we can start on any programme designed to change the status quo" (Biko 2005, 29). Biko's systematized concept of Black Consciousness finds strong phenomenological expression in what More (2023) calls "being-black-in-the world."[5] The world of apartheid brought about an ontological difference in persons' and peoples' consciousness of what it means to be. This shows once more how a racialized world and its social, cultural, political, and economic manifestations are considered a formative part of the activities of consciousness, of what makes possible a conscious mind. One may say, if Western phenomenology seeks to identify seminal structures of consciousness independent of the subject's specific conditions of living, then African and Africana phenomenology take consciousness to be constituted by such conditions in the first place. Thus the lived conditions of the conscious subject are viewed as part of the conditions of the possibility of its consciousness. It seems fair to say that the technique of de-centering the subject is intended to emphasize the constitutive effect of the subject's situatedness, particularly in oppressive conditions, as a central feature of what distinguishes African and Africana phenomenology from Western phenomenology.

Notably, Hountondji and others would accuse Western phenomenology of maintaining a contradictory notion of the constitution of consciousness. Its reasoning capacity is claimed to apply universally but, paradoxically, it is reserved for European cultures in their particularity. As Henry puts it: "Classically, European phenomenology was seen as the self-reflective practice that disclosed the latent movements of a universal reason. However, this possibility of a universal reason was, quite paradoxically, limited to a very specific cultural particularity: the cultural particularity of Europe. This particularization of universal reason was at the same time the universalizing of the European subject as its science and phenomenology would give reason a fully realized vision of itself" (Henry 2006, 2). Henry seems to have in mind specifically the way Husserl views the development of European phenomenology in *The Crisis of European Sciences and Transcendental Phenomenology* (Husserl 1970). For Husserl, so he argues, the capacity of reasoning was the primary constituting force of consciousness specifically because of "the perceived universality of its categories, positings, claims,—in short, its self- and knowledge-producing capabilities" (Henry 2006, 3). Henry objects, however, that the perceived universality of reason was in fact confined to the cultural particularity of the European subject. Following in Hegel's footsteps, for Husserl, European phenomenology was ideally "the self-reflective practice that disclosed the latent movements of a universal reason, which was also the prime constituting force operating within the core of the European subject" (Henry 2006, 3). Thus the European subject and its particular culture, and one can add science, phenomenology, politics, and economics, was considered the bearer of universal reasoning. As Henry says, this subject's particular "science and phenomenology would give reason a fully realized vision of itself" (Henry 2006, 3). The result is, paradoxically, the "particularization of universal reason" through the universalization of the European subject. This paradox demonstrates in fact the social, cultural, political, economic constitution even of what may be claimed to be the universal reasoning capacity of consciousness.

To be fair, the claim that settings or contexts, defined by social, cultural, political, and economic factors in their particularity, are constitutive of consciousness has found support by some phenomenologists in the West. They include phenomenologists who take consciousness to be situated and as such shaped by social, cultural, political, and economic contexts. Terms for such contexts are, for instance, Heidegger's "world," Merleau-Ponty's "field," Sartre's "situation," Schutz's "social world," and more recently Casey's, Malpas's, and Janz's "place."[6] The term "place" can be taken as placeholder for these terms for context. In any case, it brings to the fore a decisive difference between Western and African and Africana phenomenologists. Serequeberhan brings this well to the point. In *Existence and Heritage* (2015) Serequeberhan uses Heidegger to argue that to be human (*Dasein*) means to inherit a place in the world (Serequeberhan 2015, 107, 109, 112). To recognize one's heritage is at its core a recognition of one's historic existence as being-in-the-world, of one's possibility to retrieve the past and inhabit, or better, inherit, a place in the world as *Dasein*, with possibilities to be. Africans have witnessed a colonial denial of their heritage. This manifests, according to Serequeberhan, in the form of the imposed duplication of European technical modernity—scientifically, culturally, and economically—as universally valid, while actually hiding away the specificity of its origin. In the persistent domination of the colony through duplication, Europe has become the standard of what is worth living for or not, whose life matters or not, who has a place in society or not. Consequently, so Serequeberhan observes, African subjects have been relegated to the status of "things," they are "thingified" (Serequeberhan, 2015, 114). As he puts it: "A thing, like a colonial subject, is something that does not control itself. It has no will of its own. It is utilized and at the disposal of another. It has no power over itself" (Serequeberhan 2015, 114). Also in the neocolonial situation, so he argues, "the formerly colonized are thingified" (Serequeberhan 2015, 114). Fanon succinctly calls such denial of the African subject a submission to the "zone of non-being" (Fanon 1967, 8), to be denied a place in the world, to be, as More (2023) says, homeless from the outset. Ultimately, African and Africana phenomenologists and Western phenomenologists who share studying the "life world" are dealing with very different "life worlds" of which one is purported to be the standard and the other its denied duplication.

The way phenomenologists in the context of the African continent or African diaspora consider social, cultural, political, and economic factors to constitute consciousness thus differs decisively from how Western phenomenologists do. African and Africana phenomenology have, as Gordon says, their own unique settings and sets of "existential questions" (Gordon 2000, 10). They have in common that they can be broadly characterized by their critical focus on the lived experience of black persons and peoples African and those of African descent who were and are subjected to the formative workings of colonialism, slavery, racism, and sexism.

As subfields of African and Africana philosophy, African and Africana phenomenology are technically closely related. Lucius Outlaw makes clear this closeness in his entry "Africana philosophy" in the *Stanford Encyclopaedia of Philosophy*: "Africana philosophy is a third-order, metaphilosophical, umbrella-concept used to bring organizing oversight to various efforts of philosophizing—that is, activities of reflective, critical thinking and articulation and aesthetic expression—engaged in by persons and peoples African and of African descent who were and are indigenous residents of continental Africa and residents of the many African Diasporas worldwide" (Outlaw 2017, 1). However, as Outlaw indicates, African philosophy refers more strictly to the thought of persons and peoples African while Africana philosophy pertains more directly to the thought of the African diaspora, that is, "*peoples* of African descent in the Americas, the Caribbean, Europe, and elsewhere" (Outlaw 2017, 14). The situations of persons and peoples African and of African descent shaped their subjectivity in various particular ways. African and Africana phenomenologies serve particularly well to explain the shaping effect of these situations on subjectivity. Thus Outlaw writes: "The centuries of enslaving-relocations of millions of African peoples to the New Worlds of colonies-*cum*-nation-states created by European and Euro-American settler-colonists beginning in the sixteenth century, and the subsequent centuries-long continuations of descendants of these African peoples in, and migrations of others to, these locales, occasioned the formation of *new peoples* of African descent in the Americas, the Caribbean, Europe, and elsewhere" (Outlaw 2017, 14).

Consequently, it makes sense to say as Gordon does that persons and peoples African and of African descent will have their own unique sets of existential questions. My aim is not to explore the intricate similarities and distinctions between African and Africana phenomenologies any further. Rather, I focus in the following on African phenomenology and a brief exploration of approaches of African phenomenologists.

Approaches in African Phenomenology

Again, in my view the best way to explore African phenomenology is to examine the approaches of its proponents. Technically, one can identify in broad strokes four main approaches to African phenomenology—transcendental phenomenology, existential phenomenology, hermeneutic phenomenology, and postphenomenology. I do not claim that these approaches represent generally acknowledged schools of phenomenological thought in Africa followed by their self-proclaimed advocates. Neither do I think that there may not be other approaches. I make these distinctions on the basis of most commonly known texts offered by some authors and the methodological commitments they make in their texts. I cannot do justice to their thought in such brief space. Instead, I focus on briefly introducing what I take to be the core of their specific elaborations on these approaches. In any case, something that the suggested approaches seem to have in common is that they entertain a "critical" postcolonial attitude. One can thus add "critical" to each of these approaches as an indication of the way African phenomenologists maintain a skeptical decolonizing distance in their use of Western phenomenology. Before I move on to the four approaches, it is in order to say something more about this critical attitude.

African phenomenologists often make use of what is considered classic works of Western phenomenologists in their thinking. Hountondji, for instance, deploys the work of Husserl, More the work of Sartre, Serequeberhan works of Heidegger and Gadamer, and Mbembe works of Merleau-Ponty and Foucault. This use of the works of Western philosophers is however done throughout from the perspective of a postcolonial critique of these works. One can speak of an attitude of what Serequeberhan may agree to call a hermeneutics of suspicion. Serequeberhan is particularly known for his expansive methodological (hermeneutic) critique of the adoption of Western works and it may be worthwhile saying something in brief about his critical attitude.

Serequeberhan devotes extensive analyses of his own use of philosophers such as Kant, Gadamer, Marx, and Heidegger in both of his main works *The Hermeneutics of African Philosophy* (1994) and *Existence and Heritage* (2015). He asks himself critically why these thinkers and not others (Serequeberhan 2015, 5). His answer is that he found that these thinkers are "helpful in thinking about the situation of postcolonial Africa" (Serequeberhan 2015, 5). But "helpful" is meant in a strongly critical way.

Serequeberhan does not spare critique in his discussion of Eurocentrism and racism in Kant, Heidegger, or Gadamer and, for that matter, Levinas. Each in his own way shows how philosophers can go wrong. Nevertheless, he still thinks that these thinkers "can be gainfully employed to think about the situation of our shared present" (Serequeberhan 2015, 5). In fact, Serequeberhan seems to turn the work of these thinkers against themselves and their own parochial assumptions. Thus, he explains his subversive focus on and use of such more or less controversial thinkers to critique Eurocentrist and racist assumptions and advocates the idea of the "variegated multiplicity of our shared existence" (Serequeberhan 2015, 48). Serequeberhan, like Hountondji, More, and Mbembe, does not simply follow what Gordon (2023) calls an "application model" of thinking, which would mean the ideas of European phenomenologists such as Husserl, Heidegger, Sartre, or Merleau-Ponty are accepted as the exclusively legitimate exemplars of thought and theory. Rather, it is fair to say they all promote a subversive critical use of such thinkers to critically develop their own approaches in phenomenology. Critical can thus be taken to mean both theoretical "judgment" and "crises" (Gordon 2023). This is in particular the critical thinking called for by the crises caused by lived conditions under colonial and neocolonial racist, sexist, xenophobic, and other forms of oppression in its diversity of manifestations.

What ultimately seems to distinguish African phenomenology from other phenomenologies is its focus on the formative effect of the crisis of lived conditions on the conscious mind in but also beyond the African context—if we take seriously Serequeberhan's notion of the "variegated multiplicity of our shared existence" (Serequeberhan 2015, 48). In Hountondji's terms, the crisis of lived conditions is itself considered part of the transcendental condition of the possibility of consciousness, of what enables—or disenables—a critical conscious mind. In this sense, it seems fair to say, approaches to African phenomenology share reflections from the perspective of the crises of the constitutive effect of unjust structures and disenabling lived conditions on the genesis of consciousness in the African context as related to other contexts.

In the following subsections I give an outline of these approaches and the critical attitude they represent.

TRANSCENDENTAL PHENOMENOLOGY

The most "classic" formulation of the African phenomenological approach appears in Paulin Hountondji's *The Struggle for Meaning* and the adoption of his thought by D. A. Masolo in *Self and Community in a Changing World*. One may technically speak of their approaches as a critical *transcendental phenomenology* as they use Husserl to trace the conditions of the possibility of consciousness.[7]

In *The Struggle for Meaning*, Hountondji endorses Husserl's phenomenological appeal to return to the subject, as the condition of the possibility to generate the meaning of objects of consciousness ("the things themselves") as they are first personally experienced and intersubjectively shared through language. Thus, as Hountondji says: "All in all, the human universe is from end to end a universe of meaning where things announce themselves without ever becoming truly present" (Hountondji 2002, 59). However, Hountondji worries that, in his *Logical Investigations*, Husserl leans toward emphasizing the notion of ideal meanings at the cost of the reality of first personal experience. He argues that Husserl's universe of ideal meanings, at the end, gives way to the metaphysical notion of a universe of meanings-in-themselves. This is how Hountondji puts it: "It appears to me that this notion of 'meaning in itself' concludes a constant attempt, throughout *Investigations*, to exclude the subject, after its initial consecration as the condition and the primary source of meaning" (Hountondji 2002, 62). Hountondji does not deny that Husserl takes seriously the subject at work behind the production of ideal meaning and subjective experience as its primary source. Unlike Kant, Husserl does not submit experience to universal metaphysical categories to unify it and, in doing so, to give it meaning. Rather, Hountondji admits that for Husserl: "The unity of experience takes care of itself through a progressive and horizontal articulation, in an open, unfinishable process" (Hountondji 2002, 62). However, what Hountondji finds missing in Husserl's work is "a clear understanding of the logical motivations of Husserl's method," and his primary interest in the idealization of "logical experience" (Hountondji 2002, 62). Thus, Hountondji cautions one to see how Husserl ultimately lends toward subordinating lived experience to "logical experience." Hountondji is wary of any metaphysics of ideal universal meanings that does not account for the experiential reality of the subject, more precisely, the subject's first personal, sense-giving, and sense-fulfilling experiential act of signification. In this way, he makes a strong phenomenological appeal to return to the subject, and to the things themselves as they are first personally experienced and expressed.

Notably, Hountondji argues that the pursuit of meaning is ultimately not merely philosophical, or logical, or scientific, but social (intersubjective) and political. First, Hountondji's view is that any subjective sense-giving act anticipates an intersubjective genesis of meanings, a social act of meaning formation, so that, ideally, the meaning of the first-person singular "I experience" coincides with the first personal plural "we experience." In other words, the intersubjective genesis of meaning makes possible the formation of consciousness and its capacity to grasp meaning; it is its enabling condition. Hountondji thus subtly introduces a radical social phenomenology found only in the later Husserl. Second, in the African context, the pursuit of meaning is a political struggle to decolonize deeply entrenched neocolonial categories of concepts purported to be universal. Ultimately, Hountondji turns Husserl's phenomenological method against itself by putting it in postcolonial brackets. Husserl's phenomenology is thus bracketed for setting up the conditions of possibility of consciousness to make things appear in a particular European way. In contrast, Hountondji argues for the ideal of seeking meaning that critically accounts for the particularity of contextualized first personal experience and its possible universality across such contexts.

In *Self and Community in a Changing World*, Masolo expands upon Hountondji's idea of the return to the subject, specifically by focusing on the sociocultural constitution of African subjectivity. Given its constitutive sociocultural plurality and contingency, the African indigenous lifeworld poses a challenge to its cross-cultural representation in philosophical concepts, especially in non-African contexts. Endorsing Hountondji's ideal of intersubjective conceptual communication, Masolo develops the notion of lived intersubjectivity as the underpinning of the possibility of universally shared meaning (Masolo 2010). His focus on lived indigenous intersubjectivity and its expression appears to be less idealistic than Hountondji's notion of conceptually shared subjectivity. His focus is on the careful critical conceptual analysis of concretely lived African intersubjectivity as condition of the possibility of shared universals. The lived intersubjectivity makes intracultural and intercultural, and ultimately universal thought, an ongoing challenge and something to keep striving for. Thus, the lived particularity of indigenous intersubjectivity as what is shared between all possible subjects, is always ahead of its possible universal expression through conceptual analysis. One could say Masolo offers a transcendental African phenomenology of lived intersubjectivity.

EXISTENTIAL PHENOMENOLOGY

As a second approach in African phenomenology, one could speak of a critical *existential phenomenology*. Its main representatives can be considered

Mabogo More and Chabani Manganyi. Others include M. John Lamola and Lewis Gordon himself. More wrote, among other works, *Looking through Philosophy in Black* (2018) and *Sartre on Contingency: Antiblack Racism and Embodiment* (2021). His works have a special focus on Sartre's existentialism, Gordon and Manganyi's black existentialist phenomenology, Du Bois's and Fanon's exploration of double consciousness, and Biko's Black Consciousness. I concentrate here on aspects of More's text, "Chabani Manganyi: The Lived Experience of Difference" (2023), which brings together central features of his other work on African existentialist phenomenology.[8]

More argues that the clinical psychologist Manganyi poses a central existential-phenomenological question right at the beginning of his major work on the theme *Being-Black-in-the-World*: "Is there a black mode of being-in-the-world? Stated differently: Is being-black-in-the-world different in fundamental respects to being-white-in-the-world?" (Manganyi 1973, 4). In response, so More points out, Manganyi's first move is to establish as a primary existential given our being-in-the-world (Manganyi 1973, 25). Like Manganyi, More adopts here and in several other works of his own (More 2008, 2021) Heidegger's and Sartre's basic assumption that the human condition is the same for all human beings, one of being contingently thrown in the world. As he puts it, "We all are born and die, feel the pangs of hunger and the desire for sleep, experience joy or sadness, and so forth" (More 2023, 142). However, like Sartre, he makes strong the argument that "existence is simply not mere existence without context" (More 2023, 142). For More, like for Manganyi, "human existential experiences and problems are situational—in the Sartrean sense—for they arise in, or out of, certain historical, racial, or cultural situations" (More 2023, 142). More takes the concept of situation to be important for the understanding of racism of whatever variety (More 2023, 143). Citing Sartre's *Portrait of the Anti-Semite*, he points out that to be a Jew "is to be flung into, and *abandoned* in, the Jewish situation" (Sartre 1948, 49, 75). More argues that what applies to Jews goes also for Blacks: "to be black is to be flung into, and abandoned in, the Black situation. It is thus the 'situation' that determines the mode of 'being-black-in-the-world' and 'being-white-in-the-world' as different modes" (More 2023, 143). More consequently finds himself in agreement with Manganyi that in an antiblack racist world there are fundamentally two primary modes of existing: "a white mode of being and a black mode of being, and the relation between these modes assumes an 'Us' and 'Them' relation" (More

2023, 143). More thus puts the question of the Being of the racialized Black person at the center of any discourse about Being.

To bring to the fore the consciousness of and conscious resistance against being racialized in this way, More consequently expresses Blackness with a capital "B" in agreement with the Blackness of Biko and the Black Consciousness movement. More agrees with Manganyi's claim that where Heidegger claims that Western philosophy has forgotten Being, Western philosophy has forgotten the Being of Blacks. The Being of Blacks is one that was in the course of Western history considered too different than belonging to the white world, or for that matter, belonging to the world at all. As More puts it: "It means that the world becomes a home in which a Black person is paradoxically homeless. It also means that Blacks are considered not to have a relationship with the world" (More 2023, 141). More concludes: "the Black Question is simultaneously the Question of Being and difference," that is, of having the identity of Being-a-human-in-the-world and its difference to Being-a-black-human-in-the-world (More 2023, 128). Hence, More, like Manganyi, concur with Fanon in speaking of an existentialist "phenomenology of difference."

In exploring the phenomenology of difference, of different experiential white and black modes of existence, More sides with Fanon and goes critically beyond Sartre's notion of being-in-the-world. He claims with Fanon that Sartre's "white normativity theorizations" ultimately neglect that there are fundamentally two different modes of existence. This goes back to Sartre's notion of our experience of a "lack of Being" in *Being and Nothingness*, which constitutes the source and origins not only of human freedom but also of the desire for completeness. "Against Sartre's view of consciousness as a lack of Being and a source of freedom, Fanon argues that within an antiblack racist society, the Black man is denied consciousness and thus the capacity to be a lack, precisely because he is reduced to brute Being, a thing or object without freedom" (More 2023, 132). In fact, More concludes that, in an antiblack world, Blacks are chained to their bodies, their skins, and denied the capacity to even constitute themselves as a lack of Being in order to attain self-consciousness. Blacks are considered different, their identity being one defined by difference, but one too different to matter, and this is what an existential phenomenology of difference is about.

More asks ultimately, what difference does difference in phenomenology make? He argues that a "phenomenology of difference is by inversion a phenomenology of identity as expressed by the inclusion of

'Black' in a Eurocentric phenomenology that erases the being of Black people in its universalizing white normativity project" (More 2023, 137). In the last instance the phenomenology of difference seeks to make a difference by advocating identity, one in which one is not excluded from being-in-the-world.

Hermeneutic Phenomenology

As a third approach in African phenomenology, one can speak of African *hermeneutic phenomenology*. This approach is drawn from Serequeberhan's main works *The Hermeneutics of African Philosophy* (1994) and *Existence and Heritage* (2015). Other proponents of this approach are Theophilus Okere and Okonda Okolo. My focus here is on Serequeberhan's work. He concentrates in both major works narrowly on a critical use of the hermeneutic phenomenology of Heidegger and Gadamer, but, as indicated in the previous section, he shows clear, critical distance in his use of these philosophers and close connections to Fanon and Cabral.

Notably, Serequeberhan starts *The Hermeneutics of African Philosophy: Horizon and Discourse* by explaining its title. The book is, first, about ascribing to philosophy, specifically African philosophy, an interpretative (hermeneutic) character. Second, it is about the "horizon" and "discourse" within which African philosophy is situated. Serequeberhan follows Heidegger—and for that matter Gadamer—in developing the notion that African philosophy, like any philosophy, is at its core hermeneutical: it is "inherently an interpretative undertaking" (Serequeberhan 1994, 2). This interpretative undertaking of philosophy is grounded in "lived finitude": the limited existence of a mortal human being (Serequeberhan 1994, 2). Curiously, Serequeberhan does not mention the term "phenomenology" much in this book or his next book, but this interpretative undertaking clearly has a phenomenological underpinning. The task is to establish methods to understand, in Husserl's terminology, the experience of the "lifeworld," and in Heidegger's phrasing "our being-in-the world." Indeed, Serequeberhan shares the contention of Hountondji, Masolo, Manganyi, and More that human existence is situated in a "lived historico-cultural and political milieu—a specific horizon" (Serequeberhan 1994, 2, 6). The discourse of philosophy presupposes and is founded in this lived milieu, the lifeworld. In Serequeberhan's view, philosophy itself, no matter how neutral and universal it appears to be, is always situated in a lived context. Thus, both *The Hermeneutics of African Philosophy* (1994) and *Existence and Heritage* (2015) explore different perspectives on why philosophy is always placed in a lived context, and in particular, how to do philosophy in an African place. His focus is more specifically on interpreting limits and possibilities of the lifeworld. "Thus, from within the limits of this lived finitude, philosophical hermeneutics explores the possibilities of mortal existence" (Serequeberhan 1994, 1). In this sense, the book is about hermeneutic phenomenology: interpreting the "lifeworld" of mortal existence, its essential structures, limits, and possibilities.

Again, African philosophy is, according to Serequeberhan, like all contemporary philosophy, at the core hermeneutics—it seems fair to add, a hermeneutic phenomenology, as it is an interpretative study of lifeworld experience. However, the "horizon" of African philosophy is more specific. It is focused on the "horizon and discourse" of postcolonial Africa. Serequeberhan makes it clear: his book is about the philosophical discourse within this postcolonial horizon. In this specific sense, one can call its theme African phenomenological hermeneutics, or more precisely perhaps, African hermeneutic phenomenology. I use these terminologies here interchangeably.

Although African hermeneutic phenomenology is focused on the postcolonial African context, it is clearly not confined to this context. It rather is about a phenomenological interpretation of the shared, concrete lifeworld in which every philosophy is situated. In *Being and Time* and elsewhere, Heidegger designated such an enterprise as "phenomenological hermeneutics of facticity." One can say, in conclusion, Serequeberhan critically adopts Heidegger's "existentially aware" phenomenology for his own purposes—both in this book and in his more recent book *Existence and Heritage*. As he says: "To organically appropriate and indigenize this existentially aware philosophic thesis from within the concrete historicity of post-colonial Africa is the basic task of this study" (Serequeberhan 1994, 1).

THE POSTPHENOMENOLOGICAL APPROACH

Finally, one can speak of a critical *postphenomenological* approach, of which Achille Mbembe can be considered a main proponent. The term postphenomenology is generally used to refer to work of poststructuralists such as Derrida, Foucault, Deleuze and Guattari, and in particular Don Ihde's title *Postphenomenology: Essays in the Postmodern Context*.[9] I take the term to refer to the work of philosophers who are in conversation with mainstream phenomenology and who keep using key phenomenological concepts but in a way that both continues with and diverges from them. In this way they may regenerate these concepts in creative ways. One finds this kind of thought particularly, but not exclusively, in African phenomenology and postcolonial thought, which uses phenomenology to modify it or even go against it. Mbembe's work seems to fit the description well. In, among others, his books *On the Postcolony* (2001) and *Critique of Black Reason* (2017), he makes use of the works of Merleau-Ponty, Derrida, Foucault, and Deleuze and Guattari to offer original divergent contributions to phenomenological discourse. In the following, I would like to focus on his critique of the Anthropocene, neoliberal capitalism, and racism in his essay "Decolonising the University: New Directions" (2016), specifically because it takes some of the central themes of African phenomenological and postcolonial discourse in a new direction.[10]

Mbembe writes here that the "domination of politics by capital" has resulted in "the waste of countless human lives and the production in every corner of the globe of vast stretches of dead water and dead land" (Mbembe 2016, 45). In fact, we find ourselves, so he argues, in a new geological epoch, the Anthropocene, which is characterized by "human-induced massive and accelerated changes to the Earth's climate, land, oceans and biosphere" (Mbembe 2016, 42). This calls for rethinking of the place humans claim for themselves on the globe, in particular from the perspective of our finitude and possible extinction. Mbembe reminds us of the fact that humans are part of a history of entanglement with multiple other species with a history much longer than human history (Mbembe 2016, 42). We cannot proceed as if history is simply ours. The self-destructive effect of the Anthropocene teaches us that we are inextricably part of nature and natural history. This prompts us to question the conventional dualism drawn between the human subject and nature as its object, and the self-ascription of agency and power exclusively to humans. Mbembe consequently argues that we need to "shift away from the dreams of mastery" and concede and extend agency and power to nonhuman others (Mbembe 2016, 42). This means that we need to overcome the notion of dualism and achieve a new way of thinking about our relation with nature, which comes down to a new understanding of ontology, epistemology, ethics, and politics. This can only be achieved by overcoming anthropocentrism and humanism, the split between nature and culture.

The seminal part of questioning the dream of mastery lies in what Mbembe calls the need to "decentre" the human qua subject, and to rethink it as "object among other objects" in their own right. In his words: "The human does not constitute a special category that is other than that of the objects. Objects are not a pole opposed to humans. Humans are objects among the various types of objects that exist or populate the world, each with their own specific powers and capacities" (Mbembe 2016, 43). Mbembe makes clear that the project of decentering the human subject does not mean to degrade humans but to uproot the Western colonial ideology of human mastery. Thus he states, "Our world is populated by a variety of nonhuman actors" and claims agency also to what is typically viewed as merely objects of nature without the capacity of agency (Mbembe 2016, 43).

Subsequently, Mbembe argues that overcoming dualism and anthropocentrism has radical implications for the way race is understood (Mbembe 2016, 44). In brief, one such implication is a critique of the speciesist belief in the supremacy of the human race. Such critique brings the discussion of racism to another level and suggests a strong connection between critiques of racism and speciesism. This means most basically, says Mbembe, that we need to question the belief in the incommensurable differences between us and other species and the prejudice of human supremacy. Hence "race thinking increasingly entails profound questions about the nature of species in general" (Mbembe 2016, 44).

In conclusion, Mbembe writes: "In the last instance, non-racialism is truly about radical sharing and universal inclusion" (Mbembe 2016, 44). More specifically, Mbembe argues that nonracialism is the antithesis of the "rule of the market," of the "domination of politics by capital," which has resulted in the destruction of countless human and nonhuman lives and devastation of our natural environment (Mbembe 2016, 45). Indeed, as he says, we have to learn how to share our planet again among all humans, but also between humans and nonhumans.

Conclusion

I conclude with a short summary. I attempted to give a brief systematic introduction to African phenomenology in distinction to Western and Africana phenomenology. I ventured to show that what ultimately seems to distinguish African phenomenology from other phenomenologies is its specific critical focus on the formative effect of the crisis of the life experience of unjust structures and disenabling conditions on the conscious mind in but also beyond the African context. The best way to explore African phenomenology seems to examine the diverse approaches of its contributors. I consequently identified in outline four distinctive approaches characterizing African phenomenology, including critical transcendental phenomenology, existential phenomenology, hermeneutic phenomenology, and postphenomenology. These approaches show both commonalities and distinctions between phenomenologists inside and outside the African context. However, these, and other possible approaches, deserve more in-depth attention and anticipate much further going investigation.

Notes

1. In a note More makes references to Sithole (2016); Modiri (2017); and Hill (2015). In addition, see, for example, More (2017); Lamola (2016); and Gordon (2008b).

2. The reference is to More's contribution to this anthology. More's reference to Henry is to the latter's text "Africana Phenomenology: Its Philosophical Implications" (Henry 2006, 105). For More's own contributions to Black existential phenomenology, see More (2018, 2021).

3. See, for instance, the introductions to Africana phenomenology by Gordon (1997, 2000, 2008a), Henry (2006), and Outlaw (2017). Note there is an introductory chapter "African Phenomenology: Introductory Perspectives" in the *Handbook of African Phenomenology* (Olivier 2023), which is substantially different from this chapter in that its focus is on the work of Hountondji as related to Masolo and Wiredu.

4. See, for instance, Moran (2000) and Smith (2018).

5. For further discussion, see Lamola (2016).

6. For references, see Janz (2017).

7. For the next subsection I draw from my discussion of Hountondji and Masolo in Olivier (2023).

8. The interested reader may like to skip this subsection and read More's text in this anthology. Otherwise, this subsection may serve to briefly introduce the reader to and compare different approaches in African phenomenology.

9. For an introduction and contributions to postphenomenology, see Rosenberger and Verbeek (2015).

10. The remaining part of this subsection relies on my discussion of Mbembe's work in Olivier (2021).

References

Biko, Steven. 2005. *I Write What I Like*. Cambridge: ProQuest.
Du Bois, W. E. B. 1996. *The Souls of Black Folk*. The Project Gutenberg eBook.

Fanon, Frantz. 1967. *Black Skins, White Masks*. London: Pluto Press.

Gordon, Lewis R., ed. 1997. *Existence in Black: An Anthology of Black Existential Philosophy*. Routledge: New York.

Gordon, Lewis R. 2000. *Existentia Africana: Understanding Africana Existential Thought*. New York: Routledge.

Gordon, Lewis R. 2008a. *An Introduction to Africana Philosophy*. Cambridge: Cambridge University Press.

Gordon, Lewis R. 2008b. "A Phenomenology of Biko's Black Consciousness." In *Biko Lives! Contesting the Legacies of Steve Biko*, edited by A. Mngxitama, A. Alexander, and N. C. Gibson, 83–93. New York: Palgrave Macmillan.

Gordon, Lewis R. 2023. "Some Reflections from Africana Phenomenology on African Phenomenology." In *Phenomenology in an African Context: Contributions and Challenges*, edited by Abraham Olivier, M. John Lamola, and Justin Sands, 000–000. Albany: State University of New York Press.

Henry, Paget. 2006. "Africana Phenomenology: Its Philosophical Implications." *Worlds and Knowledges Otherwise* (Fall): 1–22. https://globalstudies. trinity.duke.edu/sites/globalstudies.trinity.duke.edu/files/file-attachments/ v1d3_PHenry.pdf.

Hill, Shannen L. 2015. *Biko's Ghost: The Iconography of Black Consciousness*. Minneapolis: University of Minnesota Press, 2015.

Hountondji, Paulin J. 2002. *The Struggle for Meaning: Reflections on Philosophy, Culture, and Democracy in Africa*. Athens: Ohio University Press.

Husserl, Edmund. 1970. *The Crisis of European Sciences and Transcendental Phenomenology*. Evanston: Northwestern University Press.

Husserl, Edmund. 1965. "Philosophy as Rigorous Science." In *Phenomenology and the Crisis of Philosophy*, translated by Q. Lauer, 71–178. New York: Harper & Row.

Janz, Bruce B., ed. 2017. *Place, Space and Hermeneutics*. Cham: Springer.

Lamola, M. John. 2016. "Biko, Hegel and the End of Black Consciousness: A Historico-Philosophical Discourse on South African Racism." *Journal of Southern African Studies* 42, no. 2: 183–194. DOI: 10.1080/03057070.2016.1135672.

Masolo, D. A. 2010. *Self and Community in a Changing World*. Bloomington: Indiana University Press.

Manganyi, Noel Chabani. 1973. *Being-Black-in-the-World*. Johannesburg: Spro-cas/ Ravan.

Mbembe, Achille. 2001. *On the Postcolony*. Berkeley: University of California Press.

Mbembe, Achille. 2016. "Decolonising the University: New Directions." *Arts and Humanities in Higher Education* 15, no. 1: 29–45.

Mbembe, Achille. 2017. *Critique of Black Reason*. Translated by Laurent Dubois. Durham, NC: Duke University Press.

Modiri, Joel M. 2017. "The Jurisprudence of Steve Biko: A Study in Race, Law and Power." In "The 'Afterlife' of Colonial Apartheid," PhD thesis, University of Pretoria, Pretoria.

Moran, Dermot. 2000. *Introduction to Phenomenology*. London: Routledge.

More, Mabogo Percy. 2008. "Biko: Africana Existentialist Philosopher." In *Biko Lives! Contesting the Legacies of Steve Biko*, edited by A. Mngxitama, A. Alexander, N. C. Gibson, 45–68. New York: Palgrave Macmillan.

More, Mabogo Percy. 2017. *Biko: Philosophy, Identity and Liberation*. Cape Town: HSRC.

More, Mabogo Percy. 2018. *Looking through Philosophy in Black: Memoirs*. London: Rowman & Littlefield International.

More, Mabogo Percy. 2021. *Sartre on Contingency: Antiblack Racism and Embodiment*. London: Rowman & Littlefield.

More, Mabogo Percy. 2023. "Chabani Manganyi: The Lived Experience of Difference." In *Phenomenology in an African Context: Contributions and Challenges*, edited by Abraham Olivier, M. John Lamola, and Justin Sands, 127–152. Albany: State University of New York Press.

Olivier, Abraham. 2021. "Decolonisation and Displacement: Mbembe on Decolonising the University." In *Decolonisation as Democratisation: The South African Experience*, edited by S. Kumalo, 187–215. Cape Town: HSRC Press.

Olivier, A. (2023). African Phenomenology: Introductory Perspectives. In *Handbook of African Philosophy*, edited by Elvis Imafidon, Mpho Tshivashe, and Bjoern Freter, 1–27. Cham: Springer, https://doi.org/10.1007/978-3-030-77898-9_37-1

Outlaw, Lucius T., Jr. 2017. "Africana Philosophy." In *Stanford Encyclopedia of Philosophy* (Summer), edited by Edward N. Zalta. Available at https://plato.stanford.edu/archives/sum2017/entries/africana/.

Rosenberger, Robert, and Peter-Paul Verbeek, eds. 2015. *Postphenomenological Investigations: Essays on Human-Technology Relations*. London: Lexington Books.

Sartre, Jean-Paul. 1948. *Portrait of the Anti-Semite*. Translated by Erik de Mauny. London: Secker & Warburg.

Serequeberhan, Tsenay. 1994. *The Hermeneutics of African Philosophy: Horizon and Discourse*. Oxford: Routledge.

Serequeberhan, Tsenay. 2015. *Existence and Heritage*. Albany: State University of New York Press.

Sithole, Tendayi. 2016. *Steve Biko: Decolonial Meditations of Black Consciousness*. Lanham: Lexington Books.

Smith, David Woodruff. 2018. "Phenomenology." In *Stanford Encyclopaedia for Philosophy*. Stanford: The Metaphysics Research Lab Center for the Study of Language and Information, Stanford University.

2

Some Reflections from Africana Phenomenology on African Phenomenology

Lewis R. Gordon

These reflections are written amid preparations for the twenty-fifth anniversary editions of *Bad Faith and Antiblack Racism* and *Fanon and the Crisis of European Man: An Essay on Philosophy and the Human Sciences*.[1] The first book, which was an expansion of my doctoral dissertation, examines the phenomena of racism and antiblack racism through resources from existential phenomenology. The second, which builds on the first, drew its inspiration from a realization of a problem involved in the study of any human phenomenon—namely, the impact of the studier's fears and prejudices obfuscating crucial critical dimensions of study. When both books were written, I had no idea of the interlocution they would afford across the global south, especially among thinkers in Africa, and the subsequent research in what today is understood as the project of shifting the geography of reason. That commitment is now a feature of theoretical inquiry across varieties of linguistic divides, as not only Africana philosophy came into its own but also new kinds of African philosophical considerations premised upon unshackling chains imposed on the status of African philosophy in the history of ideas.

In *Bad Faith and Antiblack Racism*, the argument was seemingly simple. Racism involves identifying groups of human beings under the category of a specific race and then denying their humanity on the basis of their belonging to that category or categories. It requires the denial of humanity through, at first, the identification of human subjects. This movement, I argued, is a form of bad faith because it involves lying to oneself through investing or believing in what one does not believe. This complicated phenomenon of self-lying in addition to self-deception has many implications, which range from an effort to evade freedom and responsibility to forms of misanthropy because of other human beings's role sources of accountability. The result was an exploration into the many implications of this phenomenon ranging from—as Mabogo More has written on the book not only in past essays but also in his foreword to the celebration edition and in his recent monograph on racism—the effort to deny contingency in human existence to the semiotics of Manichean impositions on human reality (More 2018, 2021).[2] The latter involves the logic of contraries—of universals of absolute positivity versus absolute negativity—suitable for apartheid and other colonial efforts to impose being and nonbeing onto human existence instead of living the dialectical realities of interaction, communication, and transcendence. Those contraries did not only have racial significance. They also revealed the convergence of gender and sexuality in every moment of racialization. To offer a proper critique of them, I argued further, one must have a sense of what is involved in the constitution of human relationships and hence human study. One must articulate what is at stake in what is lost for the loss to be significant. As racism in general and antiblack racism in particular are both attacks on human beings and our understanding of human reality, it is clear that the study of race and racism are fields of human study. Thus, the problem of bad faith requires going beyond specifically those fields and into their conditions of possibility, which are human study and human reality, that I at times refer to as philosophical anthropology.

Among my discoveries in *Bad Faith and Antiblack Racism* is the importance of existential ontology versus other kinds of ontology. Existential ontology is ironic in that it is ultimately a critique of being and Being with regard to human study; it is, in short, a critique of ontology. The human being is an existent that transcends being, which makes "being" in human being actually tentative. This is where a crucial phenomenological insight comes to the fore. In phenomenology—at least from the kind that came out of the thought of Edmund Husserl—the phenomenon described in phenomenological research is examined from the perspective of reorientation from the natural attitude, which he regards as the naïve presupposition of the being of the world and the world of being. Put differently, if one parenthesizes, brackets, suspends, or shifts from questions of the ontological status of phenomena, one is able to examine them beyond ontology. In the case of the human being and human reality, this led to an insight that I later showed is shared by African and Asian philosophers of the phenomenological kind—namely, that existence transcends being and Being. This means that the assertion of the primacy of ontology would be, in effect, a covering over of existence—and, by extension, reality—through the absolute of the positive side of a contrary. Put differently, thinking toward what could be called Absolute reality is greater than being or Being and thus radicalizes the call for responsibility over what is thought and done. In formal logical terms, reality is not a well-formed formula.

Let me now move to *Fanon and the Crisis of European Man* since it is that text that inaugurated a variety of arguments and institutions through conversations with African philosophy and, given the context here, African phenomenology that was cultivated since the mid-1990s.

Fanon and the Crisis of European Man offered (1) a conception of crisis in which colonialism and decolonization were at the forefront of thought in our times, where "European man" is his own crisis of investment in the idea that his lost hegemony supposedly equals not only the demise of reason but also the end of the world; (2) this crisis entailed a reorientation and misrepresentation of history and nature—especially in the history of science and technology—beyond what Husserl argued in his later writings (e.g., that "European man's" lack of imagination equaled for him, and even his critics ranging from Heidegger to Derrida, *the limits of what can be thought*); yet (3) the simultaneously advancement of Husserl as an object and source of critique in which at least each movement of his arguments and descriptions was an interrogation of epistemic closure and epistemic colonization; and, thus, (4) the introduction of the concepts of disciplinary and ontological suspension as a rewriting of bracketing and parenthesizing the natural attitude, especially within many if not all disciplines, as a form of decadence. Some consequences of that work were theoretical and others institutional.

The conceptual significance was what some commentators call "postcolonial phenomenology" and its impact on what are known as Africana philosophy, decoloniality, shifting the geography of reason, and Fanon studies through which also creolization arguments, as found in the writings of Jane Anna Gordon (2014) and Michael J. Monahan (2011), followed.[3] It was not that that work *created* those areas of thought. After all, decoloniality was already well on its way through Aníbal Quijano's critical work in world systems theory and dependency theory from Emmanuel Weinstein and Samir Amin. Latin American philosophy of liberation and liberation theology also preceded that work. And ideas on creolization go back, at least in linguistics theory, for more than half a century.[4] What was different about that work was the conceptual articulation of those concerns outside of a Eurocentric framework and in so doing posing a new set of arguments from which to build on what I call the human being's relationship with reality. This involved thinking of consciousness in ways that were not beholden to reductive models in which its spark rested only in the guise of Europeans or, in racialized language, whites. But more, the argument of that text was that if critique required metacritique in moments of methodological advancement, then each phenomenological act of bringing to the fore the contradictions and fallacies of ontological investment was one of decolonizing methods. This meant a commitment of going not only beyond colonial investments (epistemic and professional) but also the presupposition of negative critique as a sole objective of thought. This observation led to the argument that phenomenological reduction—or better, phenomenological critique—required decolonizing practices to become rigorous. Bear in mind that Husserl understood the importance of disorienting the inquirer in relationship to the natural attitude, which included the use of unfamiliar terms. He offered the Greek word *epoché* (*epokhē*), which, in Hellenic philosophy, referred to suspending or withholding judgment. English translations as "reduction" led to a parallel discussion of his ideas because of the many connotations of that term whose Latin etymology points to leading back and restoration. The negative interpretation as in reducing, eliminating, cutting, which in German would be *die Ermäßigung*, serves a different purpose. The meaning of suspending or withholding judgment entails moments in which hegemonic investments lose their potency. This requires, as Husserl expressed it in German, *Einklammerung* ("bracketing"). This act of disarming the force of hegemonic claims and presuppositions of legitimacy, of, in other words, not presuming ontological gravitas, is one of the reasons why I not only preferred the expression "ontological suspension" but also, in its utility, called it a postcolonial maneuver. That understanding led to my conclusion that postcolonial phenomenology was simply another way of saying rigorous phenomenology. The text also anticipated a variety of developments that are rearticulations of "European man" primarily through its critique of poststructuralism, which was very much in vogue at that time and continues to be so albeit under different nomenclature. Despite the critique of Husserlian phenomenology advanced by poststructuralism's textual and genealogical adherents, their response was to remain locked in repetitions of those arguments in which European man continued to play a central role, even under the guise of European woman, Latin American man, and negative models of black man. The new brands, of which many contemporary theorists in the humanities and social sciences are familiar, are "critical theory," "decoloniality," and "Afropessimism" (among others).[5] As this is an anthology on *phenomenology*, I will not devote much time to those developments, but I will instead contextualize their relationship to contemporary concerns of African phenomenology in the later part of these reflections.

Let us briefly identify some institutional elements. *Fanon and the Crisis of European Man* led to the Phenomenology Roundtable followed by the Institute for Caribbean Thought and then the Caribbean Philosophical Association and a variety of other organizations and publications, ranging from the journal *Radical Philosophy Review* and the transformation of *The CLR James Journal* to book series such as the past Routledge series in Africana thought to the current set of Rowman & Littlefield series: Creolizing the Canon, Global Critical Caribbean Thought, and Living Existentialism. Marilyn Nissim-Sabat's understanding of these movements summed things up well: she thought her love for Husserl was anathematic to her commitments to antiracist struggles, feminism, revolution, and social justice. She saw that work as transformative through its critique of idols and demonstration of how Husserlian phenomenology could be placed in conversation with those projects (Nissim-Sabat 1997).[6]

This is not to say that all of the institutions that emerged came from the formulations of that specific text. After all, the groundbreaking work of V. Y. Mudimbe raised critical questions of methodological critique at first through African existential philosophy and then through conversations with developments in archaeological and genealogical poststructuralism from the 1970s through the 1990s, when the influential Indiana University Press series on African Philosophy came to the fore with others' and his writings, of which two powerful achievements from the 1980s into the 1990s were Mudimbe's *The Invention of Africa* (1988) and D. A. Masolo's *African Philosophy in Search of Identity* (1994). That line of African philosophical thought eventually converged with the one inaugurated by *Fanon and the Crisis of European Man* in the writings of a group of African and Afro-Caribbean philosophers and social theorists, as is evident in Olúfẹ́mi Táíwò's *How Colonialism Preempted Modernity in Africa*, which was published in the same Indiana University Press series in 2010 and was awarded the Caribbean Philosophical Association's Frantz Fanon Outstanding Book Award in 2015.[7] Although Táíwò did not come out of the phenomenological tradition, with his earlier work being located primarily in the Marxist dialectical approaches to the study of law, his willingness to transcend methodological and disciplinary purity led not only to his conversing across the African diaspora with his award-winning book but also his explorations into more than a thousand years of West African thought in his ongoing critique of the not-out-of-Africa thesis that dominates much thought on Africa.[8]

We see, then, that work since the 1990s is more of convergence and ongoing transformation than old debates of "cause" and "effect" and "introduction" versus what could be called challenges of the *Zeitgeist*. We could call this the problem of "influence." On that, I now proceed.

On Influence

One difficulty with discussing anything African and anything black is that there is often no room for influence instead of "cause." In *Existentia Africana* (Gordon 2000), I raised this problem in the context of the relationship of experience to theory and thought. A guiding presumption in much of what we could call the Western academy is that black and indigenous peoples supposedly offer at best experience, but when it comes to reflection on that experience—thought and theory—the presupposition is that the source of such must come from elsewhere, usually the thought of a European or white thinker. The result was the presupposition of black and indigenous *thought* as oxymoronic, and this led often to discussions of Africana philosophy as primarily a focus on Africana intellectuals who "applied" the thought of European thinkers to the study of African experience. This, I argued, exemplified a form of epistemic colonization and dependency. Liberation was required, then, also of ideas. If European thinkers were building their ideas from their experience, then the appeal to those ideas as the exclusively legitimate exemplars of thought and theory meant, in effect, to delegitimate Africana people's experience as sources of ideas. Later on in *An Introduction to Africana Philosophy*

(Gordon 2008), I explicitly addressed and elaborated this problem of the deintellectualizing of Africana intellectual history. Intellectual projects require specifically intellectual problems, which connect to the unique crises stimulated from what Frantz Fanon called the attack on humanity waged by Euromodernity and the new relationship to precolonial history raised by developing a critique and going beyond that assault. That historical contextualization and critique entail at least three intellectual problematics: (1) the question of philosophical anthropology, (2) that of freedom and liberation, and (3) the metacritique of reason in which justification is, ironically, in need of justification. I will also return to these themes. For now, however, we must address the problem of influence raised from the critique of the "application" model.

The application model presumes a hegemonic white presupposition that Africana peoples are supposedly effects of European or white agents of history. They in effect treat white people as transcendental conditions of thought. The conclusion, then, is that the only way an Africana or black thinker could *think* is through the ideas of a European or white thinker. The historical fiction is that it was not only subjugation and European styles of government and extraction brought to Africa but also *thought*.

The tendency to treat African and black thought as mere application emerged from a history of active misrepresentation through which Euromodernity emerged not only as a set of historical and political expectations but also as an epistemic project. This epistemic project was advanced not by thought alone but also, as history shows, by swords, guns, and the institutionalization of radical forms of inequality premised upon the invisibility of those designated as "conquered" and "colonized." The effects were, in addition to carnage and ongoing suffering, practices of epistemic erasure. This led to the tendency to transform nearly all positive terms into European designations or racialized ones as white. To be "modern," for example—a term that simply means to belong to the present—came to be European and white. Since to belong to the present is legitimated through also belonging to the future, to be part of the direction in which humanity is going, the consequence for those African, black, and indigenous became that of belonging to, or, worse, trapped in, the past. The white belonging to the future carried an air of permanence similar to the logic of settler colonialism—a world that is settled, that is, through the permanent absence and thus eventual erasure of those whose domain is primeval. This legitimation by virtue of presumed permanence over time of avowed conquerors and settlers offered a teleology that retroactively affected the status of the present and, consequently, the past. Missing here, however, is consultation with those excluded and preempted peoples. "They" become those who are studied, not those who study and are capable of producing conditions for future study of what it means to study (think of the metacritique of reason). More radically, this line of reasoning leads to the necessity of European and white recognition as necessary conditions of legitimacy. A form of standpoint fallacy of appealing to authority (instead of that which is authoritative through having evidential legitimacy) follows. If, however, we first take the position that non-European or white thinkers are sources of thought and can thus build ideas through which belonging is a feature of their relationship to the future—and we accept consulting European thought but reject its recognition as a necessary condition and source of legitimacy—we would arrive at a set of considerations beyond Euromodernity through which the future could be transformed. This realization affords some immediate clarification of the terms under discussion thus far.

The first is to explain the use of "European or white" and "African, black, or indigenous." To that, there is also "Black." The reason is that in actual history, there were and continue to be Europeans who are not white, and there are whites who are not Europeans. Similarly, there are Africans who are not black. And, there are blacks who are not indigenous, and Africans who—for example, when they are in North America—are not indigenous. Africans in Africa are indigenous peoples. But even that is tricky, since there was no reason for any African to think of Africans as indigenous before periods of invasion from those outside of their countries, territories, or world. Similarly, there was no reason for African identity to become black until such was imposed upon Africans. The distinction between black and Black, however, requires elaboration. A black, as used here, signifies a racialized subject produced through the historical circumstances of Euromodernity and its technologies of power, which results in the black as an abject figure. A Black is a black who has transcended that abjection. That Black's understanding of self is not a function of how she or he is perceived by hostile white or other forms of antiblack eyes. That Black transcends those limits through an understanding of others beyond whiteness and potential others beyond the conceptions of people in her or his lifetime. Thus, the Black is an agent of history, one who links a future beyond the shackles of an imposed identity. This Black, then, retroactively thinks about the present in a way that is critical of European and white hegemony, in addition to other kinds of antiblack assessments. Regarding white hegemony as Eurocentric and racist, such Blacks particularize Euromodernity into one among many human possibilities. This observation, which is clearly a form of ontological suspension, is one of the contributions of Africana phenomenological thought. It is a movement from what W. E. B. Du Bois called "double consciousness" (seeing oneself through the eyes of negative hegemonic others) and what Paget Henry calls "potentiated second sight" and Jane Anna Gordon calls "potentiated double consciousness"—seeing oneself critically beyond initial double consciousness.[9] This potentiated form requires identifying the Manichean elements of an apartheid-structured episteme and offering a dialectical critique of it as one that makes people into problems instead of addressing, as elaborated in the fourth chapter of *Existentia Africana*, the problems such people face in a society premised upon cultivating such problems. This observation is, of course, shared by others who have explored the cultivation of a critical consciousness. Think, for example, of Antonio Gramsci's critique of common sense and his proffering of a critical consciousness of it. We should bear in mind, however, that convergence here of Du Bois and Gramsci is not causal but instead a shared observation. After all, Du Bois's observations preceded Gramsci's by nearly a third of a century, and others among Black phenomenology-oriented thinkers ranging from Richard Wright and Cheikh Anta Diop to Frantz Fanon offered the same relationship of convergence instead of causal effect.

Straightaway, then, Africana phenomenology would relate to phenomenology as articulated by European thinkers such as Husserl, Dilthey, Stein, Sartre, and Merleau-Ponty not as the latter standing as robust universality in relation to which the former is a particularity but instead of both as particularities of something greater than themselves. In effect, this is what phenomenology, in fidelity to *epochē*, means as a post- or decolonial practice. To make phenomenology rigorous, Husserl, for example, should have questioned his Eurocentrism in the way he articulated the relativistic fallacies of naturalism and historicism in his famous lecture "Philosophy as Rigorous Science" (Husserl 1965, 71–147). The relationship to thinking, which he later referred to as the transcendental ego, should *not* be a *European* one but, instead, an understanding of any constituted relationship of thought.[10] Thus, where there is commonality between the set of European phenomenologists and Africana phenomenologists, there should also be convergence and, in some instances, influence. This should work in both directions. For instance, G. W. F. Hegel addressed, criticized, and built on ideas from Immanuel Kant without being read in the history of ideas as a mere application of Kant's thought. The same applies to Marx's critical relationship to and inheritance from Hegel. We could think of the same with regard to Husserl when he took his transcendental turn. Kant is their influence; but he is not their master. When white thinkers use the thought of other white thinkers, the concept of influence is not only acknowledged but also taken for granted. Schopenhauer was influenced by Kant's second critique, which focused on practical reason, and his philosophy influenced Nietzsche and Freud. Later on, Michel Foucault began his career with a study of Kant's philosophical anthropology, and he examined conditions of possibility arguments, without their being reduced to Kantian transcendentalism, throughout his career. Foucault is not, however, remembered in the history of ideas as "Kantian." The same applies to his genealogical turn, attributed to his rethinking Nietzsche, but, as we see with regard to Schopenhauer's influence on Nietzsche, the road sign points back to Kant. Foucault, however, is studied by many of his adherents, from Judith Butler to Wendy Brown and Ann Stolers, often without his predecessors as causal.

Where, however, many thinkers of African descent or other Black thinkers explore what is useful from these European giants, the tendency is not the same. Take, for example, Fanon. There are texts examining whether Fanon was "Hegelian," "Marxian," "Gramscian," "Lacanian," "Sartrean," and even, despite them having been contemporaries born within five years of each other, "Derridean" and "Foucauldian," despite Fanon having made his mark nearly a decade before theirs (Gordon 2015). Fanon, as anyone who reads his work immediately notices, utilized ideas from a large variety of thinkers ranging from his countryman Aimé Césaire and the Haitian Jacques Romain through to the Catalan François Tosquelles and the Austrians Sigmund Freud, Anna Freud, and Alfred Adler. They obviously influenced his thought, but to read his ideas as an "application" of theirs would be to commit a form of injustice. It elides the originality of his thought and the influence he had on not only some of these thinkers but also others such as Sartre, Foucault, and Derrida, in addition to those in Africa and the African diaspora ranging from Steve Bantu Biko, Kwame Touré, and William R. Jones to Ngũgĩ wa Thiong'o, Chabani Manganyi, V. Y. Mudimbe, Angela Y. Davis, Souleymane Bachir Diagne, Paget Henry, Mabogo P. More, and this author. So, in the course of what follows, it should be borne in mind that it is a portrait primarily of influence, though there are moments in which "application" of the thought of one thinker on that of another is appropriate and others in which it moves along a path of reciprocity.

Africana Philosophy and Phenomenology

To talk about Africana philosophy requires also talking about philosophy. This brings up some of the fallacies already mentioned, especially that of treating terms such as "philosophy" and "Africana" as oxymoronic. As "African" is part of "Africana," the same applies to African philosophy. What makes discussions even more difficult is not only that "philosophy" is treated by its hegemonic adherents as born in what is today Southern Europe, but also that its contemporary practice tends to be far from philosophical. Professional philosophy, after all, is an academic enterprise more beholden to journals and professional demands for career advancement and location than to "wisdom." We know this because much of philosophy as practiced is "disciplinarily decadent" (Gordon 2006). This is where one ontologizes one's discipline to the point of treating its methodological framework as one created by the gods. Another way of putting this is the ontologizing of one's discipline and its methods. The result is that many philosophers would ignore truth handed to them from other disciplines and, in similar kind, other areas or kinds of philosophy. This is why many analytical philosophers, for example, would rather imagine they have invented the wheel or wait for one of them to claim its invention than simply to use wheels created by Eurocontinental philosophers and those beyond Eurocentric frameworks and get on with other matters. Among Eurocentric continentalists, a similar phenomenon emerges, as we know from the Heideggerian infamous line of philosophy as an enterprise best thought in Greek and German, and properly so only when ultimately concerned with Being.[11]

I am not alone in this critical view of much of what is called professional philosophy. Even Husserl argued that much of what was called professional philosophy in his times was not actually philosophy.[12] This was so for him because of many European philosophers' search to subordinate science and thought to its particular manifestations, which made their efforts forms of pseudo-naturalistic science, historicisms, and a variety of other areas through which, in their investments, they in effect turn away from reality. In this regard, Husserl shares much with the East Indian philosopher Sri Aurobindo and the Japanese philosopher Keiji Nishitani. Both argue, contra Heidegger, that the ontological investment in Being actually evades, elides, and, worse, covers over reality. Husserl made a similar argument in his form of transcendental turn, which he initiated from his suspension of ontological commitments in the natural attitude. Doing such, he could continue his phenomenological investigations, but the task required more if he were to radicalize this critique. Its radical-ization he called transcendental phenomenology, which for him was, ultimately, philosophy. I will return to this in my discussion of Africana phenomenology. Before doing such, however, I must make some remarks on the archaeolinguistic and historical appeal to Southern Europe as the origins of philosophy.

This appeal is usually premised on the etymology of the word "philosophy" from the conjunction of the Greek words *philo* (love of the fraternal or devotional kind) and *sophia* (wisdom). Yet, if we take that line of reasoning at its word, it quickly collapses. It is based on the pre-supposition that the search for thought, as we noticed earlier, always leads one to Europe, and that etymology, that road, leads to classical Greek and Latin. Yet those languages are, in the history of a species that is a little more than three hundred thousand years old, pretty recent. One need simply ask: On which earlier languages were Greek and Latin premised? That question inevitably leads to Africa.

We should bear in mind the cartographical fallacy of imposing onto the past the geopolitical organization of land from the present. Thus, ancient Africa is often studied as though its peoples always stopped at the site of the future Suez Canal from concern of stepping "out" of Africa. Yet strangely enough the logic does not apply to others going into Africa. Thus, Eastern African peoples up to the Mediterranean shores tend to be called "Afro-Asiatic" in contemporary literature, despite their ancient rule and reach extending up and across the Levant. Yet the peoples of the Levant through to the Arabian Sea are called "West Asian" or "Middle Eastern." Why not also call them "Afro-Asiatic"? We see here the ongoing search for a form of purity in which the African functions as a contaminant.

Mdw Ntr, an ancient African language older than Greek, was what the ancient people of Kmt spoke. Today, because of ancient Macedonian colonization, we know Kmt as Egypt. Philosophy was practiced in that society long before what is today often ridiculously and self-aggrandizingly referred to as "the Greek Miracle," as this quotation attests:

> [The lovers of wisdom are those] whose heart is informed about these things which would be otherwise ignored, those who are clear-sighted when they are deep into a problem, those who are moderate in their actions, who penetrate ancient writings, whose advice is [sought] to unravel complications, who are really wise, who instructed their own heart, who stay awake

at night as they look for the right paths, who surpass what they accomplished yesterday, who are wiser than a sage, who brought themselves to wisdom, who ask for advice and see to it that they are asked advice.[13]

I use the third-person plural in the translation because that society had philosophers who were men and women. The people of Kmt had many words to refer to wisdom of many different kinds, but the crucial one for our purposes is *Sbyt* ("wise teachings"). It is the source of the Greek word *sophia*. The related word *Sba* ("to teach" or "to be wise") was transformed through the Greek-speaking peoples' tendency to transform the Mdw Ntr *b* to *ph* or, in English, *f*. Commentaries on this genealogy are many. The layers of complexity around how *Sbyt* relates to other ancient concepts from Kmt such as *MAat*—whose meaning ranges from balance and breath to justice, right, and truth, exemplified by the role of the eponymic goddess—would require elaboration beyond the scope of this discussion. For now, these "wise teachings," which required learners, lovers, and seekers of them, precede their counterparts in the ancient Hellenic city-states by a few millennia, of which the Antef letter is a more recent example. The curious could consult writings of Ptahhotep, Peseshet, Amenemhat I, Kehty, Ani, Khun-Anup, Akhenaten, and Nefertiti.[14] Bear in mind that some of the "ancient writings" of which Antef wrote no doubt included those of Imhotep, which would date back nearly six thousand years ago.

This element of "wise teachings" is crucial for the understanding not only of philosophy but also phenomenology. As is well known, phenomenology focuses on phenomena or that which appears or is made manifest. Appearance has the structure appearance-*of*, which, as every phenomenologist knows, is a crucial feature of consciousness, which must always be *of* something. The appearance of something makes no sense without consciousness of it. This is one of the bases of suspending the ontological status of what appears. Whatever it is without appearing is another matter. The intentional theory of consciousness also raises the question of theory as a focus of consciousness. In other words, phenomenology addresses all of which there can be consciousness. There is thus not only phenomenology but also phenomenological metatheory. Theory, however, is a complicated matter. For the sake of brevity, I will just refer to theory through its etymological origins of conjoining the Greek *thea* with *orah* for the word *theoria*. The former refers not only to a god but also to sight or to seeing. The latter refers to light. Conjoined, they exemplify seeing facilitated by light, which in the infinitive was *theorein* (to view or to see). The idea is that without the light, one "sees" darkness, but this is inaccurate since paradoxically darkness is a kind of light. Really not to see is not even to see darkness. Now think of how this relates to another word built upon *thea*—namely, theater. When one goes to a theater, one sees the action when the stage is lit. But when the light is turned on or the curtains drawn, one must make decisions about that at which one looks. At the heart of all acts of seeing, then, is also choice, and, interestingly enough, a word linked to such is *krinein*, which means "to decide" or "to choose." Again, for the sake of brevity I am here sticking to the Greek etymology. This is, of course, not the entire story. For instance, *orah* is connected to the Hebrew word *Or*, which means "light." As Juda was once a Greek and then Roman colony, the influence of terminology from the colonized signifies a history of influence moving from the south. For our purposes, what is crucial here is that *krinein* is also the basis of the word *kritikos* (able to make judgments), from which we get "critic." It is also the basis of the word "crisis."

In a crisis one must make decisions. In the process of making decisions, one also learns. Thus, phenomenological movements—unfortunately popularly known, by virtue of English translations of the Greek term *epochē*, as "reductions"—are also acts of learning. Phenomenological metatheory, then, is a practice of learning about theory, and this is done through deontologizing theory—that is, not treating theory as intrinsically or ontologically fixed and legitimated. Phenomenological inquiry into theory, then, leads it to question its own efforts to assess theory. This means that phenomenology also must be subject to critique, and this requires not presuming its intrinsic legitimacy. The result, inevitably, is to arrive at a point where the inquirer faces theory as a subject of inquiry while attempting not to do so in the structural relation of intentionality (that is, the initial point of departure of phenomenology). The problem, however, is that that would be like trying not to see darkness when the light is out. But more, what one is left with is basically an intentional structure as follows:

→ (theory)

Now, if the structure of phenomenological inquiry were a variable for any subject "x," it is placed inside the parenthesis as follows:

→ (x)

The conclusion is that the structure of theorizing exemplifies the relationship of consciousness as understood in phenomenology. A critic who objects to this would simply be asked *to do otherwise*. In other words, to *show* that one could theorize without such a structure.

Husserlian phenomenology then builds on this realization to ask what would happen if we were to suspend naturalism and its correlative presupposition of reality as "outside" of us. What about the reality we experience and continue to learn from "inside" or more properly from our relationships to what is thought? For Husserl, this is the movement to transcendental phenomenology, and the discoveries here would be properly philosophical as they are learned through this practice of thought. They generate their own problems such as the evidentiality of evidence, the communicability of that evidentiality in intersubjective relationships, and the radical arrival of the structure of all relationships of thought, which he famously called the transcendental ego. The mistake many critics make of this conclusion is that they think of ego as a substance—an ontological notion—instead of a relationship to reality outside of the framework of ontological commitments such as being and substance. Difficult as this is to understand for many locked in naturalistic formulations, phenomenological consciousness is not psychological, and the transcendental ego is an even more radical rejection of such psychological containments. There is, in other words, the establishment of a relationship whose constitution we grammatically refer to as the transcendental ego.[15]

Now, if we think of philosophy in this way, we would only have part of the story of philosophical work. After all, if one arrives at such abstraction, what happens if one were to reverse each step? Here we have a curious consideration. Think back to the discussion of "theory." Notice how that analysis was steeped in the language of sight. Can one "see," however, without meaning? I bring this up because much of the effort to colonize thought involves the colonization of theory. This requires theory to stand, in effect, without myth. But myth—from the Greek word *muthos*, which means "from the mouth"—is the stuff of meaning. No meaning, as any psychoanalysis, for example, would remind us, occurs without repetition (Barratt 2013). One never initially encounters a meaning but instead eventually does so in repeated practices *as meant*. In phenomenology, this is called the practice of constitution, but in ordinary language, we could call this the process of narration (from the mouth), which involves repetition. This means, then, that meaning is always mythopoetic (think, for example, of the theological subtext of *theoria*). Thus, the effort for theory to eliminate myth leads it to the problem of seeing without meaning.

Building on this problem, we could easily see, then, the importance not only of myth but also another important ingredient of theoretical and ultimately philosophical thought—namely, allegory. Again, I will stick for now to the Greek language for the sake of brevity. "Allegory" comes from putting together the Greek words *allos* ("another," "something else," and, at times, "beyond") and *agoreuein* ("to speak openly"). It is to bring to speech its openness—its disclosure (*alethia*, which is often translated as "truth")—by means of something else. In effect, then, allegory brings us outside. But if we think of one of the most famous allegories, Plato's Allegory of the Cave in his *Republic*—which is profoundly an allegory about allegory—the subject who gets outside returns to the cave in a different relationship with its shadows. Thus, if we were to return to the phenomenological philosophical point about moving through each step from the transcendental relationship known as the transcendental ego, each step is no longer the same as it was from the initial movement. It is now allegorical, which means the eventual step back into the natural attitude is a profoundly different kind of understanding of "natural." One does not actually return since naivety, as it were, could only return through a loss of reflection. Yet, as we know, not everything is translucent even in reflection. Thus, despite not properly returning to the natural attitude, there are always elements of ignored aspects of reality awaiting attention through reflection.

Returning beyond Europe

This insight is known in many traditions outside of European-formulated phenomenology. It is a feature of ancient African thought and it is, as Kwame Gyekye showed in *An Essay on African Philosophical Thought*, at the heart of varieties of African philosophical uses of proverbs (Gyekye 1995). The details of his discussion cannot be handled here. For our purposes, what is crucial is that he used archaeolinguistic resources of Twi for the Akan context, as other African philosophers explore such in languages ranging from Wolof and Fula to IsiTswana or Setswana, IsiXhosa, and too many to list here among the Bantu-speaking peoples.

Returning to Africana philosophy, we come then to a summary of how it unfolds phenomenologically. Africana philosophy clearly emerged in Euromodernity since the designation Africana is a recent designation of that diaspora. That scattering of African peoples was primarily forced through the various kidnapping, enslavement, and selling of Africans across the globe. This historical series of attacks on the humanity of those African peoples stimulated questions on their humanity, freedom, and the practices of justification offered in the service of rationalizing their dehumanization and enslavement. This is why Africana philosophy focuses on philosophical anthropology, freedom, and critical evaluation of justificatory practices. One could explore these concerns phenomenologically through critically articulating and evaluating what it means to be human, to be free, and to be justified. Thus, the familiar array of phenomenological concerns of meaning, evidentiality, and justification comes to the fore. But, as we have already seen, there are unique considerations raised in the dehumanization of Africana peoples as a function of their racialization into black peoples. This, further, leads to the problem of being indigenous to such racialization as black while being rejected as *belonging* to the Euromodern world as human beings—even though Euromodernity was never produced exclusively by Europeans but is, instead, remembered as such through investments in rationalizations of European exceptionalism. Theorists such as Nathalie Etoke and I refer to the phenomenon of black nonbelonging to the epoch in which racialized blackness is indigenous as black melancholia.[16] Those of us who reject that nonbelonging through also paradoxically rejecting *belonging to a world premised on that rejection* seek practices of thinking and agency that, as we saw, transform black into Black and thus possibility. As this consideration is made through the process of philosophical reflection, it, too, then moves from Africana phenomenological theory into Africana phenomenological philosophy. The clear result, then, becomes one of a movement into what is well known in the South African context as Black Consciousness.

Black Consciousness and Africana Phenomenology

When I wrote earlier of disciplinary decadence, I did not mention the response I offered in my writings on it. I argued that disciplinary decadence emerges from the fetishizing of one's method and the ontologizing of one's discipline. It is, in effect, a form of disciplinary and methodological nationalism. It is also in existentialist language a form of spirit of seriousness, where one materializes or ontologizes values. Thus, to deontologize or dematerialize such values is a necessary movement from such an affliction. I call such movement *teleological suspensions of disciplinarity.*

This involves going beyond one's discipline or method for the sake of reality. As we have seen in the previous discussion, reality, at least from a phenomenological perspective, is greater than our disciplines.

Paradoxically, going beyond philosophy often produces new kinds of philosophy. It also sometimes produces new kinds of disciplines other than philosophy. The going-beyond, however, requires a form of philosophical humility through communicating with other disciplines and methodological resources and ways of thinking, learning, and feeling that may require forms of openness. This is why interdisciplinarity is not an appropriate response, since each discipline could remain in its silo. *Trans*disciplinarity comes to the fore here, since it requires communicating with others and thus transcending the idea of one's intrinsic superiority, legitimacy, or reach.

Now, to understand this form of transcendence requires rethinking language. Many of us often think of language like a vessel. It "contains" us. Many of us also think of language too purposely. We at times forget that we sometimes speak without actually saying anything. One objection to transdisciplinarity is similar to the one about limits of translation. Not every word and concept in one language is translatable into others. This is sometimes used as the basis of in effect saying others should stay in their language/discipline and I will stay in mine. This, however, is the ontologizing of language/discipline. Recall that phenomenological phenomena, whose meaning is sometimes described phenomenologically as their "essence," are without the ontological drag of substance. That means they are in fact open. This means that one can, then, arrive at a limited point that is not only an end but also a beginning. The Ghanaian philosopher Kwasi Wiredu offers a critique of the translational-closure model as follows (Wiredu 1996). Once a human being learns a language, she or he continues to learn despite not encountering terms and concepts that are translatable into those initially learned. This is only possible if one could learn through practice of a term or grammatical form instead of initial knowing of its content, nuanced use, or meaning. It is, in effect, the same argument we made about *muthos* and repetition constituting meaning. This is so as well when speakers of one language communicate with those of another language. Since the languages are not isomorphic, each speaker eventually encounters untranslatable terms. What they do, Wiredu argues, is simply learn the untranslatable terms and grammar. These practices of untranslatability are rich in pedagogical content.

For philosophers theorizing Black Consciousness, the movement from black to Black means addressing possibilities that are without precedent.

They thus have to build practices of learning from phenomena posed by unique conditions from blackness to Blackness. It also means they must, at least in the context of African societies, raise questions of linguistic and other cultural resources for understanding possibility in an epoch premised on presuppositions of their belonging to the past. It would be insufficient for such cultural defense simply to be an assertion of belonging to the future since the relationship would require *living culture*, whose adaptations are premised on possibility and new kinds of meanings that, in a word, "fit" in relational terms what is being built. This, of course, is another way of saying Afromodernity, African modernity, Black modernity, Indigenous modernity, and other kinds once covered over or curtailed by Euromodernity.

These concerns, of course, are already hallmarks of much of African phenomenology. I have written about practitioners and adherents of these issues in *An Introduction to Africana Philosophy*. In this context, however, suffice it to say that we could see these African phenomenological features at work in the rethinking of concepts posed, for instance, by V. Y. Mudimbe in his understanding of invention, which is a concept rich in content beyond contemporary notions of "construction." He took as his critical task the interrogation and unraveling of the calcified disciplinary models of an Africa in which supposedly lived, even when closely studied, no human beings. His thought offers insight and the reasons for its methodological interrogations—similar to Fanon's method of questioning method—of seeking alternative ways of knowing (which he referred to as *gnosis*) and, by implication, studying. We see here the dimensions of phenomenological movements constitutive of *sbyit*. There is so much on which to reflect from Mudimbe's thought, especially its uniqueness as a form of African existential phenomenology, but at this point, the crucial element comes from the foci of other African phenomenologists and his reflections. After all, it is not simply about the philosophical anthropological challenge of addressing the notion of no human beings in highly populated countries but also understanding the human being who comes forth in the conceptual framework of such peoples. After all, the Bantu category of languages use prefixes of personhood to articulate a form of relational humanism in which the phenomenological anthropological theory can move into a phenomenological philosophical anthropology of human dignity and value. This is evident in writings of South African phenomenologists exploring such questions of African humanity such as Mogobe Ramose, Chabani Manganyi, and Mabogo More. This is also the case among Francophone African phenomenologists other than Mudimbe, such as his countryman Théophile Obenga and country woman Nadia Yala Kisukidi, the Cameroonian linguist Bertrade Ngo-Ngijol Banoum, in addition to the philosophical literary theorist Nathalie Etoke, and those from Senegal of which Cheikh Anta Diop and Leopold Senghor were great ancestors and Souleymane Bachir Diagne and Norman Ajari, and others from nearby Benin, such as Paulin Hountondji. Again, the crucial point to stress here is that these philosophers build their own investigations with influence from instead of dependency on other African and European thinkers. Even where the aims are more structuralist and poststructuralist in appearance, the underlying question, methodologically, is one of learning through doing in ways attuned to dangers of ontological reductionism.[17]

The call to Black Consciousness also raises the question of phenomenological Africana political philosophy. None of the African philosophers I have listed here eschew political imperatives. And in the South African case, in which Steve Bantu Biko was paramount, the question of political appearance was brought forth in the understanding of the movement of black from a politically subordinated category into Black as a politically active one. As the suppression of Black could mark an abdication of rigor in phenomenological reflection—given the arguments about decolonization at the heart of each phenomenological movement made in the spirit of its demand of *radical critique*—so, too, is Black a political challenge against which antiblack racist states ultimately wage war on political life as projects of power as a manifestation of freedom instead of coercion.

Some Concluding Thoughts

I have only here touched the surface of topics explored in African phenomenology and those posed by the intersection of "African" and "phenomenology." Today, for instance, the question of "theory" continues to be marked by the influence of poststructuralism instead of phenomenology as I outlined earlier. Yet, as should be evident, one is hard-pressed to find a self-avowed poststructuralist, although one could find theorists who adhere to phenomenology without often explicitly saying so. Their commitment, in other words, is often in the form of attempting to help us not only see what we see but also overcome the impediments to admitting what is patently evident. Elsewhere I elaborate on why many poststructuralists have for the most part rebranded themselves as critical theorists, decolonial theorists, and, flowing from a strange mixture of poststructuralism and existentialism, Afropessimists.[18] Contemporary African thought is rich with debates across these three developments and more. But the specificity of phenomenology demands a form of radical critique in which the critic, as we say, does not disappear.

All this means, despite the tendency in the academy to historicize and place phenomenological inquiry more under the rubric of professional academic textual analysis, there is much African phenomenological work to do beyond such scholastic dictates, though the importance of such scholarship has its own value. Although it is important sometimes to point at a pointing figure, it is also a good idea to look at that to which the finger is pointing. Sometimes orienting thinking outside of zones that fetishize thought into a single kind of reasoning enables a shift in the geography of reason. Others have noticed the importance of such a shift and the value of the ongoing practice of shifting the geography of reason.[19] The Eurocentric model, as many of us know from Hegel, involved the spark of reason in the East and its maturation in the West. To unshackle the chains of such chauvinism through the realization that all thinking is a human affair and that human beings think everywhere—as Michael Neocosmos (2016), among others, recently reminds us—makes *African* phenomenological philosophy clearly a part of this project of shifting the geography of reason, which, as should now be obvious, is also an epistemic decolonial practice.[20] The relational elements of doing so, as we saw in discussions of communicative practices, require not only learning but also, in doing so, being affected and affecting others. There is, then, already embedded in African phenomenology, which by extension comes back to the radicalization and thus rigor of phenomenological practice, a form of creolization of its movements. If the discussion of influence shows us anything, it is that there is much to learn from our fellow human beings, even *in* movements of transcendental reflection, for the accountability of thought even under such considerations is always intersubjective without collapsing into analogical models of sameness. There is thus, as we saw in movements forward and efforts at return, always a *differentiation*, always a form of incompleteness at hand, in living thought.

What do such differences make? Humility requires not saying *everything* but, instead, through an understanding of commitment, important steps of new beginnings.

Notes

1. Lewis R. Gordon, *Bad Faith and Antiblack Racism* (Gordon 1995a), Humanities Classics edition forthcoming in 2023 with a foreword by Mabogo P. More, and *Fanon and the Crisis of European Man: An Essay on Philosophy and the Human Sciences* (Gordon 1995b).

2. Also see Mabogo More's foreword to the twenty-fifth anniversary edition of *Bad Faith and Antiblack Racism*.

3. See Jane Anna Gordon (2014) and Monahan (2011). Relatedly, in Afro-Caribbean philosophy, see Henry (2000) and, through an integration of phenomenology, feminist philosophy, Marxism, and psychoanalysis, Nissim-Sabat (2009). In South Africa, from the perspective of Black Consciousness, there is More (2021, 2018), but see also Biko (2017), and in the Latin American decolonial line, there is Maldonado-Torres (2008). There are other directions to consider, but these offer a sense of the global southern developments of creolization, Africana phenomenology, feminist phenomenology, Black Consciousness, and decoloniality. There are, as we will see, other developments, some of which are in tension with the core arguments of *Fanon and the Crisis of European Man* through urging what today is known as Afropessimistic approaches. As those approaches embrace ontological claims, they are not properly phenomenological and thus don't receive attention here.

4. See Jane Anna Gordon (2014).

5. For more developed discussion, see Gordon (2020a).

6. See also her chapter "A Phenomenological and Psychodynamic Reflection on Freedom and Oppression Following the Guiding Thread of Lewis R. Gordon's Existential Phenomenology of Oppression," in Davis (2021, 149–166), and her forthcoming essay, "Crisis and Convergence: Humanism and Method in Lewis Gordon's *Fanon and the Crisis of European Man*," in the special revised edition of *Fanon and the Crisis of European Man* (Gordon forthcoming).

7. Táíwò (2010a).

8. Táíwò's writings on these subjects are manifold; see, for example, Táíwò (2010b, 391–410).

9. Du Bois (1903), Henry (2016, 27–58); Jane Anna Gordon (2005; 2007, 143–161; 2014). I offer discussion of varieties of double consciousness in many of my writings, but see Jane Anna Gordon (2008) for summaries, especially pages 77–79 and 117. There is also the concept of doubled double consciousness: see Chandler (2014).

10. I argue this, of course, despite Husserl's unfortunate Eurocentrism in Husserl (1965). Much of what I summarize about Husserl's approach, despite himself, is available in *Husserliana* (The Hague: Nijhoff, 1973–2012). Despite its discussion in a variety of his writings on transcendental phenomenology, Husserl's most well-known discussion is in *Husserliana 1*; see also *Husserliana 17*.

A wonderful summary is also available in Natanson (1973). I also discuss this concept in Gordon (2012b).

11. For more discussion, see Gordon (2021).

12. See *Cartesianische Meditationen*, First Meditation (Husserl 1931).

13. "Inscription of Antef," twelfth dynasty, Kmt/Ancient Egypt, 1991–1782 BCE. I amended the translation into pluralized subjects because Antef was not referring exclusively to male philosophers. This well-known inscription (among Egyptologists) is discussed by Théophile Obenga in Obenga (2003, 35). See also Obenga (1990).

14. See, for example, Obenga (2016), especially part 11.

15. See Gordon (2012b), and Nissim-Sabat (forthcoming).

16. Etoke (2019) and Gordon (2012b, 96–105).

17. See, for example, Ramose (1999); Manganyi (1977); More (2021), and the foreword to the Humanities Classics edition of *Bad Faith and Antiblack Racism* (Gordon 2023); Mudimbe (2013); Obenga (1990); Kisukidi (2013) and Kisukidi (2014, 1–10); Banoum (2004, 445–458); Etoke (2019); Diop (2003); Senghor (1964); Diagne (2016); Ajari (2019); Hountondji (1983).

18. See Gordon (2021).

19. For elaboration of this concept, see, in addition to *Freedom, Justice, and Decolonization*, Gordon (2021; 2011, 96–104; and 2020b, 42–47) and Headley and Robino (2007).

20. For Michael Neocosmos's recent reflection, see Neocosmos (2016).

References

Ajari, Norman. 2019. *La dignité ou la mort: Éthique et politique de la race.* Paris: La Découverte.

Banoum, Bertrade Ngo-Ngijol. 2004. "Bantu Gender Revisited through and Analysis of Basaá Categories: A Typological Perspective." In *Proceedings of the 4th World Congress of African Linguistics,* edited by Akinbiyi Akinlabi and Oluseye Adesola, 445–458. Cologne: Rüdiger Köppe Verlag.

Barratt, Barnaby B. 2013. *What Is Psychoanalysis? 100 Years after Freud's "Secret Committee."* London: Routledge.

Chandler, Nahum Dimitri. 2014. *X—The Problem of the Negro as a Problem for Thought.* New York: Fordham University Press.

Diagne, Souleymane Bachir. 2016. *The Ink of the Scholars: Reflections on Philosophy in Africa.* Dakar: CODESRIA.

Diop, Cheikh Anta. 2003. *Cheikh Anta Diop: L'homme et l'oeuvres.* Paris: Présence Africaine.

Du Bois, W. E. B. 1903. *The Souls of Black Folk: Essays and Sketches.* Chicago: A. C. McClurg.

Etoke, Nathalie. 2019. *Melancholia Africana: The Indispensable Overcoming of the Black Condition*. Translated by Bill Hamlett. London: Rowman & Littlefield International.

Gordon, Jane Anna. 2005. "The General Will as Political Legitimacy: Disenchantment and Double Consciousness in Modern Democratic Life," PhD dissertation, University of Pennsylvania, Philadelphia.

Gordon, Jane Anna. 2007. "The Gift of Double Consciousness: Some Obstacles to Grasping the Contributions of the Colonized." In *Postcolonialism and Political Theory*, edited by Nalini Persram, 143–161. Lanham, MD: Lexington Books.

Gordon, Jane Anna. 2008. *An Introduction to Africana Philosophy*. Cambridge: Cambridge University Press.

Gordon, Jane Anna. 2014. *Creolizing Political Theory: Reading Rousseau through Fanon*. New York: Fordham University Press.

Gordon, Lewis R. 1995a. *Bad Faith and Antiblack Racism*. Atlantic Highlands, NJ: Humanities International Press.

Gordon, Lewis R. 1995b. *Fanon and the Crisis of European Man: An Essay on Philosophy and the Human Sciences*. Special revised edition with essays by Nigel Gibson, Greg Graham, Paget Henry, Michael Monahan, Marilyn Nissim-Sabat, Julia Suàrez-Krabbe, and Catherine Walsh. New York: Routledge.

Gordon, Lewis R. 2000. *Existentia Africana: Understanding Africana Existential Thought*. New York: Routledge.

Gordon, Lewis R. 2006. *Disciplinary Decadence: Living Thought in Trying Times*. New York: Routledge.

Gordon, Lewis R. 2008. *An Introduction to Africana Philosophy*. Cambridge: Cambridge University Press.

Gordon, Lewis R. 2011. "Shifting the Geography of Reason in an Age of Disciplinary Decadence." *Transmodernity: Journal of Peripheral Cultural Production of the Luso-Hispanic World* 1, no. 2: 96–104.

Gordon, Lewis R. 2012a. "Black Existence in Philosophy of Culture." *Diogenes* 59, nos. 3–4: 96–105.

Gordon, Lewis R. 2012b. "Essentialist Anti-Essentialism, with Considerations from Other Sides of Modernity." *Quaderna: A Multilingual and Transdisciplinary Journal* no. 1: http://quaderna.org/wp-content/uploads/2012/09/Gordon-essentialist-anti-essentialism.pdf

Gordon, Lewis R. 2015. *What Fanon Said: A Philosophical Introduction to His Life and Thought* New York: Fordham University Press.

Gordon, Lewis R. 2019. "Decolonizing Philosophy." *Southern Journal of Philosophy* 57, Spindel Supplement: 16–36.

Gordon, Lewis R. 2020a. *Freedom, Justice, and Decolonization*. New York: Routledge.

Gordon, Lewis R. 2020b. "Shifting the Geography of Reason in Black and Africana Studies." *Black Scholar* 50, no. 3: 42–47.

Gyekye, Kwame. 1995. *An Essay on African Philosophical Thought: The Akan Conceptual Scheme*, rev. ed. Philadelphia: Temple University Press.

Headley, Clevis, and Marina Banchetti Robino, eds. 2007. *Shifting the Geography of Reason I*. London: Cambridge Scholars Press.

Henry, Paget. 2000. *Caliban's Reason: Introducing Afro-Caribbean Philosophy*. New York: Routledge.

Henry, Paget. 2016. "Africana Phenomenology: Its Philosophical Implications." In *Journeys in Caribbean Thought: The Paget Henry Reader*, edited by Paget Henry, Jane Anna Gordon, Lewis R. Gordon, Aaron Kamugisha, and Neil Roberts, 27–58. London: Rowman & Littlefield International.

Hountondji, Paulin. 1983. *African Philosophy: Myth and Reality*. Translated by Henri Evans with the collaboration of Jonathan Rée and introduction by Abiola Irele. Bloomington: Indiana University Press.

Husserl, Edmund. 1931. *Cartesianische Meditationen*. Hamburg: Meiner Verlag.

Husserl, Edmund. 1965. "Philosophy as Rigorous Science." In *Phenomenology and the Crisis of Philosophy: Philosophy as Rigorous Science and Philosophy and the Crisis of European Man*, translated and with an introduction by Quentin Lauer, 71–147. New York: Harper & Row.

Husserl, Edmund. 1973–2012. *Husserliana 1*. The Hague: Nijhoff.

Husserl, Edmund. 1974. *Formale and transzendentale Logik* (Husserliana 17). The Hague: Nijhoff.

Kisukidi, Nadia Yala. 2013. *Bergson ou l'humanité créatrice*. Paris: CNRS Éditions.

Kisukidi, Nadia Yala. 2014. "Négritude et philosophie." *Rue Descartes* 83, no. 4: 1–10.

Maldonado-Torres, Nelson. 2008. *Against War: Views from the Underside of Modernity*. Durham, NC: Duke University Press.

Manganyi, Chabani. 1977. *Alienation and the Body in Racist Society: A Study of the Society That Invented Soweto*. New York: NOK.

Masolo, D. A. 1994. *African Philosophy in Search of Identity*. Bloomington: Indiana University Press.

Monahan, Michael J. 2011. *The Creolizing Subject: Race, Reason, and the Politics of Purity*. New York: Fordham University Press.

More, Mabogo P. 2017. *Biko: Philosophy, Identity and Liberation*. Cape Town, SA: HSRC Press.

More, Mabogo P. 2018. *Looking through Philosophy in Black: Memoirs*. London: Rowman & Littlefield International.

More, Mabogo P. 2021. *Sartre on Contingency: Antiblack Racism and Embodiment*. London: Rowman & Littlefield.

Mudimbe, V. Y. 1988. *The Invention of Africa: Gnosis, Philosophy, and the Order of Knowledge*. Bloomington: Indiana University Press.

Mudimbe, V. Y. 2013. *The Invention of Africa and On African Fault Lines: Meditation on Alterity Politics*. Scottville, SA: University of KwaZulu-Natal Press.

62 | Lewis R. Gordon

Natanson, Maurice. 1973. *Edmund Husserl: Philosopher of Infinite Tasks*. Evanston, IL: Northwestern University Press.

Neocosmos, Michael. 2016. *Thinking Freedom in Africa: Toward a Theory of Emancipatory Politics*. Johannesburg, SA: Wits University Press.

Nissim-Sabat, Marilyn. 1997. "Appreciation and Interpretation of the Work of Lewis Gordon." *The CLR James Journal* 5, no. 1: 118–135.

Nissim-Sabat, Marilyn. 2009. *Neither Victim nor Survivor: Thinking toward a New Humanity*. Lanham, MD: Lexington Books.

Nissim-Sabat, Marilyn. 2021. "A Phenomenological and Psychodynamic Reflection on Freedom and Oppression Following the Guiding Thread of Lewis R. Gordon's Existential Phenomenology of Oppression." In *Black Existentialism: Essays on the Transformative Thought of Lewis Gordon*, edited by Danielle Davis, 149–166. London: Rowman & Littlefield.

Nissim-Sabat, Marilyn. Forthcoming. "Crisis and Convergence: Humanism and Method in Lewis Gordon's *Fanon and the Crisis of European Man*." In the special revised edition of Lewis Gordon's *Fanon and the Crisis of European Man*.

Obenga, Théophile. 1990. *La Philosophie africaine de la période pharaonique: 2780–330 avant notre ère*. Paris: L'Harmattan.

Obenga, Théophile. 2003. "Egypt: Ancient History of African Philosophy." In *A Companion to African Philosophy*, edited by Kwasi Wiredu, 31–50. Oxford: Blackwell.

Obenga, Théophile. 2016. *Writings from Ancient Egypt*. Translated by Toby Wilkinson. London: Penguin Classics.

Ramose, Magobe B. 1999. *African Philosophy through Ubuntu*. Harare, ZI: Mond Books.

Senghor, Léopold. 1964. *Liberté: I*. Paris: Editions Seuil.

Táíwò, Olúfẹ́mi. 2010a. *How Colonialism Preempted Modernity in Africa*. Bloomington: Indiana University Press.

Táíwò, Olúfẹ́mi. 2010b. "'Love of freedom brought us here': An Introduction to Modern African Philosophy." *Southern Atlantic Quarterly* 109, no. 2: 391–410.

Wiredu, Kwasi. 1996. *Cultural Universals and Particulars*. Bloomington: Indiana University Press.

3

Why Husserl in Africa?

Autobiographical Reflections

PAULIN J. HOUNTONDJI

The highest interests of human culture demand the elaboration of a rigorously scientific philosophy, therefore . . . if a philosophical revolution is to prove itself in our time, it must always be animated by the intention to found philosophy anew in the sense of rigorous science.

—Husserl, *Philosophy as Rigorous Science*

Guilty or not guilty? Why was I so strongly impressed by Husserl's doctrine during the very first years of my studying philosophy and in some of my writings? I have no problem acknowledging that my critique of ethnophilosophy was based among other demands on the idea of philosophy defended by Husserl, especially in his *Philosophy as Rigorous Science* (Husserl 1965, 71–178). I already made this clear in *The Struggle for Meaning*. In this chapter, I offer some more autobiographical reflections on my encounters with Husserl's work. This includes an exposition of the beginnings of my studies in France that led to working on Husserl, my encounter with other thinkers,[1] my ethnocritique, and my critical adoption of Husserl's view of what I call the struggle for meaning. In the first section, I start with a portrayal of my studies and encounters that brought me to writing a doctoral thesis on Husserl's work. In the following two sections, I give accounts of the way I met and was influenced by Louis Althusser, a militant philosopher who intended to free his own political party from the shackles of its official ideology, and Alioune Diop, who had been able to offer African thinkers of the time an invaluable platform for exchanges and meetings. In the fourth section, I turn to my critique of ethnophilosophy. In the final section, I close by giving a brief discussion of my critical adoption of Husserl's phenomenology and the struggle for meaning.

Getting to Husserl

In 1959–1960 I was in the last year of high school in Lycée Victor Ballot in Porto-Novo, Dahomey (today's Benin Republic). The curriculum included an initiation into philosophy, and I became fond of this subject matter. After passing the baccalaureate (equivalent to what was known in the English-speaking area as the General Certificate of Education [GCE, A-level]), I got a scholarship, which enabled me to travel overseas and register at Lycée Henri IV in Paris. During my three years there, I was able to prepare for the competitive examination to enter Ecole Normale Supérieure, an institution specific to the French educational system, which at the time was considered the highest school for training teachers. I attended classes in various disciplines, including Latin, Greek, French literature, English language and literature, history, philosophy. The pedagogical tradition in philosophy was to encourage students to read the authors themselves instead of being satisfied with just summaries and/or commentaries on their works. My classmates and I were lucky enough to have as our teacher André Bloch, a brilliant and enthusiastic instructor who introduced us chiefly to thinkers like Descartes, Kant, Husserl, Hegel, Kierkegaard, and other modern and contemporary authors. His course on Husserl consisted mainly of an enthusiastic explanation of, and commentary on, Husserl's famous 1911 essay *Philosophy as Rigorous Science*. Another teacher of mine was Jacques Muglioni, who gave us an intense exposure into Kant and general Kantianism.

I passed the entrance exam to the Ecole Normale Supérieure in 1963. Then I had to choose *one* discipline to prepare for *agrégation* (a national competitive exam to select a limited number of confirmed high school teachers). I had reservations. The easiest for me would have been to prepare for an *agrégation* in the classics (including Latin and Greek) but I felt these disciplines would take me too far from African realities (both mine and others). I preferred philosophy, which I held to be a more universal discipline, but on the other hand *agrégation* in philosophy was said to be rather tough and difficult. Louis Althusser was then the tutor (the "caiman") in philosophy (fellows of ENS both in the arts and the science sections were compared to the red fishes of the basin in the school's garden) and was assisted by Jacques Derrida. I consulted with Althusser. He gave me a topic for a short dissertation, which I submitted two days later. He called me back a day or two days after. I was so happy with his verdict: *you can prepare for an* agrégation *in philosophy*.

I set at work reading greedily but critically some of the most famous philosophers, trying to understand whatever could be understood in their works, flushing out occasionally contradictions and other inconsistencies within each doctrine and incompatibilities between the doctrines.

A time came when I had to formulate a topic for the first real research work in academia for the *Diplôme d'études supérieures*, which is similar to an MA dissertation. I decided to work on Husserl. Derrida had organized a most exciting seminar at ENS on authors like Hume, Kant, Husserl. He had himself written his MA dissertation some eleven years earlier under the supervision of Professor Maurice Patronnier de Gandillac at the University of Paris (the Sorbonne) on "The Problem of Genesis in the Philosophy of Husserl." He oriented me toward an issue that he thought was still to be researched on, "The Notion of *Hylè* in Husserl's Phenomenology."

Hylè was the Greek word for "matter." In the history of Western philosophy, Aristotle is known for his celebrated distinction between *hylè* and *morphè*—matter and form—and his doctrine of "hylomorphism," meaning that matter and form cannot be separated. For Aristotle, the mind and the body are inseparable and form a substantial unity. Hylomorphist unitarianism was opposed to Platonic dualism and the notion that the essence of an individual object or person is far away, in the intelligible heaven of eternal ideas.

The same word *hylè* is used by Husserl in the context of his radical turn back to consciousness to designate the nonintentional content of the latter. While insisting again and again that *all consciousness is consciousness of something* (in other words, that *all consciousness is intentional*), Husserl acknowledges at the same time that intentionality is not self-evident and should be perceived itself as a problem. One has to wonder about its origin and conditions of possibility.

After successful completion of my *agrégation* Derrida recommended me to Professor de Gandillac, who agreed to supervise my work and take me on as his student. Thus, I first registered at the Institute of History of Science and Technology, an institute that was part of the Sorbonne, for a "State Doctorate" on "The Theory of the Relationship between Social Structure and the Birth of Scientific Spirit since the Early Nineteenth Century." To me, it was research in the sociology of science. I wanted to read and analyze all the available literature on the topic since the *Course on Positive Philosophy* and other celebrated works by Auguste Comte. The aim was to understand the conditions for the (new) rise of science and technology in Africa, the birth or rebirth, development or new development of scientific culture and technological inventiveness both necessary to empower the continent beyond the parenthesis of the slave trade and colonization.

I never achieved this ambitious project. I did not even start writing the thesis itself though I took a lot of notes while going through and reading carefully substantial pieces of the available literature on the topic. Meanwhile I decided to prepare an intermediate doctorate (*doctorat de troisième cycle*) on Husserl. I had met Paul Ricoeur during his brilliant lectures on Husserl at the Sorbonne, and he accepted my request to supervise my PhD thesis on "The Idea of Science in Husserl's *Prolegomena to Pure Logic* and the First Logical Investigation."

My interest in Husserl was motivated first and foremost by his idea of philosophy, his ambition that philosophy should be a rigorous science. There are also other entries to this oeuvre of course, for example, the theory of subjectivity whereby Husserl appropriates in his own way and transforms the Cartesian *Cogito* and Kant's transcendental philosophy, or the philosophy of history as developed in *The Crisis of the European Sciences and Transcendental Phenomenology*.

Althusser's Lesson

Besides Husserl, I must also confess how fascinated I was by Louis Althusser's approach to Marxism. Few people realize that he was not just a leftist activist, but also and foremost a keen philosopher. I cannot forget two brilliant seminars he gave on Spinoza and Rousseau. His small book on Montesquieu was an original approach to this eighteenth-century political philosopher. He often quoted Aristotle, Kant, Freud, Bachelard, not to mention contemporary thinkers like Lévi-Strauss, Lacan, Foucault, Canguilhem, and many others. When he came to Marx therefore one could not expect him to maintain a catechetical relationship to the doctrine as so many Communist activists did.

My class at Ecole Normale Supérieure (1963) had the chance to attend the birth of some of Althusser's most celebrated works. *Pour Marx* was published in 1965 and its foreword, entitled "Today," was a kind of intellectual autobiography, which told the fascinating story of a long resistance to attempts at doctrinal enrollment and the corporatization of thought from within the workers' movement itself. Althusser's effort to "think in Marx" was something truly unheard of at that time; many forget that Marxism was generally perceived as a closed doctrine having an answer to everything and responding to any imaginable question. To Althusser, though, the problems that Marx highlighted were not yet solved and there was still room for free discussion within the intellectual legacy that Marx had left us. My class also attended the seminar on *Capital*, which was to give birth to *Reading Capital*, the collective book of two volumes published in 1966. We attended in 1967 the exciting and somewhat experimental "Philosophy course for scientists" introduced by Althusser's preliminary remarks later published as *Philosophy and the Spontaneous Philosophy of Scientists* (1974).

I quickly understood that, first, Althusser's fight within the French Communist Party and the workers' movement in Europe had a universal meaning. We also needed in African political parties mass organizations and throughout our various forms of activism to combat all kinds of intellectual laziness. We needed to develop knowledge. We needed to produce theory as opposed to ideology in Althusserian terms.

Second, I was highly sensitive to a specific question that runs throughout Althusser's work and that he gives in his early texts a very clear answer: What is philosophy? His initial answer was that philosophy serves as a theory of science, but not in the sense of a doctrine that would provide science with a metaphysical foundation. Rather, philosophy gave science a theory, which a posteriori recognizes and identifies in conceptual clarity the necessary and sufficient methodological procedures of science. This answer was complemented or completely revised later on. After May 1968 Althusser's followers at the University of Vincennes liked to define their discipline: *théorie de la science et du politique* (theory of science and the political). Althusser himself redefines it in his *Elements of Self-Criticism* (1972) as class struggle in the realm of theory.

There is, of course, a massive distance between Husserl and Althusser. The "caiman" of Rue d'Ulm rarely quoted Husserl as far as I remember. However, being a careful reader of both, I could not help being impressed by their common demand for rigor and certainty, their rejection of what the former calls *Weltanschauung* (worldview) as opposed to philosophy and the latter ideology as opposed to theory and science.

Alioune Diop and the African Elite

I would be remiss if I did not mention here all I owe to a man about whom little is said but who was a great figure in modern African culture: Alioune Diop, founder of the journal *Présence africaine*, organizer of the two world congresses of black writers and artists, the first of which was held in Paris in 1956 and the second in Rome in 1959.

I already knew the *Présence africaine* magazine at the Porto-Novo high school. I quoted almost by heart entire paragraphs of communications by Aimé Césaire and Léopold Sédar Senghor to the First International Congress of Black Writers and Artists. "Présence Africaine" was, however, also the name of a bookstore and publishing house. As soon as I arrived in Paris in 1960, I knew that the Présence Africaine bookstore was one of the best places to go. Here I personally met many writers, many poets that I had only known by name until then, including Aimé Césaire and Léon-Gontran Damas.

But my great luck was to meet Alioune Diop himself. He invited me to an international conference organized at the University of Perugia, Italy, in the summer of 1964, as a prelude to many other meetings and conferences like the one held in 1967 on a hotel boat in Copenhagen, Denmark. Here I was to meet someone like Cheikh Anta Diop, among many other people whom I deeply admired. Through Alioune Diop, I was also able to eventually meet Léopold Sédar Senghor, albeit much later in life . . . Alioune, therefore, was a network unto himself and a tireless, passionate unifier. And Présence Africaine, a place of convergence and meeting.

When he asked me, on my return from Perugia, to lead the Inter-African Philosophy Commission of the "African Cultural Society" (an NGO created by Présence Africaine) he left me free to direct its work as I saw fit. I made it an inter- and multidisciplinary meeting place. People such as Elikia Mbokolo, Marcien Towa, and many others have participated actively or occasionally in our work. Alioune the Sphinx must have had fun, deep down, with our passionate attacks on *négritude* and ethnophilosophy. Just like his friend Jacques Howlett, the philosopher of the house. They obviously had their opinion on the matter, but they listened patiently. For Alioune was a man of listening, of great tolerance—say, of great charity—toward those who held opinions contrary to his own. Not all of his colleagues were of the same persuasion, unfortunately. A quarrel was soon to break out between one of the managers and us, which resulted in a collective resignation and self-dissolution of the Philosophy Commission. Meanwhile, however, I had been able, as editor of the philosophy section of *Présence africaine* magazine, to open this section with a short note introductory to a most controversial article by Fabien Eboussi-Boulaga, "Le Bantou problématique" (Eboussi-Boulaga 1968).

From Husserl to the Critique of Ethnophilosophy

To come back to Husserl, the founder of phenomenology notes repeatedly that the demand for certainty is not anything new, it is as old as philosophy itself. He observes, however, that this ambition has never been fulfilled: "From its first beginnings philosophy has claimed to be rigorous science, and in fact to be the science that satisfies the highest theoretical needs. . . . In no epoch of its development philosophy has been able to satisfy the claim to be rigorous science" (Husserl 1965, 227). One could have expected the 1911 essay therefore to propose at least some of the specific methods and techniques through which philosophy can at last achieve this age-old ambition. Of course, this was not the case. Instead, *Philosophy as Rigorous Science* comes to terms with two deviations easily recognizable in those times: naturalistic philosophy and historicist philosophy. While he accused naturalist philosophy of neglecting the influence of subjective assumptions in science, he accused historicist philosophy, specifically, the worldview philosophy (*Weltanschauungsphilosophie*) of delivering science to the relativity of subjective historic views. The idea that every historical period produces the kind of wisdom it needs, a wisdom that is different from that of another period or place, is for Husserl a typical form of relativism and skepticism. It is self-contradictory and just unacceptable.

My critique of ethnophilosophy derives from Husserl's view (Ndoye 2021, 749–756).[2] I actually read Tempels's *Bantu Philosophy* in the same period. The title was so promising! I very much expected an exciting account of philosophical discussions among the Bantu people. Instead, the book was a laborious reconstruction of the collective worldview of the Bantus, "a philosophy without philosophers" (Kagame 1976).[3] I did not deny that such collective worldviews exist in Africa as well as any other part of the world, but I could not understand why they should be assimilated to what is known as philosophy in the West.

I first expressed this view at the aforementioned Copenhagen conference. The topic of the conference was "African Humanism—Scandinavian Culture," and within this framework I was invited to present a paper on "African Wisdom and Modern Philosophy." My whole approach consisted in questioning the proposed theme itself, wondering why we should compare wisdom to philosophy instead of wisdom to wisdom and philosophy to philosophy (Hountondji 1970b, 183–193).

I do not know why and how a need appeared at that time to take a panoramic view of the state of philosophy in the world. Professor Georges Canguilhem told me one day, in 1967 or '68, about Raymond Klibansky, an eminent professor at McGill University in Canada. The latter wanted to edit an exhaustive work on contemporary philosophy in the world and was looking for someone who could present the situation in Africa. Having accepted this challenge, I started gathering as many available texts as possible, both published and unpublished, and established a bibliography. It became immediately obvious that the vast majority of these texts were trying to define what they called "African philosophy" in the sense of a system of thought shared by all Africans. In this context, African philosophy was perceived first and foremost as the tireless search for a collective identity. This was wholly different to the philosophical approach and motivations within European and American contexts, and, to me, it presented a problem (Hountondji 1971, 613–621).

In the same period, UNESCO embarked on a vast project on the main trends of research in the social and human sciences. The Senegalese scholar Amadou-Mahtar M'Bow was then director general and the deputy director general in charge of the social science section was a French philosopher, Jacques Havet. The project was divided into four parts: (1) anthropological and historical sciences, (2) aesthetics and art sciences, (3) legal science, (4) philosophy.

Paul Ricoeur was in charge of coordinating the last part on philosophy. He asked me to contribute an article on philosophy in Africa, which was published with his permission in *Diogenes* in 1970 (Hountondji 1970a, 109–130). He acknowledged it in his foreword to the fourth section of the book published eight years later as an outcome of the whole project (Ricoeur 1978).

So, I owe a lot to the global approach of both of Raymond Klibansky and Paul Ricoeur. I adopted this approach, and it allowed me to see that there was indeed in Africa, as anywhere else, a philosophical activity, a debate that left traces. These traces often go unnoticed: we take the existing literature independent of its context and jump straightaway to what it says, to the question it poses, typically, for example, "What is our identity?" "What distinguishes our system of thought?" Instead, the approach that is both comparative and inclusive, which wants to appreciate the state of philosophy in the world in all its nooks and crannies without excluding any continent or group of countries, obliges us to take into account, first and foremost, the existing literature within its context, even if it means analyzing it rigorously afterward to perceive its strengths and weaknesses. The very first statement of the *Diogenes* article made this clear: "I term a group of texts 'African philosophy': to be precise, the group of texts written by Africans and defined as 'philosophic' by the authors themselves" (Hountondji 1970a, 109). This article launched a serious debate. *Diogenes* had a large audience and it appeared at that time in at least three languages: French, English, Spanish. In the wake of this article and under the crossfire of critics, I was quick to publish other texts in various reviews, newspapers, magazines. My three-year stay in Congo-Kinshasa, baptized Zaire while I was there, was rich in lessons. Zaire, Father Tempels's chosen land, was, as one might expect, the capital of ethnophilosophy, as Dakar was the capital of *négritude*.

The debate continued after I returned home to Dahomey in 1972, enriched by a new experience and a direct political commitment that I could not make in other countries (Hountondji 1973).[4] The idea appeared at one point to gather into a volume a selection of the articles I had published that far on the question. Thus appeared a book published in 1977 in Paris (Hountondji 1977) and republished three years later by Clé editions in Yaoundé.

I owe the late Abiola Irele, a good friend of mine, for the fact that this book was soon translated into English. Abiola was then professor of Romance languages and civilizations at the University of Ibadan, Nigeria. He had me invited in the late seventies or early eighties to a seminar hosted by the Rockefeller Foundation Conference Center in Bellagio, Italy. The program included, among other things, a lecture by himself on recent developments in French-speaking African literature. I was supposed to be his "discussant," but I did not know anything about the content of his talk. Great was my surprise to hear him comment copiously, in the last section of his presentation, on my book. And as one might expect, he did not deprive himself, as an admirer of Césaire and Senghor, of putting in its place, in the name of *négritude*, the critique of ethnophilosophy (Irele 2001). I improvised a long response in my own stuttering English. There was a lively discussion. The next morning, during the break after the first session, I overheard a conversation in a group that included Henri Evans, then head of the Department of Modern European Languages at the University of Ibadan. They said it was a pity that such a book was not available in English. I did not imagine that it would actually be translated into English by Henri Evans and published in 1983 (Hountondji 1983a). I did not expect either that once available in the USA it would be awarded the Herskovits Prize by the African Studies Association at its annual meeting in 1984. Besides, a German translation was published in 1993, based on the English version (Hountondji 1993). All in all, I owe all of this to Abiola Irele.

A Serbo-Croatian translation by Daniel Bucan was published the same year as the English one in 1983 in Zagreb, Yugoslavia (Hountondji 1983b). But this is another story. As everyone knows, Yugoslavia no longer exists. The war has been there with its devastation and its destructive power.

A Continental Debate

I will not expand here on the argument and actual content of my critique of ethnophilosophy. Those interested may refer to a lecture that I gave at the University of Calabar, Nigeria, in 2017 under the title: "How African Is Philosophy in Africa?" (Hountondji 2017).

Let me just recall this. The worldview philosophy that was first popularized in Africa by Tempels's book was soon taken up by an increasing number of African scholars, starting with Father Alexis Kagame from Rwanda (Kagame 1956). I mentioned some examples in my *Diogenes* article that became the first chapter of *African Philosophy: Myth and Reality* under the title: "An Alienated Literature" and in other chapters of the same book. I mentioned, among others, people like Alassane Ndaw and Assane Sylla from Senegal, John Mbiti from Kenya, William Abraham from Ghana. It is clear however that this approach is still thriving today and is not about to stop.

My critique was twofold. First, these scholars assume that in Africa, or in the specific ethnic groups they are dealing with, that everyone agrees with everyone. I called this wrong assumption a "unanimism." I contend that nowhere in the world is there total unanimity between people within a single culture, and yet this monolithically appears to be the case when it comes to African philosophy (or so it was at the time and often still is). There is always in various degrees some diversity of opinions, and this is a condition for progress. We have therefore to (re)discover and value as an asset the internal pluralism and intellectual diversity of African societies, instead of lamenting it as a curse.

Second, this discourse seemed to me based on some kind of exclusion. This was clear in Tempels's *Bantu Philosophy* where the seventh and last chapter was entitled: "Bantu Philosophy and Our Mission to Civilize" (Tempels 1949)[5] and where it appears clearly that the book did not address a Bantu but a European audience. Mutatis mutandis, works by African scholars describing their people's system of thought were not intended first, in my view, for their fellow Africans but primarily for a Western audience. To me these scholars were extraverted, that is, externally oriented.

I have only mentioned so far my own criticism. It converged however with similar criticisms by a number of colleagues throughout Africa. The late Marcien Towa published in 1971 a powerful booklet, *Essai sur la problématique philosophique dans l'Afrique actuelle* (An essay concerning philosophical inquiry in today's Africa), in which he also used the word "ethnophilosophy" in a derogatory sense, as I did, to question the dominant way of philosophizing in Africa. Odera Oruka from Kenya, known at that time as Henry Odera, published in 1972 an article under the title "Mythologies as African Philosophy."

The critique of ethnophilosophy, however, raised a vivid controversy. A countercritique quickly developed—a kind of second order ethnophilosophy, which was no longer satisfied with naïvely describing African customs and projecting behind them a hypothetical system of thought but tried to argue further on that this way of doing philosophy was the only legitimate way in Africa. A good example of this powerful counterattack could be seen during a conference organized in December 1976 in Addis Ababa by Father Claude Sumner. That is where I met for the first time Koffi Niamkey, then head of the Philosophy Department at the University of Abidjan. He presented two papers, one on "Controverses sur la philosophie africaine" (Controversies over African philosophy) and the other on "L'impensé de Towa et de Hountondji" (The unthought of

Towa and Hountondji). Though I had announced that I was not going to present a paper, I couldn't help after listening to him but improvise a quick response under the title: "Sens du mot 'philosophie' dans l'expression 'philosophie africaine'" (Meaning of the word "philosophy" in the phrase "African philosophy").

The countercritique of course did not stop there. Many issues were raised, some of them serious. I dealt with some of these issues in a number of articles and gave a summary of the whole debate in a preface written for the second edition of *African Philosophy: Myth and Reality* (Hountondji 1996).

The Struggle for Meaning, published in French in 1997 and excellently translated by my good friend the late John Conteh-Morgan from Sierra Leone, recontextualized my critique of ethnophilosophy in its historical context (Hountondji 2002). The very structure of the book is highly significant. Part 1 is entitled "Discovering Husserl," part 2 "Critique of Ethnophilosophy," and part 3 "Positions." The title itself is based on a subtle distinction made by Husserl in the Fourth Logical Investigation between three kinds of expressions or utterances: those that make sense (whether true or false), those that are self-contradictory, and those that do not make sense at all, which he calls in German *Sinn*, *Widersinn*, and *Unsinn*, translated in French as *sens*, *contre-sens*, *non-sens*, and in English as sense, nonsense, senselessness.

The title of my book thus referred to the Husserlian project of a pure logical grammar aimed at establishing the a priori laws governing the domain of meaning. From this domain is excluded the immense sphere of nonsense, combinations of words that mean absolutely nothing. Husserl gives an example. If I say: "a round square," this expression has a meaning, although it is contradictory, absurd. But if I say: "a circle or," "a man and is," I am just uttering a collection of words, a simple *flatus vocis* that has no meaning.

Based on these indications by Husserl, I realized that the field of *Unsinn* (senselessness, Nonsense with a capital N) is immense, that the meaning that we produce by speaking, by writing, by arranging signs in various ways to make ourselves understood by the one facing us or by anyone else, in short, the domain of meaning in general is never more than a tiny island floating on the immense ocean of Nonsense.

Beyond language *stricto sensu*, I realized that, in our daily environment, our social, economic, and political life, even the life of our religious communities, in all sectors of our individual and collective experience, we are always already stuck in a pool of Nonsense from which we aim to extract Sense.

So, we have to fight, again and again. Producing meaning is not that easy. The political struggle is also a struggle for meaning if it is to oppose the crushing of the weak by the strong, injustice, and all forms of dehumanization.

This is basically what I learned from Husserl. Others have learned different lessons from his teaching, sometimes diametrically opposed to those I have learned. Phenomenology, a pure description of lived experience, has been invoked in particular, in support of attempts at analyzing collective wisdoms, attempts at defining or redefining various notions deemed essential to any philosophy in general but placed in the linguistic, social, cultural context of such and such African people: for example, the notion of person, the notion of life, the experience of death, and so on. Phenomenology, a real do-it-all, could be seen as the most appropriate method to account for collective experience, immediately presented as a philosophy.

Finally, my admiration for Husserl did not prevent me from recognizing what is unacceptable for an African or non-Western reader in a whole aspect of his work, namely his philosophy of history. Great thinkers have sometimes spoken nonsense. We find at least one example in the famous "Vienna lecture," a lecture given by Husserl on March 7, 1935, under the title: "Philosophy and the Crisis of European Mankind." Wanting to underline Europe's vocation to cultivate philosophy, understood as a determining element of its identity, he writes something like this: if man is, as Aristotle says, a reasonable animal and if in this sense even the Papuan is a man, it is also true that philosophical reason represents a higher degree of rationality. It's a safe bet that there was no Papuan in the audience, nor any Viennese who knew Papua and its culture enough to be offended to hear Husserl so generously concede humanity to Papua. It is to be bet that Husserl would never have expressed himself thus if he had suspected for a single moment that he would one day be read by Papuans or people who feel close or united in some way with Papuans. The content of a speech is always a function, directly or indirectly, of the audience to which it is addressed. Nobody can reproach Husserl for feeling challenged by the serious crisis that was going through in his time what he calls "European humanity." It is all the more regrettable, however, that this legitimate concern has led him to a form of Eurocentrism that is simply unacceptable.

Notes

1. Some works referenced were not widely published and were more essays disseminated among a very few. Therefore, we have no citations or references to give to them.

2. My colleague Bado Ndoye from Cheikh Anta Diop University in Dakar has very well perceived the influence of Husserl on my critique of ethnophilosophy and the deep impact of his thought on the philosophical debate in Africa. See Ndoye (2021; forthcoming).

3. These words are taken from Kagame (1976). Don't believe that the Rwandan philosopher and Catholic priest uses these words ironically or with some amount of humour. He uses this phrase without any embarrassment and doesn't perceive it as self-contradictory. He positively claims that he is trying to describe a collective wisdom, a philosophy without philosophers, and that he is not doing philosophy properly so-called but ethnophilosophy.

4. Soon after I came back, a military coup wiped out the "Presidential Council" that had been set up two or three years earlier to force the three historic leaders to govern together by exercising in turn the function of head of state with the prerogatives attached to it. The spokesperson for the junta, after this "three-headed monster" (*sic*) was defeated, exclaimed, at the end of his solemn proclamation: "Long live the revolution!" Youth organizations were immediately invited to come together to come up with a government program. On the sidelines of this collective exercise, I preferred, after discussing it with some of my comrades and friends, to isolate myself to write an extremely simple article under the title: "What Is a Revolution?" The article was immediately published in three successive issues of the only daily newspaper at the time, *Daho-Express*. Journalists read it on national radio without asking my opinion (television did not yet exist). Other articles of circumstance followed. Result, a small book: Hountondji (1973). While sharing the collective enthusiasm aroused by this unexpected coup, I warned against the risk of authoritarianism and fascism inherent to such a regime.

5. This chapter was added in the 1949 edition by Présence Africaine and was not part of the initial version published in Elisabethville (present-day Lubumbashi) in 1945.

References

Eboussi-Boulaga, Fabien. 1968. "Le Bantou problématique." *Présence africaine*, no. 66: 4–40.

Hountondji, Paulin. 1970a. "Comments on Contemporary African Philosophy." *Diogenes* 71: 109–130.

Hountondji, Paulin. 1970b. "African Wisdom and Modern Philosophy." In *African Humanism—Scandinavian Culture: A Dialogue*, 183–193. Copenhagen: Danish International Development Agency.

Hountondji, Paulin. 1971. "Le problème actuel de la philosophie africaine." In *La philosophie contemporaine: chroniques*, tome 4, edited by Raymond Klibansky, 613–621. Florence: La Nuova Italia Editrice.

Hountondji, Paulin. 1973. *Freedoms: Contribution to the Dahomean Revolution*. Cotonou: Renaissance.

Hountondji, Paulin. 1977. *Sur la philosophie africaine: critique de l'ethnophilosophie*. Paris: Maspéro.

Hountondji, Paulin. 1983a. *African Philosophy: Myth and Reality*. Translated by Henri Evans and Jonathan Rée, introduction by Abiola Irele. London: Hutchinson, and Bloomington: Indiana University Press. Second edition with a preface by the author, Bloomington: Indiana University Press, 1996.

Hountondji, Paulin. 1983b. *O "africkoj filozofiji."* Zagreb: Skolska Knjiga.

Hountondji, Paulin. 1993. *Afrikanische Philosophie: Mythos und Realität*. Translated by G. Hoffmann, C. Neugebauer, and F. Wimmer. Berlin: Dietz Verlag.

Hountondji, Paulin. 2002. *The Struggle for Meaning: Reflections on Philosophy, Culture and Democracy in Africa*. Translated by J. Conteh-Morgan, foreword by K. Anthony Appiah. Athens: Ohio University Press.

Hountondji, Paulin. 2017. "How African Is Philosophy in Africa?" *Filosofia Theoretica: Journal of African Philosophy, Culture and Religions* 7, no. 3: 9–18.

Husserl, Edmund. 1965. *Philosophy as Rigorous Science*. In *Phenomenology and the Crisis of Philosophy*, translated by Quentin Lauer, 227–246. New York: Harper & Row.

Irele, Abiola. 1990. *The African Experience in Literature and Ideology*. Bloomington: Indiana University Press.

Irele, Abiola. 2001. *The African Imagination: Literature in Africa and the Black Diaspora*. Oxford: Oxford University Press.

Kagame, Alexis. 1956. *La philosophie bantu-rwandaise de l'être*. Brussels: Académie royale des sciences coloniales.

Kagame, Alexis. 1976. *La philosophie bantu comparée*. Comparative Bantu Philosophy. Paris: Présence Africaine.

Ndoye, Bado. 2021. "Africa." In *The Routledge Handbook of Phenomenology and Phenomenological Philosophy*, edited by Daniele de Santis, Burt Hopkins, and Claudio Majomino, 749–756. Oxon: Routledge.

Ndoye, Bado. Forthcoming. *Phénomenologie et philosophie en Afrique: la leçon de Paulin Hountondji*. Paris: Présence Africaine.

Ricoeur, Paul. 1978. "Avant-propos: la philosophie et les philosophies aujourd'hui." In *Tendances principales de la recherche dans les sciences sociales et humaines*, 1135. Paris/New York: Mouton/UNESCO.

4

Hountondji and Husserl

Subjectivity, Responsibility, and Phenomenology in the Critique of Ethnophilosophy

PATRICK ELDRIDGE

Paulin Hountondji abandoned his scholarly work on Husserl's phenomenology to mount his own critique of ethnophilosophy (Hountondji 2002, 73–75; 1996b, 81). With this critique he drew battlelines between philosophy conceived as an element of culture on the one side, and philosophy as a professional discipline on the other; he supported the latter, to the chagrin of many who took the cultural view as the surer path to self-affirmation and autonomy for postcolonial Africa. This chapter is not an intervention in that debate. It is rather a reconstruction and critical evaluation of Hountondji's critique of ethnophilosophy as a phenomenological project; it is an attempt to show that Hountondji did not so much abandon his work in phenomenology as drastically refashion it.[1] His work *The Struggle for Meaning* forges a few connections between phenomenology and the critique of ethnophilosophy but leaves a number of tensions unresolved. My aim is to provide a synoptic reading of Hountondji and Husserl, demonstrating how phenomenology organically unites the seemingly disparate impulses of Hountondji's work: the elaboration of a philosophical theory of objective knowledge, the critique of theoretical extraversion in Africa, and the call for a sociological theory of collective representations. This demonstration will consist in drawing out answers to four interrelated questions posed to Hountondji: For what is the philosophizing subject responsible? Who is the responsible, philosophizing subject? To whom is the philosophizing subject responsible? In light of its responsibilities, what then must the subject do? The answers to these questions make manifest the task that Hountondji sets for the African philosopher: to combat the destructive intellectual legacies of colonization by reinvigorating the thoughts and practices of their community by their own radical commitment to truth.

Responsibility for What?

What makes Hountondji's work on Husserl distinctive in the broader field of phenomenological research is his embrace of Husserl's "resolute objectivism," and his discipline in reading all of Husserl's analyses of subjectivity in light of that objectivism (Hountondji 2002, 27–29). Husserl's phenomenology occupies a precarious space between the rejection of (objectivist) formalism and the rejection of (subjectivist) psychologism. To paint with a broad brush, it seems that Husserl's rejection of naïve, positivistic objectivism has proved far more attractive than his rejection of introspective, relativistic subjectivism, with the consequence that the name "phenomenology" is more closely linked to descriptions of experience than to claims about the necessary features of objects. Hountondji, in contrast, makes the rejection of psychologism the sine qua non of phenomenological research, which may obscure rather than highlight the phenomenological dimension of his thought.[2]

In his account of the *Logical Investigations*, Hountondji argues that we must first of all understand Husserl's conception of the transcendence of intentional objects in the light of the universal validity of logical laws. The first and decisive sense of intentional objectivity is manifest in the validity of, say, syllogisms—it would be false to claim these are relative to any subject or any culture. These laws are objective *Wahrheiten an sich*, and to the extent a subject understands them, they are obliged to recognize them as transcendent, objective correlates of their thought. These cannot, a priori, be dissolved into subjectivity's own immanence, hence their decisive status for the determination of intentional transcendence, and their propaedeutic status for phenomenology, which could otherwise be considered as just a philosophy of consciousness and not a theory of being. Not all intentional objects have this sort of validity, but it is this type of validity that guarantees the transcendence that makes all other forms of intentionality intelligible (Hountondji 2002, 30–32, 48–49).

Hountondji emphasizes how this view of intentional objectivity allows one and the same object to be the point of convergence for many different approaches by consciousness (i.e., it is the same across different experiences and acts of thinking). If we consider scientific knowledge in its objective existence as an ideal system of truths, then that allows for, on the subjective side, a potentially infinite number of knowing scientists, who can have potentially infinite embodied practices and infinite cognitions (Hountondji 2002, 42, 47). This infinity must be possible if truth is not to be exhausted by, and therefore dissolved into, the plurality of subjective, cultural practices and cognitions. Yet this very infinity also threatens to devolve into arbitrariness. Why this approach, this experiment, this laboratory tool, and not some other? From a Husserlian standpoint, the threat of arbitrariness intensifies once we move from the rigorous sciences like formal logic to the exact sciences like physics, whose objects are always capable of being otherwise, and whose results must therefore always remain merely probable (Hountondji 2002, 51–52).

The philosopher's awareness of the contingency of their own practices and cognitions carries with it a negative moral self-evaluation of their own arbitrariness. The responsible philosopher strives to minimize if not eradicate arbitrariness. Thus, the philosopher and the scientist order their cognitions and refine their embodied experimental practices. Hountondji writes that philosophical responsibility bears within it "the hope for a new order where . . . the vertical agreement of minds with the universal structures of being would lead to a horizontal agreement of minds between themselves, and to transparency, justice, and peace" (Hountondji 2002, 36). Philosophical reason, as the desire to grasp the things themselves, in their own being, is the manifestation of a desire to live in accordance with rational norms. There are still potentially infinite theoretical practices, but the philosopher and scientist strive to achieve a privileged, normative shape in their very thought and embodiment out of responsibility for objectivity, which in turn is the core of respect for their cotheorizers operating under the weight of the same objectivity.

Hountondji's conception of philosophical responsibility, insofar as it is shaped by Husserl's account of intentionality and theory of knowledge, is not a moral emotion in any empirical sense. Philosophical responsibility is not a feeling of obligation in the subject but rather a way that the subject produces itself, synthesizing its cognitions and organizing its immanence, under the normative guidelines of a transcendent objectivity. Thus, Hountondji endorses Husserl's infamous intellectualism, to the extent he interprets this intellectualism as an ethics of self-effacement (Hountondji 2002, 42). To take responsibility for truth claims is to place oneself under the rule of objectivity, and thus to subordinate personal preferences and contingent features of one's own consciousness to the legality of truth. In short: What is the philosopher responsible for? They are responsible for organizing their actions, speech, and thought around the striving for truth that transcends them.

Who Is Responsible?

Hountondji has always been clear that his critique of ethnophilosophy rests on a view of philosophical responsibility; we now see how his view of responsibility rests on a theory of intentional subjective consciousness. For Hountondji, there can be no such thing as an unconscious, a-subjective philosopher—no more than there can be an unconscious, a-subjective geometer (Hountondji 1996a, 48). Philosophical thought requires the form "I consciously assert this truth, and I must answer when asked why or how it is so." Philosophical thought is allergic to unanimity, anonymity, and unconscious expressions; it cannot say "one affirms this truth, and one affirms it unconsciously, because it is so much agreed upon no-one need justify it, because no-one may question it" (Hountondji 1996a, 37–38, 47; 1996b, 83).

The philosopher is responsible for what they say. They must acknowledge that the claim they assert is their offspring, and that they speak as its originator and guardian (Hountondji 1996b, 79–80). We can protest that a philosopher who claims to be the originator of their assertions is in fact taking credit for views they have likely appropriated from their own community. The philosopher begins to resemble a bourgeois individual, profiting off the labor of others with their claims of ownership (Hountondji 2002, 169–170, 179, 188). Yet the demand of philosophical responsibility is not to be original or to own statements like products.[3] According to Hountondji: "[Even if] I am nothing more than a translator and spokesperson, I remain nevertheless responsible for my affirmations in the literal sense of the word."[4] To "own" one's assertions as a philosopher is not to copyright them but to take on the task of defending their truth, to respond to all who question them in good faith. Responsible philosophical speech begins with the silent prologue: "No matter who said it before, or how many times, I now claim this to be true." If we can now say what the subject is responsible for, we cannot yet say what, or rather who, the subject is. Does Hountondji follow Husserl by positing a transcendental ego? Hountondji repeatedly acts as an apologist for idealism and transcendental subjectivity. In *African philosophy* he criticizes Nkrumah's alignment of idealism with political oligarchy (Hountondji 1996a, 153–154). In his address to the APA, Hountondji defended Husserl's turn to the transcendental subject against Sartre's criticisms (Hountondji 1996b, 80). In *The Struggle for Meaning* Hountondji highlights how Lenin's criticisms of idealism failed to make idealism seem incoherent (Hountondji 2002, 144–146). And contrary to Tran Duc Thao, Hountondji finds no break between the early and later Husserl, no discontinuity between a purportedly realist Husserl of the *Logical Investigations* and the transcendental idealist Husserl of *Ideas I*, thereby defending the properly phenomenological character of Husserl's transcendental idealism (Hountondji 2002, 29–30). If Hountondji appears ready to defend forms of transcendental subjectivity against external criticisms, it is not so clear that he is willing to advance its cause by giving a positive account of transcendental subjectivity or detailing the philosophical methods of laying it bare. He doggedly keeps the option open but does not actually take it.

For Husserl, a phenomenological account of the transcendental subject must be supported by insight, not a Kantian deduction, and it is the phenomenological reduction that allows us to catch sight of the transcendental subject performing its constitutive syntheses.[5] By reducing all real existence to the status of a merely phenomenal correlate of consciousness, the phenomenologist puts out of play their entrenched and dogmatic belief in the existence of transcendent reality—not for the sake of a Cartesian drama of negation and resurrection, but for the sake of studying how their consciousness contributes to the meaningfulness of that reality. Hountondji has a highly original but peculiar reading of the phenomenological reduction. He approaches the reduction through Husserl's idea of science. Since the truth of logical laws does not presuppose any truth about the real existence of a world, the subject is permitted to neutralize their own factual, worldly existence in their project of developing a theory of knowledge. Thanks to the truth-in-itself of the intentional object, subjectivity sees that it can excuse itself from the world (Hountondji 2002, 32–33). By Hountondji's lights, the idea of science guides the development of the reduction since it affirms the independence of truth from the contingent existence of subjective consciousness. Now if this were Hountondji's sole interpretation of the phenomenological reduction, it would amount to an evasion—not investigation—of subjectivity. If we look at the reduction in *Ideas I*, we find it is the subject who is necessary, and the world contingent (*Hua* III/1 1950c, 63–73).[6] Hountondji does, however, offer another view of it. He states that apart from a theory of knowledge, Husserl's phenomenology was also an attempt to provide a scientific foundation for the study of the mind, such that it would not generate the relativism and skepticism that empirical psychology and psychologism do. Looked at in this way, the phenomenological reduction is part of a project to give a descriptive account of the essential structures of subjective experiences, without committing oneself to mundane, causal (and therefore merely probable) explanations. The phenomenologist is permitted to perform the reduction and study their own experiences, just insofar as the reduction renders these experiences as mere examples of essential ways of intending transcendent objects. In this way, Hountondji's interpretation seamlessly unites the project of the *Logical Investigations* with that of *Ideas I*, where so many of Husserl's contemporaries and followers saw an aberration (Hountondji 2002, 33–34). Looking for a phenomenological conception of the subject in Hountondji's work, we pick up two threads that correspond to his two readings of the reduction. The first is a notion of the subject who organizes their thoughts and actions in accordance with a duty to truth. This is a personal consciousness who must become a subject; the philosophical "I" does not preexist the adoption of responsibility. The second is the subject who neutralizes the contingent reality of their own being, to uncover their own essential structures, that is, what is true about their sort of being. Here the subject preexists their act of reflective imagination. It is not evident that these two threads are entirely complementary: the organizational idea suggests the production of a transcendental subject over and above their empirical life, while the neutralization idea suggests an uncovering of a transcendental subject behind their empirical life. Was the one who says "I" always already this subject, or is this the creation of a new self? We cannot decide this matter in Hountondji's oeuvre and it is, besides, a rather sore point in the work of Husserl as well. We can, however, say in either case that the subject emerges in the philosophical act of self-effacement, whether by shaping their actions and thoughts to accord with objective truth, or by stripping away the merely contingent and personal aspects of their consciousness to reveal the structural elements.

Responsible to Whom?

The very appearance of the words "African" and "philosophy" side by side concentrates within it the problem of the relationship between the empirical and the transcendental in Hountondji's work. On the one hand, Hountondji insists that the qualifier "African" cannot change the meaning of the word "philosophy." Any cultural or geographical qualifier is an accidental and therefore effaceable qualification of the discipline "philosophy" (Hountondji 2002, 135–137). On the other hand, he writes passionately about the challenges and duties of the African philosopher, ones they do not share with, say, their European counterpart. The qualifier "African" cannot limit the possible topics and problems that fall under "philosophy," yet the term "African" does limit who the author and audience of the philosophical discourse can be (Hountondji 1996a, 66). The figure of "the African philosopher" in Hountondji's thought must assume responsibility for living in accordance with truth but must do so with and before a very specific audience: other persons who share a contingent, empirical determination—who conduct their lives on the same continent. The urgency and difficulty of Hountondji's attempt to unite the meanings of "African" and "philosopher" become clearer if we consider the most insidious problem the figure of the African philosopher must solve: the extraversion of knowledge in Africa, perpetuated by ethnophilosophy. By Hountondji's lights, the ethnophilosopher seeks to promote the wisdom of a particular culture. They do not take responsibility for any claims to truth that transcend them, and as such they lack the personal responsibility of the genuine philosopher. Yet this is not their sole failing. They also fail in a particular form of interpersonal responsibility. The ethnophilosopher writes about Africans but not to them. They address an audience in the industrial North to their benefit, arguing on behalf of a people who are excluded from the discussion (Hountondji 1996a, 34; 1996b, 83; 1990a, 12). Here the issue is not that what the ethnophilosopher says about, say, the Yoruba people is *de jure* false[7]—the information the ethnophilosopher gathers about them may very well be true, but they are excluded from the "production" and "distribution" of this knowledge; their questions and needs are not addressed in the research. Hountondji characterizes extraversion as a theoretical exploitation akin to economic exploitation. Raw resources (data about Africans) are gathered in Africa and sent to the industrial North for processing, where disproportionately greater value is added and consumed, and so the benefits remain where the factories and research centers are, while the periphery is stripped (Hountondji 1995, 7–8; 1990a, 7–9).This aspect of the critique of ethnophilosophy tells us that beside the philosopher's responsibility for their relationship to the truth is their responsibility to their community. Hountondji's critique of extraversion is itself an act of responsibility to Africa. This is not a responsibility to an academic community, in the sense of an ideally possible collective of rational coinvestigators. What is at stake is a political community who calls the philosopher to responsibility for them. The Other to whom the African philosopher is responsible is empirically determined and is not merely a second transcendental ego. Who is the Other confronting the African philosopher with the problem of extraversion and demanding a response to it? To sort out the tangle of empirical and transcendental issues at play in this appeal, we must depart from our exegetical procedure and attempt an extrapolation: we must draw out the phenomenological sense (which Hountondji never articulated) of the Other suffering under theoretical extraversion (of whom Husserl knew not). We will give a three-step progressive, concretizing analysis—in the spirit of Husserl—to arrive at an account of the phenomenality of this Other who appears in Hountondji's writings. First, this Other must form a particular kind of "We" with the philosophizing subject, since this Other appears to the philosopher as a "fellow of the same community." Following Husserl, any sort of intersubjective union must have certain foundations, for instance, an expressive kind of embodiment that motivates empathetic pairing between self and Other, a pairing in which each is aware that they are appearing to one another, and that each has before it appearances of common objects, situated in a common lifeworld (*Hua* XIV 1973a, 55–73). These foundations of "we-consciousness" only provide us with the sort of "We" that can be formed between the ego and any Other whosoever, but it is not just any Other who creates the demand that the African philosopher address their words first and foremost to their shared community. Second, it is not sufficient to have a mere juxtaposition of two consciousnesses, who are aware they are both intentionally oriented to a common world; we must allow for an interweaving of intentions, where each subject is able to direct and influence the Other's intentions.[8] To go from a "we" with merely adjacent intentions to a "we" with interwoven intentions—a "we" capable of making demands on each other—communication is required.[9] Third, the African philosopher and the Other who calls them to responsibility do not communicate just in any way, about just any objects. They communicate in their own way, about objects that make up their own "homeworld" (*Heimwelt*), to use an expression of the later Husserl (*Hua* XV 1973b, 161–163, 176–177, 207–214, 625–627). Their ability to relate to each other as individuals is conditioned by a shared kind of upbringing in a shared milieu. The specificity of this we-consciousness consists in how both the I and the Other are born into and die out of the same homeworld and thus are parts of a generational community (*Hua* XV 1973b, 138–139). Turning back to Hountondji, as fellows of the same community, the philosophizing subject and this Other are aware that they share a "complex heritage that is transmitted through education, and that predisposes us to prefer certain forms of behavior to others, certain objects to others, independently of our choices and will" (Hountondji 2002, 203). They share notions of what counts as normal, familiar, and "right" relative to their community, which other subjects in other communities may not share. They share what Hountondji calls a primary passivity, comprised of collective representations, which he characterizes as "the implicit horizon of all possible forms of discourse—quotidian or learned, mythical or rational, religious or profane, philosophical or non-philosophical, scientific or crazy, etc." (Hountondji 2002, 202–203). This primary passivity preexists and in some way conditions the "secondary activity" of the subject's responsible speech (Hountondji 2002, 204). The call to responsibility for the philosopher's own community has an ambiguous philosophical status: the call to the philosopher resounds in an a-philosophical region of their being, but the response to be given is a philosophical one (Hountondji 2002, 203). Under the specific circumstances of theoretical extraversion, the African philosophizing ego sees the Other as being limited and harmed, and following the life if not the letter of Hountondji's work, we must understand this harm as an appeal: "You must speak to me, you must direct your philosophical care to the community in which we both move and have our being, you must care for our own relationship to truth and falsehood, as shaped by the gifts and challenges of our heritage." This is a formal sketch of the foundational, constitutive, phenomenological sense of the Other to whom Hountondji's African philosopher responds, that is, the expressive, embodied, communicative, home-world comrade whose theoretical capacities are being preyed upon and not exercised for their own benefit. Admittedly, in this account, the Other is not specifically African but is indeed postcolonial. This appeal—to care for those suffering under the prolonged intellectual consequences of colonialism—need not come from a person living on any particular continent, yet this call cannot resound in the voice of just anyone from any community. On this view of the Other's phenomenality, the transcendental and empirical aspects of their being are neither contradictory nor indifferent to one another, but they do make the African philosopher's practice of their discipline inherently more complex. The figure of the African philosopher would have to go through two stages of self-alienation in order to be responsible for their relationship to the legality of truth and responsible to their fellow African. First, the dedication to objectivity leads them to cast a critical eye on the heritage they previously took for granted. Second, the responsibility to their community diverts them from a direct, unadulterated pursuit of that objectivity in order to care for the endogenous theoretical demands of a homeworld, which is not, strictly speaking, a community of philosophers. It would be more accurate, at this point, to speak only of the "postcolonial philosopher" in Hountondji, and not the "African philosopher," but I hope in the next section to show how this philosopher can take on greater social, cultural, and political specificities without losing their philosophical vocation.

What Must the Subject Do?

The relationship of the philosopher to their community is one of the central problems of Hountondji's oeuvre. At times, Hountondji clearly enjoins the philosopher to speak to and hear the needs of their community. At other times, he is extremely skeptical of the political import of philosophical work. In the "engaged intellectual" who believes in the revolutionary import of their journal articles, Hountondji sees an immodest academician who is trapped in the illusion that their purring will do anything to change the material conditions of the proletariat they claim to support (Hountondji 1987, 189–193). If we are to determine what Hountondji would have the subject—as the African philosopher—do in light of their dual responsibilities, we must look at the relationship of philosophy to the cultural, political community from which it emerges. Once again, a contrast between an ethnophilosophical understanding of this relationship and a proper understanding is instructive. The ethnophilosopher sees the discipline of philosophy as part of a cultural, philosophical worldview, which they take to be a greater whole, whose science is ethnography. In doing so, "they mistake the relationship of part and whole. It is a science of the part (ethnography) that claims to be a science of the whole (philosophy)" (Hountondji 2002, 219). Philosophy is the theory of the whole; it provides the theory of knowledge, such that all particular parts of knowledge (e.g., the knowledge of this or that particular culture, or even laws of culture generally) fall under it (Hountondji 1987, 169). To become an apologist for the achievements of a particular community is tantamount to becoming lost in the part, abandoning the proper critical perspective on how or whether this fits into the whole of knowledge (Hountondji 1990b, 190). Philosophy in the genuine sense transgresses any attempt to make it into something partial and subordinate: claims to objective validity necessarily transgress the boundaries of particular communities. To produce philosophical meanings, you must call into question the validity of the meanings that structure your prephilosophical life. This sort of questioning does not allow the philosopher to be simply a participant in their own culture. Insofar as the philosopher strives for objectivity, they relativize the beliefs and values of their community. Philosophy can neither be entirely immanent to the culture of a political community, nor can it be simply exterior to it. Philosophy has a non-place with respect to culture; it is always a rupture. Ethnography or ethnophilosophy, on the other hand, is a science of the part and nothing impels it to transgress the boundaries of the part it studies. Hountondji has promoted the study of traditional knowledge in African communities, but he does not call this philosophy. Hountondji's advocacy for such a study of endogenous knowledge comes with the major caveat of calling it not philosophy but a sociology of collective representations (a project he admits he never carried out) (Hountondji 1990b, 187–192, 205). The issue with Hountondji's strategy here is that, by this line of reasoning, as soon as one is working on a part, even with the proper awareness that this is not the whole, one is no longer doing philosophy. As soon as we deal with anything particular, it seems we lose our status as philosophers (and become instead, say, sociologists or political scientists). It is true a priori that no part can contain the whole, but is it really possible to obtain the whole if one must relinquish each and every part one gets a grasp of? Hountondji has proclaimed the unlimited scope of reason but is constantly describing the realm of culture and politics as something less than rational, so that it is unclear that there can really be a properly rational account of those regions of human existence and activity.[10]

Hountondji does have a partial answer here. Acknowledging that the cultural heritage of pre-theoretical beliefs and values shapes the very being of the philosopher, he argues the philosopher can only become a self-responsible subject by explicitly grasping that heritage and submitting it to critique (an admittedly infinite task). The act of taking responsibility for one's existence as it relates to truth always happens after one has already led a prephilosophical life, and so there is an ineluctable necessity to pass through the primary passivity of collective, cultural representation on the way to the transcendence of genuine philosophy. But how does this determine what the philosopher must do for their community? To answer this, I offer a corrective criticism of Hountondji that runs counter to most of his critics, that is, rather than saying he is overcommitted to traditional Western philosophical figures (like Husserl) in his intervention in African philosophy, his intervention there would have benefited from a more intensive engagement with Husserl. In short, supplementing his work on ethnophilosophy and theoretical extraversion with an alternative reading of Husserl is a fruitful way of unifying and extending his philosophical project.

A return to Hountondji's phenomenological roots here is helpful. Hountondji's early work on Husserl did not at all neglect the problems of primary passivity (albeit understood as affectivity and not collective representations) (Hountondji 2002, 14–15, 23–24). While he recognized the necessity of such analyses, his reading of the reduction prevented him from seeing how such analyses could be properly philosophical, that is, how they contribute to the whole. This is due to what I would call his "reductive" reading of the reduction. There is an alternative method of reduction that more organically unites the realm of primary passivity and responsible, philosophical judgment.

I cannot provide a history of the transformations of Husserl's phenomenological reduction. I will limit myself to contrasting two versions of it—the Cartesian path and the path via the ontology of the lifeworld.[11] Husserl's early attempts to articulate the reduction followed a Cartesian path, in which consciousness and its correlated phenomena have the status of residua, once the dogmatic view of existence is neutralized. Transcendental consciousness and its phenomena, then, are ineradicable remainders after the loss of mundane being (*Hua* II 1950b, 9; III/1 1950c, 70) (Kern 1977, 128). This is problematic in that a remainder is precisely a part of a whole.[12] Husserl meant for phenomenology to be a theory of the whole, the discipline to which all other disciplines must appeal. Trying to establish a science of the whole of existence by reducing the field of objects to only a part of that whole is absurd. Hountondji's reading(s) of the reduction has this much in common with the Cartesian path: it is meant to uncover the necessary structures of subjectivity and objectivity that radically ground all knowledge by casting off the contingent layers of existence (whether by variation or world-negation). His version of the reduction also consists in a cutting away to expose an essential remainder.

Husserl's path through the ontology of the lifeworld, in contrast, is an operation of completion. Indeed "reduction" is a misnomer. This path to the transcendental phenomenological reduction treats the lifeworld as an index of actual and possible experiences, both intrasubjective and intersubjective (*Hua* VIII 1959, 434–435). The existence of the world (and the empirical, partial knowledge thereof) is not reduced so much as it is treated as a clue that leads back to constituting consciousnesses (*Hua* VIII 1959, 225).[13] Phenomenalizing the existence of mundane objects means that they become virtual manifolds that accrue unto them actual and possible meaningful givennesses to a community of actual and possible transcendental subjects. Kern likens this operation of projecting the object into the community of transcendental subjectivities to expanding the object into another dimension (Kern 1977, 137).

Husserl's path to a fully phenomenalized objectivity—an objectivity for which subjects may be responsible—resembles his surprising account in *Ideas II* of the modern-scientific notion of the physical object, that is, a meeting point of physical forces lacking any subjective-relative qualities. Rather than supposing this is achieved by an abstraction of all subjective-relative givenness, Husserl contends the constitution of the physicalistic thing is achieved by an amplification of subjectivity. The scientist becomes more aware of the contingency of their own perceptual capacities by entering into real or imagined communication with other consciousnesses with differing perceptual capacities. In order for an ideal community of scientists to responsibly generate determinations of the same object, while sharing only partially overlapping modes of givenness, they must restrict themselves to those determinations that are accessible to the entirety of their diverse community of coinvestigators—hence the object as bare meeting point of calculable forces. The subject constitutes the physicalistic object not by absurdly trying to remove everything relative to itself, but by a massive amplification of that relativity to ever more diverse subjects (*Hua* IV 1952, 89–93).

The upshot of this view of Husserl for our reading of Hountondji is that it shows us a version of the reduction that organically unites the investigation of particular, relative modes of consciousness and the positing of objective truth. The phenomenalization that the reduction achieves is not an abstraction but a concretization. This runs against Hountondji's reading of Husserl—or, better, exceeds it—and yet helps to ease the tension in his work between the need to strive for the absolute and the need to pass through the relative. In this version of the phenomenological method, the phenomenologist would not put their community's partial and relative values and knowledge out of play; rather they complete them with an account of the correlated, subjective, intentional acts and experiences that that knowledge and value system presuppose. The phenomenologist can remain a philosopher while attending to the claims and demands of their community—and the members of the phenomenologist's community see themselves reflected in the phenomenologist's discourse, even while the phenomenologist exposes the assumptions that are concealed by their naïve orientation to their home-world. This interpretation of the reduction does not level the difference between the contingent and the necessary but preserves the legitimacy of the philosophical movement through the contingent on the way to the necessary.

That said, the amplification of partial and relative views only becomes philosophically beneficial if it is performed under the yoke of responsibility. A mere increase of perspectives is an invitation to become lost in the contingent and relative, if not guided by the demands of the critical, rational striving for truth. The phenomenologist, in this context, does not only relate the truth claims prevalent in their home-world back to the subjective acts that constitute them; the phenomenologist also relates those truth claims to a goal of objectivity. What the philosopher must do—both for themselves and for their community—is introduce a teleological perspective into their home-world (Hountondji 2002, 141). To become a philosopher is not to possess truth in advance; it is to be shaken out of complacency and to set oneself the task of progressing toward ideal objectivity. Hountondji, following Husserl, characterizes the ideal of objective knowledge toward which philosophers orient themselves, and toward which they attempt to orient their interlocutors, as teleological in the prescriptive sense: a standard that ought to be realized, against which one's attempts may be measured (Hountondji 2002, 30, 35). As a standard, it has a critical function, and to the extent the philosopher introduces it into their familiar, heritage-bound discourse with their home-world comrades, they are performing an immanent critique: critiquing the heritage that belongs to them by introducing a standard that belongs to everyone and to no one—universal objectivity.

If we combine the acts of "phenomenalization-as-amplification" and the immanent, rational, teleological critique of the own-community, we can characterize the philosopher's task as one of renewal—surprisingly this is a term and a project we find articulated in both Hountondji and Husserl. The agreement between the two thinkers on this point is all the more striking once one considers that Husserl's texts on cultural renewal only became widely available after Hountondji had given up Husserl scholarship. Hountondji—instantiating the figure of the "African philosopher" himself—calls for a renewal of African cultures when he laments how colonialism has deprived African endogenous knowledge "of its internal dynamism and power of self-regeneration and self-criticism" (Hountondji 1990a, 7). Consonant with this, Husserl's idea of renewal is essentially a project of self-development through self-critique, guided by the demand of reason: to become responsibly self-regulating (*Hua* XXVII 1989, 29, 36, 55).

The reason both Hountondji and Husserl believe the philosopher's immanent critique renews their home-world is that it invests the beliefs and values of the community with greater import by raising the stakes. They are not taken for granted as cultural curios but are tested, measured against the ideal of grasping the whole of existence. Where the ethnophilosopher's taxonomies and defensive valorizations have a deadening effect, the immanent and radical intervention of the philosopher in their own culture unsettles and stirs their comrades. This invests more life into a community's intellectual heritage than the ethnophilosopher's advocacy work, because it restores the dynamism needed to stimulate engagement within the community, which regenerates their traditions (Hountondji 1990a, 12). In Hountondji's words: "The facile apologia for our systems of belief and other collective representations cannot but lead to an impasse. What we need to do today is not to make a spectacle of our cultures to others and to ourselves. It is to embark on a renewed creativeness on all fronts, in all fields. . . . [One must] take root in a tradition, but at the same time, one must be capable of keeping one's distance from—and entertain a critical and free relation with—that cultural tradition. One must invent again and again" (Hountondji 2002, 217–218). For Husserl, the phenomenologist's analysis of constitutive acts and insistence on the telos of reason in their home-world is not a matter of uncovering static truths, but of generating the ideal community, of producing the best, richest, most optimal cultural practices.[14] The immanent critique that the philosopher operates upon the sedimented meanings of their own culture is not just a matter of laying out the unwarranted assumptions that are latent in one's cultural axioms; it is rather to revitalize them by showing everyone their edges, by intimating a greater whole in which they are a part (Steinbock 1995, 201).

In this synoptic reading of Hountondji and Husserl we outlined an alternative version of the phenomenological reduction that has a less worrisome relationship to the study of culturally bound representations and sketched Husserl's view of the philosopher's task of cultural renewal—which Hountondji arrived at separately. We can now understand and even bolster the phenomenological core of Hountondji's critique of ethnophilosophy. The phenomenologist, through the study of intentionality, analyzes all the implicit ways they relate to an order of being that transcends them and takes care to relate themselves responsibly to that transcendent order. In the phenomenologist's own community, the phenomenologist is not responsible only for themselves but for the community that has produced and shared in the systems of values and beliefs that shaped them. Under the phenomenologist's own teleological perspective, it is good that they transform themselves in accordance with reason, but it is obviously better—culturally, politically, philosophically—to transform their community (*Hua* XXVII 1989, 45–47).

Notes

1. For overviews of the critiques of Hountondji and responses to them, see: Apter (1992); Bondurin (1981); Dübgen and Skupien (2018); Ikuenobe (1997); Janz (2010); Keita (1981); Osha (2005). For reasons of space, I can offer my evaluation of "Hountondji-as-phenomenologist" but cannot situate it in this broader debate.

2. This unified reading of Husserl protects Hountondji against the criticism that Irele levels at him, where he interprets Husserl's later development as an approximation of vitalism and an abandonment of his intellectualism (Irele 2004, 164).

3. Concerning originality: Hountondji (1996a, 44–45).

4. Hountondji (1990b, 190–191; my translation).

5. I cannot address the contrast within transcendental philosophy between Kant's deduction and Husserl's reduction. For the reader curious about how Husserl's reduction is supposed to open a philosophical dimension within everyday experience, I recommend Bernet (2016, 311–333).

6. Henceforth, I refer to Husserl's publications in the *Husserliana* as *Hua*.

7. Hountondji has expounded on how much of ethnophilosophy is de facto false. To the extent ethnophilosophy affirms the "primitive unanimity" of

the people it studies, and to the extent this unanimity nowhere in fact exists, ethnophilosophy is a science without an object and thus amounts to "a crazed language." Hountondji (1996a, 60–62).

8. See the classical if dated study: Toulemont, "The Specific Character of the Social according to Husserl" (Toulemont 1981, 226–242).

9. This is not to suggest that, for Husserl, there is any sort of presocial ego who somehow thinks their way into a social "we"; this progressive presentation is just meant to highlight some different foundational layers of sociality in which the (always already) empathic and social ego lives.

10. Cf. Hountondji (2002, 254–255).

11. See the classic study: Kern (1977, 126–149).

12. See *Hua I*, §7 (Husserl 1950, 7).

13. Admittedly I have not given an account of what exactly the ontology of the lifeworld is and how it relates to the positive sciences founded upon the lifeworld, and in the context of this chapter I cannot provide one. For the curious reader who is not a Husserl expert, I refer you to: *Husserliana VI* (1954, 132–141) and Carr (1970, 331–339).

14. I am borrowing from Steinbock (1995, 202).

References

Apter, Andrew. 1992. "Que faire? Reconsidering Inventions of Africa." *Critical Inquiry* 19, no. 1: 87–104.

Bernet, Rudolf. 2016. "The Phenomenological Reduction: From Natural Life to Philosophical Thought." *Metodo* 4, no. 2: 311–333.

Bondurin, Peter. 1981. "The Question of African Philosophy." *Philosophy* 56, no. 216: 161–179.

Carr, David. 1970. "Husserl's Problematic Concept of the Life-World." *American Philosophical Quarterly* 7: 331–339.

Dübgen, Franziska, and Stefan Skupien. 2019. *Paulin Hountondji: African Philosophy as Critical Universalism*. London: Palgrave Macmillan.

Hountondji, Paulin. 1981. "Que peut la philosophie?" *Présence africaine* 119: 47–71.

Hountondji, Paulin. 1987. "Le particulier et l'universel." *Bulletin de la société française de la philosophie* 81, no. 4: 145–189.

Hountondji, Paulin. 1990a. "Scientific Dependence in Africa Today." *Research in African Literatures* 21, no. 3: 5–15.

Hountondji, Paulin. 1990b. "Pour une sociologie des représentations collectives." In *La pensée métisse: Croyance africaine et rationalité occidentale en question*, edited by R. Horton et al., 187–192. Paris: PUF.

Hountondji, Paulin. 1995. "Producing Knowledge in Africa Today." *African Studies Review* 38, no. 3: 1–10.

Hountondji, Paulin. 1996a. *African Philosophy: Myth and Reality*, 2nd ed. Translated by Henri Evans. Bloomington: Indiana University Press.

Hountondji, Paulin. 1996b. "Intellectual Responsibility: Implications for Thought and Action Today." *Proceedings and Addresses of the American Philosophical Association* 70, no. 2: 77–92.

Hountondji, Paulin. 1997. "Introduction: Recentering Africa." In *Endogenous Knowledge: Research Trails*, edited by Paulin Hountondji and translated by Ayi Kwesi Armah, 1–39. Dakar: CODESRIA.

Hountondji, Paulin. 2002. *The Struggle for Meaning*. Translated by John Conteh-Morgan. Athens: Ohio University Press.

Husserl, Edmund. 1950a. *Cartesianische Meditationen und Pariser Vorträge. Husserliana I*. The Hague: Martinus Nijhoff.

Husserl, Edmund. 1950b. *Die Idee der Phänomenologie: Fünf Vorlesungen. Husserliana II*. The Hague: Martinus Nijhoff.

Husserl, Edmund. 1950c. *Ideen zu einer reinen Phänomenologie und phänomenologischen Philosophie: Band I. Husserliana III/1*. The Hague: Martinus Nijhoff.

Husserl, Edmund. 1952. *Ideen zu einer reinen Phänomenologie und phänomenologischen Philosophie: Band II. Husserliana IV*. The Hague: Martinus Nijhoff.

Husserl, Edmund. 1954. *Die Krisis der europäischen Wissenschaften und die transzendentale Phänomenologie. Husserliana VI*. The Hague: Martinus Nijhoff.

Husserl, Edmund. 1959. *Erste Philosophie: Band II. Husserliana VIII*. The Hague: Martinus Nijhoff.

Husserl, Edmund. 1973b. *Zur Phänomenologie der Intersubjektivität: Dritter Teil (1929–1935). Husserliana XV*. The Hague: Martinus Nijhoff.

Husserl, Edmund. 1973a. *Zur Phänomenologie der Intersubjektivität: Zweiter Teil (1921–1928). Husserliana XIV*. The Hague: Martinus Nijhoff.

Husserl, Edmund. 1989. *Vorträge und Aufsätze (1922–1937). Husserliana XXVII*. The Hague: Martinus Nijhoff.

Ikuenobe, Polycarp. 1997. "The Parochial Universality Conception of 'Philosophy' and 'African Philosophy.'" *Philosophy East and West* 47, no. 2: 189–210.

Irele, Abiola. 2004. "Philosophy and the Post-Colonial Condition in Africa." *Research in African Literatures* 35, no. 4: 160–170.

Janz, Bruce. 2010. "The Folds in Paulin Hountondji's 'African Philosophy: Myth and Reality.'" *Philosophical Papers* 39: 117–134.

Keita, Lansana. 1981. "The Debate Continues: A Reply to Olabiyi Yaï's 'Misère de la philosophie speculative.'" *Présence africaine* 120: 35–45.

Kern, Iso. 1977. "The Three Ways to the Transcendental Phenomenological Reduction in the Philosophy of Edmund Husserl." In *Husserl: Expositions and Appraisals*, edited by F. Elliston et al., 126–149. Notre Dame: Notre Dame University Press.

Osha, Sanya. 2005. "Legacies of a Critique of Ethnophilosophy: Hountondji's 'African Philosophy: Myth and Reality' Revisited." *Quest: An African Journal of Philosophy* 17: 13–34.

Steinbock, Anthony. 1995. *Home and Beyond: Generative Phenomenology after Husserl*. Evanston: Northwestern University Press.

Toulemont, René. 1981. "The Specific Character of the Social according to Husserl." In *A priori and World: European Contributions to Husserlian Phenomenology*, edited by W. McKenna et al., 226–242. Dordrecht: Martinus Nijhoff.

5

Philosophical Universality in Crisis

Hountondji's Interruption of Husserlian Phenomenology

CARMEN DE SCHRYVER

The text that, for many philosophers, most readily comes to mind as examining the themes of philosophical universality and crisis is Husserl's 1935 Vienna Lecture, "Philosophy and the Crisis of European Humanity."[1] Writing during a period in which it was politically urgent to condemn the pervasive irrationalism threatening to propel Europe into a second world war, Husserl offers a diagnostic treatment of what he calls the crisis of European humanity, which is first of all a crisis of universal philosophical reason.[2] In the course of this lecture as well as a number of other writings from the time, Husserl takes a stand against an increasingly vogue relativism and issues an impassioned plea on behalf of philosophy's unique vocation to become "a science [that produces] truths that are valid, and remain so, *once for all and for everyone*."[3]

Husserl's context and concerns are no doubt quite far removed from the contemporary intellectual landscape. And yet, it is equally undeniable that a discussion of philosophical universality in crisis strikes a definitive chord today. As Nadia Yala Kisukidi and Seloua Luste Boulbina have each noted, the question of the universal is once again the "central question" of our time, and a very vexed one at that.[4] On the one hand, universality has rightly been subjected to criticisms exposing the Eurocentric biases

99

lurking behind this ideal; from this perspective, to invoke the "universal" is to rehearse the historical elision of marginalized forms of thought. On the other hand, taking stock of the increased fragmentation of global public discourse, certain commentators have lamented the loss of universality under the pressures of multiculturalism and the supposed "racism of anti-racism,"[5] championing what they take to be a distinctively European emphasis on the universal.[6] On either side of the equation, the assumption is that universality belongs exclusively to what is now referred to as the "Global North"; despite the opposition between these two perspectives, there is a shared premise that the choice is between a relativism often ascribed to post- and decolonial theorizing and a reassertion of Western exceptionalism.

It is against this background that a number of decolonial thinkers have questioned the anti-universalist current of much decolonial theorizing.[7] Souleymane Bachir Diagne, for example, asks: "Is the postcolonial anti-universal? Shouldn't we rather say that only in a post-colonial world can the question of the universal truly be posed"?[8] According to this line of thought, the critique of Eurocentric universalism, far from necessitating a commitment to relativism, becomes a step in the direction of a decolonial thinking aimed at the discovery of "a more universal universal."[9]

A key voice among these decolonial thinkers interested in developing a non-Eurocentric notion of the universal is the Beninois phenomenologist Paulin J. Hountondji, whose criticism and ultimate departure from Husserl's treatment of the crisis of philosophical universality forms the topic of this chapter. Throughout his philosophical oeuvre, Hountondji has held together a penetrating critique of philosophical Eurocentrism as well as a commitment to a form of universality that would be, for the first time, truly universalist by dint of being truly global. The central argument put forward in this chapter is that a decolonial, phenomenological universality involves a powerful and extraordinarily pertinent vision of cross-cultural contact in a neocolonial, globalized world.[10]

Both Hountondji's abiding interest in universality, as well as his operating within a broadly Husserlian framework, have long been recognized in the literature. There is an unfortunate tendency, however, to treat Hountondji's interest in the universal as *simply* a residual Husserlianism; the suggestion is that Hountondji, in spite of his departure from Husserlian phenomenology, nonetheless derives from Husserl the view of philosophy as "rigorous science" and its concomitant universalistic orientation, and that this importantly inflects his work on African philosophy.[11] While this interpretation has its merits, it is grounded in a deeper methodological orientation covertly operative in much scholarship focused on non-European philosophers: namely that insofar as the philosopher in question has some relationship to the European "canon," this relationship is one of simple, direct influence and plays a pivotal, if not exhaustive, explanatory role in elucidating the non-European thinker's core commitments and intellectual development.[12]

There is a marked difference in the way philosophical influence is understood *within* a European context. It has been noted that the itineraries of post-Husserlian, European phenomenology may be described as a series of "heresies";[13] that is to say, the development of Husserlian phenomenology in the work of, for example. Martin Heidegger and Maurice Merleau-Ponty is understood to involve a substantial transformation of Husserl's framework, even as this framework remains a key influence. The discussions of Hountondji's relationship to Husserl, by contrast, tend to imply that even in his move away from Husserl, Hountondji is *essentially* continuing the Husserlian project by adopting without modification the latter's notion of universality. Once again, then, the non-European world is cast as a recipient rather than a producer of truly innovative philosophical knowledge. Substantively, this implicit methodological tendency has the result of dampening a recognition of the novelty of the Hountondjean approach, the acuity of his insights, and his pertinence to the task of thinking in a global situation marked by a quite different crisis of philosophical universality.

This chapter arrives at its central argument regarding the pertinence of Hountondji's vision of phenomenological universality by staging a methodological intervention. My suggestion is that we effect an explicit reversal of perspective—rather than reading Hountondji with a Husserlian framework in mind, this essay revisits Husserl's texts, especially those that deal with the metaphilosophical themes that have claimed Hountondji's interest throughout his career, from the positions articulated in Hountondji's broader philosophical project. This shift allows us to move beyond the standard interpretation of the Husserl-Hountondji relationship, enabling both a more immanent explanation for the ways in which Hountondji departed from Husserl's thinking, as well as a deeper appreciation for the distinctiveness of Hountondji's approach to philosophical universality in crisis. Therefore, in addition to generating these interpretive insights, this essay speaks to ongoing discussions of philosophical methodology by providing one example of a decolonial approach to historical-philosophical analyses with an expansive geographical scope.[14]

In looking at Husserl's *Crisis* texts through the perspectives afforded by Hountondji's work, what emerges is a novel criticism of the uncomfortable coupling, in Husserl's philosophical thinking, of an unquestioned Eurocentrism and a claim to universality. Indeed, it is not merely that the Husserlian crisis of philosophical universality is played out on the European continent; for Husserl, the cure to Europe's sickness is to be sought *within* the European tradition. It is on this question that I locate Hountondji's interruption and, indeed, heretical transformation of phenomenology. For Hountondji, any satisfactory response to the crisis of philosophical universality will involve a novel, emphatically *global* vision of the universal. Hountondji's proposed resolution to the contemporary crisis hinges on a demand to move beyond an exclusive reliance on the European tradition of thought and toward a universality that, as Hountondji writes, would "finally put in its place the false universal wearing the mantle of universalism [in order to] open up avenues which will allow us to construct a rationality that is *more* comprehensive, that is *more* universal."[15]

The Critique of Ethnophilosophy:
Hountondji on the Presumed Particularism of African Philosophy

Hountondji's *African Philosophy: Myth and Reality* is indisputably a foundational text in modern African philosophy, and few if any contributions to the literature fail to cite its significance.[16] In this text and the publications surrounding it, Hountondji expresses a deep reservation about the anthropology-like approach taken toward African philosophy. This is Hountondji's now well-known critique of "ethnophilosophy," which he develops through a close reading of the influential work of Belgian missionary Placied Tempels, as well as a number of discourses that continue in Tempels's wake.[17]

It was Tempels's book, *Bantu Philosophy*, that first introduced the idea of African philosophy within a European academic context. At the time of its publication in 1945, *Bantu Philosophy* was roundly celebrated by African intellectuals as heralding the rehabilitation of African cultures: Léopold Senghor quickly declared it "indispensable for any library worth its name," and in its French translation it was the first book to be published by the newly founded Présence Africaine.[18] The "axial" significance of *Bantu Philosophy*, to borrow Lucius Outlaw's description, is owed to the fact that Tempels attributes a philosophical system to an African people—specifically, the Baluba of the present-day Democratic Republic of Congo (DRC), whom he terms the "Bantu."[19]

The cultural and intellectual context surrounding the publication of this book explains its largely positive reception: the paradigm for understanding the colonized, at the time, was Lucien Lévy-Bruhl's notion of a "primitive" mentality, based on his studies of Papuan culture.[20] According to Lévy-Bruhl, the mind of the so-called "primitive" man and that of the so-called "civilized" European are distinct in kind; he argues that "primitive" mentality is unresponsive to the principle of noncontradiction and the laws of causality.[21] Tempels's book thus seemed to usher in a renewed spirit of inclusion through its insistence that the Bantu—and, by hypothesis, all so-called "primitive" communities—were by no means categorically distinct and indeed in possession of an implicit philosophical system.[22] As Diagne has noted, then, Tempels's attempt to show that "the African Weltanschauung could not be reduced to that 'primitive mentality' " is a direct response to the Lévy-Bruhlian thesis.[23]

The broadly positive reception of Tempels's *Bantu Philosophy* among African intellectuals, however, was by no means unanimous. Prominently among Tempels's early detractors, Aimé Césaire undertook to expose the political motivations animating the text.[24] As Césaire points out, *Bantu Philosophy* emerges in a context in which Belgian colonists and missionaries were prepared to abandon the underlying philosophical commitments of the "civilizing mission," namely the view that philosophical reason is universal even as it admits of radical differences in its developmental trajectory. Tempels himself is indeed quite forthcoming about the fact that his "revelation" of an ontological system among the Bantu people is a response to the growing disquiet among Belgian authorities regarding the aptness of the civilizing mission. Discussing a meeting of colonial authorities in the present-day DRC, Tempels explains the motivation of his work as follows: "The decision reached by these gentlemen was the following: that the dissemination of Christianity, after so many decades, appears unsuited to the task of civilizing the Bantu."[25]

The Lévy-Bruhlian thesis that there exists a radical disparity in *kind* between the mind of the European and what is called "primitive mentality" is thus one, albeit a very telling, intellectual symptom of a broader anxiety regarding the tenability of European universalism, and, by extension, European colonialism. Césaire's withering criticism highlights this discomfiting motivational background, making clear that Tempels's *Bantu Philosophy* is, in itself, *a discourse on universality in crisis*. Against the felt sense that the civilizing mission had run its course, Tempels's text attempts to confirm, now empirically, that philosophical reason is *indeed universal*; "even" the Bantu population has a philosophy, with the caveats that this collective philosophy is (1) implicit, (2) historically lagging, and (3) can be systematically adumbrated only by the benevolent European.[26]

Tempels thus argues that the colonized are not outside the realm of reason, but simply, as an earlier no less racist view had it, developmentally inferior. Deploying a strikingly teleological vocabulary, Tempels writes that the worldview of the Bantu people is *remarkably* well suited to Christianization, being only a more primitive form of Christian metaphysics that "longs" for its "final destination," that is, Christian "civilization."[27] It follows that the missionary task of "raising up" the colonized, in Tempels's disturbing phrase, remains feasible.[28] *Bantu Philosophy* is ultimately in service of colonial policy: rather than setting the colonized and the colonizers on an equal footing, Tempels looks to welcome in a new era of colonization supported firmly by the continuing relevance of the civilizing mission and its universalistic outreach.[29]

For Hountondji and a new generation of critics, Césaire's points, while surely correct, did not go far enough.[30] This is because Césaire's target was not *Bantu Philosophy* as such, but rather the ideological purposes for which it was intended.[31] The methodological presuppositions subtending the work were therefore left intact, and indeed reiterated in a number of postcolonial African philosophical texts that took Tempels's book for their inspiration.[32] For Hountondji, then, the critique of Tempels must take the form of a radical *theoretical* problematization.

Hountondji begins by pointing out a fateful equivocation central to Tempels's work and the body of literature inspired by it: applied to the African context, the word "philosophy" no longer designates a specialized field of methodical inquiry, as in the West, but rather a collective worldview or *Weltanschauung*.[33] Put differently, when "philosophy" is qualified by the word "African," it apparently changes its meaning from a theoretical discipline oriented toward universal truth to a summative enterprise, the reconstruction of a "purely local curiosity that has no effectiveness outside its particular context."[34] This is why Hountondji dubs both Tempels's *Bantu Philosophy* and the work of Tempels's African successors as "ethnophilosophical": these texts present their content as philosophical, when in fact what they discuss are collective worldviews, that is, the traditional subject matter of ethnology.[35]

This equivocal use of the term "philosophy" flows directly from what Hountondji variously calls the "alienated" or "extraverted" nature of ethnophilosophical texts. At issue is the audience to whom these texts are addressed: both Tempels's *Bantu Philosophy* and the writings of his "African successors" are intended primarily for a European public, in a manner that importantly inflects the content of these texts.[36] For, in order to consolidate an audience and assure their dissemination and transmission, this writing is compelled to answer to the European public's desire, to the "Western craving for exoticism."[37] As Hountondji writes: "Their objective has been to describe the main features of African civilization for the benefit of [Europe] . . . *but on Europe's own terms*. In the circumstances, it was inevitable that they should have ended up by inventing, as a foil to European philosophy, an African "philosophy" concocted from extra-philosophical material."[38]

Although Hountondji does not make this entirely explicit, his use of "extra-philosophical material" here is telling. For the issue is not merely that the work of Tempels and others are responsive primarily to a European public and therefore determined in part by Western tastes.[39] The deeper issue is that ethnophilosophical literature plays Europe's game in the sense of consolidating, under a different guise, the key premise of philosophical Eurocentrism: the idea that European humanity is uniquely endowed with the ability to develop properly *philosophical*, that is, universally valid, systems of thought. The non-European world, by contrast, is thought to remain enmeshed in the realm of the mythical or religious—that is, the extraphilosophical—and this in such a way as to inhibit the thought of the colonized from having any appeal beyond the particular time and place of its emergence. The European interest in African systems of thought under the aegis of ethnophilosophical literature, then, is not driven by any presupposition that these traditions might contain important insights. Instead, it follows the pattern of keeping well stocked, in Frantz Fanon's very apt phrase, "the inventory of particularisms."[40]

As Hountondji puts this point, "ethnophilosophy" responds to Western desires in the further and significant sense that it confirms the "thesis that non-Western societies are absolutely specific."[41] Hountondji thus pulls the rug out from under those who think Tempels's work is a salutary step in the direction of a truly universal discourse of philosophy, arguing that it achieves no more than a replacement of the Lévy-Bruhlian myth with yet another myth.[42] For "ethnophilosophy" confirms, now with a humanist veneer, the key tenant of philosophical Eurocentrism; the assumption that, as Natalie Melas has put it, "the species is unevenly divided between those who are bound to particular territories and particular customs and manners, and those who can be detached from their place of birth, literally and figuratively, in the fullest sense, since this detachment itself constitutes an ideological legitimation for Europe's incursion into [non-European] territory."[43]

Europe in Crisis: Husserl's Ethnophilosophy

As Hountondji himself makes clear in his philosophical autobiography, *The Struggle for Meaning*, his critique of ethnophilosophy marked something of a turning point in his academic career: prior to the publication of *African Philosophy*, Hountondji was preoccupied with Husserlian phenomenology, devoting his graduate research to Husserl's early thought. In spite of encouragement from his mentors, Hountondji refrained from publishing his doctoral work, actively opting *not* to participate at a professional level in a "non-African philosophical tradition."[44] Nonetheless, most commentators agree that the influence of Husserl is palpable in Hountondji's critique of ethnophilosophy in the form of the restrictive conception of philosophy that Hountondji defends, as well as more generally in Hountondji's commitment to universality.[45]

On this view, Hountondji's turn away from Husserl and toward African philosophical discourse is (1) motivated by reasons extrinsic to Hountondji's work on Husserl, and (2) represents no more than a shift in philosophical attention, since Husserl's work is considered to remain significantly influential even as it recedes into the background of Hountondji's thinking. This view has garnered support from Hountondji's own comments on the development of his critique of ethnophilosophy in *The Struggle for Meaning*, where he notes that "to publish on Husserl was not the obvious thing for an African academic" and describes his departure from Husserl as "a political decision of sorts."[46]

The remainder of this section puts into action the reading strategy proposed at the outset of this chapter, looking at Husserl's texts *through* the concerns articulated by Hountondji. This has the upshot of providing a fuller, more immanent explanation for why Hountondji departed from Husserl than has so far been suggested. For while Hountondji's interest in the universal is certainly consistent with Husserl's hopes that phenomenology would realize the promise of a "rigorous science," reading Husserl through Hountondji makes clear that Husserl's commitment to universality is compromised by a distinctive *ethnophilosophical* element in his thinking. Specifically, in looking at Husserl's *Crisis* texts against the background of Hountondji's critique of Tempels, we see that Hountondji's two main complaints against Tempels, namely that his vision of "universal" philosophy remains Eurocentric, and that his retort to the Lévy-Bruhlian myth of "primitive mentality" institutes another myth, *can also be applied to Husserl.* To Jacques Derrida's provocative question as to whether the critique of ethnophilosophy should not be extended to Europe—for our purposes, whether and to what extent elements of Hountondji's critique of ethnophilosophy apply equally to Husserl—this chapter thus answers in the affirmative.[47]

To be sure, Husserl's phenomenology is *not* ethnophilosophical in the following sense: in *content*, Husserl's texts never venture into providing summative statements of collective worldviews, attending instead to the intentional correlation between consciousness and what is given to it. Nor is Husserl equivocal regarding the term philosophy; indeed, he is at pains to make a sharp distinction between philosophy proper, which in his eyes is strictly scientific and therefore *universal*, and worldviews, which remain tied to practical interests and, consequently, beset by particularity.

And yet, precisely the same bias that Hountondji discerns in Tempels is at play in Husserl's demarcation between "philosophy" and "worldviews," for these are each given a geographical determination.[48] The universal *telos* of philosophy is said to be "innate only in our Europe," while the non-European world is understood as producing mere "worldviews," that is, cultural data that while no doubt interesting cannot hope to command any allegiance beyond the particular site of their enunciation.[49] In other words, from a Husserlian perspective, what Tempels terms Bantu "philosophy" is decidedly not philosophy; nonetheless, Husserl and Tempels are in fundamental agreement that the intellectual productions of the non-European world have no claim to a context-transcending, universal truth.

In the *Crisis* texts in particular, Husserl affirms his commitment to a view of philosophy as the universal prerogative of humanity, at the same time as he indexes this prerogative firmly to the European continent. As Hountondji writes: "One of the most fascinating teachings in Husserl is the way he views science as an infinite task of humanity. . . . However, the humanity he talks about is specified as European humanity."[50] On the one hand, Husserl's focus on Europe is clearly related to his political and social context; Europe is uniquely threatened by the forces of irrational-ism, one aspect of this crisis being Hitler's rise to power.[51] On the other hand, however, Husserl's weaving together of "philosophical universality," "crisis," and "Europe" bespeaks a deeper metaphilosophical commitment of his: for Husserl, the crisis of philosophical universality is a crisis of *Europe* not only because European rationality is thrown into question by homegrown intellectual and political movements, but because, as one Husserl commentator has put it, "Europe coincides with the very idea of [philosophical] universality itself."[52] The crisis of philosophical universality is, for Husserl, a markedly European affair, first and foremost because he understands thought that has a universal scope to have originated in, and to remain the exclusive property of, European humanity.

Significantly, while historicism, psychologism, and Nazism each show up the predominance of a relativism threatening to topple Euro-pean universalism, a further symptom of this crisis is the popularization of what was at the time a novel ethnological idea: Lévy-Bruhl's thesis of "primitive" mentality. In March 1935—two months prior to the delivery of the *Vienna Lecture*—Husserl wrote a letter to Lévy-Bruhl in which he expressed his appreciation for the latter's newest publication, *Primitive Mythology*. This is not to say that Husserl was convinced of the conclusions drawn by Lévy-Bruhl; instead, he regarded the Lévy-Bruhlian thesis of categorical difference as mounting an important challenge to phenome-nology's universalistic aspirations.[53] Husserl's engagement with Lévy-Bruhl is given its most explicit expression in another publication written a year later, *The Origin of Geometry*, in which he seeks to affirm the possibility of universality by tracing a "historical a priori." Husserl here insists that his method of imaginative variation secures the geographically and tem-porally invariant structures—the historical a priori—of what he calls the lifeworld.[54] As intimated earlier, however, it is the European environing world that uniquely provides insight into these "invariant structures": other societies and cultures take part in this universality only *in potential*. In other words, while the invariant structures first identified within the European context are superficially lacking in culturally distant societies, this is merely because they are lying in wait, as it were, behind the façade of difference. The historical a priori is paradigmatically on display in what Husserl calls "our Europe" because, in a troubling repetition of the key argument of the civilizing mission—and one that, it must be noted, closely parallels the claims made by Tempels—European culture is further along the developmental trajectory, bearing witness to the "first breakthrough of what is essential to humanity *as such*."[55]

The exceptionality of Europe is justified by reference to its unique possession of philosophy, of a cultural phenomenon that is no longer historicized. That is to say, the philosophy that allegedly bursts into existence in ancient Greece aims at the universal: its pronouncements are to be valid for all places and all times, its achievements are not transitory. As Husserl writes, "No other cultural form in the prephilosophical historical horizon is a culture of ideas in the above-mentioned sense."[56] Here we see in paradigmatic form the manner in which Eurocentric commitments operate under the guise of philosophical universality: Europe is the privileged site of the unfolding of the universal. The paradox involved in anchoring the universal viewpoint of philosophy to a particular territory is well expressed by Kisukidi: "[it involves] the assimilation of a theoretical practice, which is supposed to demonstrate the very excellence of humanity as such, to *one* territory, the West, and to *one* body, the white body."[57] And Husserl stubbornly insists on the special election of Europe in this regard. He writes: "Here we meet the obvious objection that philosophy, the science of the Greeks, is not, after all, distinctive of them. . . . They themselves tell of the wise Egyptians, Babylonians, etc. . . . Today we possess all sorts of studies on Indian, Chinese, and other philosophies."[58]

Tellingly refraining from citing any texts or thinkers within these "equally notable oriental philosophies," Husserl goes on to argue that the distinctiveness of Europe remains intact, for these other "philosophies" remain entangled in the mythical-religious worlds in which they emerge— and this in such a way as to inhibit them from having any appeal beyond their particular time and place.[59] In the words of Edward Said, the view is that non-European peoples are relegated "to a particularity from which they cannot free themselves . . . and so [there is no sense in which] the colonized people should be heard from, their ideas known."[60] In this way, non-European thought is seen as a worldview out of which no universal insight can be generated.

Both Tempels and Husserl articulate a response to a "crisis of universality" prompted in part by the popularization in Europe of Lévy-Bruhlian anthropology. And the attempt to "save the honor of reason" against the onslaught of relativism, to borrow a phrase of Derrida's, hinges for both Tempels and Husserl on a revamped ethnocentrism that upholds Europe as the unique crucible of universalistic thinking.[61] The only difference between Tempels and Husserl on this score is that, while the former generously extends the title "philosophy" to worldviews, the latter chooses to be more semantically precise with his Eurocentrism. In both cases, however, underlying what is at first blush a comprehensive universalism is the stubborn conviction that "the universal quality of the human is vested . . . in the European, while the particular resides in all the rest."[62] Regarding Hountondji's comment that "Tempels's approach in *La philosophie-Bantoue* seemed to me an attempt to debunk Lévy-Bruhl, but in the worst way possible," and that it amounts to "the art of 'combatting a myth by another myth,'" it should by now be clear that precisely the same charge might be leveled at the Husserl of the *Crisis* period.

This then begins to put serious pressure on the standard interpretation of the Husserl-Hountondji relationship and its suggestion that Hountondji simply adopts Husserl's vision of universal science as a tool with which to interrogate Tempels. For the Husserlian notion of universality is itself plagued by a Eurocentrism strikingly similar in form to that evinced by the writer of *Bantu Philosophy*. Much like Tempels, Husserl actively participated in the marginalization of Africa and its constitution in the European-philosophical imagination as a geographical site outside of the frontiers of scientific thought. It would therefore be odd, to say the least, for Hountondji to unquestioningly marshal this framework in order to move beyond Eurocentric universalism.

The reinterpretation of the Husserl-Hountondji relationship offered here finds textual support in Hountondji's later work, specifically in a 2015 presentation of Hountondji's titled "Constructing the Universal: A Transcultural Challenge."[63] In this presentation, Hountondji argues that Husserl's texts are constitutively Eurocentric on account of the narrow scope of their audience, just as he had previously argued with regard to Tempels. Hountondji here focuses on Husserl's comments about the manner in which the "Papuan of New Guinea," while understood to be a rational animal, nonetheless lacks the philosophical reason proper to European humanity. Hountondji notes that in evaluating such a claim, it is important to "ask first what kind of audience [is being addressed]." As commentators such as Dismas Masolo and Katrin Flikschuh have pointed out, then, Hountondji's concern with the "false universality" of European philosophy is a prescient insight into the issue of epistemic injustice and this field's characteristic concern with issues of uptake. As Flikschuh in particular notes, philosophy cannot consistently hope to raise universally valid claims while at the same time "arbitrarily restricting the scope of its possible participants and addressees."[64] Hountondji articulates this concern as follows:

> However scientific, objective, or rational a discourse claims to be, it is always, directly or indirectly, shaped by its potential audience. As a matter of fact, [Husserl] never suspected that [he] could someday be read by . . . the Papuans of New Guinea. [He] felt free, therefore, to talk about the latter without fearing to be contradicted . . . What I say depends on whom I am *not* talking to as well as whom I *am* addressing. Such exclusions are usually made spontaneously, without any question about their legitimacy.[65]

That Husserl circumscribed the range of philosophical interlocution to the European continent is made very clear in those passages where he puts forward a "resolution" to the crisis of philosophical universality.[66] Given that Husserl, like Tempels, reserves for Europe the special role of developing universalistic thinking, it is perhaps not surprising that the resolution to the crisis is to be sought within the Western tradition, specifically in a reactivation of its Greco-European origin. As Lewis Gordon has noted, then, Husserl's "sermon on European reason" ends with a call for a *return*: "resuscitation became the order of the day."[67]

The response to a philosophical universality in crisis is thus, ironically, a renewed insistence upon philosophy's provincialism. Husserl's repeated pronouncements of the non-European world as primitive and prephilosophical imply that the contributions of other traditions of thought on the issues of universality and crisis are seen as irrelevant. As Nelson Maldonado-Torres expresses this point: "The voices of other people and their views on history, humanity, reason and crisis are declared insignificant."[68] To the extent that there *is* a global dimension to Husserl's proposed response to the immanent disappearance of universal reason, Husserl speaks, in an alarmingly colonialist register, of the submission of the "rest" to Europeanization: "There is something unique here that is recognized in us by all other human groups, too, something that, quite apart from all considerations of utility, becomes a motive for them to Europeanize themselves . . . whereas we, if we understand ourselves properly, would never Indianize ourselves, for example."[69]

Tempels is similarly inured to the necessary unsettling of European epistemic privilege in his own proposed resolution to the crisis. In the final pages of his *Bantu Philosophy*, Tempels writes of two possibilities: "Either we will contribute to a Christian Bantu civilization, or we will witness a superficial Europeanization that will gradually wipe out Bantuism. There exists no other way out."[70] Husserl, in his turn, concludes the Vienna Lecture as follows: "The crisis of European existence can end in only one of two ways: the ruin of a Europe alienated from its rational sense of life, fallen into a barbarian hatred of spirit, or in the rebirth of Europe from the spirit of philosophy."[71] The startlingly close mirroring of these concluding passages drives home the point that Husserl and Tempels cannot see beyond a *European* resolution to the crisis of philosophical universality. In neither thinker is there any inkling that a movement toward genuine universality will involve moving beyond an exclusive reliance on the European tradition of thought.

Decolonial Universality and the Margins of Philosophy

In one of her essays on the ongoing work of decolonizing philosophy, Nadia Yala Kisukidi poses a number of provocative questions regarding various decolonial strategies. As she recognizes, the act of "bursting [philosophy's] geographies, real or imagined," is in itself a significant decolonizing move.[72] From a certain perspective, Kisukidi argues, the decolonization of philosophy amounts to an exposure of its various paradoxes: "geographies of spirit, philosophical nationalisms, racial anthropologies, etc."[73] The force of Hountondji's work with respect to this critical aim is, *on any reading*, undeniable: what the critique of ethnophilosophy discloses is the widespread operation of philosophical Eurocentrism's central paradox whereby the universality of philosophy is said to reside, exclusively, in the West.

Kisukidi ultimately claims, however, that there is another perspective from which the "bursting of [implicit] philosophical geographies . . . is not sufficient for an effective decolonization of philosophy."[74] Kisukidi goes on: "Seen in this light, the decolonizing gesture [would be] more radical still . . . decolonizing philosophy would have no other meaning than asserting, once again, *the necessity of an exit*."[75] In the remainder of this chapter, I argue that the reading strategy deployed previously allows us to see that Hountondji's thinking on the universal does indeed partake of this more radical gesture.

In the preface to *The Struggle for Meaning*, Hountondji expresses in no uncertain terms the intentions underlying his critique of ethnophilosophy, writing of opening up the horizon of African philosophizing beyond the implicit demand that its insights be reduced to the particularisms of the ethnological. Hountondji writes: "The researcher could once again claim . . . the duty to truth and the desire for apodictic certainty. . . . The philosopher, in particular, could once again assert a claim for universality that is the foundation of his discipline, by refusing to yield to cultural relativism, and by clearly acknowledging his vocation to enunciate propositions that are valid across frontiers."[76]

The stakes of the critique of ethnophilosophy and its metaphilosophical implications thus concern the philosophical demarginalization of Africa and the assertion of a *"right to the universal*, the possibility of raising independent questions that are not a mere restatement of those raised on Africa by Western curiosity."[77] Hountondji's exposure of the paradox whereby the universal is the special privilege of Europe does not lead him, in other words, to condemn as irremeably Eurocentric the aspiration to universality as such. To borrow an incisive formulation of Sekyi-Otu's, "to abjure universalism *tout court* because of imperialist, Eurocentric and discriminatory auspices of certain versions . . . is the last word of the imperial act [by] conceding ownership of universalism to the West."[78]

Hountondji discusses this "right to the universal" in strikingly Husserlian terms; his reference to "apodictic certainty" is very clearly a nod to Husserl. This type of comment has authorized those interpretations according to which Hountondji effectively retains intact Husserl's vision of phenomenology as universal science. My claim has been that when we shake off the methodological habit of reading Hountondji as though he is simply derivative of Husserl, a different, more nuanced, and, importantly, *new* account of universality in crisis comes to the fore. Specifically, while it is clear that a certain Husserl exerts influence on Hountondji's work, exploring the Husserl-Hountondji relationship *on the basis of* Hountondji's work shows that Hountondji's assumption of the right to the universal involves something of a heresy, to invoke Ricoeur's comment, vis-à-vis Husserlian phenomenology.

Husserl, as we have seen, evinces a prototypical response to philosophical crisis by suggesting that its resolution lies in a *return*, or, more precisely, a reactivation of the supposed Greco-European origin of universalistic thinking. In the process, "the privileged viewpoint of post-Hellenic, European consciousness is never for a moment put into question."[79] Hountondji, by contrast, shows up the necessity of an exit from the Western philosophical inheritance in order to adequately respond to the crisis of philosophical reason. What is required is a "work on the margins," as Hountondji puts it, a metaphilosophical endeavor that questions European philosophy's self-narrative as the historical privilege of European man.[80] Explicitly taking off from the positionality of the philosophical margin, this is emphatically not a questioning of European philosophy by European philosophy, as in the traditional discourses of crisis. Instead, Hountondji speaks of the necessity of the "paradoxical task consisting in getting out of philosophy, in transgressing continually its limits."[81] Schematically put, what this involves is twofold.

On the one hand, at stake is the shifting of the geography of philosophy with a concerted effort to dislodge the global philosophical conversation from its often-implicit locus.[82] Given the tenacity of the philosophical and institutional privileging of the Global North, Hountondji recognizes that a preliminary step in this direction is the promotion of horizontal, inter-African dialogue. He thus speaks of the necessity of "open[ing] up in Africa a new space of research and discussion, an *autonomous space* where the themes explored would no longer be a distant echo of those developed by Western knowledge," and recommends to this end a strategy of "delinking."[83] The effect of delinking would thus be to breathe new life into the "inner tensions and dynamism" of African cultures artificially rendered inert by the Western imagination.[84] As Hountondji writes, in a language that suggests the Fanonian inspiration of his concerns: "Pluralism is first of all a fact. It is not invented, it is acknowledged . . . it is necessary to recognize the internal dialectic, the creative pluralism at work in contemporary African culture and in each of its components."[85]

But the inter-African debate is not, for Hountondji, the end of the story. Hountondji looks toward debate on a worldwide scale, and he envisions the delimitation of "new spaces of scholarly discussions within Africa . . . as concentric circles starting from limited points and widening progressively to encompass the whole continent and . . . eventually the whole world."[86] Hountondji is nonetheless careful that the expansion of the debate should not involve an emptying out of particularity. Of this shift to the global level, Hountondji writes that it would not be a question of a "sort of supra-culture, which will synthesize all regional cultures and smooth over their differences."[87] Instead, by acknowledging the connection between the universal and the internal dynamism of particular cultures, "the reality of world civilization will be conceived no longer as a system of universally accepted values but rather as an extension of the debate to a world scale."[88]

On the other hand, the disciplinary bounds of philosophy must also be interrogated and eventually crossed. That which philosophy has consigned to the extra- or nonphilosophical must be reevaluated in the interest of a global dialogue oriented to the ideal of universal validity.[89] A key dimension of Hountondji's philosophical work since the critique of ethnophilosophy has thus involved the critical *reappropriation* of endogenous systems of knowledge, of that which has been routinely understood on the dimension of "worldviews." At issue here is the reevaluation of so-called "traditional" corpuses of knowledge, now liberated from the ethnophilosophical paradigm wherein they are treated as no more than local curiosities that do not, in principle, contain any universalizable insights. Recall that a central premise of ethnophilosophy is its condescending attitude vis-à-vis indigenous systems of knowledge: "it does not ask any questions about the truth of local knowledge systems. It just describes them and leaves them as they are."[90] Within the intra-African debate, Hountondji wagers that it becomes possible to adopt a different attitude vis-à-vis what he calls these epistemic "counter-systems," approaching endogenous knowledge systems with an eye toward that which is potentially context-transcendent.[91]

In sharp contrast with Husserl's insistence on the intellectual bounty of a European tradition assumed to contain ample resources for addressing the crisis of universality, Hountondji thus argues that the pursuit of a truly universalist philosophical discourse presupposes the full participation of Africa. Moving away from what Fanon shrewdly termed the West's "narcissistic monologue with itself," Hountondji's resolution to the contemporary crisis of philosophical reason insists on global inclusivity as the sine qua non of a genuine universality.[92] Yoking together the two elements involved in his turn to the margins of European philosophy, Hountondji writes: "Above all we need, beyond the individual co-optation of such and such a scholar in the field of discourse that is entirely controlled by the North, to put in place an ambitious strategy of appropriation of knowledge by our own societies."[93]

In the course of this transgression of philosophy's limits, Hountondji articulates a novel conception of the universal that traverses the path between rootedness within a particular situation and universality as an orienting ideal. Put otherwise, Hountondji's explorations into universality seek to ferret out the "modes of co-existence of the particular and the universal."[94] In this endeavor, Hountondji is in dialogue less with Husserl, and, as briefly intimated, more with an Afrocentric genealogy of universalistic thinking that includes Aimé Césaire and Frantz Fanon.[95] While an in-depth exploration of this dimension of Hountondji's thinking lies outside the scope of this chapter, it bears mentioning that in engaging with this set of interlocutors, Hountondji is setting into action his own conviction that a resolution to the crisis of universality can under no circumstances rest content with an exclusive reliance on the European tradition. Instead, an expansion of the geographical and disciplinary traditions standardly used in philosophical thinking is to give rise to a universalism that, to give the last word to Hountondji, "is not given in advance. It is still to be built. It is not behind us, but before us. No culture is predestined to it, and none is barred from it. Hence the immense responsibility of contemporary generations: that of contributing together, in a thoughtful manner, in a spirit of solidarity and sharing, to the building of the common edifice."[96]

Notes

1. References to this text throughout this chapter will be to the edition published in Husserl (1965, 149–192).

2. For Husserl, reason is threatened on two counts: first, by the lopsided development of reason in the form of a scientistic objectivism that severs reason from meaning and thereby foments relativism, and, second, by a historicism that works to undermine all claims to universality. Although Husserl does not explicitly link these endemic threats to reason to Germany's situation in the interwar years, a number of commentators have established the significant explanatory force of this sociopolitical context: irrationalism in the particular form of anti-universality was very much in "vogue" under the Nazi regime. On this, Diagne (2013); Moran (2011); Derrida (2004, 118–159).

3. Husserl (1995, 12, italics original).

4. Boulbina (2011). See also Kisukidi (2020/21).

5. This phrase is a reference to Sartre's quip that *Négritude*, in affirming Black particularity, involves an antiracist racism, Sartre (1964–1965, 48).

6. Kisukidi (2020/21, 48). Two examples of views of this nature include Žižek (2016) and Amselle (2008).

7. Some prominent examples include Diagne (2013); Sekyi-Otu (2019); Diagne and Amselle (2020); Melas (2016); Boulbina (2019); Dübgen and Skupien (2019).

8. Diagne (2013, 2).

9. Immanuel Wallerstein in *European Universalism or the Rhetoric of Power* (New York: New Press, 2006), cited by Diagne (2013, 2).

10. The version of universality of interest here is universality qua validity across contexts. It thus belongs to insights and knowledge claims rather than being a property of certain entities. In this chapter and elsewhere I remain neutral as to whether such validity is intersubjectively discovered or constructed.

11. See for example Bongmba (2004); Irele (2004); Dübgen and Skupien (2019); Masolo (2003).

12. As Boulbina has remarked of the Fanon-Sartre scholarship, there is a preference "to make Fanon into a reader of Sartre rather than Sartre into a reader of Fanon. Fanon's reading of Sartre thereby appears essential, while Sartre's reading of Fanon appears inessential. Thus, the same division is reproduced, the same hierarchy, and, in the end, the same coloniality. When Sartre reads Hegel, he is considered first as an author, even when he is visibly also a reader. One must therefore decolonize both gazes and forms of knowledge" (2019, 269).

13. The expression is Paul Ricoeur's, from his seminal study of Husserl. See Ricoeur (2007, 4).

14. For similar examples of decolonial or "creolizing" reading strategies, see Belausteguigoitia and Gutiérrez Magallanes (2013, 95–106); Belausteguigotia (2013); Gordon (2014); Monahan (2017); Gordon (1995).

15. Hountondji (2007, 4). Translations are mine unless otherwise noted.

16. As Kwasi Wiredu notes, because Hountondji's critique of ethnophilosophy has "precipitated and constituted quite a large part of the concerns of contemporary African philosophy" one could pick "almost at random" the studies that engage or are indeed entirely devoted to this work and the controversy surrounding it. A few notable examples include: Appiah (1989); Gyekye (1987); Masolo (1994). See Wiredu (2004, 3).

17. Hountondji (1987a).

18. This was accompanied by a preface by *Présence africaine* founder Alioune Diop, who noted that "this little book (c'est petit livre)" was to his mind the most important publication on Africa to date. On this, see Tomaz Carlos Flores Jacques (2011); Diagne (2016, 9). On *Présence africaine*, see Mudimbe (1992).

19. Outlaw (1987, 20).

20. For an in-depth discussion, see Bernasconi (2005); see further Masolo (2010, 85–101).

21. Lévy-Bruhl (2018). See also Alexander Koyré, "Review of Lucien Lévy-Bruhl, *Die Seele der Primitiven*," *Deutsche Literaturzeitung* 14 (1930), cited by Bernasconi (2005, 235).

22. Tempels (1946).

23. Diagne (2016, 13); see also Hountondji (1987a, 34).

24. Césaire (1972, 58–59).

25. Tempels (1946, 111).

26. Diagne (2016, 12).

27. Tempels (1946, 113).

28. Tempels (1946, 6). The resonances of this phrase—"opvoeden"—in the Dutch language leave no doubt that Tempels is describing the relationship of the Belgian colonist to colonial subjects as one of paternalistic authority.

29. Diagne (2016, 12).

30. For other, contemporaneous critiques of ethnophilosophy, see Boulaga (2014); Towa (2012).

31. Hountondji (1987a, 37).

32. Hountondji (1987a, 58).

33. The Husserlian resonances of Hountondji's invocation of the distinction between a worldview or *Weltanschauung* and philosophy properly understood should not be ignored. I argue in the following section, however, that an over-emphasis on this inheritance obscures the fact that Husserl himself misuses this distinction. On this, see Hountondji, "Why Husserl in Africa? Autobiographical Reflections," chapter 3 in this volume; see also Lamola (2020).

34. Hountondji (1997, 18). See also Hountondji (1987a, 60).

35. Reflecting on his critique of Tempels, Hountondji writes, "To make it clear that this way of doing philosophy was not the standard one, I described it as ethnophilosophy, i.e. a branch of ethnology mistaken for philosophy" (2004, 530).

36. Hountondji (1987a, 50). "Primarily" is a key term here, as Tempels's *Bantu Philosophy* was energetically taken up by the Jamaa religious movement of the Katanga (now Shaba) region of the present-day DRC. This was with Tempels's full consent and encouragement. On this see Fabian (1971). I thank the anonymous reviewer of this chapter for bringing this to my attention.

37. Hountondji (1987a, 54; see also 52, 80).

38. Hountondji (1987a, 50, italics added).

39. Hountondji (1987a, 80).

40. Fanon (2004, 160).

41. Hountondji (1987a, 61).

42. Hountondji (2002, 84–85).

43. Melas (2016, 134).

44. Hountondji (2002, 89).

45. This has been the source of some controversy, with commentators leveling a charge of Eurocentrism at Hountondji on account of his commitment to Husserl. See, for example, Owomoyela (1987); Ikuenobe (1997); Koffi (1980); Gyekye (1995); Serequeberhan (1994).

46. Hountondji (2002, 74).

47. Derrida (2002, 108). Katrin Flikschuh suggests something similar in her reading of Hountondji, noting that Hountondji's trajectory raises the following question: "Is Western philosophy a science or is it itself a kind of 'ethnophilosophy'—a construction based on the constants of Western culture mistakenly packaged as a form of universal knowledge?" (2017, 146).

48. On Husserl's Eurocentrism, see Diagne (2013); Mignolo (2018); Masolo (2010, 85–101); Bernasconi and Cook (2003, 8–19); Moran (2011); Gasché (2009); Dussel (1995); Derrida (2003, 154–159).

49. Husserl (1965, 155; see also 163–164).

50. Paulin J. Hountondji, "Constructing the Universal: A Transcultural Challenge," Keynote Address, Department of Philosophy, University of Ghana. Cited in Flikschuh (2017, 137).

51. For an extensive analysis of the sociopolitical background to Husserl's late work, see Moran (2011).

52. Gasché (2009, 21). See also Guénoun (2013, 16–24).

53. On this see Masolo (2010, 85); Bernasconi (2005, 234–237).

54. Husserl (1970, 373).

55. Husserl writes: "We are heirs and cobearers of the direction of the will which pervades this humanity; we have become this through a primal establishment which is at once a reestablishment and a modification of the Greek primal establishment. In the latter lies the *true beginning*, the true birth of European spirit as such" (1970, 71). Here the question cannot be refused as to why the "we" who bear this heritage are specified as Europeans. Husserl contributes to no small extent to the appropriation of the Greek legacy for Europe, and for Europe alone. To speak in Martin Bernal's terms, Husserl participates in popularizing the highly politicized "Aryan model" of Greek historiography, which obscures the Egyptian-Phoenician influences on Greek culture. See Bernal (2020).

56. Husserl (1965, 163).

57. Kisukidi (2015, 86).

58. Husserl (1965, 164).

59. Husserl (1965, 169).

60. Said (1993, 50).

61. Derrida (2004, 118–124).

62. Melas (2016, 130).

63. Published in article form as Hountondji (2017).

64. Flikschuh (2018, 110). See also Masolo (2010, 24–25).

65. Hountondji, "Constructing the Universal," cited by Flikschuh (2017, 137–138).

66. It bears remarking that this implicit restriction of audience is indeed made more or less *explicit* by Husserl in his delimitation of those who are engaged in and by the constitution and transmission of ideal objectivities to "normal" subjects. On this see Derrida (1962, 79–83). See also Bernasconi (2005, 239–240).

67. Gordon (1995, 6–7).

68. Maldonado-Torres (2002, 285).

69. Husserl (1970, 275).

70. Tempels (1946, 114).

71. Husserl (1965, 192).

72. Kisukidi (2015, 86).

73. Kisukidi (2015, 85).

74. Kisukidi (2015, 92).

75. Kisukidi (2015, 92, italics added).

76. Hountondji (2002, xviii).

77. Hountondji (2002, 138, italics added).

78. Sekyi-Otu (2019, 14).

79. De Man (1983, 16).

80. Hountondji (2002, 75).

81. Hountondji (1987b, 22).

82. "Shifting the geography of reason" is the motto of the Caribbean Philosophical Association (CPA). See Lewis Gordon (2011).

83. Hountondji (2004, 241). Hountondji intentionally borrows this term from world-systems theory.

84. Hountondji (1987a, xvii).

85. Hountondji (2002, 107–108).

86. What such an emphasis inevitably leads to, according to Hountondji, is a "deepening perception" of pluralism: rather than appearing only at the level of transcultural dialogue (and indeed, Hountondji's questioning suggests that it is precisely here that pluralism tends to be undermined), pluralism is revealed to be proper to each culture. The effect of delinking would thus be to breathe new life into the "inner tensions and dynamism" of African cultures artificially rendered inert by the Western imagination. As Hountondji writes: "Pluralism is first of all a fact. It is not invented, it is acknowledged . . . it is necessary to recognize the internal dialectic, the creative pluralism at work in contemporary African culture and in each of its components." On this, see Hountondji (2019, 175); Hountondji (1992, 239).

87. Hountondji (1987a, 166).

88. Hountondji (1987a, 167).

89. Hountondji (2002, 28).

90. Hountondji (2004, 536).

91. Hountondji (1997, 14). While the contours of the appropriate epistemic attitude vis-à-vis endogenous systems of knowledge is left rather vague by Hountondji, we can extrapolate that it would be one of humility, involving an openness to being surprised and having one's methodological and, importantly, disciplinary and metaphilosophical commitments and presuppositions radically transformed. Rather than approaching epistemic counter-systems by way of ethnophilosophical exoticization, or equipped with the presupposition that modern science will be the final arbiter, Hountondji looks toward the possibility of an encounter that would cause "shifts and shake-ups in the [existing body of knowledge], of which we have no way of predicting either the scope or the impact." These quotes are pulled from another edition of this essay, translated as "Recapturing." See Hountondji (1992, 132).

92. Fanon (2004, 51).

93. Hountondji (2002, 222).

94. Hountondji (2002, 206).
95. Hountondji (2002, 86); see also Hountondji (2000).
96. Hountondji (2002, 258).

References

Amselle, Jean-Loup. 2008. *L'occident décroché: Enquete sur les postcolonialismes (pluriel)*. Paris: Éditions Stock.

Appiah, Anthony Kwame. 1989. *Necessary Questions: An Introduction to Philosophy*. Englewood: Prentice Hall.

Belausteguigotia, Marisa. 2013. "Strategies for a Transnational Reading of Border Writers: Pairing a Triangle." In *Translocalities/Translocalidades: Feminist Politics of Translation in Latin/a Americas*, edited by in S. E. Alvarez and C. de Lima Costa et al., 107–112. Durham: Duke University Press.

Belausteguigoitia, Marisa, and María del Socorro Gutiérrez Magallanes. 2013. "Chicana/o and Latina/o Literary Studies in México." In *Routledge Companion to Latino/a Literature*, edited by Suzanne Bost and Frances R. Aparicio, 95–106. London: Routledge.

Bernal, Martin. 2020. *Black Athena: The Afroasiatic Roots of Classical Civilization, Volume 1: The Fabrication of Ancient Greece 1785–1985*. New Brunswick: Rutgers University Press.

Bernasconi, Robert. 2005. "Lévy-Bruhl among the Phenomenologists: Exoticisation and the Logic of the 'Primitive.'" *Social Identities* 11, no. 3: 229–245.

Bernasconi, Robert, and Sybol Cook, eds. 2003. *Race and Racism in Continental Philosophy*. Bloomington: Indiana University Press.

Bongmba, Elias K. 2004. "Whither African Philosophy?" *African Studies Review* 47, no. 2: 119–123.

Boulaga, Fabien Eboussi. 2014. *Muntu in Crisis: African Authenticity and Philosophy*. Trenton: Africa World Press.

Boulbina, Seloua Luste. 2011. "Lettre Ouverte à Pierre Nora." *Médiapart*, October, 17. https://blogs.mediapart.fr/edition/les-invites-de-mediapart/article/171011/lettre-ouverte-pierre-nora.

Boulbina, Seloua Luste. 2019. *Kafka's Monkey and Other Phantoms of Africa*. Translated by Laura E. Henhegold. Bloomington: Indiana University Press.

Césaire, Aimé. 1972. *Discourse on Colonialism*. Translated by Joan Pinkham. New York: Monthly Review Press.

De Man, Paul. 1983. *Blindness and Insight: Essays in the Rhetoric of Contemporary Criticism*, 2nd ed. Translated by Wlad Godzich. Minneapolis: University of Minnesota Press.

Derrida, Jacques. 1962. *Edmund Husserl's Origin of Geometry: An Introduction*. Translated by John P. Leavey Jr. Lincoln: University of Nebraska Press.

Derrida, Jacques. 2002. "The Crisis in the Teaching of Philosophy." In *Who's Afraid of Philosophy: Right to Philosophy I*, translated by Jan Plug, 99–116. Stanford: Stanford University Press.

Derrida, Jacques. 2003. *The Problem of Genesis in Husserl's Philosophy*. Translated by Marian Hobson. Chicago: University of Chicago Press.

Derrida, Jacques. 2004. *Rogues: Two Essays on Reason*. Translated by Pascale Anne-Brault and Michael Naas. Stanford: Stanford University Press.

Diagne, Souleymane Bachir. 2013. "On the Postcolonial and the Universal?" *Rue Descartes* 2, no. 78: 7–18.

Diagne, Souleymane Bachir, and Jean-Loup Amselle. 2020. *In Search of Africa(s): Universalism and Decolonial Thought*. Translated by Andrew Brown. Cambridge: Polity Press.

Diagne, Souleymane Bachir. 2016. *The Ink of the Scholar: Reflections on Philosophy in Africa*. Translated by Jonathan Adjemian. Dakar: CODESRIA.

Dussel, Enrique. 1995. *The Invention of the Americas: Eclipse of the "Other" and the Myth of Modernity*. Translated by Michael Barber. New York: Continuum.

Dübgen, Franziska, and Stefan Skupien, eds. 2019. *Paulin Hountondji: African Philosophy as Critical Universalism*. London: Palgrave Macmillan.

Fabian Johannes. 1971. *Jamaa: A Charismatic Movement in Katanga*. Evanston: Northwestern University Press.

Fanon, Frantz. 2004. *The Wretched of the Earth*. Translated by Richard Philcox. New York: Grove Press.

Flikschuh, Katrin. 2017. *What Is Orientation in Global Thinking: A Kantian Inquiry*. Cambridge: Cambridge University Press.

Flikschuh, Katrin. 2018. "Philosophical Racism." *Aristotelian Society* 92, no. 1: 91–110.

Gasché, Rodolphe. 2009. *Europe, or the Infinite Task: A Study of a Philosophical Concept*. Stanford: Stanford University Press.

Gordon, Jane Anna. 2014. *Creolizing Political Theory: Reading Rousseau through Fanon*. New York: Fordham University Press.

Gordon, Lewis. 1995. *Fanon and the Crisis of European Man: An Essay on Philosophy and the Human Sciences*. London: Routledge.

Gordon, Lewis. 2011. "Shifting the Geography of Reason in an Age of Disciplinary Decadence." *Transmodernity*: 95–103.

Guénoun, Dennis. 2013. *About Europe: Philosophical Hypotheses*. Translated by Christine Irizarry. Stanford: Stanford University Press.

Gyekye, Kwame. 1987. *An Essay on African Philosophical Thought*. Cambridge: Cambridge University Press.

Gyekye, Kwame. 1995. *African Philosophical Thought: The Akan Conceptual Scheme*. Philadelphia: Temple University Press.

Hountondji, Paulin J. 1987a. *African Philosophy: Myth and Reality*. Translated by Henri Evans. Bloomington: Indiana University Press.

Hountondji, Paulin J. 1987b. "What Philosophy Can Do." *Quest: Philosophical Discussions* 3, no. 2: 2–30.

Hountondji, Paulin J. 1992. "Recapturing." In *The Surreptitious Speech: Présence Africaine and the Politics of Otherness, 1947–1987*, edited by V. Y. Mudimbe, 238–248. Chicago: University of Chicago Press.

Hountondji, Paulin J. 1997. "Recentering Africa." In *Endogenous Knowledge: Research Trails*, edited by Paulin J. Hountondji, translated by Ayi Kwei Armah, 1–39. Dakar: CODESRIA.

Hountondji, Paulin J. 2000. "La 'Fin Du Monde': Césaire et L'Invention de La Liberté." *Renaissance Noir* 3, no. 1: 166–185.

Hountondji, Paulin J. 2002. *The Struggle for Meaning: Reflections on Philosophy, Culture and Democracy in Africa*. Translated by John Conteh-Morgan. Athens: Ohio University Press.

Hountondji, Paulin J. 2004. "Knowledge as a Development Issue." In *A Companion to African Philosophy*, edited by Kwasi Wiredu, 529–537. Oxford: Blackwell.

Hountondji, Paulin J., ed. 2007. *La rationalité, une ou plurielle?* Dakar: CODESRIA.

Hountondji, Paulin J. 2017. "Construire l'universel: un défi transculturel." *Méthode: African Review of Social Sciences Methodology*: 1–17.

Hountondji, Paulin J. 2019. "Appendix: Interview with Paulin Hountondji." In *African Philosophy as Critical Universalism*, edited by Franziska Dübgen and Stefan Skupien, 166–177. London: Palgrave Macmillan.

Husserl, Edmund. 1965. "Philosophy and the Crisis of European Man." In *Edmund Husserl, Phenomenology and the Crisis of Philosophy*, edited by Quentin Lauer, translated by Quentin Lauer, 149–192. New York: Harper & Row.

Husserl, Edmund. 1970. *The Crisis of European Sciences and Transcendental Phenomenology*. Translated by David Carr. Evanston: Northwestern University Press.

Husserl, Edmund. 1995. *Cartesian Meditations: An Introduction to Phenomenology*. Translated by Dorion Cairns. Dordrecht: Kluwer Academic.

Ikuenobe, P. 1997. "The Parochial Universalist Conception of 'Philosophy' and 'African Philosophy.'" *Philosophy East and West* 47, no. 2: 189–210.

Irele, Abiola. 2004. "Philosophy and the Postcolonial Condition in Africa." *Research in African Literatures* 35, no. 4: 160–170.

Jacques, Tomaz Carlos Flores. 2011. "Philosophy in Black: African Philosophy as Negritude." *Sartre Studies International* 17, no. 1: 1–19.

Lamola, M. John. 2020. "Paulin Hountondji, Knowledge as Science, and the Sovereignty of African Intellection." *Social Epistemology*: 1–15.

Kisukidi, Nadia Yala. 2015. "Décoloniser la philosophie, Ou de la philosophie comme objet anthropologique." *Présence africaine* 192: 83–98.

Kisukidi, Nadia Yala. 2020/21. "L'universel dans la brousse." *Éditions Esprit*: 47–59.

Koffi, N. 1980. "L'impensé de Towa et de Hountondji." In *La Philosophie Africaine*, edited by C. Summer, 165–188. Addis Ababa: Chamber.

Maldonado-Torres, Nelson. 2002. "Postimperial Reflections on Crisis, Knowledge, and Utopia: Transgresstopic Critical Hermeneutics and the 'Death of European Man.'" *Review (Fernand Braudel Center)* 25, no. 3: 277–315.

Masolo, D. A. 1994. *African Philosophy in Search of Identity*. Bloomington: Indiana University Press.

Masolo, D. A. 2003. "Philosophy and Indigenous Knowledge: An African Perspective." *Africa Today* 50, no. 2: 21–38.

Masolo, D. A. 2010. *Self and Community in a Changing World*. Bloomington: Indiana University Press.

Melas, Natalie. 2016. "Re-Imagining the Universal." In *Unpacking Europe: Towards a Critical Reading*, edited by Salah Hassan and Iftikhar Dadi, 134–151. Rotterdam: Museum Boijmans Van Beuningen, NAi.

Mignolo, Walter D. 2018. "Decoloniality and Phenomenology: The Geopolitics of Knowing and Epistemic/Ontological Colonial Differences." *Journal of Speculative Philosophy* 32, no. 3: 360–387.

Monahan, Michael, ed. 2017. *Creolizing Hegel*. London: Rowman & Littlefield.

Moran, Dermot. 2011. "'Even the Papuan is a Man and not a Beast': Husserl on Universalism and the Relativity of Cultures." *Journal of the History of Philosophy* 49, no. 4: 463–494.

Mudimbe, V. Y., ed. 1992. *The Surreptitious Speech: Présence Africaine and the Politics of Otherness, 1947–1987*. Chicago: University of Chicago Press.

Outlaw, Lucius. 1987. "African 'Philosophy': Deconstructive and Reconstructive Challenges." In *Contemporary Philosophy, Volume 5: African Philosophy*, edited by G. Fløistad, 9–44. Dordrecht: Martinus Nijhoff.

Owomoyela, Oyekan. 1987. "Africa and the Imperative of Philosophy: A Skeptical Consideration." *African Studies Review* 30, no. 1: 79–100.

Ricoeur, Paul. 2007. *Husserl: An Analysis of His Phenomenology*. Translated by Edward G. Ballard and Lester E. Embree. Evanston: Northwestern University Press.

Said, Edward W. 1993. *Culture and Imperialism*. New York: Vintage Books.

Sartre, Jean-Paul. 1964–1965. "Black Orpheus," translated by John MacCombie. *Massachusetts Review* 6: 48.

Sekyi-Otu, Ato. 2019. *Left Universalism: Africacentric Essays*. London: Routledge.

Serequeberhan, Tsenay. 1994. *The Hermeneutics of African Philosophy: Horizon and Discourse*. London: Routledge.

Tempels, Placied. 1946. *Bantoe-Filosofie*. Antwerp: De Sikkel.

Towa, Marcien. 2012. "The Idea of a Negro African Philosophy." In *Marcien Towa's African Philosophy: Two Texts*, edited by Tsenay Serequeberhan, 15–98. Amara: Hdri.

Wiredu, Kwasi. 2004. "Introduction: African Philosophy in Our Time." In *A Companion to African Philosophy*, edited by Kwasi Wiredu, 1–27. Oxford: Blackwell.

Žižek, Slavoj. 2016. "A Leftist Plea for Eurocentrism." In *Unpacking Europe: Towards a Critical Reading*, edited by Salah Hassan and Iftikhar Dadi, 112–130. Rotterdam: Museum Boijmans Van Beuningen, NAi.

Part 2

Consciousness, Identity, Existence, and Embodiment

6

Chabani Manganyi

The Lived Experience of Difference

Mabogo Percy More

In his autobiographical offering, *Apartheid and the Making of a Black Psychologist* (Manganyi 2017), Noel Chabani Manganyi, perhaps out of modesty or out of disdain, elides articulation of his discursive contributions to a philosophical tradition known as Africana phenomenology or Africana existential psychology in which he stands as one of the main pillars and pioneers. I am certainly not interrogating Manganyi for not acknowledging his early philosophical work in his memoirs. His modesty notwithstanding, he remains one of the forerunners of what recently has come to be known in general as "Black phenomenology," or Africana existential phenomenology, in South Africa. By Black or Africana phenomenology, to use Paget Henry's definition (Henry 2016, 28), I refer to a discourse that has been conditioned by and draws on a specific set of lived experiences and the cultural traditions of Africans and African-descendent people in the world. In this sense it is quite different from Western phenomenology, which is conditioned exclusively by white peoples' lived experiences. This chapter aims not only to explain Manganyi's contribution to South African phenomenology but also to articulate its difference from phenomenology in general.

In Manganyi's terms we may thus speak, from a phenomenological perspective, of "Being-Black-in-the-world" and "Being-white-in-the-world."

The difference is evident from the classic formulation by Kant, Hegel, and even Husserl, who conceptualized phenomenology as "the self-reflective practice that disclosed the latent movements of universal reason, which was also the prime constituting force operating within the core of the European subject" (Henry 2016, 28). Paradoxically, this universal reason was limited to a very specific cultural particularity: the cultural particularity of Europe and thus constituting Europe as the geography of reason. Hence, for Husserl, the expansion of European phenomenology was attached to the question of whether "European humanity bears within itself an absolute idea, rather than being merely an empirical anthropological type like 'China' or 'India'" (Husserl 1970, 16). For Africana phenomenology, on the contrary, the governing telos has been a fundamental focus on racial liberation and the problems of racial domination from which it emanates.

Heidegger (1962), Sartre (1956), and even Hegel (1977) leave the question of Being unattended as it concerns black(ness). All of them proceed as if the question of Being has been settled and that we no longer need to question it. The Being of Black people as victims of colonization and apartheid antiblack racism is a different Being from the Being integral in the subjectivity articulated by Western philosophers such as Hegel, Heidegger, Sartre, Merleau-Ponty, or Camus, and psychoanalysts and psychologists such as Sigmund Freud, Alfred Adler, or Jacques Lacan. For both Fanon and Manganyi, by contrast, the Being of the Western subject, or what Alexis de Tocqueville describes as "MAN preeminently so called" (1981, 169) does not portray the Being of "the black man" because, within colonial and apartheid situations, "the black is not a man" (Fanon 1967, 8), that is, the Black man is a black man and not man.[1] Thus, the question of the Being of the Black subject *qua* human raises its head. Manganyi seeks to put the question of the Being of the Black back in its proper place: at the center of any discourse about Being. When Heidegger claims that Western philosophy has forgotten Being, Manganyi's claim is that Western philosophy has forgotten the Being of Blacks. This means that the Black Question is simultaneously the Question of Being and difference, that is, Being-man-in-the-world and Being-a-black-man-in-the-world. Manganyi's *Being-Black-in-the-World* is thus a meditation about the presumed nonrelation between blackness and Being. He contends that to the extent that Blackness is in the world, it *is* through its Being a Being different from the Being of Western phenomenology's originary subject. Thus, as I will argue, Manganyi concurs with Fanon in articulating a phenomenology of difference.

Manganyi and Africana Phenomenology

Phenomenology and existentialism among African people in South Africa have a long history, which unfortunately has not been explicitly thematized or philosophically engaged. Recently, a lot of work has been done on Steve Biko as an Africana existentialist philosopher.[2] Unfortunately, very little, if at all, attention has been directed to the entire Black existential-phenomenology tradition in this country, a poeticist tradition fashioned and sustained in the great literary production of South Africans that took the form of what Paget Henry describes as "the imagistic phenomenology" (Henry 2000, 105) of consciousness. First to outline a comprehensive phenomenology in South Africa, however, was Chabani Manganyi, who in his various early works explicitly thematized the phenomenology of Africana self-consciousness. In the tradition of Frederick Douglass, Ida B. Wells, Edward Blyden, Marcus Garvey, W. E. B. Du Bois, Frantz Fanon, Steve Biko, and Charles Johnson, Manganyi is interested in the "psychopathological and philosophical explanation of the state of being a Negro" (Fanon 1967, 15). Given the neglect of existential-phenomenological tradition in his country, I shall argue that Manganyi is the quintessential African(a) existential-phenomenological psychologist in whose work a very large number of influences converge. Even though he has benefited from and engaged the ideas of, among others, Western psychologists and phenomenologists such as Victor Frankl, Johan van den Berg, Albert Camus, Martin Heidegger, Maurice Merleau-Ponty, Sigmund Freud, Herbert Marcuse, Erik Erikson, David R. Laing, Erich Fromm, Erich Neumann, Jean-Paul Sartre, and others, and Africana existential phenomenologists such as Frantz Fanon, Léopold Sédar Senghor, and others, I take the position that he thinks with and against them. For reasons that will be evident later, I briefly put him in conversation with them—especially—Heidegger and Fanon.

There is simply no question about Manganyi's status as a Black existential-phenomenological psychologist. His early work brings forth an assortment of Fanon's phenomenology of blackness, Heidegger's phenomenological ontology, Sartre's existential phenomenology, Maurice Merleau-Ponty's phenomenology of the body schemas, Viktor Frankl's logotherapy (existential psychology), van den Berg's historical psychology (metabletics), Albert Camus's notions of rebellion and absurdity, and Aimé Césaire's and Léopold Sédar Senghor's Negritude. His engagement with the leading existentialists (especially Sartre, Camus, Merleau-Ponty,

Heidegger, and Fanon) is plainly expressed in his choice of the titles for his books and the chapters therein. For example, the title of his first book, *Being-Black-in-the-World* (1973), explicitly echoes Heidegger's and Sartre's phenomenological ontology of "being-in-the-world." Contained in that text are chapter titles such as "Us and Them," "Black Consciousness," "Being-Black-in-the World," and "Nausea" (the title of Sartre's celebrated first novel), all of which have an existential, phenomenological, and onto-logical ring to them that combines Heidegger's and Sartre's philosophical concerns. His subsequent text, *Looking through the Keyhole* (1981), is clearly reminiscent of Sartre's famous example of a man who, driven by intense jealousy, is caught peeping through the keyhole in the famous section of *Being and Nothingness*: "The Look." Two of his other books, *Alienation and the Body in Racist Society* (1977), *Mashangu's Reverie and Other Essays* (1977)—besides reminding us of Fanon's *Black Skin, White Masks* (1967) and Merleau-Ponty's *Phenomenology of Perception*—contain chapter titles with an existentialist flavor, for example: "The Body-for-Others," "Alienation: The Body and Racism," and "The Body-World and the Ontogenesis of Racism." The chapter "The Edge of the Precipice" also reminds one of Sartre's articulation of the feeling of vertigo in the face of radical freedom in *Being and Nothingness*. In the next section I want to briefly focus on Manganyi seminal text, *Being-Black-in-the-World*, mainly for its richness in phenomenological significance. This, however, does not mean that the other early texts with phenomenological density will suffer marginalization. To appreciate the richness and significance of this text, a consideration of Fanon and Heidegger is necessary. First, a brief detour on Fanon ideas will help in situating Manganyi within the realm of the phenomenological psychologist of radical difference.

Frantz Fanon's Phenomenology of Blackness

Like Fanon, Manganyi is a psychologist and has repeatedly described himself as such, and he sees his approach as "psychophenomenological"; he sees his work as "a philosophical orientation which may be described as existential-phenomenology" (Manganyi 1977, 8). In the same manner as Fanon, Manganyi uses phenomenological and existential psychoanalysis to understand the complex effects of racism on the personality and identity of the oppressed Black subject. His fundamental point of departure, "being-black-in-the-world," is an idea that has long been articulated in the form of "On Being Black" by earlier Black theorists such as W. E. B. Du Bois, Eric D. Walrond, among others, and Black psychologists such as Alvin F. Poussaint, Kenneth B. Clark, and others, in the USA. Indeed, the very title of his text, *Being-Black-in-the-World*, besides invoking Heidegger's ontological-phenomenological concept of "thrownness," is in many ways an articulation of Fanon's climactic fifth chapter, whose literal translation is "The Lived Experience of the Black" in *Black Skin, White Masks*.

Manganyi's early work, just like Fanon's early text, has become central in discussions on racism, alienation, identity, and sociality, but very rarely do scholars engage it as philosophy. This essay provides such a reading not only to articulate the dimensions of Black phenomenology, but also to recognize Manganyi as a unique phenomenologist with an approach to Blackness and ontology that is ambitious and provocative. What I am calling "Black phenomenology" or "Africana phenomenology" is a philosophical orientation scattered across the arch of Manganyi's early writings and explores the lived experiences of being Black or African in an antiblack or Anti-African world. I think of Manganyi as an Africana phenomenologist because he extends Heidegger's neutralist universalistic ontology and Merleau-Ponty's presumed universalistic conception of corporeality to the specificity of the Black (African) mode of being. Because of this intervention, Manganyi's theory may, borrowing Jeremy Weate's phrase, be described as a "radical phenomenology of difference" (Weate 2001, 170).

Besides W. E. B. Du Bois's groundbreaking contributions to existential phenomenology through the concept of "double consciousness," Frantz Fanon is without doubt the most celebrated Black phenomenological psychologist of the twentieth century. The most commonly commented upon chapter of Frantz Fanon's book *Black Skin, White Masks* is "L'expérience vécue du Noir," famously translated as "The Fact of Blackness." However, a more accurate translation of the chapter title, "The Lived Experience of the Black Man" (Fanon 2008), succinctly captures and expresses the phenomenological character of Fanon's work. In this chapter, Fanon aims to understand the experience of being black and being defined by your race through the perception of others. This theorization constituted Fanon as the first phenomenologist to problematize and reorganize Maurice Merleau-Ponty's classical phenomenological theories in order to discuss and theorize race. His radical inclusion of race and racism into phenomenological theory, issues that were left untheorized by European phenomenologists, translated his work into what may be described as corrective or radical phenomenology.

Rather than merely being influenced by the phenomenology of Hegel, Sartre, and Merleau-Ponty, Fanon seriously confronted, interrogated, and engaged their phenomenological theories in relation to the situation of the Black person in an antiblack context. While appreciating Hegel's *Phenomenology of Spirit* (1977), Sartre's phenomenological ontology of *Being and Nothingness* (1956), and Merleau-Ponty's *Phenomenology of Perception* (1962), Fanon considered their phenomenological ontology inadequate when applied to the situation of the Black person. For instance, in *Black Skin, White Masks*, in a section titled "The Negro and Hegel," Fanon argues that in Hegel, the master and the slave have a reciprocal relation that constitutes the slave into an Other. When it comes to Blacks and Whites, the relation of self-Other is simply not as Hegel portrays it; instead it changes into a relation of self-non-Other: "Here the master differs basically from the master described by Hegel. For Hegel there is reciprocity; here the master laughs at the consciousness of the slave. What he wants from the slave is not recognition but work" (Fanon 1967, 220). In other words, Fanon insists that while Hegel says, "Man is human only to the extent to which he tries to impose his existence on another man in order to be recognized by him" (Fanon 1967, 216), and since in an antiblack racist society the Black man is reduced to a nonperson, not a man, what Hegel asserts about man does not pertain to the Black man.

Concerning Sartre, Fanon laments: "Jean-Paul Sartre had forgotten that the Negro suffers in his body quite differently from the white man." This is because, as a Black man and because of the color of his body, he is "overdetermined from without" (Fanon 1967, 116). As a footnote on the same page, Fanon bemoans the fact that "though Sartre's speculations on the existence of The Other may be correct . . . their application to a black consciousness proves fallacious. That is because the white man is not only The Other but also the master, whether real or imaginary" (Fanon 1967, 138). According to Sartre's existential ontology, human being is a lack of Being. As a lack of Being, human reality is the being that lacks coincidence or identity with itself by "being what it is not and not being what it is." As he puts it: "Human reality by which lack appears in the world must be itself a lack. For lack can come into being only through lack" (Sartre 1956, 87). As a lack, human reality desires what it lacks. Since human reality lacks self-identity, coincidence with itself, it therefore desires that being which possesses these qualities—in short, brute Being. If human reality's desire can be satisfied, then it would be a synthesis of both consciousness and brute Being, two entities that are oppositional and contradictory. As a contradiction, this desire cannot be fulfilled, for in the event that consciousness can merge with brute Being to achieve identity with it, there would occur the demolition and annihilation of consciousness *qua* consciousness because the appropriation of brute Being, that which is opaque, substantial, and impenetrable requires the elimination of consciousness, which is emptiness or nothingness. It is this lack of Being, Sartre contends, that constitutes the source and origins not only of human freedom but also of the desire for completeness, fullness, and opacity. Against Sartre's view of consciousness as a lack of Being and a source of freedom, Fanon argues that within an antiblack racist society, the Black man is denied consciousness and thus the capacity to be a "lack," precisely because he is reduced to brute Being, a thing or object without freedom. Within this situation, the Black man is denied the capacity to even constitute himself as a lack of Being in order to attain self-consciousness. The Black man is "chained to his being, to his body, more particularly to his skin" (Oliver 2004, 14) by colonial and antiblack values. What Fanon is fundamentally claiming here is that there are two modes of existence within antiblack societies that both Hegel and Sartre ignore because of their white normativity theorizations: being-white-in-the-world and being-black-in-the-world. Developing the category of Black "world-hood," Manganyi, picks up Fanon's position and articulates a Black radical phenomenology of difference that critiques the universalistic and nondifferentiating phenomenology of European thinkers.

Heidegger and Being-in-the-World

An intelligible appreciation of Manganyi's existential phenomenology, especially the significance of his text *Being-Black-in-the-World*, requires an equal grasp of the existential-ontological notion, particularly Heidegger's formulation, of "being-in-the-world" in *Being and Time* (1962). The original ground of phenomenological ontology is the fundamental consciousness of being-in-the-world. The hyphenation in Heidegger's formulation serves a major philosophical function that indicates a primordially primitive, unitary, and irreducible relatedness between *Dasein* (human reality) and the world. *Dasein* exists ecstatically, as always already embedded within the world. However, it may be prudent to quickly bring to light each of its constituent structures separately in order to appreciate their connectedness. In Heidegger's *Dasein's* "*In-der-Welt-Sein*" (being-in-the-world), "Being" *qua* an ontological foundation assumes significance because, for him, traditional philosophy has forgotten "Being." Husserl's phenomenology, Heidegger argues, has its main focus on consciousness and how phenomena appear to consciousness. But Heidegger does not make as strong an onto-epistemic commitment to the paradigm of consciousness as Husserl. For him, privileging consciousness as Husserl does marginalizes Being. Thus, when Husserl implores us to phenomenologically go "back to the things themselves" as they primordially appear to consciousness, Heidegger urges us to go "back to Being itself"; that is, philosophy must return to the question of Being itself. Philosophy for Heidegger, therefore, becomes phenomenological ontology as the disclosure and unconcealment of Being. But the intelligibility of Being is conditional on the intelligibility of the nature of the ontic being (Existentialle) that understands. The being that possesses this understanding Heidegger calls *Dasein* or human existence. *Dasein* literally means "being there," that is, being situated somewhere *qua* self. To the question: "Being there" where? The answer is: "In the world." *Dasein* can thus be described as always already situated consciousness.

How is the "world" to be understood? The world, Heidegger insists, because we use words such as "in-the-world" should never be understood as a container of human beings in the manner of an enclosedness of spatial objects. A glass, as a container, can be filled with water and can be emptied of its contents, which is water. There exist two entities related to each other externally in space, that is, the presence or absence of one does not affect the other. This relation is a relation of exteriority such that the glass can exist without affecting water and water can be somewhere outside the glass without affecting the existence of the glass whatsoever. Unlike the glass and the water, the world cannot exist without the human subject precisely because human beings do not have the categorical structure of objects. "Being-in" involves a much richer relation than merely a spatial one of locatedness in a world container. The relationship between *Dasein* and the world is a relation of interiority. The world and *Dasein* entail, and are primordially connected to, each other. Without the world there is no *Dasein* and without *Dasein* there is no world. At the core of Heidegger's phenomenology, therefore, is the idea of relationships. It is the essence of *Dasein* to always be *Dasein*-in-the-world. Human existence is intrinsically in and of the world. *Dasein* cannot exist without the world and the world cannot be without *Dasein*. If there is no *Dasein* (human reality) that exists, says Heidegger, there is no world. All of us are always already thrown in the world, involved and living in the world, and we cannot separate ourselves from the world. The relation between *Dasein* and world expresses the irreducibly interwovenness, inter-involvement, and mutual implication of being-in-the-world. The "Being-in" that is fundamentally our relation, or better still, our attitude to the world, Heidegger describes as "concern" or "care." As indicated earlier, Fanon's and Manganyi's works function as critiques of Heidegger's universalization of an idealized White consciousness of the world. Even though explicit references to Whiteness are scarce in his works, Heidegger deploys it implicitly in the tropes he uses. In Heidegger's ontology, Being covers reality. On the contrary, Manganyi understood that reality and Being are not, as Heidegger claims, identical. This difference between Heidegger and Manganyi does indeed serve as an ingress to the philosophical dimensions of Manganyi's work as articulated in his groundbreaking text: *Being-Black-in-the-World*.

Being-Black-in-the-World

Africana phenomenology, like all phenomenology, undercuts the dualistic metaphysics of empirical realism and idealism and begins with the individual person being-in-the-world. If we follow Heidegger, phenomenology means "to let that which shows itself be seen from itself in the very way in which it shows itself from itself" (Heidegger 1962, 58). Put differently, phenomenology is to "let us see," to uncover, to explicitly exhibit that which "proximally and for the most part does *not* show itself at all" (Heidegger 1962, 59). It is fundamentally a stripping away of concealment and distortions so that we are able to see that which lets itself be seen for what it is, that which is hidden, covered up, disguised, or concealed. Phenomenology, therefore, involves the disclosure, revelation, exposure, and uncovering of the Being of that which is concealed or hidden to consciousness. Heidegger's "Being-in-the-world," phenomenological as it is, is however—from Manganyi's point of view—a phenomenology of sameness, a transcendental phenomenology that implicitly succumbs to White normativity or the White transcendental norm. Because of its latent Eurocentrism, it is thus still inadvertently a concealment of that which appears to a Black consciousness. It is a phenomenology that in historical terms may be likened, for example, to the original Constitution of the United States in which the phrase "all men" did not include Black people, who are considered two-thirds human. How then does Heidegger's maxim "Being-in-the-world" fail to disclose or even implicitly conceal the reality of Black subjects?

According to Heidegger, what being human (*Dasein*) means is to let things *to be*, that is, let things reveal themselves in their nakedness to consciousness. Letting things *be* is to allow them to invade presence, to make themselves be present. However, letting a phenomenon present itself as itself is paradoxically to cover, or to conceal, other phenomena. For example, when I pick up or look for my car keys, I let their meaning come forth or let them show themselves as themselves to the exclusion, disappearance, or concealment of all other things. Every disclosure of being is simultaneously a concealment of others. When we are actively engaged with things in the world, that which makes them possible gets covered up. When I jump onto my bed, what reveals itself (*qua* bed) covers up something else. When the bed becomes an object of my consciousness, then the space within which the bed exist recedes into the background or disappears. What, then, does Heidegger's phenomenology of Being conceal or fail to disclose?

Given what the dominant figures in Western philosophy—for example, Kant, Hume, Hegel—have pronounced about Black people, given also the universalistic pretension of Western philosophy, Africana philosophers such as Fanon, Manganyi, and others began to question whether the African functioned as a genuine Other or actually a non-Other within the context of Western phenomenology. They thus became phenomenologists by attempting to disclose or unmask what the English translation of Fanon describes as "The Lived Experience of the Black Man" from concealment in the realm of the "present-at-hand" (substantiality, the untouchables) and particularly "the ready-to-hand" (the exploitables, the usables, instrumentalities). The focus of Africana phenomenologists therefore—by virtue of slavery, colonization, apartheid, and antiblack racism—has historically been the stripping away, the clearing away of concealment and distortions about the reality of Black *Dasein* (human reality) so that we are able "to see that which lets itself be seen for what it is" (Heidegger 1962, 59). Since *Dasein*, according to Heidegger *is* existence, Manganyi qua *Dasein* phenomenologically thinks and understands himself as existence. As a phenomenologist, he sets forth the basic structures of Black human existence as these structures are disclosed or uncovered or laid bare before us in our own existence. *Dasein*, Heidegger declares, "always understands itself in terms of its existence—in terms of a possibility for itself: to be itself or not itself. Dasein has either chosen these possibilities itself, or gets itself into them, or grown up in them already. Only the particular Dasein of existence never gets straightened out except through existing itself" (Heidegger 1962, 33). Hence, as "a being whose being is always an issue for itself" (Heidegger 1962), by introducing the word "Black" within Heidegger's formulation of "being-in-the-world," Manganyi questions the concealment of his Black existence, of the Black mode of "being-in-the-world." In current temperament, Manganyi is almost saying: "Black Lives matter"! We here encounter a serious critique of Heidegger's universalist presuppositions and an introduction of a phenomenology of the difference of identity.

What difference does difference in phenomenology make? Manganyi's phenomenology of difference is by inversion a phenomenology of identity as expressed by the inclusion of "Black" in a Eurocentric phenomenology that erases the being of Black people in its universalizing White normativity project. Because the governing telos of Africana phenomenology, as Henry contends, has been racial liberation from racial domination, the uniqueness of Manganyi and Fanon lies in the displacement of the problem of Western rationality by the problem of racial liberation as the source of an occasion for self-reflection. There is much in Blackness that requires defense against erasure. A phenomenology of difference, therefore, contains creative responses of resistance to totalitarian regimes (e.g., the apartheid regime that Manganyi was confronting) by marginalized, oppressed, and discriminated upon groups. Manganyi's phenomenology of difference is such an oppositional resistance against the decentering Eurocentric discourse that parades as an incarnation and expression of universal human rationality.

In phenomenology, one does not simply accept what one sees. Doing phenomenology requires a vigilance on the part of the subject on its object of consciousness. In my view, phenomenology requires a suspension of the habitual ways of seeing—of ways of doing. For instance, in what Husserl calls the "natural attitude" we encounter human beings as Chinese, Whites, Indians, or Blacks. These are simply different human beings in our world. However, they all, qua different beings, prereflectively or nonpositionally participate in Being. This is what in Plato's formulation can be called the many in one or *E pluribus unum*. But the moment I apply Husserl's principle of "bracketing" or suspension of the phenomena of the natural attitude, I constitute them into phenomena or objects of consciousness. Instead of "What is a Black person?" I phenomenologically shift to: "What does it mean *to be* Black-in-the-world?" The question of meaning then comes into play. A similar approach has been made by Ruth Frankenberg in her book *White Women, Race Matters: The Social*

Construction of Whiteness (1993) in which she addresses the situation of being a White woman in a patriarchal but racist society. Frankenberg is facing the same phenomenological question that Manganyi is posing: "What does it mean *to be* a White woman in a patriarchal society?" Phenomenologically, Frankenberg's concern amounts to: "What does it mean *to be* a White-woman-in-the-world?" Embedded in Manganyi's theory is Sartre's concept of the *situation*, which can be rephrased as: "What is the situation of the Black human being in an apartheid world?" Sartre's concept of situation may be translated in Manganyi's "Being-Black-in-the-world" as the equivalent of "Black situatedness in the world" and in Fanon as "the lived experience of the black man." Drawing from Sartre's description of the situation of the Jew in the *Portrait of the Anti-Semite* (1948), Manganyi reaches the following social constructionist conclusion: "Likewise, the African or Afro-American lives in a world that takes him for a 'nigger' or a 'kaffir' while he believes himself to be simply a black man. The black man is inassimilable. In South Africa, for example, Africans who have the situation common to blacks are seen as a very real threat to whites even at the peak of political disarray. Again Sartre strikes the nail on the head when he observes: 'It is therefore the idea of the Jew that one forms for himself which would seem to determine history, not the 'historical fact' that produced the idea'" (Manganyi 1977, 53 note 2). Thus the title, *Being-Black-in-the-World*, is significant in two ways: First, in addition to Heidegger's being-in-the-world thesis, that being-in-the-world is existence itself and that the self and world are irreducibly related in a fundamental manner, Manganyi adds the category "black" in this relation, thereby explicitly thematizing a phenomenology of Africana self-consciousness that implicitly suggests alterity. Thus, instead of Heidegger's three operative concepts ("Being," "World," and "Self"), Manganyi's title contains four discourse-constitutive fundamentals, namely: *Being*, *World*, *Self*, and *Black*, with the fourth assuming a different operative concept and thematization from those of Heidegger. These four discourse-constitutive fundamentals do not function as independent and separate concepts but significantly appear as a hyphenated, and therefore connected, concept. The differences are both thematic, such as the issue of racialization, and metaphysical as indicated by the different rules guiding the prioritizing and systematizing of discourse-constitutive fundamentals.

Being-Black-in-the-World, therefore, brings in a complex element to Heidegger's maxim of "Being-in-the-World" and even Husserl's characterization of phenomenology as "Back to the things themselves." It introduces the category of "Blackness" into these two phenomenological principles. Husserl's maxim is transformed into "Black to the things themselves" instead of "Back to the things themselves." Why introduce Blackness in these ontologico-phenomenological formulations? Because Manganyi, just as any other existing being, has the ability to interrogate his Being. Human reality, Sartre and Heidegger remind us, is being such that in its own being its being is always in question, or a being whose very being is always an issue to itself. By inserting "Black" in Heidegger's formulation, Manganyi introduces a structure that European phenomenologists completely ignore, the concrete (ontic) corporeality of being in the world and not simply its abstraction. Lacking in Heidegger's phenomenological ontology, for example, is a serious engagement with the body as a phenomenological category in terms of which *Dasein* manifests itself ontically as presence. To say that human being is "Being there" (*Dasein*) calls attention to human finitude, that is, bodily dimension or mode because consciousness proximally and for the most part manifests itself in the world through corporeality. Unlike Heidegger, Manganyi proclaims the specificity of African incarnation, the corporeality of existence and thus considers the body as the nexus of worldhood in his theory. In other words, in relation to Heidegger—to use Sartre's formulation from another register—Manganyi "marks a progress towards realism, since he insists, above all on the *primacy* of the specifically real over thought, that the real cannot be reduced to thought" (Sartre 1968, 12). Rather than simply wallowing in Heideggerian categories, Manganyi stretches Heidegger to the limit.

What is the "Black," the *beingness* of which Manganyi proclaims? Is it biology, color, race, politics, culture, or all of these? Blackness, it is now universally acknowledged—except of course by antiblack racists—is not biological. What about color, cultural, social, political, existential Blackness? From an epidermal perspective, the paradoxical issue about "Blackness" in the modern world is that once color is introduced and attached to people, then race becomes an issue. It then means that we bring into existence other colors, such as for example "white" and "black," which in a racist society are considered in terms of contraries. In contraries, Blackness becomes the necessary condition for Whiteness to exist and vice versa: "For not only must the black man be black, he must be black in relation to the white man" (Fanon 1967, 110). To then define someone as black in an antiblack society is to posit that person as absolutely not white. The relation between these two colors assumes a relation of negativity. For example, Black people had no reason to consider themselves "black" before the emergence of circumstances that referred to them as black. In Africa, for example, they considered themselves only in terms of their linguistic and cultural affiliations such as, among others, Sotho, Tswana, Igbo, Yoruba, Hausa, Ashanti, Akan, Tshona, or Xhosa people and so on. In *The Second Sex*, Simone de Beauvoir insists that the verb "to be" must be understood in its correct meaning, "It is bad faith to give it a static value when it really has a dynamic Hegelian sense of 'to have become'" (Beauvoir 1989, xxx). Embracing this warning, being-black-in-the-world translates to "to-have-become-black-in-the-world." "*Being*-black," in Manganyi's formulation, should consequently not be taken in terms of substantiality but in terms of "*to have become* Black" because Blacks have Blackness imposed on them from without. Color as such is, for Manganyi, not the issue in the world; it is the *meaning* attached to color that determines racist attitudes and practices. Blackness is a racialized character of being bodily in the world. The epidermal meaning of race is skin. Challenging the view that color is a necessary and sufficient condition for race, Manganyi explains: "My own interpretation is that skin colour in itself and of itself is insignificant. What is important is what the skin actually signifies in sociological and psychological terms" (Manganyi 1973, 18). We realize here with Stuart Hall that the introduction of "Black" leads to race, which functions as a producer of differences. As he puts it, race is "one of those major or master concepts that organize the *great classificatory systems of difference* that operate in human societies" (Hall 2017, 32–33, italics added).

Becoming Black as a condition has a historical character rather than an ahistorical one. In Manganyi's world, this history is a history of slavery, colonialism, and apartheid. Blackness is an imposed identity on Africana subjects. We thus end up with an exteriority and interiority of Blackness. The imposed Blackness is from without and thus is an exterior black, a stigmatized, dehumanized Blackness. When Blackness is appropriated by those designated black, it becomes interiorized Blackness. Interiorized Blackness may or may not be a radical counterhegemonic Blackness that can be expressed with a capital "B," the Blackness of Biko and the Black Consciousness movement. Similarly, White people had absolutely no reason to consider themselves White until they created the colonial circumstances that required that they designate themselves "White" vis-à-vis created Blacks, even though in strict terms of the color spectrum there *are no* white, red, or yellow people.

In *Black Skin, White Masks*, Fanon insists: "As long as the black man is among his own, he will have no occasion . . . to experience his being through others. The black man among his own in the twentieth century does not know at what moment his inferiority comes into being" (Fanon 1967, 109, 110). Like Fanon, Manganyi believes that Blackness cannot be understood in the context of the Black among his or her own. The point made here is that it is only in the encounter with Whiteness, more especially the White imagination, in a colonial, apartheid, or antiblack society, that the analysis of the experience of racial difference of being-Black-in-the-world—the non-Other—can be undertaken. Blackness, therefore, is invariably connected to a history constructed by a White imaginary. In a significantly historical context, Manganyi has the following to say about the meeting of Europeans and Africans and the emergence of the meaning of colors—black and white—and antiblack racism in a colonial situation: "Indeed, in the beginning was the word. The word was *written* and *spoken* and it was, as blacks know so well, about God and whiteness, the devil and blackness. . . . It was the power of the word, the power of language, the tyranny of the symbolic, which introduced psycho-social dominance of the blacks by the whites" (Manganyi 1981, 67). In another register Manganyi introduces embodiment as a source of historical antiblack racism: "One of the legacies of colonialism in Africa has been the development of the dichotomy relating to the body, namely, the 'bad' and 'good' body. The white man's body has been projected as the standard, the norm of beauty, of accomplishment. Not only the body proper, but its periphery; its embellishments have been recognised as such. On the contrary, the black body, projected as the 'bad' body, has always been projected as being inferior and unwholesome" (Manganyi 1973, 28).

When Black people became "black" in the modern antiblack world, they found themselves faced with a paradoxical situation of becoming "Black" in a world that rejected blackness. If existing is being-in-the-world, what then does it mean to belong to a world in which one does not belong? For Fanon and Manganyi, the nonbelonging of the black subject is the product of the "historico-racial" and the "sociological" schemas respectively. It means that the world becomes a home in which a Black person is paradoxically homeless. It also means that Blacks are considered not to have a relationship with the world. Their appearance in the world automatically amounts to an unjustified appearance, an illegitimate presence that requires justification. The problem with this demand is that once one exists, one does not need any justification for one's existence besides the very fact that one exists. As Heidegger indicates earlier, "The question of existence never gets straightened out except through existing itself" (Heidegger 1962, 33). Tendayi Sithole puts it graphically when he declares: "The place of blackness in the antiblack world is placelessness. It is the belonging without. It is to be without a place, to be displaced. Place and blackness are rendered, in the antiblack world, oxymoronic" (Sithole 2020, 17). This constitution of Blackness and Black people is an expression of invidious antiblack racism. What we then gather from the preceding, is that "Blackness" cannot be black without being epidermal. To stretch this conclusion further, neither can "Blackness" be black without being political, social, religious, cultural, racial, and existential. Blackness in an antiblack world simply signifies racialization, that is, to be Black-in-the-antiblack-world is to be raced, named, marked, considered nonrational, criminal, emotional, deviant, pathological, different.

Modes of Being-in-the-World

In the same manner as Fanon's objection to Hegel and Sartre, Manganyi laments the fact that psychology and its many theories do not take the experience of Black people seriously; their universalistic posture is in fact a European particularism that excludes Black experience. He then sets himself the project of exploring the lived experiences of Black corporeality and incarnated subjectivity, applying, as it were, the various theories in psychology and existential phenomenology. He poses an existential-phenomenological question right at the beginning of his text *Being-Black-in-the-World*: "Is there a black mode of being-in-the-world? Stated differently: Is being-black-in-the-world different in fundamental respects to being-white-in-the-world?" (Manganyi 1973, 4).

In response, his first move is to establish the primordiality of human reality as being-in-the-world, the unreflective, nonthetic or nonpositional consciousness of being in the world, such that "the primary mode of being-in-the-world, of existing, is a given" (Manganyi 1973, 25). He recognizes that the human condition is indeed the same for all human beings. We all are born and die, feel the pangs of hunger and the desire for sleep, experience joy or sadness, and so forth. But existence is simply not mere existence without context. For him, human existential experiences and problems are situational—in the Sartrean sense—for they arise in, or out of, certain historical, racial, or cultural situations. Hence in his phenomenological description of being-Black-in-the-world, he adopts Sartre's idea that human beings are beings "in situation." He writes: "The concept of *situation* is important for the understanding of racism of whatever variety" (Manganyi 1977, 53). For Sartre in the *Portrait of the Anti-Semite*, to be a Jew "is to be flung into, and *abandoned* in, the Jewish situation" (Sartre 1948, 49, 75). The Jewish situation is neither constituted by Jewish religion or history but by an ensemble of structures and restrictions produced by a collectivity that regards the Jew as a Jew. The same applies for Blacks; to be Black is to be flung into, and abandoned in, the Black situation. It is thus the "situation" that determines the mode of "being-Black-in-the-world" and "being-White-in-the-world" as different modes. While Heidegger argues that there are different modes of "being-in-the-world," such as "Being-with-others," "authentic and inauthentic" modes of being, Manganyi, in agreement with Sartre, argues that although this is true in general, in an antiblack world, however, there are fundamentally two primary modes of existing: a White mode of being and a Black mode of being, and the relation between these modes assumes an "Us" and "Them" relation.

Further, existence is simply not mere existence in abstraction. To exist is to exist as something, that is, for human reality, to be is to-be-there, "there in the classroom," "there next to the car," and so on. Being-there (*Dasein*) can thus only be possible through bodily presence. Corporeality is thus the primary medium through which we are present to and engaged in the world. It bestows upon each one of us our existential identity. Since Whiteness and Blackness are essentially qualities belonging to corporeal-ity, the body therefore assumes primacy in the determination of being-White-in-the-world or being-Black-in-the-world. It is for this reason that the body becomes a central category of Manganyi's phenomenological account of being-in-the-world. The centering of the body happens out of the recognition of its fundamental position in existence. "We make our approaches to the world through our bodies: the body is movement inwards and outwards" (Manganyi 1973, 6). In other words, the body constitutes our primary relation with the world. I am conscious of the world through the mediation of the body.

In phenomenological terms, Manganyi's question may be rephrased in this manner: Is there a Black way of experiencing the world, a Black "mode of intentionality"? By mode of intentionality is meant: "What it is like to experience things, oneself, others, events, nature, children, etc.—the world—out of historical location of [one's skin color] produced by what might be called the relations of race formation" (Vasey 1998, 4). Arguing that indeed there exists a White or Black or Latino "mode of intentionality" Vasey's explanation supports Manganyi's thesis: "In spite of the scientific truth that there is no such thing as a white race, and no racial essences at all, it would be absurd to deny that in the world which we inhabit, it is possible to be white, and that if one is white, one experiences the world in a white way" (Vasey 1998, 4). Similarly, being defined as Black, one experiences the world in a Black way, that is, being-Black-in-the-world. Given that the answer to the preceding question is affirmative, further questions emerge: What does it mean to *live* "Blackness" in a world that rejects Black people? or What does it mean to *experience* "Blackness" in a White supremacist society? What are the consequences (psychological, philosophical, moral, social, political, cultural, and religious) for Black people internalizing (interiorizing) antiblack racism? The lived experience of Black people in a racist society, Manganyi contends, is an experience of alienation caused by a condition known as "psychic splitting" or "Double Consciousness" in Du Bois's formulation. In existential terms, "psychic splitting" is a fissure in an individual's experience of her Being "associated with the societal devaluation of the body" (Manganyi 1977, 39).

The problem of the body, Manganyi argues, is central in an antiblack world, for it is through the body that I am present in the world and to others. This problem originates primarily with the dualistic nature of the "old ethic" of Western civilization, a dualistic worldview in which a polarization between the spiritual (soul, psychic) and the bodily (physical) exists. I think Manganyi is here referring to the Cartesian bifurcation of *res cogitantes* and *res extensae*, an indication of Western ontological division between higher (spirit, mind, soul) and lower (body). Throughout human history, Manganyi contends, "the body has been the object of disturbing ambivalence. It has always been real or substantial enough for it not to be ignored completely. But under the conditions of the old ethic—which is generally still operative—the body has been experienced as an object that could stand in man's way to eternal life" (Manganyi 1977, 39). In time, the body became vulgarized by being reduced and devalued to the realm of the unwanted, the base, and the appetites. The mind or spirit, on the other hand, was elevated to the realm of thought or rationality. It is this "rejected portion of the individual and social existence" that, for Manganyi, "creates tensions not only in the individual but also in the life of whole groups and nations" (Manganyi 1977, 32).

Manganyi asks, "To what extent does the body determine the experience of being-black-in-the-world or being-white-in-the-world?" (Manganyi 1973, 6). In response to this question that he regards as "crucial," he introduces the concepts of the "individual schema" and the "sociological schema" notions made popular by Merleau-Ponty and Fanon. Besides the Manichaean epidermalization of the body, each individual develops a concept or image of his or her body: the "individual schema," what in Sartre's language can be called "the body as being-for-itself," that is, the body as we nonthetically or prereflectively exist in it, or the body as one's perspective on the world. Manganyi defines the body image, or individual schema, as "the mental representation of one's body," or "*the primary body reality*" (Manganyi 1977, 9, 51). In most general terms, the body image may be described as an individual's internalized conception or experience or image of his/her physical self. The experience of our body-for-the-other is the source of what Manganyi calls the "sociological schema," that is, the socialization of our body image that is culture bound and specific. If, for instance, an individual is Black, "he begins to know, through various subtle ways, that his black body is unwholesome, that the white body is the societal standard of wholesomeness" (Manganyi 1973, 6). Consequently, there is an African as well as a European sociological schema of the body constituted by these two different cultures. However, in a White supremacist culture, the Black body schema is socially constructed as a negative sociological schema. Manganyi writes: "What in terms of the African experience of being-in-the-world does it mean to talk about the socialisation of the body image? It means . . . that in the African experience there has over time developed a sociological schema of the black body prescribed by white standards. The prescribed attributes of this sociological schema have . . . been entirely negative" (Manganyi 1973, 51). For a well-integrated personality, harmony should exist between the two body schemas. Disharmony results in a rupture or split in the individual's perception of self, a divided self, an alienated self. However, in race-supremacist or antiblack societies, the sociological schema may express itself in the form of body stereotype, either expressive of *overvaluation* or *undervaluation* of the body. To Black subjectivity, it is attributed the contents that White consciousness itself fears to contain or confront: bestial sexuality, uncleanliness, criminality, all the purported "dark things." The stereotypes, Manganyi argues, are developed from childhood, during which Whiteness is equated with mind while Blackness is associated with the body, which in turn is equated to dirt/feces. "Like the body of the Jew, the black body was tagged with all the anti-values of the Caucasian body. In the colonial and following situations of black-white interaction, the black body has become the repository of and target for all the bad objects in the collective psyche of the West—the stereotype for everything from dirt to evil" (Manganyi 1977, 76).

The consequence of such sociological schemata is the disintegration of the individual body schema and the sociological schema that leads to the splitting process or alienation. This condition involves the experience of the body primarily as the body-for-others and not as the body-for-me. In other words, alienation is for Manganyi primarily the lack of balance, wholeness, and unity between the two body schemata. Because of this disequilibrium the Black's body is experienced as a burden, as an object and a lived weight of subordination and therefore as an alienated body.

In his later work, *Alienation and the Body in Racist Society: A Study of a Society That Invented Soweto*, Manganyi offers "psychophenomenological" responses to these critical questions. In dealing with the issue of alienation and racism, Manganyi claims that formal psychological methods, or even a sociopsychological approach, though necessary, are however not sufficient to deal effectively with the phenomenon of alienation in its varied and complex reality. A more promising approach to the rampant alienation that is characteristic of modern-day Western societies, Manganyi suggests, is psychophenomenological method. This is "the study of alienation and racism, viewed from the vantage point of the body-world. Put in another way, the approach here is that of a psychologist who thinks and conceptualizes psychosocial reality in a phenomenological way" (Manganyi 1977, 8).

His project is, first of all, the attempt to legitimize the relationship between Black people and the world, to insist that Black existence in the world is just as justified as any other and that Black humanity cannot be put into question at all, as the apartheid system does. The apartheid demand for justification for Black people's existence throws us directly into the realm of race and inevitably the corporeal realm. Manganyi's *Being-Black-in-the-World* is thus a text about antiblack racism, specifically apartheid society, which he consistently describes as a "race supremacist society." The titles of the chapters in his work speak to this racial orientation; for example: "Alienation: The Body and Racism," "The Body-World and the Ontogenesis of Racism," and "Alienation and the Body in a Racist Society." At the phenomenological level, "being Black" refers to a certain consciousness in the world. Since phenomenologically, consciousness is always consciousness of something, the Black person's consciousness is proximally and for the most part (always already) a consciousness of the self that is constituted as Black. Black consciousness is thus a consequence of being constituted as Black in a "race supremacist world." This explains Manganyi's inclusion of the chapter "Black Consciousness" in his book.

For reasons of space, I shall not offer a critique of some of Manganyi's ideas except to hurriedly mention that, in my opinion, he is guilty of conflating anti-Semitism with antiblack racism in his phenomenology of the body. Furthermore, his suggestion for the transcendence of racism is predicated on Black solidarity, which he curiously defines as "Mutual Knowledge," an epistemic category if ever there was any. It is therefore strange for Manganyi to explain solidarity in terms of "mutual knowledge" (More 2006, 2017) and to make a logical entailment statement such as "where there is mutual knowledge it should come as no surprise if there should be solidarity" (Manganyi 1973, 19). Having said this I wish to immediately put to rest a criticism that always accompanies the work of Black thinkers. In a paper titled "The Psychologist and Black Consciousness in South Africa: The Work of N. C. Manganyi" (1984), presented in the Department of Psychology at the University of Cape Town, Cyril Couve criticized Manganyi for using Western categories to articulate Black experience. He writes: "There is a particular paradox appearing in writers like Manganyi who derive their inspiration from a BC [Black Consciousness] perspective. In trying to articulate a black experience or a black self which would be unique they seem in fact captive of conceptual categories which have profound roots in Western philosophies such as empiricism and phenomenology" (Couve 1984, 42). The issue here translates into Audre Lorde's question: "Can the master's tools dismantle the master's house?" The problem with this kind of critique is that it implicitly deprives Black people of knowledge production. It naïvely assumes, as it is mostly the case, that philosophy and its theories and categories are Hellenistic or of Western origins. Apparently Couve was not familiar with the work of Cheik Anta Diop, Theophile Obenga, Martin Bernal, Molefi K. Asante, Marimba Ani, Yosef Ben-Jochannan, George James, Lewis Gordon, Richard King, Ivan van Sertima, among others.[3] Although Manganyi was influenced by Western existential phenomenology, psychoanalysis, and logotherapy, it would nevertheless be an error to assume that this influence functions as a "cause" rather than a consequence; he is not a Husserlian, a Sartrean, a Freudian, or a Franklean. His lived experiences in apartheid South Africa, the native country he so clearly describes in his memoirs, had already provided him with sufficient grounds to raise existential questions of being-Black-in-the-world, Black identity, authenticity, or Black liberation.

Couve's critique further assumes that Western or European philosophers constitute the conditions of possibility not only for Black thought but also for all thought. The problem with this is that it imagines that the only way Black thinkers can think is through the ideas, theories, doctrines, or categories of European Western philosophers. In short, this view echoes Kant, Hume, Hegel, and many Enlightenment philosophers about the rational capacity of Black subjects. It is the same argument used to question the existence of African and Black philosophy in the academy. As imitators of European philosophers, Black philosophers then are assumed to be incapable of original thought, let alone thinking at all, such that the notion of Black/African/Africana thought becomes oxymoronic. In his *An Introduction to Africana Philosophy* (2008) Gordon, reiterating George James, Asante, van Sertima, and Bernal, argues that as a matter of fact, the term "philosophy," contra popular presumption of its Greek origins, is in fact Kemetic (Egyptian/Nubian) and that Greek philosophy itself could not have developed had it not exchanged relations with other civilizations around it. Gordon also argued explicitly against the relegation of Blacks to experience and their presumed dependence on White thought. He argued that thought is a necessary element of liberatory work and thus belongs to everyone (Gordon 2000).

Conclusion

Given what the dominant figures in philosophy (Kant, Hume, Hegel, et al.) claim about the rationality and thus the humanity of Black people, given also the fact that the theorization of these Euromodern philosophers about what it means to be human pretends to be universalistic while in fact it is particularistic through the exclusion of Black people, Black philosophers such as W. E. B. Du Bois, Frantz Fanon, George Yancy, Robert Birt, Naomi Zack, Lewis Gordon, Tommy Curry, Paget Henry, Linda Martin Alcoff, Aimé Césaire, Léopold Sédar Senghor, Steve Biko, and more importantly for my purpose, Noel Chabani Manganyi and many others, have conceptualized their existence phenomenologically and existentially by attempting to disclose or reveal what in Fanon's words is "the lived experience of Blackness" from concealment in the space of the human. As if speaking for the many mentioned Black philosophers, Manganyi declares: "Each one of us in his own way is forced to be a philosopher of existence" (Manganyi 1981, 123). What Manganyi and most Black phenomenologists therefore share, is a deep understanding of the relationship between Blackness, ontology, and racism—a relation that Heidegger and most European phenomenologists could not, or would not, envision because of their Eurocentric perspective of Being and *Dasein*. Thus Manganyi's project, in fundamentally being a stripping away of concealment and distortions so that Black people are able to see that which lets itself be seen for what it is, articulates a phenomenology of difference and diversity.

Notes

1. I am here using "man" in an inclusive sense in accordance with Fanon's usage in his text.

2. See for example the following twenty-first-century publications on Biko: More (2017); Sithole (2016); Modiri (2017); Hill (2015).

3. See for example the following texts: Diop (1974); Obenga (1989); Bernal (1987); Asante (1990); King (1987); James (1992 [1954]); van Sertima (1983); Ani (1994); Gordon (2008); among others.

References

Ani, Marimba. 1994. *Yurugu: An African-Centered Critique of European Cultural Thought and Behavior*. Trenton: Africa World Press.

Asante, Molefi K. 1989. *Kemet: Afrocentricity and Knowledge*. Trenton: Africa World Press.

Beauvoir, Simone de. 1989. *The Second Sex*. Translated by H. M. Parshley. New York: Vintage Books.

Bernal, Martin. 1987. *Black Athena: The Afroasiatic Roots of Classical Civilization* (*The Fabrication of Ancient Greece 1785–1985, vol. 1*). New Brunswick: Rutgers University Press.

Couve, Cyril. 1984. "The Psychologist and Black Consciousness in South Africa: The Work of N. C. Manganyi." Paper presented in the Department of Psychology, University of Cape Town.

Diop, Cheik Anta. 1974. *The African Origin of Civilization: Myth or Reality*. New York: Lawrence Hill.

Fanon, Frantz. 1967. *Black Skin, White Masks*. Translated by Charles Lam Markmann. New York: Grove.

Fanon, Frantz. 2008. *Black Skin, White Masks*. Translated by Richard Philcox. New York: Grove.

Frankenberg, Ruth. 1993. *White Women, Race Matters: The Social Construction of Whiteness*. London: Routledge.

Gordon, Lewis R. 2000. *Existentia Africana: Understanding Africana Existential Thought*. New York: Routledge.

Gordon, Lewis R. 2006. *Disciplinary Decadence: Living Thought in Trying Times*. Boulder: Paradigm.

Gordon, Lewis R. 2008. *An Introduction to Africana Philosophy*. Cambridge: Cambridge University Press.

Hall, Stuart. 2017. *The Fateful Triangle: Race, Ethnicity and Nation*. Cambridge, MA: Harvard University Press.

Hegel, Georg Wilhelm Friedrich. 1977. *Phenomenology of Spirit*. Translated by A. V. Miller. Oxford: Oxford University Press.

Heidegger, Martin. 1962. *Being and Time*. Translated by John Macquarrie and Edward Robinson. Oxford: Basil Blackwell.

Henry, Paget. 2000. *Caliban's Reason: Introducing Afro-Caribbean Philosophy*. New York: Routledge.

Henry, Paget. 2016. *Journeys in Caribbean Thought*. Edited by Jane Anna Gordon, Lewis R. Gordon, Aaron Kamugisha, and Neil Roberts. London: Roman & Littlefield.

Hill, Shannen. 2015. *Biko's Ghost: The Iconography of Black Consciousness*. Minneapolis: University of Minnesota Press.

Husserl, Edmund. 1970. *The Crisis of European Sciences and Transcendental Phenomenology*. Translated by D. Carr. Evanston: Northwestern University Press.

James, George G. M. 1992 [1954]. *Stolen Legacy: Greek Philosophy Is Stolen Egyptian Philosophy*. Trenton: Africa World Press.

King, Richard. 1987. "African Origins of Psychology." Lecture at City College, New York.

Manganyi, Noel Chabani. 1973. *Being-Black-in-the-World*. Johannesburg: Spro-cas/Ravan.

Manganyi, Noel Chabani. 1977. *Alienation and the Body in Racist Society: A Study of a Society That Invented Soweto*. New York: Nok.

Manganyi, Noel Chabani. 1981. *Looking through the Keyhole*. Johannesburg: Ravan Press.

Manganyi, Noel Chabani. 2017. *Apartheid and the Making of a Black Psychologist*. Johannesburg: Wits University Press.

Merleau-Ponty, Maurice. 1962. *Phenomenology of Perception*. Translated by Colin Smith. London: Routledge and Kegan Paul.

Mills, Charles W. 1998. *Blackness Visible: Essays on Philosophy and Race*. Ithaca: Cornell University Press.

Modiri, Joel M. 2017. "The Jurisprudence of Steve Biko: A Study in Race, Law and Power in the 'Afterlife' of Colonial Apartheid." PhD thesis, University of Pretoria, Pretoria.

More, Mabogo P. 2006. "Fanon, Apartheid and Black Consciousness." In *Shifting the Geography of Reason: Gender, Science and Religion*, edited by Marina Paola Banchetti-Robino and Clevis Headley, 241–254. Newcastle: Cambridge Scholars Press.

More, Mabogo P. 2017. *Biko: Philosophy, Identity and Liberation*. Cape Town: HSRC.

Obenga, Theophile. 1989. "African Philosophy of the Pharoanic Period." In *Egypt Revisited*, 2nd ed., edited by Ivan van Sertima, 286–324. New Brunswick: Transaction Press.

Oliver, Kelly. 2004. *The Colonization of Psychic Space: A Psychoanalytic Social Theory of Oppression*. Minneapolis: University of Minnesota Press.

Sartre, Jean-Paul. 1948. *Portrait of the Anti-Semite*. Translated by Erik de Mauny. London: Secker & Warburg.

Sartre, Jean-Paul. 1956. *Being and Nothingness*. Translated by Hazel E. Barnes. New York: Philosophical Library.

Sartre, Jean-Paul. 1968. *Search for a Method*. Translated by Hazel Barnes. New York: Vintage Books.

Sithole, Tendayi. 2017. *Steve Biko: Decolonial Meditations of Black Consciousness*. Lanham: Lexington Books.

Sithole, Tendayi. 2020. *The Black Register*. Cambridge: Polity Press

Sithole, Tendayi. N.d. *Fugitive Tapes: Poetics of Black Sonic Imagination*. Unpublished manuscript. Manuscript provided by the author.

Tocqueville, Alexis de. 1981. *Democracy in America*. New York: Modern Library.

van Sertima, Ivan. 1983. *Blacks in Science: Ancient and Modern*. New Brunswick: Transaction.

Vasey, Craig. 1998. "Being and Race." Paper presented the Twentieth World Congress of Philosophy, Boston, August 10–15, http/www.bu.edu/wcp/Papers/Soci/SociVase.htm. Accessed January 28, 2000.

Weate, Jeremy. 2001. "Fanon, Merleau-Ponty and the Difference of Phenomenology." In *Race*, edited by Robert Bernasconi, 169–183. Oxford: Blackwell.

7

A Post-Sartrean Reflection on Being Black in the World

Reading Steve Biko through Slavoj Žižek

M. John Lamola

Introduction

This chapter postulates the ontological condition of the Black African within her protracted colonial milieu. It is a reflection on the postcolonial African as a being with a quixotic ontology. On the one hand, she is a subject susceptible to doubting her humanity as this humanity is ontically questioned and denied by others; on the other, this state of being black in the world is a state that is forever yearning for freedom for self-actualization. The reflection the reader is invited to join in here is a discovery of a locus of this anticolonial and antiracist African consciousness that, against the immanent negativity surrounding being-black, perversely endures as a threatened-but-defiant self-affirming existence that is laden with an inherent potential to redeem humanity qua nonracial humanity. I here explicate the theoretical dynamics and historic manifestations of this state of being through an experimental reading of Bantu Stephen Biko through the Slovenian philosopher and cultural critic Slavoj Žižek.

The theorization of the psychophilosophical state and historic mission of Blacks in a White world as seminally broached by Frantz Fanon was systematically attempted in the setting of apartheid South Africa by Chabani Manganyi in his *Being-Black-in the World* (Manganyi 1973). Mtu-tuzeli Matshoba monumentally dramatized the essence of this condition in the epigraph to his 1979 anthology of short stories about Black life under apartheid, "Call me not a Man / For neither am I man before the law / Nor before the eyes of my fellowmen" (Matshoba 1979). Fanon's youthful meditations and Matshoba's poetic despair at the contradiction of his fraught existence, I here aim to demonstrate, were to be given theoretical value by Archibald Mafeje in his "Africanity: A Combative Ontology" (Mafeje 2008 [2000]),[1] and by a string of contemporary interpretations of the writings, life, and death of Biko (see Lamola 2016; More 2017).

Going beyond Fanon's pioneering analysis of the psychophilosophical state of the Black African colonized subject in his remonstrations against Jean-Paul Sartre in *Black Skin, White Masks* (Fanon 1986 [1952]) and Biko's application of this Fanonian insight on the condition and struggle of Blacks against apartheid, I focus on finding a sufficient theoretical framework to the *resolution*[2] of this peculiar Black human condition. The result is an explication of Black existentiality through a philosophical disquisition that begins with Sartre and eventually incorporates a reinterpretation of Georg W. F. Hegel's dialectical logic by Žižek.

In *Absolute Recoil: Towards a New Foundation of Dialectical Materialism* (2014), Žižek expounds a novel reinterpretation of the meaning and conceptual potency of Hegel's dialectical schema. He discerns as the essence of Hegel's *dialektika* the "Absolute Recoil" (*absoluter Gegenstoss*). He explains this Absolute Recoil as the qualitative subsistence and value of negativity as this negativity acts as the motor of the positivity that arises as an unanticipated outcome against what at an initial consideration was perceived or experienced as a deleterious condition (something akin to a boomerang). I found this rereading of Hegel within the context of Žižek's internationalist political project to be in coherence with the analytical conclusions arrived at by Biko, and even Fanon, in the final versions of their articulation of the political mission (*telos*) of Black Consciousness. The conclusion of this reading of Biko through Žižekian lenses, I discovered, corroborates Mafeje's identification of Africanity, as Black Consciousness, as the positivity that arises out of the negativity of the racist denial of the humanity of Black Africans. He postulated that "Africanity" is a history-negating combative ontology that is shaped by "prior exclusivist ontologies such as white racist categorisations and supremacist European self-identities in particular" (Mafeje 2008 [2000], 107). He asserted that we would not be talking of Africanity if African humanity was in the first place not denied (Mafeje 2008 [2000], 31).

Collaterally, I claim that during the development of Black Consciousness into a pragmatic political program, Biko's thought transitioned from its theoretical dependence on Sartre's existentialism and embraced what Biko identified as "the Hegelian theory of dialectical materialism" (Biko 2004 [1971], 55) as the theoretical grid that shaped the political goal of "his" movement.[3] This turn to Hegelian political heuristics, mediated through his affinity with Fanon's work, revolved around the appreciation of the dialectical triad as it eventuates into the "synthesis" of the new reality that emanates out of the antagonisms of White antiblack racism and Black inferiority complex. The logical political implications of this, the ideal of a nonracialized "True Humanity . . . South Africa with a human face" was inspirational for Biko (Biko 2004 [1973, 99, 103). This chapter distills the structure of this logic through the prism of Žižek's fresh reading of Hegel.

I will start with a narration of the intellectual peregrination that led my political African philosophy to Slavoj Žižek. This is followed by a cryptic characterization of Black existence as viewed from Martin Heidegger's classic postulation of being-in-the-world from a perspective that assesses Abraham Olivier's article "Heidegger in the Township" (Olivier 2015). I will expound Olivier's article as an unwitting existentialist embellishment of Biko's analysis of the Black human condition (life in South Africa's townships) as a Being deprived of its possibility to *be*. With this statement of the reality of Black Being on hand, I proceed to posit and demonstrate the Hegelian-Žižekian epistemological framework as the efficacious analytical tool through which the universal value of the denied potential of Black Being could be appreciated. Imbued with Mafeje's notion of "Africanity as combative ontology," I then recast Biko's enunciation of Black Consciousness, in my concluding section, as an apt typology of a recoiled revolutionary ontology that produces unanticipated results in a manner predicted in Žižek's reconceptualization of Hegel's dialectic as the Absolute Recoil.

Theoretical Journey: Nothingness, Possibility, and Being,

At first glance, the title of Sartre's *Being and Nothingness* (Sartre 1992 [1943]) evokes what appears to be a dialectical hypothesis on the ontological status of the Being of persons with a fractious lived experience such as that of the African colonial subject. However, the severity of the critical reflection demanded by the graveness of our mission impelled me to move beyond the Sartre of 1943 as I found inspiration in my reading of John Russon's 2008 essay "The Self as Resolution: Heidegger, Derrida and the Intimacy of the Question of the Meaning of Being." Sartre had explained: "Being is. Being is in-itself. Being is what it is" (Sartre 1992 [1943], 22). Russon, an accomplished Hegel scholar (Russon and Baur 1997; Russon 2004, 2010), extended this Sartrean view and Heidegger's definition of Being as "the most universal, the most self-evident concept, and inherently undefinable" (Heidegger 1962 [1927], 21). He further conceptualized "Being as possibility," a possibility that is never exhausted by "Being as actuality" (Russon 2008, 105). I found this Russonian exposition of Being aptly instrumental for my agonized project.

Russon's assertion on infinite possibility is a qualitative extension of Heidegger's statement that "being means 'being possible'" (Heidegger 1962 [1927], 183), which for my purposes has a special valence when read with Olivier's "Heidegger in the Township" (Olivier 2015), which I discuss later on. In Russon's explication, "Being is not just the actuality of what actually is, but also the as yet unrealised power to be otherwise" (Russon 2008, 107). In the light of this insight, the motif of our reflection becomes a search of *how to be* otherwise as a Black African in a Black-Being-potentiality-denying, racialized world.

This observation of the inherent potentiality of *Being* led me to propel Heidegger's question of Being beyond Sartre's 1943 abstract existential phenomenology to a post-Marxian study of Being that conceptualizes the human condition as a materialized or situated consciousness. This realizes being human as a dialectical existentiality that progressively resolves itself in actual history (Marcuse 1941). I concurred with Paulo Freire that "authentic reflection considers neither abstract Man nor the world without people, but people in their relations with the world" and that "in these relations, consciousness and world are simultaneous: consciousness neither precedes the world nor follows it" (Freire 2005 [1970], 85).[4] These reflections, including Herbert Marcuse's critique of Sartre, in his 1948 "Sartre's Existentialism" (in Marcuse 1973 [1948], 157–190), led to the discovery of Žižek's radical reconceptualization of Hegel's dialectical logic as the conceptual framework that could be instrumental in the quest for the ownmost potentiality of the Black African Being.

Žižek (2014, 1–3, 148–156) identified the essence of the Hegelian dialectic as being its hypostasis as the Absolute Recoil, whereby in the dialectical triad of thesis-antithesis-synthesis, the resolution of negativity (self-alienation) is the raison d'être of the thesis/reality. The negativity latent in the *antithesis* always produces the unintended positivity (synthesis-thesis), which is then immediately lost as thesis turns into a new antithesis. Conscious reality (*Dasein*?), according to Žižek, is negative recoil that inexorably produces unintended results (historically progressive consciousness) in a manner akin to a boomerang effect.[5]

The distillation of the *absoluter Gegenstoss* (recoil) as the central logic of Hegel's *dialektika* presents us with a framework of reflection on the *ontology* of the ontology of the (self-)conscious Subject: how the self-knowing Subject, patently a negativity, opposes itself and deals with negations of itself, as it attains new forms of consciousness. Žižek explains:

> The full scale of absolute recoil, of a thing emerging through its very loss, is thus that of the subject itself, as the outcome of its own impossibility. In this precise Hegelian sense, the subject is the truth of the substance: the truth of every substantial thing is that it is the retroactive effect of its own loss. . . . Not only is the subject co-substantial with its loss, the subject *is* the loss. . . . There is no such thing as lost innocence, only the choice of Evil makes us aware of the Good as that which was lost in making this choice. (Žižek 2014, 150–151)[6]

Applied to the ontology of the colonized/racialized subject who is in the state of a loss of her ontological counterpush against her Master, trapped in the "zone of non-being" (Fanon 1986 [1952], 83), Žižek's insights produce a revolutionary phenomenology. It valorizes the sense of loss of the dehumanized and inspires affirmative self-knowledge, a self-ontologization into a combative being.

This phenomenological reconceptualization of negativity as a dynamic feature of what Žižek was impelled to classify as the "New" dialectical materialism availed itself as a prism through which I revisited Hegel's *Science of Logic* and *Phenomenology of Mind* and reinterpreted Mafeje and Biko. The result posited here is how the Žižekian schema, with the material derived from our reading of Heidegger, Sartre, and Russon, resolves the ambiguity of Black African being from an impotent nonbeing into a possibility of a revolutionary ontology.

I hope I have in the foregoing traced how I arrived at the theoretical prism that I now shall proceed to demonstrate and apply in the following sections that build our expository argument.

The Reality of Being Black

In a 1970 essay, "We Blacks," Biko describes the social ontology of a Black person in South Africa in these words:

> To a large extent the evil-doers have succeeded in producing at the output end of their machine a kind of Black man who is man only in form. This is the extent to which the process of dehumanisation has advanced. . . . Reduced to an obliging shell, he looks with awe at the white power structure and accepts what he regards as the "inevitable position" . . . celebrated achievements by whites in the field of science—which he understands only hazily—serve to make him rather convinced of the futility of resistance and to throw away any hopes that change may ever come. All in all the Black man has become a shell, a shadow of man, completely defeated, drowning in own misery, a slave, an ox bearing the yoke of oppression with sheepish timidity. (Biko 2004 [1970], 30–31)

Delving more directly into the existentiality of what he is describing with Sartrean existentialist pessimism, Biko then turns specifically on the psychophilosophical effect of apartheid's residential segregation on Black minds: "The streets are different, the lighting is different [no electricity], so you tend to begin to feel that there is something incomplete in your humanity, and that completeness goes with whiteness" (Biko 2004 [1970], 101).

In *Being and Nothingness*, Sartre introduced a unique philosophic import to the terms: incompleteness, emptiness, negativity, lack, annihilation, nonbeing (Sartre 1992 [1943]: 36–70, 673). These categories assume a pertinently evocative relevance when applied to the existentiality of Black selfhood against the background of what we noted about "loss" in Žižek's explication of the dialectic as Absolute Recoil.

In "Heidegger in the Township," Olivier (2015) juxtaposes Heidegger's postulations on *Dasein* to the meanings emanating from the lived experience of persons living in South Africa's squalid residential areas traditionally populated by Black people, eponymously called "townships" relative to the upper-class "suburbs." Focusing on Heidegger's emphasis on the possibility of Being as dependent on an enabling environment, Olivier observes that "the township represents a vital aspect of the *human condition*, the predicament of people living permanently in a disenabling environment," and thus precluded from being-in-the-world in fulfillment of their full potential (Olivier 2015, 245). In Olivier's observation, unlike Heidegger's world that is permeated by the desire to care, township folk are forever struggling for survival and living with apprehension and anxiety. He concludes: "Heidegger's ordinary world and the ordinary world of the township seem to be worlds of a different kind. Heidegger's world is a space that manifests as an enabling network of possibilities. . . . If one has no choice but to live in a shack, go to an abusive school, take an odd job, visit a pitiable medical clinic, walk dangerous streets, one can hardly speak of a network of possibilities that constitute the enabling space Heidegger calls the world" (Olivier 2015, 244–245). Olivier's article is vitally important in that it draws attention to both the existential reality (actual living conditions) as well as the existentiality (life-meaning emanating from lived experience) of people forced by economic deprivation to reside in the Black townships of South Africa in the post-apartheid dispensation, well away in time from Biko's depiction of life in 1970 we opened this section with. It is also a fact, of course, that the vast majority of the Black population, globally, live in conditions akin to what Olivier, and his referent, Sharlene Swartz (2009), describe.

In Olivier's application of Heidegger, we find Black South Africans in their living conditions as structurally precluded from attaining their ontological possibility, *being-in-the-world* in pursuit of their potentiality to *be*. Theirs is the "possibilities-depraved world" (Olivier 2015, 246). They are trapped, in the words of Fanon, in the "zone of non-being," into an abyss of Nothingness. Instead of being in an enabling world to pursue their ownmost potential to be (cf. Russon 2008), the *Being* of these Black[7] people

> become dispersed by impulsively grabbing the very first best and closest possibilities that are on offer for the sake of survival . . . in a headless scramble for scarce options. In this sense one can speak of a scattered existence. Adjacent to scattering is "shattering," To shatter is to demolish, pull down, devastate, ruin, smash, tear down, waste, or desolate. In one way or the other, people who have had to grow up in an environment which makes them not to realise their ownmost potential are shattered. (Olivier 2015, 250)

To Sartre's existentialist lexicon of Nothingness, we can now add "a shattered being," and a "scattered existence" when describing the ontology of the postcolonial and post-apartheid Black African as in-itself (as opposed to the yet to be recuperated "for-itself").

What is to be done or is to happen with this deleterious condition? To help us in grappling within the context of the utility of Žižek's postulation, we will first have to consider Russon's axiom: "It is only in its embracing of its not-being-able-to(yet)-be-itself that the self is properly itself" (2008, 103). Is it in our Nothingness that we are? How? Also, what are we to make of Hegel's declaration that "there is nothing in heaven or on earth which does not contain in itself being and nothingness."[8] Does this mean that the "nothingness" (Zone of nonbeing) of African selfhood as presented in the foregoing is necessarily *the* substance? The given anticipatory antithesis of what could be?

In the same essay in which Biko mournfully decried "the Black man [as] a shell, a shadow of man, completely defeated, drowning in own misery, a slave, an ox bearing the yoke of oppression with sheepish timidity," he hastened to add: "The first step then is to make the Black man come to himself; to pump back life into his empty shell; to infuse him with pride and dignity, to remind him of his complicity in the crime of allowing himself to be misused and therefore letting evil reign supreme in the country of his birth. This is what we mean by an inward-looking process. This is the definition of Black Consciousness" (Biko 2004 [1970], 31). With this elaboration by Biko, we now have the seeds of a schema of a threatened-but-defiant Black ontology. The ambiguity of Black African ontology is introduced as a Being in an anguished emergence from a degraded selfhood to a possibility of revolutionary self-creation. To Olivier's rationalization of the possible relationship between "care" and "struggle" in Heidegger (Olivier 2015, 246), we can now have a vision of Being-in-the-township as Being-in-struggle.

To explicate the emergence of this Being-in-struggle, let us consider Mafeje's appreciation of the revolutionary value of negativity in the section that follows.

The Antithesis in Being Black African

In "Africanity: A Combative Ontology," Mafeje ventured: "We would not talk of freedom, if there was no prior condition in which this was denied; we would not be anti-racist if we had not been its victims; we would not proclaim Africanity, if it had not been denied or degraded; and we would not insist on Afrocentrism if it had not been for Eurocentric negations"

(2008 [2000], 31). In anticipation of Žižek, here we have an articulation of the inexorable nexus between the status of what has been historically denied and the potentiality of the same to transform that negative denial into not only a positive self-affirmation but a creative force for universal liberation. It is the discernment of negativity realizing its positivity in a scale and form whose quality surpasses the original reality in an unanticipated proportion.

As a pertinent illustration, the foregoing statement of Mafeje, when appreciated within the Hegelian-Žižekian dialectics of "being and nothingness" draws us to the combative political content of the self-naming of Malcolm Little as Malcolm X. By declaring his ancestry as X, the unknown, nonexistent, he simultaneously mobilized contemporaneous consciousness to the historical injustice of the transatlantic slave trade, which he drew attention to every time he answered to the name Malcolm (X 1973 [1965]).

What am I as John Lamola? Why do I, an African born Black in a South African township, allow people to call me "John"? Who gave me the name John? Was my great-great-grandfather a Christian? I am John. Malesela, my ancestral name, is sublimated and generally nowhere. Lost. What does this continued use of a Christian name say about the psychophilosophical state of modern African consciousness in the postcolony? Am I in the state of Nothingness? Bad Faith? Does this psychical state, riddled as it is with contradictions, have any potential for positive self-negation and eventual actualization as a combative ontology?

What is the value of the negative, dehumanizing symbols of our oppression in an era or at a stage when we consider ourselves liberated? Do we need to preserve them to keep us reminded and motivated to fight on and not slide back into our state of slavery? Is it even ethical to proudly assert one's Black racial identity in a progressively cosmopolitan age? In "Black Orpheus," Sartre wrote: "The Negro cannot deny that he is negro, nor claim this abstract colourless humanity; he is Black. Thus he is driven to authenticity: insulted, enslaved, he straightens up, he picks up the name 'negro' that was thrown to him like a stone, and he claims to be Black, in front of white, in pride."[9] How does this act of embracing negativity with the purpose of transcending that very negativity operate in an anti-Black social reality in which "the Blacks" are embedded? Read with Sartre's averment of the embrace of the negative connotations of "being Black" by protagonists of *Négritude*, where is the following exhortation by Biko leading? "Merely by describing yourself as Black you have started on a road towards emancipation, you have committed yourself to fight against all forces that seek to use your Blackness as a stamp that marks you out as a subservient being" (2004 [1971], 52). A Being-in-struggle is instantiated.

The gist of our disquisition, however, is that beyond the discernment of the advent of Black combative ontology, Biko and Mafeje's proclamation of the genitive negativity of Black Consciousness makes sense only when set onto an observation of the operation of the Absolute Recoil. As it plays itself out, we find Black Consciousness as not only the resolution of the ambiguity of Black social ontology but as a consciousness that in an *unanticipated way*, nurtures a vision of the recovery of the humanity of the White oppressor as well. It becomes a trail from a racialistically-denied-but-combative ontology of the oppressed to a nonracial ontology for all, "True humanity" (= nonracial consciousness). Out of the historically dehumanized Africans, Biko declares: "We believe that in the long run, the special contribution to the world by Africa will be in this field of human relationship. The great powers of the world may have done wonders in giving the world an industrial and military look, but the great gift still has to come from Africa—giving the world a more human face" (Biko 2004 [1973], 108). The systematic valorization of negativity in Žižek's interpretation of Hegel, inexorably, bears unintended liberatory potential as and when applied to concrete historical situations. This point will progressively be amplified by my conclusions on the import of Biko's philopraxis.

Hegel Redeems Anticolonial Theorization

Sartre's conceptual substantiation of Nothingness as "non-being," "anguish," and "bad faith" resonated with the existential condition of Black-lived-experience and served as the foundational analytical tool for South African Black Consciousness. However, at the matured stage of the politicization of the Black Consciousness movement, Biko found Hegel's thought system readily useful as the frame of describing the vagaries of *humanity* in a racialized society. A precedent to this, and certainly the conduit of Biko's exposure to Hegel, was Fanon's devotion of a discussion on "The Negro and Hegel" in *Black Skin, White Masks* (1967, 168–174).

In the foundational essay "The Definition of Black Consciousness," Biko categorically states:

The overall analysis therefore, based on the Hegelian theory of dialectical materialism, is as follows. That since the thesis is a white racism there can only be one valid antithesis, i.e., a solid Black unity to counterbalance the scale. If South Africa is to be a land where Black and white live together in harmony without fear of group exploitation, it is only when these two opposites have interplayed and produced a synthesis of ideas and a modus vivendi. We can never wage a struggle without offering a strong counterpoint to the white [racism] that permeates our society so effectively. (Biko 2004 [1971], 55)

And in his most celebrated essay, the 1973 "Black Consciousness and the Quest for a True Humanity," Biko further exhibited his reading of Hegel, as he employs the dialectical schema as a framework for unraveling the conundrum of the racial dynamics of the anti-apartheid struggle at the time. He wrote:

The thesis, the anti-thesis and the synthesis have been mentioned by some great philosophers as the cardinal points around which any social revolution revolves. For the liberals, the thesis is apartheid, the antithesis is non-racialism, but the synthesis is very feebly defined. They want to tell the Blacks that they see integration as the ideal solution; Black Consciousness defines the situation differently. The thesis is in fact a strong white racism and therefore, the antithesis to this must, ipso facto, be a strong solidarity amongst the Blacks on whom this white racism seeks to prey, out of these two situations we can therefore hope to reach some kind of balance—a true humanity where power politics will have no place. (Biko 2004 [1973], 99)

There is a mysterious contradiction here. How does Hegel, a notorious intellectual progenitor of an anti-African Euro-American civilization, become such a crucial component of a philosophic inventory for African emancipation? Žižek accidentally addresses this riddle in a New York University lecture entitled "Hegel's Wound," which is the subject of a chapter in Žižek (2014).[10] This happens as he deploys an idiomatic phrase from Wilhelm R. Wagner's *Parsifal* to illustrate the import of the Absolute Recoil as the essence of the hypostasis of the dialectic. He quotes Wagner, "The wound can be healed only by the spear that smote it [*Die Wunde schliesst der Speer nur der sie schlug*]" (2014, 131) and then concludes illuminatively: "It is precisely apropos the wound of colonialism that the final message of Wagner's *Parsifal* holds." Žižek ricochets this analytical schema at Hegel against his complicity in "the wound colonisation" as seminally perpetrated in his introduction to the *Philosophy of World History*. He observes how this "properly Hegelian ambiguity of colonialism" (Zizek 2014, 135) finds itself confronted by "the anti-colonial recoil" (132).

What is hidden here is an esoteric message that it is through Hegel's *dialektika* that the ramifications of the colonization of Africa can be healed.[11] The radical rediscovery of Hegel's dialectic is the spear that may heal "the Wound of colonialism," in the infliction of which Hegel bears substantial complicity.

We can now turn to appreciating how the conception of the dialectical recoil as the kernel of Hegel's phenomenology, ironically, serves the attainment of a revolutionary Black social ontology.

Back to Hegelian Phenomenology via Žižek

The notion of the necessity of contradictions/negation as a vital feature of reality (Being, *da Sein*) and the progressive self-resolution of this contradiction through sociohistorical institutions are central features of Hegel's philosophy.[12] Evidently, it is upon this inspiration that Mafeje proclaimed that "it is the historical juncture which defines us socially and intellectually . . . of necessity, under the determinate global conditions, an African renaissance must entail a rebellion—a conscious rejection of past transgressions, a determined *negation of negations*" (Mafeje 2008 [2000], 32).

Cognate with the principle of negation are notions of possibility and actualization. The Hegelian Being is a being burdened with potentiality, never perfect but simultaneously pregnant with possibilities of its full actualization, which, in turn, simultaneously devolves into an imperfect being with potentiality, ad infinitum.[13] Being, according to Hegel, is the substantive negation of the negation of the negation. And it is in this sense that that "there is nothing in heaven or on earth which does not contain in itself being and nothingness."[14] This statement of Hegel on the relation between being and nothingness is radically different from Sartre's thought. In Sartre's existentialism "being presupposes non-being" (Sartre 1992 [1943], 39). You continue being what you are not while you are what you are. It is not a dialectic of the sublation of Nothingness into

Being. It is an ontology of perpetual annihilation, a descent into a series of consciousnesses haunted by nonbeing. The adumbration of rebirth, a new ontology is absent from this Sartrean assertion.

In contrast, in Hegel self-negation is at the core of the hypostasis of being and nothingness. This self-negation is not only substantive, it is determinate (*bestimmt*); it has a purpose. According to Michael Rosen, this determinate negation is the foundation of Hegel's entire philosophy (Rosen 1982, 30). It is the negation of "the given," that is, of the thesis, that constitutes the antithetical action or moment, which is the motor of the dialectical process. But the antithesis is not independently temporal. It is merely a moment in which the experienced and the idealized coincide in a productive trajectory.

For an illustration, let us allude to an example drawn from political praxis. Resistance against some political cause qua *resistance* is intrinsically an act of negation. But, or hence, resistance cannot be resistance for the sake of resistance. It has a teleology embedded within it. It has an ideal that is simultaneously *a priori* and *teleological*. It is propelled to produce the idealized alternative out of the given reality that is being negated/resisted. The purpose implied in the teleology is the initiating and driving force of the negation or change.

Epistemologically, the enigma of Hegel's Absolute Reason, which is the resolution of the dialectical (thinking) process, occurs at this overarching moment of the conjunction of the a priori (potentiality) and the teleological—the presupposed actuality. This resolution of the dialectic is, in fact, always a recoil of *den Geist*; hence it can only be an *Absolute* Recoil. It is *understanding* losing itself within the object of its cognition and inexorably producing new, unanticipated knowledge or enlightenment. Indeed, as originating from and within the context of Hegel's *Science of Logic*, Absolute Recoil originally relates to what Hegel calls "absolute reflection": a reflection that is no longer external to its object, presupposing it as given, but which, as it were, closes the loop and posits its own presupposition.[15]

Accordingly, as Žižek asserts, Absolute Recoil is a notion Hegel only used "at a crucial point in his logic of reflection to designate the speculative coincidence of opposites in *the movement by which a thing emerges out of its own loss*" (Žižek 2014, 1, my emphasis). It goes beyond the standard exegesis of the triad of thesis-antithesis-synthesis as being in a linear and smooth progression, by indicating the force and importance of the turn of negativity into a positivity that ultimately and inexorably also degenerates into its own negativity. Positivity is both lost and regained, always arising out of the negation of the negation. "*Absoluter Gegenstoss* thus stands for the radical coincidence of opposites in which the action appears as its own counter-action, or, more precisely, in which the negative move (loss, withdrawal) itself generates what it 'negates'" (Žižek 2014, 148).

In the *Encyclopaedia of Philosophical Sciences*, Hegel explains the process of negation or self-negation, that is, the passing of the thesis into its opposite, as "self-sublation," *Aufheben*. The word means both to cancel and preserve at the same time (Maybee 2020). Negativity, laden with is ownmost potentiality to be the acceptable condition is synthesized (*aufgehoben*) with its actuality. In this way, "nothingness" is teleologically substantiated.

As a Hegelian phenomenology that is sensitized by Marxian epistemology would later maintain, the revolutionary Self arises out of the Self-in-its-passivity embracing its negativity, its self-alienation, and self-sublating. The Self-in-its-passivity (nonbeing) does not transcend; it negates (self-sublates) this passivity to assume a teleological consciousness. In this conceptual scheme, Nothingness is not merely nihilated (rearranged in consciousness); it is annihilated (it is negated, *aufgehoben*) so that the resulting reality logically degenerates into another Nothingness. In this Hegelian dialectics the potentiality within Nothingness is always retained in what is being negated and recreated.

Against the *transcendence* of Husserl, Heidegger, and Sartre, we have the *Synthesis* of Hegel. This synthesis is not only the resolution of the opposites of thesis and antithesis; it is the thesis *becoming*, that is, realizing the ideal inert within itself. It is self-actualization through the pursuit of retaining its telos and in the process becoming anti-thesis. The negativity is neither denied nor lost but valorized into a new reality that would, in the course of the ensuing process, meet its synthesizing negation. It is in this sense that Russon's axiom we referred to earlier is proven, namely: "It is only in its embracing of its not-being-able-to(yet)-be-itself that the self is properly itself."

In all of Biko's oeuvre, his comprehension of the import of the concept of the synthesis demonstrates his glittering brilliance as a twenty-six-year-old medical student reading Hegel. In "Black Consciousness and the Quest for a True Humanity" (Biko 2004 [1973]), he eloquently contends that in the multiracial integration thesis then propounded by White liberal anti-apartheid activists during the mid-1960s "the synthesis is very feebly defined." In contradistinction, he posits a pure Hegelian synthesis: the negativity of Black inferiority complex is *aufgehoben* into a rebellious deprivation of the false consciousness of White superiority complex as subservient black consciousness rises into Black Consciousness, collapsing both the erstwhile mutually dehumanized black inferiority complex and white superiority complex into a True Humanity.

Accordingly, in line with the modus vivendi of the dialectic as the Absolute Recoil, the colonial evil and resultant tragedy of dehumanized Africans is not only negated into merely a synthesis of a new self-consciousness, a restoration to some original state that was perceived to be the correct one. A "Good," something positive sprouts out of what "the evil doer" (Biko 2004 [1970], 30) did not intend. In an Absolute Recoil, the tragedy of the objectification of the African Subject is de-tragicized in an attainment of a true humanity that ironically even the oppressor did not have. This harks back to the cry of Fanon who in the conclusion section of *The Wretched of the Earth* charges African intellectuals to work for the new paradigm of humanity as the racialized European one had historically failed (Fanon 1991 [1961], 312–313).

Rightly interpreted, the "phenomenological ontology" presented in Sartre's *Being and Nothingness* may be read as leaving the colonial subject in a perpetual state of anguish and overwhelmed with the challenge for self-situation within their facticity, which esoterically, is declared as the state of nonbeing (inauthentic self, "bad faith") and thus Nothingness (Sartre 1992 [1943], 59, 67–70). Contra this, following our application of Žižek's Hegelianism, we realize an activist Subject who is purposeful ("conscientized" instead of "intentional"), resolute about her social ontology while acknowledging and exploiting the contradictions of her colonially formed being-in-the-world. This is an ontological negativity of a Malesela who tactically answers to John Lamola and thereby constantly provokes the uncomfortable confusion about the politico-historical context of his personal identity, and that of Christianized Africans in general.

From the foregoing convoluted exposition of how the dialectic subsists as the negativity best captured as Absolute Recoil, we can now proceed to an illustrative manifestation of this crucial aspect of Hegel's thought in the construction and telos of Biko's philosophy.

The Absolute Recoil of Black Consciousness

In the 1973 "Black Consciousness and the Quest for a True Humanity" Biko makes a noteworthy attempt at systematizing the practical vision of his political philosophy. Among a number of interesting conceptual advancements endeavored in that essay, the following distillation of the definition of Black Consciousness is the most historically valuable: "Black consciousness is an attitude of mind *and a way of life*, the most positive call to emanate from the Black world for a long time. Its essence is the *realisation* by the Black man of the need to rally together with his brothers around the cause of their oppression, the Blackness of their skin, and to operate as a group to rid themselves of the shackles that bind them to perpetual servitude" (Biko 2004 [1973], 91–92). This political statement is a repetition of what he had written in the 1970 "We Blacks" essay. Significantly, this time gone is the sole emphasis on "the attitude of mind," a phenomenological-type obsession with "consciousness." With the addition of "a way of life," objective social ontology is asserted.

As a way of life, Biko underscores that Black Consciousness is a *realization*. It is both a consequence of a reflection and a state of being; enlightenment on what one is, who he or she should be, and what should be done within a concrete political arena. It is an awakening that demands action, a *conscientization*. The antithesis to the status quo—the political impulsion to rise and rally together, that is Black Solidarity—emerged at the mantra of the Black Consciousness movement's political formations, SASO (South African Students' Organisation) and BPC (Black Peoples Convention).

Being conscientized is a step beyond being merely aware. The equivalent of a Conscious Black person is a conscientized laborer under capitalism who turns into a proletariat that rallies together in a trade union. So, while overlaid with the identitarian sense of "consciousness," Black Consciousness is an *organized realization*. It is a state of being and a reflection of what one is as a signifier of an objectified community and what one can be as a negation of this. The realization is not to be merely conscious of the situation; it is a commitment to transform the status quo.

Black Consciousness—having at its core the notion of Black solidarity—thus arises as a deliberate political-dialectical negation of the institutionalized white racism of apartheid as a cause and result of the consciousness of White racial supremacy. Even as a psychological process, it is pushed out of the realm of Sartrean Nothingness (the ontological ambiguity or susceptibility of languishing as either being-for-Itself or being-for-Others). Positive consciousness as a negation of Nothingness is envisioned and unambiguously affirmed as an a priori teleological standpoint. To this end Biko wrote in "We Blacks," and we repeat: "The first step, therefore, is to make the Black man to come to himself: to pump life back into his empty shell; to infuse him with pride and dignity; to remind him of his complicity in the crime of allowing himself to be misused and therefore letting evil to reign supreme in the land of his birth. This is what we mean by an inward process. This is the definition of Black Consciousness" (Biko 2004 [1971], 31). The negativity of self-alienation is negated. "Black man to come to himself," and with immediacy, beyond this, to realize his social ontology of a being complicit in its own annihilation in "letting evil to reign supreme in the land of his birth." The victim is chastised; it is a drama of the negation of the negation.

This is Black Consciousness crafted not merely as a natural negation; it has a purpose, it is teleological in construction. Like Hegel's negativity, it is determined, *bestimmt*. Its ultimate goal is to combat the racial superiority complex among Whites by ridding society of Blacks willing to be treated as perpetual children or slaves. Black Consciousness is, thus, a priori, a combative consciousness. It is a new ontology of being Black: revolutionary Blackness. The "bad faith" of a self-deceptive, defective, and passive black consciousness is actively negated, not merely transcended, by a combative consciousness of responsibility of being Black in a land where "evil reigns supreme." In the process, this sublates, frustrates, and transforms the thesis/ negativity/reality of "strong white racism" into its direction toward its synthesis.

Revolutionary Black Being, therefore, I have sought to demonstrate, is the state of consciousness that embraces the negativity imposed on Black skin, and simultaneously countervailing a mental state of lack and of being awed and fascinated by White Power as the *mysterium tremendum et fascinans*. At one and the same time, it is a rejection, an embrace, a resistance, and new construction, all wrapped into a singular process of the recovery and self-actualization of the Black person as the Subject of history—a Subject ontologically mobilized as an agent of change, a change whose nature may even supersede his or her own parochial ideal and interests.

But if Black Consciousness is resistance, it follows that in our Hegelian-Zizekian schema, it is negativity that awaits its self-sublation. What nature would this synthesis, the *aufheben* to the new thesis, take? What is the practical political implication of this? The answer to this lies in the discernment of the modus operandi of the Absolute Recoil within the rubric of Biko's thought. This Absolute Recoil, at the risk of repetition, is here discernible in a dually pronged symbiotic act: In that, in attaining their full human consciousness, "the envisaged self, which is the free self" (Biko 2004 [1971], 53), the annihilated Black Being is not only transformed into a conscientized combative Africanity: White racist complex is now starved of the subservient Black inferiority complex it had to prey on.

In this way the false consciousness of White superiority complex is negated by the negation of the false consciousness of Black inferiority complex through its sublation by a combative Black ontology. Both Blacks and whites are redeemed from their twin false consciousnesses. One of inferiority, and the other of superiority complex. The colonizer is redeemed from subjective supremacism and attains authentic subjectivity as they are conscientized of their historical positionality, while the colonized regain their ontological sovereignty over their subjectivity. An equilibrium and unity of social ontologies is attained.[16] A notion of "true humanity" is birthed. This is the cry and gist of the closing paragraph of Biko's 1973 essay: "We have set out on a quest for true humanity, and somewhere on the distant horizon we can see the glittering prize. Let us march forth with courage and determination, drawing strength from our common plight and our brotherhood. In time we shall be in a position to bestow upon South Africa the greatest gift possible—a more human face." This is a quest for a world that enables the possibility to *be*, to attain nonracialized Being. It is a vision of a world without racial minorities and majorities, superior Whites and subjected Blacks, an ideal mediated through the mobilization of the dehumanized into a combative Being.

What the evildoer had wished for ill has turned for good!

Notes

1. For Mafeje's life and oeuvre, see Nyoka (2019, 2020).

2. The notion of "resolution" is here employed as an existential-phenomenological construct as used, among others, in Russon (2008). It denotes the self-directed process that inexorably leads to a qualitatively new epistemic reality, such as is achieved in the self-resolution of cognition through the dialectical triad of thesis-antithesis-synthesis.

3. The claim is not that Biko or the Black Consciousness movement evolved into a Marxian project; nor is the disquisition here oblivious to the fact that in

its generic and classic sense, Hegel's dialectic is essentially a dialectical idealism. The context of the utility of dialectical materialism is based on Zizek's insightful "post-Marxian" reconceptualization of the latter, as the full title of our key text (Zizek 2014) suggests.

4. This is a veiled retort against the mantra of Sartre's existentialism: "Existence precedes and perpetually creates essence" in *Les lettres franfaises*, November 24, 1945 (cited in Marcuse 1973 [1948], 161). See Sartre (2007 [1945], 22).

5. For other related writings of Žižek, see Žižek (1989, 1991).

6. For an exegesis of how Subject is substance in Žižek's thought, see Chen (2019). The act of critical (dialectical) thinking objectifies the thinker (Subject) in her negativity, which is her true, substantial state of being.

7. Curiously, Olivier's article refers only once to the racial identity of these people who occupy "a world of the township" (Olivier 2015, 242–244) and just briefly makes reference to how White racial disdain and exploitation of these Blacks is what historically motivated and maintained this "possibilities-depraved world." The objectification of Blacks as human beings ordained for "a world of the township" is an inverse of the sense of entitlement of White subjecthood to a life of luxury and privilege.

8. Hegel quoted by Sartre in *Being in Nothingness* (Sartre 1992 [1943], 37).

9. Sartre (1964–1965, 18).

10. https://www.youtube.com/watch?v=DRsrYi-wXro; and in Žižek (2014, 117–147).

11. For my dedicated elaboration of the import of Hegelian thought on the philosophy of Black Consciousness, see Lamola (2016).

12. Besides the later materialization of the dialectic by Karl Marx (during 1844–1857), the subject and content of Hegel's *Philosophy of Right* (1820) is a clear demonstration of this fact.

13. According to Žižek's interpretation: "Every historical situation harbours its own unique utopian perspective, an immanent vision of what is wrong with it, an ideal representation of how, with the necessary changes, the situation can be rendered much better" (2014, 37).

14. Hegel quoted in Sartre (1992 [1943], 37).

15. Hegel (1969 [1812], 402) quoted in Žižek (2014, 148): "Reflection therefore *finds before it* an immediate which it transcends and from which it is the return. But this return is only the presupposing of what reflection finds before it. What is thus found only *comes to be* through being *left behind* . . . the reflective movement is to be taken as an absolute recoil [*absoluter Gegenstoss*] upon itself. For the presupposition of the return-into-self—that from which *essence* comes, and *is* only as this return—is only in the return itself."

16. "Superiority? Inferiority? Why not the quite simple attempt to touch the other, to feel the other, to explain the other to myself?" (Fanon 1986 [1952], 181).

References

Biko, Steve. 2004 [1970]. "We Blacks." In *I Write What I Like*, edited by A. Stubbs, 29–35. Johannesburg: Picador.

Biko, Steve. 2004 [1971]."The Definition of Black Consciousness." In *I Write What I Like*, edited by A. Stubbs, 52–57. Johannesburg: Picador.

Biko, Steve. 2004 [1973]. "Black Consciousness and the Quest for a True Humanity." In *I write What I Like*, edited by A. Stubbs, 96–108. Johannesburg: Picador.

Chen, Zhiang. 2019. "The Absolute Not Only as Substance, but also as Subject." *International Journal of Žižek Studies* 13, no. 2: https://philpapers.org/rec/CHETAN-3?ref=mail.

Heidegger, Martin. 1962 [1927]. *Being and Time*. Translated by J. Macquarrie and E. Robinson. Oxford: Blackwell.

Hegel, Georg Wilhelm Friedrich. 1969 [1812]. *Science of Logic*. Translated by A. V. Miller. London: George Allen & Unwin.

Fanon, Frantz. 1986 [1952]. *Black Skin, White Masks*. Translated by Charles Lam Markmann. Sidmouth: Pluto Press.

Fanon, Frantz. 1991 [1961]. *The Wretched of the Earth*. Evergreen ed. New York: Grove Weidenfeld.

Freire, Paulo. 2005 [1970]. *Pedagogy of the Oppressed*. Translated by Myra Bergman Ramos. New York: Continuum.

Lamola, M. John. 2016. "Biko, Hegel and the End of Black Consciousness: A Historico-philosophical Discourse on South African Racism." *Journal of Southern African Studies* 42, no. 2: 183–194.

Mafeje, Archibald. 2008 [2000]. "Africanity: A Combative Ontology." in René Devisch, Francis Nyamnojoh eds, In *The Postcolonial Turn*, edited by René Devisch and Francis Nyamnojoh, 31–44. Bameda: Langaa.

Manganyi, Chabani. 1973. *Being-Black-in the World*. Johannesburg: Ravan Press.

Marcuse, Herbert. 1941. *Reason and Revolution: Hegel and the Rise of Social Theory*, 2nd ed. London: Routledge & Kegan Paul.

Marcuse, Herbert. 1973 [1948]. "Sartre's Existentialism." In *Studies in Critical Philosophy*, 157–190. Boston: Beacon Press.

Marx, Karl. 1974 [1867]. *Capital: A Critical Analysis of Capitalist Production*, vol. 1. London: Lawrence & Wishart.

Matshoba, Mtutuzeli. 1979. *Call Me Not a Man*. Johannesburg: Ravan Press.

Maybee, J. E. 2020. "Hegel's Dialectics." In *The Stanford Encyclopedia of Philosophy* (Winter), edited by Edward N. Zalta, https://plato.stanford.edu/archives/win2020/entries/hegel-dialectics/.

More, Mabogo Percy. 2017. *Biko: Philosophy, Identity and Liberation*. Cape Town: Human Resource Research Council Press.

Nyoka, Bongani. 2019. *Archie Mafeje: Voices of Liberation*. Cape Town: HSRC Press.

Nyoka, Bongani. 2020. *The Social and Political Philosophy of Archie Mafeje*. Johannesburg: Wits University Press.

Olivier, Abraham. 2015. "Heidegger in the Township." *South African Journal of Philosophy* 34, no. 2: 240–254.

Rosen, Michael. 1982. *Hegel's Dialectic and Its Criticism*. Cambridge: Cambridge University Press.

Russon, John. 2004. *Reading Hegel's Phenomenology*. Bloomington: Indiana University Press.

Russon, John. 2008. "The Self as Resolution: Heidegger, Derrida and the Intimacy of the Question of the Meaning of Being." *Research in Phenomenology* 38: 90–110.

Russon, John. 2010. "Dialectic, Difference, and the Other: The Hegelianizing of French Phenomenology." In *Phenomenology: Responses and Developments*, edited by Leonard Lawlor, 17–42. Chesham: Acumen.

Russon, John, and Michael Baur, eds. 1997. *Hegel and the Tradition: Essays in Honour of H. S. Harris*. Toronto: University of Toronto Press.

Sartre, Jean-Paul. 1964–1965 [1948]. "Black Orpheus." *Massachusetts Review* 6, no. 1, http://massreview.org/sites/default/files/Sartre.pdf. Accessed August 12, 2019.

Sartre, Jean-Paul. 1992 [1943]. *Being and Nothingness: An Essay on Phenomenological Ontology*. Translated by Hazel E. Barnes. London: Routledge.

Sartre, Jean-Paul. 2007 [1945]. *Existentialism Is a Humanism*. Translated by Carol Macomber. New Haven: Yale University Press.

Swartz, Sharlene. 2009. *iKasi: The Moral Ecology of South Africa's Youth*. Johannesburg: Wits University Press.

X, Malcom. 1973 [1965]. *The Autobiography of Malcom X*. London: Penguin.

Žižek, Slavoj. 1989. *The Sublime Object of Ideology*. London: Verso.

Žižek, Slavoj. 1991. *For They Know Not What They Do: Enjoyment as a Political Factor*. London: Verso.

Žižek, Slavoj. 2014. Absolute Recoil: Towards a New Foundation of Dialectical Materialism. London: Verso.

8

Blackness as a Conundrum
for Phenomenology

KEOLEBOGILE MBEBE AND THABANG DLADLA

Slavery and colonialism constitute two extremely violent moments in African existence that ruptured African ways of being and relating to the world (Mbembe 2003). In this regard, these moments can be considered world-making: the making of both the new world and the colonized world in the image of the White. This process in turn created Blackness and Blacks as denigrated and degenerate ways of being. African philosophy and Black philosophy, as philosophies necessarily concerned with liberation and born of the struggle to exist, have had the task of extricating Africans from such entanglements. This has necessitated the subjection of the European archive to a negative critique and to mapping an independent path toward liberatory practices of philosophy.

In this chapter, we offer some reflections on how Blackness presents a conundrum for phenomenology not only as a condition about which to theorize, but also as a position from which one may theorize. Our central claim is that Blackness offers an alternative phenomenology to Western phenomenology by giving a point of view from those who do not die but end. In order to do so, we will explicate the notion of violence used by Orlando Patterson and adopted by the Afropessimist school. We will be using the concept of *gratuitous violence* encapsulated in the phenomenon of social death as employed by Afropessimism for our analysis of Blackness as a position of *nonbeing* from which one may theorize.

Against Eurocentric Negations

The exclusion of conquered and colonized peoples from equal normative consideration by Western philosophers such Aristotle and Kant can only serve the political interest of European male *dominance* over these groups. As colonizer, Europe presents the White man as knower and everyone else as those who should be studied. What has been referred to as the age of reason in the West coincides with the enslavement and colonization of Africa, Asia, and Latin America by the West as part of what the West considers its "discovery" of the New World. Modernity, as Oyeronke Oyewumi illustrates, is hallmarked by the "expansion of Europe and the establishment of Euro/American cultural hegemony throughout the world," with gender and race as "two fundamental axes along which people were exploited and societies stratified" (Oyewumi 2002, 393). According to Oyewumi, with Euro-American institutions and social categories being dominant in the writing of human history, this process has profoundly impacted the production of knowledge about societies, human behavior, history, and cultures (Oyewumi 2002). Tsenay Serequeberhan has defined this Eurocentrism as a "pervasive bias located in modernity's self-consciousness of itself. It is grounded at its core in the metaphysical belief or idea (*idee*) that European existence is qualitatively superior to other forms of human life" (Serequeberhan 1997, 65). Indeed, this amounts to the racialization of knowledge that Oyewumi has identified as distinctive of the modern age: "Europe is represented as the source of knowledge and Europeans as knowers," which Oyewumi has designated as the privileging of the White male experience in the generation of knowledge (Oyewumi 2002, 65).

This epistemology of the Europeans as superior is informed by Aristotle's assertion that "man is a rational animal," and that this assertion was not spoken of anyone else other than the European man (the true human) (Ramose 1999). Others such as Africans and Native Americans are not included in the equation and are not rational; meaning that they are not "men" (true humans).

The measure of being rational came with a scale of civilization for different people, measured by their capacity for self-determination, that is, "maturity." Maturity, in the Kantian sense, is an individual's ability to restrain the influence of impulses, desires, and external forces on behavior and thinking by willing in accordance with principles one has assessed and accepted on the basis of empirical evidence and logical reasoning. Maturity is demonstrated in an individual's courage to "use one's intelligence without being guided by another"; an intelligence that is the capacity for free thought. When a civil society is characterized by this free thought, according to Kant, "the free thought, the spirit of the people can develop to its full capacity" (Wood 2001, 135, 141). If the abstract European idea of proper human political society was not discernible in a non-European population, it was seen as proof that that population's capacity to self-govern was either deficient or nonexistent, thus making them perpetually in need of tutelage and/or mastery and not equally deserving of moral treatment. African/black philosophy as a philosophy of liberation describes a position of interpretation from the perspective of the indigenous people conquered in the unjust wars of colonization.

As Serequeberhan has noted, as a practice of resistance

> African philosophy has a double task: destructive and con-
> structive. In this it is a practice of resistance, for it is engaged
> in combat on the level of reflection and ideas, aimed at dis-
> mantling the symmetry of concepts and theoretic constructs
> that have sustained Euro-American global dominance. It is a
> resistance focused on challenging the core myths of the West—
> its self-flattering narratives—in terms of which its domination
> of the earth was justified. The practice of African philosophy
> is consequently internal to the very process through which the
> formerly colonized world is presently reclaiming itself. It is, in
> this sense, a concrete practice of resistance. (Serequeberhan
> 1997, 141)

It is from such a realization that a philosophy of resistance and liberation is born, which is also a liberation of philosophy insofar as it challenges the oppressive, exploitative, patriarchal, and colonial character of modern Western philosophy or Western philosophy in general; a philosophy that is responsible for or provides justification for the domination of women and non-Europeans (Serequeberhan 1997; Mills 2007).

Blackness as a Threat to Reason

The Black radical tradition as defined by Cedric Robinson considerers itself a critique of Western civilization, which coincides with the critical negative project that is African philosophy (Robinson 1987). This is because Western civilization negates Africa and its contribution to civilization, and the first step toward real liberation entails the unshackling of the chains of slavery and colonialism. Black philosophy needs to move against the subsumption of Black experience to a White philosophical anthropology that extends the concerns of White philosophers to the problems of race and giving the Western canon credibility (Curry 2011). In its classical definition, classic philosophy is "*theoria* as opposed to *praxis*, contemplation rather than activity, leisure rather than labour" (Veroli 2001, 242). Accordingly,

> it belongs to the realm of freedom, while its opposite belongs to the domain of necessity. John Dewey once shrewdly suggested that this definition was no doubt indebted to the *division of labor* in Ancient Greece between *citizens* and *slaves*. The citizens, unfamiliar with the physical process of creating forms—something which the servants did on an everyday basis—developed the strange notion that all forms were eternal and uncreated so that they need only be contemplated. Conveniently this enabled them to justify their *social dominance* by differentiating their own activity (philosophical contemplation—the contrary of practical activity) from that of their servants (servile labour). (Veroli 2001, 242, emphasis added)

Classic Western phenomenology assumes the ability to extricate oneself from corporeality in order to experience a thing as a phenomenon.[1] A relationship between the subject and thought is formed by the intentionality of the subject. This presupposition privileges the idea that the individual can think qua individual, can recognize oneself as such, and engage in a material suspension that affords the subject a unique relationship to the nature of the phenomenon. The body is laden with "meanings and significations," which "sets the parameters for what constitutes the reasonable response from others," creating a particular experience of life and phenomena (Lee 2014, 1). Epistemological presuppositions about the nature of theory that proceed from a Eurocentric social world first and foremost designate the White man—its standard of humanity—as the master of thought and of Blacks. In contrast, the Black is antithetical to humanity because it is "a site of questioned humanity" (Gordon 2010, 198). Instead of being capable of rational thought, "the Black is a site without reason or worse—a threat to reason" (Gordon 2010, 198). And instead of the Black being a master of oneself, "the Black emerged as a site whose freedom is challenged" (Gordon 2010, 198). Blacks are burdened with the identification of Blackness as corporeality. There can be no material suspension of that which cannot transcend the body. There can be no thought. Blackness confounds theory because Blackness is corporeality; it is some*thing* from which reason cannot be expected as it threatens reason.

Therefore, thinking from a place of Blackness, as Gordon avers, forces theory to "face itself," meaning that it forces theory to be self-reflective (Gordon 2010, 197). It forces *Whiteness* to be self-reflective. Theorizing from a place of Blackness is doing what is supposedly unreasonable; it confounds the bounds of theory. It manifests presence; it becomes being-in-itself. Says Gordon, "Blackness . . . is the dark side of theory, which, in the end, is none other than theory itself, understood as self-reflective, outside itself" (Gordon 2010, 198). The proposition is that Blackness not only critiques the idea of European monopoly on reason, but also capsizes this confidence.

To grapple with this idea of theorizing from a place of Blackness, we turn to certain themes in the school of Afropessimism. Afropessimism concerns itself with analyzing the ways in which the structural violence against Blacks in the global antiblack racist society is based on the human-nonhuman paradigm instead of the oft-used paradigm of human-subhuman (Douglass, Terrefe, and Wilderson 2018). It attempts to give "a diagnosis of Black suffering" and "a paradigmatic critique . . . that reckons civil society's perverse and parasitic relation to the hydraulics of anti-Black violence" (Wilderson 2016). The foundational claim for Afropessimists is that Blackness is social death since it is "coterminous with slaveness" (Wilderson 2016). The conception of slavery as social death to which Afropessimists refer is inspired by that used by Patterson (1982). Patterson identifies two historical kinds of social death, *intrusive* and *extrusive*. While the latter refers to "the dominant image of the slave [as] that of an insider who had fallen, one who ceased to belong," the former refers to the state of "the slave [who] was ritually incorporated as the permanent enemy on the inside [who] did not and could not belong because he was the product of a hostile, alien culture" (Patterson 1982, 39). It is intrusive social death to which Afropessimism refers. To be in a state of social death is to subtend a society but not be part of its civic life. This is reminiscent of the aforementioned idea of Blacks as mere being-among-beings and not beings-in-themselves, taking up space but not in human form, with their abjection being necessary for civic life. To suffer social death is to be a nonhuman in the antagonism between human and nonhuman, a position from which the Black can be liberated only through the end of the world. From an Afropessimist lens, in a state of social death there is no point at which Blackness can be redeemed, which is different from other identities such as indigenous identities, where for instance the return of the land can offer a form of redemption, a return to plenitude. To think of it as emplotment, Blackness does not conform to a romantic narrative whereby the protagonist overcomes an obstacle and there's a resolution at the end, nor does it conform to a comedic narrative whereby the protagonist overcomes numerous challenges over and over again. Blackness also does not conform to a tragic narrative where the protagonist finds meaning in their impossibly tragic circumstances and comes to form some sort of meaningful survival within those circumstances (White 1973, 7–11). All these narrative emplotments hold space for the kind of existential meaning that comes from the possibility and experience of hope of a linear trajectory; the hope of redemption—denouement—from being-black-in-the-world. Afropessimism is consistent with the narrative emplotment of satire. With satire the lack of a teleological movement toward denouement creates a world that is illegible and incoherent because it stands out of the framework of time that is necessary for narrative to develop. The black "life" is satirical and is marked by the social death of the slave. Patterson asserts that slavery, as a form of social death, is composed of three traits: natal alienation, general dishonor, and gratuitous violence (Patterson 1982). With regard to natal alienation, the slave suffers because they cannot have a family or kinship ties. This means any former kinship ties that the slave may have had are not recognized and are insignificant and unsubstantial insofar as slaves are disposable, as they do not form part of any moral community that would make this disposability unethical. The slave suffers general dishonor "because of the origin of his status, the indignity and all-pervasiveness of his indebtedness, his absence of any independent social existence, but most of all because he was without power except through another" (Patterson 1982, 10). The third component, gratuitous violence, involves "a master-slave relation where the antagonism is that of total power and domination for the master and total powerlessness for the slave." This relation "involves the use or threat of violence in the control of one person by another" (Patterson 1982, 1–2). The violence "is unusual, first, both in the extremity of power involved . . . and in the qualities of coercion that brought the relation into being and sustained it" (Patterson 1982, 2).

The Prelogic of Gratuitous Violence against Blacks

From an Afropessimistic angle, in an antiblack racist society the violence described by Patterson is akin to that suffered by Blacks. Antiblackness "[signifies] not only the particularity of racism against those deemed Black but also the centrality of such racism to all paradigms of racial domination" (Olaloku-Teriba 2018, 105). It is a philosophy grounded on the conviction that the fight against White supremacy is not the same as that against antiblack racism. The latter notion resists the tendency to describe White supremacist society within the paradigm of human-subhuman and asserts instead that the actual paradigm is human-nonhuman. For instance, the dominant position in theories about White supremacy aver that "the categories of capitalist and worker, male and female, are in a sense secondary to the more fundamental categories—appearing "natural," the result of biological law—of human/subhuman" (Mills 2012, 34). However, although Blacks can be oppressed as indigenous people or workers or women or queer people, their Blackness is the essence of these orientations (Douglass, Terrefe, and Wilderson 2018). Wilderson makes a distinction between contingent and gratuitous violence to show the slaveness of Blacks. Contingent violence is that which is inflicted in proportion to the transgression committed *when* the transgression *has* been committed. It is contingent on the nature of the transgression of established laws within the social order. It is rational because it is inflicted for a reason. There is a rational justification for it. The categories of nonblack oppressed people, accordingly, have the possibility of having what they have lost to Whites returned, such as land or labor or even recognition for the subaltern; what is demanded is the respect for the consent of all such groups. They have an experience of plenitude before the advent of White conquest, a plenitude to which they may return or that they may emulate. Blacks have no such possibility. There was never a plenitude for the Black, the slave (let the reader understand that what is not talked of here is not a place where blacks can return). This is because although slaves existed before Blackness, the blueprint for the creation of Blackness was slavery itself. Blacks, as slaves, cannot lose what they never had—consent, ownership of, and sovereignty over oneself. "Humanity," argue Douglass, Terrefe, and Wilderson, "is made legible through the irreconcilable distinction between humans and Blackness . . . [if] Blackness is seen as a paradigmatic position, rather than an ensemble of cultural, social, and sexual orientations" (Douglass,

Terrefe, and Wilderson 2018). As Wilderson argues, "[Gratuitous] anti-Black violence is an ensemble of necessary rituals that are performed so that the human race can know itself as Human and not as slave, meaning not as Black" (Wilderson 2020a). Humanity's fulfillment of the need to maintain the symbolic order is dependent on the condemnation of the Black, the nonhuman made flesh. As such, Blacks suffer a gratuitous violence that goes beyond the proportion needed for the punishment of a transgression. It is a violence "that produces . . . the antithesis of the Human, and, in so doing, also secures the coherence of what it means to be Human" (Wilderson 2020a). Without anti-Black gratuitous violence, there is no coherent schema in the social order. Acts of gratuitous violence inflicted on Blacks are the rituals that make intelligible what it means to be Human. This gratuitous violence the Black suffers is irrational and disproportionate when meted out for the punishment of a wrong, and it is also meted out when there is no wrong (Sexton 2010a). Wilderson posits that this gratuitous violence is "prelogical" and "conceptually incoherent" (Wilderson 2020a). It is prelogical because it is performed before reason and it is conceptually incoherent because the only thing it can extract is the life of the Black and not a tangible resource like land (as a basis for oppression against indigenous nonblacks) or labor (as a basis for oppression against the nonblack working class). When Blacks die, they have not lost their lives because they were never in possession of it. As Sexton explains, Blacks cannot lose their lives because they suffer from "a never having had—the literal inability to lose (because unable to own, to accumulate, to have and to hold, to self-possess) at all" (Sexton 2010a, 16). As those who suffer from "never-having-had," blacks are required to manage the fear that the "haves" have toward them—Whites' fear of Blackness. It is a fear that is the result of the absolute otherness and nonhumanity to which Blacks have been relegated. Notions prevalent in the White consciousness such as *Die Swart Gevaar* (Afrikaans for "The Black Danger/Peril") and *Nag van die Lang Messe* (Afrikaans for "Night of the Long Knives") speak to this fear. *Die Swart Gevaar* refers to the fear that Blacks, an incomprehensible and lustful horde (symbolizing nonhuman bloodlust), would take over the White world and displace Whites from their rightful place of mastery. The legend of the *Nag van die Lang Messe* in White communities is testament to the fear of White South African society in general that the paradigm of Human versus Black would be turned on its head, and Whites would become the new abject, purged and massacred senselessly by a Black mob in a widescale genocide—most probably by machetes, the weapon of choice for the "African savage"—when Mandela dies. This is the fear of an unimaginable force, pure terror, fear of being Human yet consumed like an animal. Anti-Black racist society, therefore, is preoccupied with managing the anger of Blacks in order to maintain the Human-nonhuman structure. Gratuitous violence against Blacks serves to reinforce this antagonism. The infliction of gratuitous violence on the Black is thus always potentiality until it is actualized. They are culpable before they commit any transgression, hence their very existence is a transgression, so they exist as problems themselves that they have to solve themselves. Although Blacks cannot possess reason, they supposedly do possess "a criminal will, a criminal reasoning, a criminal intent, a criminal rationality: with these erstwhile human capacities construed as indices of culpability before the law" (Sexton 2010a, 15). Thus, the violence and killing is justified before it happens because the Black is the scene of the crime. It is irrelevant that they must have done something to deserve death, as they exist in a state of nonhuman where the notion of desert does not fit. The force against Blacks is then justified before it is inflicted. The skin asks for the blows to hit. It provokes violence. It is a given that the Black—a slave—must yield and obey at all times to state machinery as an implement of White desire. "The forced submission of the slave is absolute," so violence against Blacks leads to sympathy for the maimers and/or killers of Black bodies (Sexton 2010b, 51). Absolute submission begets absolute force and vice versa. "You did what you had to. The circumstances are irrelevant. It was a Black." Obedience to the law for Blacks is irrelevant to their suffering. Obedience does not extinguish or allay the predictability or inevitability of violence. Black suffering is tautology; to be Black is to suffer. Blacks are guilty and are incapable of innocence and so they are outside the realm of vindication or acquittal. Black death is thus always warranted because culpability is part of Blackness itself. Hence proportional punishment is out of the picture. This supposed inherent criminality of Blacks gives an explanation for why the prevalence of media showing the violence meted out against Black bodies in recent years does not elicit sympathy but actually ends up doing the opposite, creating a spectacle out of Black death. This is seen with the bodies of Emmett Till in 1955 and Steve Biko in 1977, bodies mutilated at the hands of Whites and shown in open caskets. These spectacles generate an all-too-familiar ontological outrage and despair within Black communities given how Blacks engage the world through a state of abjection.

The Social Death of Collins Khosa

Due to the spread of the COVID-19 pandemic, the South African government enforced a lockdown from March 27 to April 16, 2020, which prohibited the sale of alcohol, although the consumption of one's own liquor on their own premises was allowed. On the 11th of April, Collins Khosa was drinking alcohol at his home when two government soldiers noticed an alcoholic beverage just outside his home and then entered his home. By the time the soldiers left Khosa was in the last few moments of his life (Mokhoali 2020). His family, who were with him at the time, reveal that soldiers attacked the family with sjamboks and then proceeded to "kick [Khosa] and beat him against the wall" outside and in the street (Mokhoali 2020). He "was later found dead in his bedroom after suffering from internal injuries" (Mokhoali 2020). The soldiers involved were suspended with full pay pending an internal investigation, which eventually exonerated them of any responsibility for Khosa's death despite his grievous injuries at their hands (Zulu 2020). Although the death of Collins Khosa and the gratuitous violence and torture he suffered ignited a level of anger from Blacks across South Africa, it is not surprising. South Africa is an anti-Black society founded on an agreement between the Boer and British colonial settlers to relegate Blacks to the status of nonhuman noncitizens in their own territory. Gratuitous violence against Blacks in such a violence arrangement is not just a part of daily life, it is necessary for the maintenance of the very life of societies such as this where Blacks (corporeal chaos) are the antithesis of Whiteness (rationality and logic). Khosa suffered from the law. The law is a tool to put the Blacks in place. Using the police was not enough, the military was used to come into the townships where Blacks are in their status as criminal nonbeings controlled by impulses and unable to regulate themselves. This understanding is characterized by the Setswana adage "Ba utlwa ka letlalo," which is literally translatable as "they only hear through their skins," meaning that violence is the only language they understand. This is illustrated by the utterances by the South African defense minister Nosiviwe Mapisa-Nqakula that the military's approach would be to "skop, skiet, and donder" (Afrikaans for kick, shoot, and assault) people in townships not abiding by lockdown regulations.

The irony is that this same rhetoric led the apartheid military strategy against Blacks, even those not committing any transgression against the law of the day, and it was to townships and settlements of Black in particular that the military were deployed this time as well. The idea is that the nature of the Blacks is that of predictable chaos, but also that the violence against Blacks will preempt this chaos. Blacks in civil society deserve to be ill-treated by the state because blacks are a societal problem that necessitates law, that necessitates mastership. They are a problem not because they cause problems with how they act or with their demands, "but being a problem in one's very existence" (Sexton 2010a, 13). Under legal apartheid policy, both legal and extralegal acts of state violence were the norm against blacks. They existed not only under the law as the target of a myriad of laws removing them from the public sphere except only as tools for White needs and wants, but they also existed as potential enemies of the state whose rebellion could come into actuality at any point (Sitze 2013, 32). This duality put them at the mercy of violence by state police, the military, as well as White citizens, who were "a race of people with a private army under the command of their fantasies" (Wilderson 2020b, 90). The role of the military as an implement of the state was to reinforce not necessarily the law but Blackness in the Human-nonhuman paradigm. In this light, the question "Who is Collins Khosa?" is the same question as "What is Collins Khosa?" Collins Khosa was not murdered, he was ended. The Black is outside the realm of moral regard.

Blacks suffer gratuitous violence because they are always required to account for their presence. Their presence is in itself a transgression. Questions such as "What are you doing in this White part of town?" become "What are you doing on the street?" to "Why are you not in your house?" Khosa held liquor in his hand before he ever touched it, because he was prelogically culpable before any rational judgment. His torture and killing was the fulfillment of an eventuality. Blacks cannot be law-abiding in any substantial sense as Blackness is a legal problem requiring state violence to be mitigated. As a result, Khosa was not a victim of state violence but rather a target of state violence. Victimhood requires a state of wholeness before deprivation of rights, but blacks cannot be violated where violence is the law (Wilderson 2020b, 89).

Blackness as Absence and the Problem of Ontology

Wilderson interprets Gordon in *The Problematic of Presence*:

> The world cannot accommodate a black(ened) relation at the level of bodies—subjectivity. Thus, Black "presence is a form

of absence" for to see a Black is to see the Black, an ontological frieze that waits for a gaze, rather than a living ontology
moving with agency in the field of vision. The Black's moment
of recognition by the Other is always already "Blackness," upon
which supplements are lavished—American, Caribbean, Xhosa,
Zulu, etc. But the supplements are [not] substantive, they do
not unblacken. (Wilderson 2008, 98, emphasis added)[2]

Wilderson continues:

The inverse is even more devastating to contemplate vis-à-vis
the dim prospects for Blacks in the world. For not only are
Whites "prosthetic Gods," the embodiment of "full presence,"
that is, "when a White is absent something is absent," there
is "a lacuna in being," as one would assume given the status
of Blackness but Whiteness is also "the standpoint from which
others are seen"; which is to say Whiteness is both full Presence
and absolute perspectivity. To look at a Black body is to look at
a mere being-among-beings. . . . [But] the White body, being
human (Presence), doesn't live as a mere-being-among-beings.
It lives with the potential to be a being that stands out from
mere beings. Its being-in-itself ironically enables it to be a
being-for-itself. (Wilderson 2008, 98, emphasis added)

White perspectivity as theory or philosophy constitutes the core of
the modern project of Western philosophy, which provided the justificatory
apparatuses for the domination of the world. The philosophical subject of
modern philosophy is the subject that colonizes and enslaves. It is a being
that has the world as its object of contemplation and manipulation, pro-
ceeding on its way to invisibilize its "other." Discourses on "phenomenology,"
as implied by the name, concern themselves with "what appears and how
it appears from the horizon of the world, the system, Being" (Dussel 1983,
16). Precisely because the oppressed are rendered invisible by the world
and discourses concerning them cannot proceed in the same vein as that
constituted as being by the world, which is why Dussel would advance a
theoretical posture that reveals the underlying nature of the world and the
oppressed: "Epiphany, on the other hand, is the revelation of the oppressed,
the poor never a mere appearance or a mere phenomenon, but always maintaining a metaphysical exteriority. Those who reveal themselves transcend
the system and continually question the given. Epiphany is the beginning

of real liberation" (Dussel 1983, 16). In short, Blackness cannot speak or be spoken of in the language of ontology, precisely because it is a being that is not. Discourses of ontology can only speak and decipher what is—what in effect exists. Blackness on the other hand is not (Marriot 2020).

Our central claim in this chapter has been that Blackness offers an alternative phenomenology to Western phenomenology by giving a point of view from those who do not die but end. We employed the notions of Blackness and Blacks as targets of gratuitous violence to subject European phenomenological logic to a negative critique. We argued that blacks as targets of gratuitous violence experience social death in a way that excludes the denouement of narrative and thus blacks do not die but end, presenting Blackness as a conundrum for Western phenomenology as the experience of life. To furnish our critique, we explored the example of the death/end of Collins Khosa using the school of Afropessimism and suggested that his death was not only inevitable but anticipatory. Our critique expands the logic of Afropessimism in a way that further describes Blackness as a position of *nonbeing* from which one may theorize. To this end, the task of African philosophy and Black philosophy is to map an independent path toward liberatory practices of philosophy by interrogating Blackness not only as a position about which to theorize, but also as a position from which one may theorize.

Notes

1. Later interpretations and further development of the phenomenology tradition would challenge such a view, for example, Merleau-Ponty's *Phenomenology of Perception*.

2. Wilderson demonstrates this by further quoting Gordon thus: "There is 'something' absent whenever Blacks are present. The more present a Black is, the more absent is this 'something.' And the more absent a Black is, the more present is this something." Blackness, then, is the destruction of presence, for Blacks "seem to suck presence into themselves as a Black hole, pretty much like the astrophysical phenomenon that bears that name" (Wilderson, 2008).

References

Curry, Tommy. 2011. "The Derelictical Crisis of African American Philosophy: How African American Philosophy Fails to Contribute Towards the Study of African Descended Peoples." *Radical Philosophy Review* 14, no. 2: 139–164.

Douglass, Patrice, Selamawit Terrefe, and Frank B. Wilderson. 2018. "Afropessimism." In *Oxford Bibliographies*, August 28, 2018. https://www.oxfordbibliographies.com/view/document/obo-9780190280024/obo-9780190280024-0056.xml. Accessed August 18, 2020.

Dussel, Enrique. 1983. *Philosophy of Liberation*. Translated by Aquilina Martinez and Christina Morkovsky. Eugene, OR: Wipf and Stock.

Gordon, Lewis R. 2005. "Through the Zone of Nonbeing: A Reading of *Black Skin, White Masks* in Celebration of Fanon's Eightieth Birthday." *CLR James Journal* 11, no. 1: 1–43.

Gordon, Lewis R. 2010. "Theory in Black: Teleological Suspensions in Philosophy of Culture." *Qui Parle* 18, no. 2: 193–214.

Lee, Emily. 2014. *Living Alterities: Phenomenology, Embodiment, and Race*. Albany: State University of New York Press.

Marriot, David. 2020. "Blackness: N'es Pas?" *Propter Nos* 4: 27–51.

Mbembe, Achille. 2003. "Necropolitics." *Public Culture* 15, no. 1: 11–40.

Mills, Charles. 2007. "White Ignorance." In *Race and Epistemologies of Ignorance*, edited by S. Sullivan and N. Tuana, 13–28. Albany: State University of New York Press.

Mills, Charles. 2012. "Materializing Race." In *Living Alterities: Phenomenology, Embodiment, and Race*, edited by Emily Lee, 19–41. Albany: State University of New York Press.

Mokhoali, Veronica. 2020. "Family Accuse Police of Murdering Man in Alexandra during COVID-19 Lockdown." *Eyewitness News*, April 12, 2020. https://ewn.co.za/2020/04/12/alexandra-family-want-justice-after-man-dies-allegedly-at-hands-of-police. Accessed November 1, 2020.

Olaloku-Teriba, Annie. 2018. "Afropessimism and the (Un)Logic of Anti-Blackness." *Historical Materialism* 26, no. 2: 96–122.

Oyěwùmí, Oyèrónkẹ́. 2002. "Visualising the Body." In *Philosophy from Africa: A Text with Readings*, edited by P. Coetzee and A. P. J. Roux, 319–415. Cape Town: Oxford University Press.

Patterson, Orlando. 1982. *Slavery and Social Death: A Comparative Study*. Cambridge: Harvard University Press.

Ramose, Mogobe. 1999. *African Philosophy through Ubuntu*. Harare: Mond Book.

Robinson, Cedric. 1987. *Black Marxism: The Making of the Black Radical Tradition*. London: ZED Books.

Serequeberhan, Tsenay. 1997. "The Critique of Eurocentrism and the Practice of African Philosophy." In *Postcolonial African Philosophy*, edited by E. Eze, 141–161. Cambridge: Blackwell.

Sexton, Jared. 2010a. "The Curtain of the Sky: An Introduction." *Critical Sociology* 36, no. 1: 11–24.

Sexton, Jared. 2010b. "People of Color Blindness: Notes on the Afterlife of Slavery." *Social Text* 28, no. 2: 31–56.

Sitze, Adam. 2013. *The Impossible Machine: A Genealogy of South Africa's Truth and Reconciliation Commission*. Ann Arbor: University of Michigan Press.

Veroli, Nicolas. 2001. *Imagination and Politics: A Study in Historical Ontology*. Binghamton, NY: Binghamton University.

White, Hayden. 1973. *Metahistory: The Historical Imagination in Nineteenth-Century Europe*. Baltimore: Johns Hopkins University Press.

Wilderson, Frank B. 2008. "Biko and the Problematic of Presence." In *Biko Lives: Contesting the Legacy of Steve Biko*, edited by A. Mngxitama, A. Alexander, and N. Gibson, 95–114. London: Palgrave Macmillan.

Wilderson, Frank B. 2016. "Afropessimism and the End of Redemption." Frank Humanities Institute, March 30, 2016. https://humanitiesfutures.org/papers/afro-pessimism-end-redemption. Accessed November 1, 2020.

Wilderson, Frank B. 2020a. "Afropessimism and the Rituals of Anti-Black Violence." *Mail and Guardian*, June 24, 2020. https://mg.co.za/article/2020-06-24-frank-b-wilderson-afro-pessimism-memoir-structural-violence. Accessed July 16, 2020.

Wilderson, Frank B. 2020b. *Afropessimism*. New York: Liveright.

Wood, Allen. 2001. *Basic Writings of Kant*. New York: Modern Library.

Zulu, Sifiso. 2020. "SANDF Inquiry into Collins Khosa's Death Contradicts Recent Court Ruling." *Eyewitness News*, May 28, 2020. https://ewn.co.za/2020/05/28/sandf-inquiry-into-collins-khosa-s-death-contradicts-recent-court-ruling. Accessed May 1, 2021.

9

Merleau-Ponty, Embodied Subjectivity, and (White) Women Dancing

Rianna Oelofsen

Introduction

As a white South African woman, my contribution to a collection on African phenomenology should be called into question. In terms of situating my chapter, I would argue that, due to the role that "white supremacy" plays in Africa, an analysis of the phenomenon is relevant. Thus, this contribution adds an investigation of the embodiment of white womanhood. I investigate white womanhood as a way of *being-in-the-world*, which is at once a result of, and supports, the structures of white supremacy. This analysis is gained through the lens of seeing ourselves as embodied subjects à la Maurice Merleau-Ponty, which is to realize that we should treat our bodies as part and parcel of our subjectivity. I argue that as white women, a particular comportment and spatiality is prescribed in terms of "feminine whiteliness" and prescriptions under patriarchy to avoid gender-based violence. This prescription in comportment and spatiality both supports and is perpetuated by white supremacy and patriarchy.

From the interrogation of the example of dancing, I argue that "white womanness" can be understood as inhabiting the world in a whitely feminine way, which assumes "white feminine" values and priorities. I argue that the construction of the subjectivity of "white womanness" relies on social structures and a whitely discourse of structural gestures in a society that systematically deny and undermine the recognition of the black "other" as equal. This means that "whiteliness" (white supremacy) can be (and is) present even where individual agents do not have the conscious intentions to harm, or diminish, the "other."

Embodied Subjectivity, Habituation, and Culture

As embodied subjects, our actions, body language, and gestures are an important part of our subjectivity. This has the implication that culture plays a significant part in the formation of our subjectivity, as culture is partially conveyed through specific body language. I will argue that body language is *an expression of intentionality that manifests through our bodies.* I am using the term intentionality to mean *both* in the phenomenological and the teleological senses. In terms of the phenomenological meaning, the fact that my intentionality is about the gestures of others means that the meaning of these gestures are incorporated into my own gestures (or intentions in the teleological sense). This means that if gestures of someone with particular intentions are copied (which is how children learn) and then internalized, the intentions and worldsense[1] of that person is (at least partially) adopted as well, even if not on a conscious level. Habitual gestures are copied and adopted from people within one's social group through our experience of these habitual gestures in terms of *intentionality* in the phenomenological sense, and it is this fact that makes us more comfortable with that group than with another group with gestures that are foreign to us.

Maurice Merleau-Ponty understands habit to be a type of "sedimentation of action" that is grounded in our physical intelligence to become prereflective when we are not attending to the action. In *Phenomenology of Perception*, he explains the concept of embodied subjectivity and its relationship to habituation through the example of an organ player who has to do a performance on a new organ (Merleau-Ponty 2002, 168). Organs can be very diverse in their constitution and makeup, and the organ player needs some time to adjust to his new instrument. He does this not through studying the organ and making mental notes of the differences. Instead, he sits down and "tinkers" with the new instrument. He lets his body adjust to the differences; it is his *body* that needs to get to *know* the new instrument.

Thus, part of what it means to be embodied subjects is to realize that we should treat our bodies as part of our subjectivity. Since we are embodied subjects, our body language and gestures are an important part of our subjectivity, and it partly constitutes our identity and determines our stance and reactions to the world. Cultural identity, for example, is constituted by the practices of a culture, and this includes a specific body language and discourse of gestures. The body is (*body-*)subject and therefore has overall intentions (which might be conscious or not). In the case of habitual action, our bodies act in accordance with our overall intentions, but without our conscious control. Gestures are not mere *representations* of intentions (in the teleological sense), but an *expression of* intentionality (in the phenomenological sense—the meaning of phenomena being included in our experience of these phenomena) through our bodies. In other words, as embodied subjects, intentions find expression through our bodies, even if these intentions are not necessarily clear to ourselves intellectually. This means that if the gestures of someone with certain intentions are internalized by others (through the meaning of these gestures internalized through intentionality in the phenomenological sense), then the intentions and worldsense of that person is adopted as well, even if it is not on a conscious level.

Merleau-Ponty's work on child psychology could be useful in order to explain why gestures might be important in the formation of our cultural and individual identities. The forming of subjectivity is for Merleau-Ponty a kind of habituation, and the gestures that are imitated by the child during early years have a profound impact on her subjectivity and intentions. As opposed to an intellectualistic understanding of how the child learns, Merleau-Ponty argues that "in imitating others, in learning to walk, in becoming familiar with an environment, what occurs cannot be explained by the notion that there is first an intellectual act of 'knowing' rules, maps or words and then to move to use them" (Cobb [translator's note], Merleau-Ponty 1964, 96).

The point is that our intentions and subjectivity are formed, through and in the body, in relation and as a reaction to our human and nonhuman environment. Merleau-Ponty claims that our "functions of cognition" such as our intelligence, perception, and imagination are actually all the function of "activity that is prior to cognition properly so called, a function of organizing experiences that imposes on certain totalities the configuration and the kind of equilibrium that are possible under the *corporeal and social conditions* of the child himself" (Merleau-Ponty 1964, 99, italics mine).

This means that we relate to the gestures (of ourselves and others) *not on an intellectual* but on an embodied level. The relations we have with others are central to the formation of our subjectivity. Our subjectivity is limited to a number of possibilities by the environment we live in, and therefore, even though the environment does not determine our intentions, it can (and does) severely limit them. Habituation into a particular set of cultural gestures shows how it is possible that prejudice and "judgment" in the form of being closed to the humanity of the "other" can be pre-reflective, as we inhabit a social space with bodies that are prejudiced in certain ways. So, if we inhabit a social space with people who are closed to the humanity of others, this influences us to also be closed to this difference. Our ability to be open to and accepting of different others is undermined through such early habituation.

This points to the importance of historical and cross-cultural studies to highlight the use of the labels of "normal" and "abnormal" and as such allows us to foster a healthy skepticism about our own use of such labels since they are, as Martha Nussbaum claims, "often just ways of wrapping the deeply habitual into mantels of sanctity" (Nussbaum 1999, 16). The normalization process has a strong influence on what we are willing and able to do.

This can be related fruitfully, I believe, to discussions of "whiteliness."[2] Whiteliness can be understood as having gained one's subjectivity through copying body language that represent inhabiting the world in a whitely way, which assumes certain "white" values and priorities. This means that "whiteliness" can be present even where individual agents do not have conscious intentions to harm or diminish the "other." Whiteliness relies on social structures and a whitely discourse of gestures in a society that systematically deny and undermine the recognition of the black "other" as equal.

An Example of Embodied Subjectivity, Habituation, and Culture: Perception

I make the claim in the previous section that cultural identity is constituted by the practices of a culture, and this includes a specific body language and discourse of gestures. This claim is supported by Merleau-Ponty's work on child psychology, as he argues that the gestures that are imitated by the child during early years have a profound impact on her subjectivity and intentions.

But, how much can our culture really influence our subjectivity? In order to answer this question, I will reflect on the senses, and the central role they play in our acquisition of knowledge—having no senses necessarily means that I can have no knowledge. But, you might argue, this is perfectly clear and does not prove anything about our subjectivity being deeply culturally constituted—after all, we (mostly) all have the same five senses, which means that we can with relative certainty say that we perceive things in a similar manner. What it is like to be a person of another culture is not the same kind of problem we might encounter as when we ask what it is like to be a bat.[3]

However, here we should pause and take into account Oyèrónké Oyêwùmí's claim that Western cultures' view of the world is just that: a view, it is sight oriented. This is related to what Oyêwùmí calls the "world-sense" of different cultures, as opposed to a "worldview" that is specifically Western. Oyêwùmí goes further and states that this Western conception of the "universality of the emphasis on sight" is not questioned when confronted with African systems of thought because Western ideology has been deeply ingrained into African studies in systems of knowledge production (Oyêwùmí 1997). In line with this claim, Kathryn Geurts argues that "in the west, we often treat the domain of sensation and perception as definitively precultural and eminently natural, one of the most basic of the human psychobiological systems. That is the approach in fields of neurology, biology, physiology, psychology, and even philosophy" (Geurts 2002, 3).

However, as Geurts argues, there are problems with this assumption. In the West, most people would say there are five senses, and perhaps a "sixth sense." However, we do not have five senses. This belief turns out to be Western folk ideology and is not based on science as most Westerners (read culturally whitely people) would assume.[4] The sense of balance, for example, is treated as a "sense" in biology textbooks, and even has a corresponding "organ" (the vestibular organ). The sense of balance is the most easily recognized sense outside of the usual repertoire of five taught to (Western, whitely, but also colonized) children in preschool. How we perceive the world, it turns out, is in fact very culturally determined if we do not value a sense enough to include it in our folk psychology, this is an indication that our culture does not value it as highly as the others.

In comparison to Western culture, Geurts's study of the Anlo-Ewe-speaking people in Ghana provides her with evidence to argue for what could be categorized as another sense, namely, *seselelame* (an Anlo-Ewe term that can be translated roughly as *feel-feel-at-flesh-inside*), which reveals "close links among sensation, perception, emotion, cognition, and so forth" (Geurts 2002, 43): "Seselelame can be described as 'feeling in the body' and is often used to capture the way many west Africans fore-ground bodily feeling as a vital source of information about environment, self-making, and moral knowing. As a local iteration of a broad African foundational schema, seselelame spawns a fusion rather than atomization of the senses, an integration rather than splitting of mind–body communi-cation" (Geurts and Komabu-Pomeyie 2016). Other Anlo-Ewe "phenomena such as 'hearing in the skin' or 'hearing odor' [Geurts claims] were not merely problems of language and translation but suggested a difference in embodied experience or aspects of a different *being-in-the-world* (to use Merleau-Ponty's phrase)" (Geurts 2002, 49).[5] In addition to these different explanations of lived experience, several of Geurts's "cultural guides" also insisted that "morality" was a sense, and one that "Anlo-Ewe people hold dear.[6] One of the reasons [the Anlo-Ewe claimed] . . . that morality had sensorial qualities was . . . a close association between kinaesthetic sen-sations (. . . one's movement) and dispositional feelings (. . . one's moral character)" (Geurts 2002, 75).

With regard to this claim, Geurts gives evidence from her engage-ment with the Anlo-Ewe people, that, for example, balance is an extremely important sense in this culture and forms a core metaphor for their understanding of the world. "For instance, [Geurts] often heard caregivers say to infants, '*Do agba! do agba!*' which was an imperative statement encouraging babies to "Balance! Balance!" . . . Anlo-ewe people considered balancing (in a physical and a psychological sense, as well as in literal and metaphorical ways) to be an essential component of what it meant to be human" (Geurts 2002, 4). More examples with regard to balance and its importance for morality can be found in other cultures, past and present. For example, balance was at the center of morality for the Nahua of Central America.[7] The central understanding of morality for the Nahua is one of "balancing on the slippery earth."

This is not to say that in white(ly) culture we do not have some metaphors with regard to balance, and that it is not important at all in Western culture. However, the pervasiveness of the concept in Anlo-Ewe (and other) language(s), metaphor, and understanding is striking. So, it would seem that there is evidence that bodily ways of knowing in other cultures can be said to be quite different from bodily ways of knowing in Western whitely culture.

The claim of embodied subjectivity posits that we relate to the gestures of others not on an intellectual, but on an embodied level. Therefore, the relations we have with others as we are habituated into particular embodied ways of being are central to the formation of our subjectivity. We could even, at this point, make a connection between this understanding of the body-subject and the thought in African philosophy: "I am a person because of other people."[8] Not only is it possible to draw a parallel as to what this claim of cultural constitution of subjectivity could mean, but the "African subjectivity" that such a claim sometimes refers to could be given a concrete, yet nonessentialist foundation in culture.[9] In other words, the understanding of our subjectivity being culturally constituted could account for a radically different kind of subjectivity without appeal to any essential features of the "African."[10]

In order to make clear the extent to which our own perceptions are culturally constructed, a comparison with a culture that perceives the world in very different (yet, still not mutually exclusive to my, whitely womanly cultural) ways proves helpful. So, with the idea in mind that our perceptions are culturally determined, are there ways we can say whitely women perceive the world? Is there a "white womanly" way of *being-in-the-world*? And if so, how is this embodied?

White Supremacy and the Embodied Subjectivity of Whitely Women

I understand the term "white supremacy" from critical race theory (CRT) as the political and socioeconomic configuration in which white people have a structural advantage over other groups, both on a collective and individual level. So, "white supremacy is conceived as a comprehensive condition whereby the interests and perceptions of white subjects are continually placed centre stage and assumed as 'normal'" (Gillborn 2006, 318). In terms of this claim, it is possible to understand white supremacy as a particular culture. Culture is a notoriously difficult concept to pin down (Spencer-Oatey 2012), but the definition I work with is the "shared set of (implicit and explicit) values, ideas, concepts, and rules of behaviour that allow a social group to function and perpetuate itself" (Hudelson 2004).

Elsewhere I have argued that there is the need for a "decolonization of the mind" (Oelofsen 2015). Here I want to argue that, seeing as we are embodied subjects, the decolonization of the mind (of both black and white) cannot occur without the decolonization of the body as body-subject. Decolonization can be understood as one way to undermine white supremacy, and the colonized body-subject perpetuates the values of white supremacy through body language and gestures. The decolonization of the body-subject therefore requires a change in *being-in-the-world* and not merely an intellectual, cerebral commitment. Gestures are *an expression of intentionality that manifests through our bodies*, and so, as an expression of intentionality (in the phenomenological sense that our experiences are about particular phenomena, and importantly, that these phenomena carry particular meanings), a particular body language is part of a culture. We learn a culture through observing and copying the body language and gestures of others, as much as their language and actions. Remind yourself of the organ player Merleau-Ponty uses to explain how the body is part of our subjectivity. In the same way, in any new situation, we draw on our previous (body)knowledge with regard to how to react. So, if you are exposed to, and habituated into, the gestures and body language of white supremacist culture, you are expressing the intentionality of the valuation of white lives above others. While you are not exposed to all the different situations in which white supremacy can be instantiated during your habituation, you adapt and tinker with new situations in order to apply your (body)knowledge of the normalization of centering white interests and "perceptions."[11]

In the case of a culture, there are particular preferred interests and perceptions, and it is my contention that these preferred interests and perceptions are cemented through exposure to a particular value system and environment. In order then to change and broaden our interests and perceptions as white people, we need our *bodies* to get to know how to react within different value systems and environments so as to undermine, instead of perpetuate, the habituation of white supremacist culture.

"Color-blind" white feminism is a global phenomenon, which manifests itself in ignorance of black women's particular experience of patriarchy as a result of also being subjected to white supremacy. This phenomenon is apparent in a Hulu series entitled *The Handmaid's Tale* (Miller 2017), based on the novel of the same title by Margaret Atwood (Atwood 1985). This series in its depiction of patriarchal oppression of women in a postdemocratic society ignores the links in ideology between white supremacy and patriarchy. In the series, all women and men of different races are treated as either equally privileged or oppressed in terms of their gender and sexuality—that race is a category of oppression is ignored. The question is whether, with the fiction starting in the present day, and envisaging a different future from there, it is possible to imagine a future in which race does not play a hierarchical oppressive role. The claim that it is even possible to imagine such a future (at least without an explanation of how white supremacy was defeated), when extrapolating from the present, is a result of white feminism that ignores the particular oppressions of black women.

Kimberlé Crenshaw, in her theory of intersectionality (2016), sets out the way in which the experiences of oppression of black women differ from those of white women. Intersectionality should not be understood as the addition of different oppressions, but rather as the way in which the combination of different oppressions fundamentally changes the experience of the relevant person from the experience of the person who is subject to only one type of oppression. This can be understood with the illustration that each oppression is visualized as a particular color of light. When you overlap the green (say, patriarchy) and red light (say white supremacy), you end up with a completely different color, namely yellow.[12]

In order to illustrate how intersectionality operates in terms of the *being-in-the-world* of white and black women, I will draw on the example of how, stereotypically, white and black people dance.[13] Iris Marion Young, in her article "Throwing Like a Girl," did not analyze "structured body movement which does not have a particular aim—for example, dancing" (Young 1980, 140). Her reasons for this include her confidence that "it is the ordinary purposive orientation of the body as a whole toward things and its environment which initially defines the relation of a subject to its world" (Young 1980, 140). This assumption, however, is in itself a whitely assumption, which presupposes that actions with aims of "getting things done" (as the Protestant work ethic prescribes) are inherently more valuable, and thus form subjectivity in deeper or more essential ways than other forms of "nonpurposive" movement such as dancing. As opposed to seeing it as "nonpurposive," dancing can be understood as a form of communication—a type of language (Tortora 2005). The human being's response to music through dancing, research has shown,[14] is a universal response by all infants.[15] As such, perhaps the analysis of how (in general) different cultures move according to rhythmic music could tell us something central about their subjectivity, and could be as important as the "purposive" actions Young pays attention to.[16]

Stereotypical whitely dancing[17] entails being unable to "let go," overthinking, and overintellectualizing. This is a reflection of the way in which the body in general is devalued in Western culture, and the mind is valued. Simply being in, sensing, and experiencing the body and "letting go" means letting go of the "mind," which culturally we have been habituated to value more.

But apart from this, if we understand dancing as a language that white people are not fluent in, perhaps we can postulate that dancing emphasizes the (unrecognized and underemphasized) senses of *seselelame* and balance. In terms of *seselelame*, is there perhaps a way in which rhythm can be perceived through a "feel-feel-of-the-flesh-inside"? Can the communication between people through dance be understood as a "feeling in the body"? Is *seselelame* not recognized in whitely culture as a result of the mistrust and devaluation of the body in whitely culture? In terms of the sense of balance, which is crucial for dancing, perhaps whitely people do not have a predilection for dancing as balance is not emphasized and deemed as central in whitely culture.

While dancing and how you dance is not necessarily under your conscious control, precisely because of the fact that if you concentrate on your dancing body your motility and spatiality is affected,[18] this does not negate the importance of the meaning of how we dance. This can be seen as parallel with the phenomenon of "white tears," which is also an involuntary bodily reaction and not under our conscious control.[19] Just like in the instance of white tears though, the fact that how we dance is involuntary does not detract from its meaning.

This example is meant to show how the seemingly innocuous comportment and spatiality of whitely dancing can support and perpetuate the culture of white supremacy. To show how this seemingly innocuous example plays itself out in terms of black women's oppression, I next analyze how the stereotypes associated with white and black women dancing play itself out in the area of gender-based violence (GBV).

All women are under attack in South Africa, with high rates of rape, femicide, intimate partner violence, and so forth.[20] However, in accordance with intersectionality, in our shared experience of our oppression as women subjected to gender-based violence (GBV), white women have an advantage. White women, in general, as a result of white privilege, have more resources in order to face GBV. In accordance with both white privilege and the patriarchal ideology of white feminine purity, white women stand a better chance to have their reports of GBV taken seriously and believed.

This is in line with Miranda Fricker's epistemic testimonial injustice (2007).

The stereotypical *perceived* fragility and purity of white women (as opposed to black women, who are perceived to be tough and overly sexual[21]) means that they are also perceived to be valuable and thus in need of protection.[22] This perception of the white woman as fragile and pure is supported through whitely dancing, as whitely dancing enacts such a body that is not in touch with their bodies, and thus sexuality.

In South Africa, the perceived purity and chastity of white women is also linked to white supremacy in accordance with the apartheid narrative in South Africa of the *swart gevaar*.[23] According to this narrative, GBV is again conceived as the white woman being fragile and pure—having to be protected against the perceived "savage black man."[24] The white man is not seen as the face of a perpetrator in actions of GBV. As Pumla Gqola, argues, black women are *perceived* as "unrapeable" (Gqola 2007). "Unrapeability" is a result of the perception of black women as objects, mere possessions (as in slavery), impure, and exclusively sexual. Objects do not have agency, and as such black women are understood as not being the kinds of creatures to which consent applies. Black women being perceived as "unrapeable," while white women are perceived as pure and chaste, influences the testimony of black women in obvious ways. Through the very action of not being able to dance (well), the white woman expresses her difference from black women who are stereotypically understood as overly sexual. Not being able to dance (well) means that the whitely woman plays into the stereotype of white women as pure, due to perceived links between dancing and sex.

Conclusion

White women need to be cognizant that the way in which we experience the world is deeply constituted by our whiteliness.[25] This chapter was an analysis that points out a particular way in which white women support and perpetuate white supremacy and patriarchy, through an innocuous activity such as whitely dancing. As whitely women, we are in a double bind with regard to dancing—you cannot pay attention to dancing in order to overcome whitely dancing, since paying attention and not being able to "let go" through experiencing the music through your body is exactly what whitely dancing entails. To work against the structures of white supremacy and patriarchy, which support our dancing and culture, will not have anything to do with focusing on the way we dance. While dancing whitely supports and perpetuates stereotypes that support and perpetuate white supremacy and GBV, tackling the structural underpinnings of white supremacy and patriarchy needs to be central—and perhaps dancing could one day be a gauge of whether whitely culture has reached its demise. This example of dancing whitely, and how it can support white supremacy unconsciously, shows that white supremacy can be (and is) present even where individual agents do not have the conscious intentions to harm or diminish the "other." If we see morality as a sense related to comportment, then the way in which we move and the way in which we move with others can take on a moral meaning.

Notes

1. I use "worldsense" as opposed to worldview, following the work of Oyeronke Oyewumi. This will be explained in more detail later in the chapter.

2. See Marilyn Frye (2001) for an account of "whiteliness." Frye writes: "Being whiteskinned (like being male) is a matter of physical traits presumed to be physically determined; being whitely (like being masculine) I conceive as a deeply ingrained way of being in the world. Following the analogy with masculinity, I assume that the connection between whiteliness and light-colored skin is a contingent connection: this character could be manifested by persons who are not 'white'; it can be absent in persons who are" (Frye 2001, 87).

3. Reference to Thomas Nagel's famous paper "What Is It Like to Be a Bat?"

4. "Despite the belief of many Euro-Americans, the five senses model is not a scientific fact, and the enumeration of the senses has been a subject of debate among scholars and philosophers for many centuries. . . . The reduction of the sensorium into five senses was first determined by Aristotle, perhaps for neat numerological reasons rather than physiological ones; but Galen said there were six, Erasmus Darwin thought there were twelve, and Frey reduced them down to eight. From Aristotle to Aquinas to Descartes, however, cultural traditions have sustained a five-senses model that privileges mental representations and external modes of knowing. This construct, I argue, is essentially a folk ideology" (Geurts 2002, 7).

5. It is interesting to note that in the West, phenomena such a "hearing in the skin" or "hearing odor" is known and classified as synesthesia. While people with synesthesia are not viewed as deficient, they are perceived as "abnormal" in Western culture. (This is in contrast to synesthetic experience of the integration of the modalities being central to what Merleau-Ponty calls normal experience.) It is therefore possible to find evidence for different *being-in-the-world* from one

with five specific senses not only when making cross-cultural comparisons but also when looking at particular Western people.

6. Guerts refers to them as *mofialawo*, an Anlo-ewe term (more traditionally known in ethnography), which the informers also used to refer to themselves.

7. Maffie ("Aztec Philosophy").

8. I am referring here to the long tradition of Afro-communitarianism, such as for example John Mbiti's claim: "I am because we are, and because we are therefore I am" (Mbiti 1990 [1969], 41).

9. Accordingly, one might then argue that some of the insights of the Negritude movement do, in fact, hold true, but not in the "essentialist" manner in which Negritude has historically been interpreted. See Diagne (2010) for an argument that Negritude should not be interpreted in a manner that essentializes blackness.

10. I only sketch the possibility of this link here in the broadest terms. The link could be explicated in much more detail and with more attention to the subtleties in Afro-communitarian personhood. Space constraints however do not allow for this here, and I hope to turn my attention to this in future research.

11. Note the ambiguous use of "perceptions" here—it refers to both perceptions as perspectives but also perceptions as the senses.

12. See the pictorial illustration of this understanding of intersectionality in Kang et al. (2017).

13. To clarify, I recognize that the question of who can and cannot dance is not only a question of bodily movement but also involves times, place, custom, and subcultures. As a result, it is possible that someone who is deemed to not be good at dancing in one context is in fact a very good dancer in another context. In terms of the current project, I am specifically speaking about the context of present-day South Africa and what constitutes "good" and "bad" dancing in mainstream culture.

14. See Zentner and Eerola (2010). The findings, based on the study of infants aged between five months and two years old, suggest that babies may be born with a predisposition to move rhythmically in response to music.

15. How does the fact that something is a predisposition make it important for our subjectivity. Our predispositions are shaped by culture as we grow up. Either there is a focus on music and dance in the culture, or there is not.

16. None of what I am saying here is meant to be essentialist, but rather it is meant to capture cultural ways of existing in the world. What I am doing here is trying to expose and address the *culture* of "whiteliness."

17. While it may not be true that white people can't dance, there is the definite perception (and reproduction of the stereotype in popular culture) that they cannot. See Tsai (2018) who investigates the dancing body as gendered and racial ideology in American popular culture. This perception perpetuates white supremacy—it shows how white people differentiate themselves from black people, even if the intentions are not conscious or voluntary (as they were created by culture).

18. Young (1980) argues that women's motility and spatiality is affected in this way as a result of perceiving themselves as objects as opposed to subjects in the midst of an action. In the same way, concentrating on the dancing body as object will interrupt the "flow" of the dancing. Try taking a "normal step" when you concentrate on it, and you will find that your attention on the action interferes with the way in which the action is executed.

19. See Accapadi (2007) for an analysis of the phenomenon of white tears. In essence, white tears occur when white women cry as a response to being called out on being racist in some way, or, as a response to hearing about black people's experiences of oppression. The response of crying might be involuntary, but it has the result that instead of the black experience of oppression being the central issue in the situation, the white woman's feelings and experience is centralized.

20. See Gqola (2015) for an analysis of rape in South Africa.

21. This perception of white and black women as different in terms of these categories is treated in detail in hooks (1981).

22. This protection perpetuates patriarchy, in the way that women are expected to trade independence for protection by the very group who oppresses them. However, it does make the experience of white women different from that of black women.

23. An Afrikaans term literally translated as "black danger." The term was a political slogan introduced in the South African elections of 1929 and refers to the threat that white people would be overrun by black people in the country. It has come to mean a general fear that white people as a group will be annihilated by black people. See *Dictionary of South African English* (DSAE) online. See also Steve Biko's discussion of this concept in "Black Consciousness and the Quest for a True Humanity" (2004 [1978]).

24. An example of the inability of the public to see white men as capable of GBV was the Oscar Pistorius saga (Langa et al. 2018), during which many white women joined "we stand with Oscar" groups. Note that in this situation, the reason Pistorius gave for shooting was that he thought his partner, Reeva Steenkamp, was an intruder in the house. This narrative in his defense plays into the *swart gevaar* narrative of the "savage black man."

25. See Vice (2010).

References

Accapadi, Mamta Motwani. 2007. "When White Women Cry: How White Women's Tears Oppress Women of Color." *College Student Affairs Journal* 26, no. 2: 208–215.

Atwood, Margaret. 1985. *The Handmaid's Tale*. Toronto: McClelland & Stewart.

Biko, Steve. 2004 [1978]. "Black Consciousness and the Quest for True Humanity." In *I Write What I Like*, edited by A. Stubbs, 96–108. Johannesburg: Picador.

Biko, Steve. 2004 [1978]. "Fragmentation of the Black Resistance." In *I Write What I Like*, edited by A. Stubbs, 36–43. Johannesburg: Picador.

Crenshaw, Kimberlé. 1989. "Demarginalizing the Intersection of Race and Sex: A Black Feminist Critique of Antidiscrimination Doctrine, Feminist Theory and Antiracist Politics." *University of Chicago Legal Forum* 1, article 8.

Crenshaw, Kimberlé. 2016. *On Intersectionality: Essential Writings*. New York: New Press.

Diagne, Souleymane Bachir. 2010. "In Praise of the Post-racial: Negritude beyond Negritude." *Third Text* 24, no. 2, *Beyond Negritude: Senghor's Vision for Africa*: 241–248.

Fricker, Miranda. 2007. *Epistemic Injustice: Power and the Ethics of Knowing*. New York: Oxford University Press, 2007.

Frye, Marilyn. 2001. "White Woman Feminist 1983–1992." In *Race and Racism*, edited by B. Boxhill, 83–100. New York: Oxford University Press.

Gillborn, David. 2006. "Rethinking White Supremacy: Who Counts in 'White-World.' " *Ethnicities* 6, no. 3: 318–340.

Gqola, Pumla Dineo. 2007. "How the 'Cult of Femininity' and Violent Masculinities Support Endemic Gender-Based Violence in Contemporary South Africa." *African Identities* 5, no. 1: 111–124.

Gqola, Pumla Dineo. 2015. *Rape: A South African Nightmare*. Johannesburg: Jacana Press.

Geurts, Kathryn. 2002. *Culture and the Senses: Bodily Ways of Knowing in an African Community*. Berkeley: University of California Press.

Geurts, Kathryn, and Sefakor Komabu-Pomeyie. 2016. "From Sensing Disability to Seselelame: Nondualistic Activist Orientations in Twenty-First-Century Accra." In *Disability in the Global South: The Critical Handbook*, edited by Shaun Grech and Karen Soldatic, 85–98. New York: Springer.

Hudelson, Patricia M. 2004. "Culture and Quality: An Anthropological Perspective." *International Journal for Quality in Health Care* 16, no. 5: 345–346.

Hooks, bell. 1981. *Ain't I a Woman: Black Women and Feminism*. Brooklyn, NY: South End Press.

Israel, Shayna. 2007. *Why, I Say, White People Can't Dance*. https://serendipstudio.org/exchange/white-people-cant-dance. Accessed March 26, 2021.

Kang, Miliann, Donovan Lessard, Laura Heston, and Sonny Nordmarken. 2017. *Introduction to Women, Gender, Sexuality Studies*. Amherst: University of Massachusetts Amherst Libraries.

Langa, Malose, Adele Kirsten, Brett Bowman, Gill Eagle, and Peace Kiguwa. 2018. "Black Masculinities on Trial in Absentia: The Case of Oscar Pistorius in South Africa." *Menand Masculinities* 23, nos. 3–4: 499–515.

Liebow, Nabina, and Trip Glazer. 2019. "White Tears: Emotion Regulation and White Fragility." *Inquiry: An Interdisciplinary Journal of Philosophy* 66, no. 1: 122–142.

Maffie, James. "Aztec Philosophy." *Internet Encyclopedia of Philosophy*. http://www.iep.utm.edu/aztec/.

Matthews, Sally. 2011. "Becoming African: Debating Post-Apartheid White South African Identities." *African Identities* 9, no. 1: 1–17.

Mbiti, John S. 1990 [1969]. *African Religions and Philosophy*. African Writers Series. Portsmouth, NH: Heinemann.

Merleau-Ponty, Maurice. 1964. "An Unpublished Text by Maurice Merleau-Ponty: A Prospectus of His Work," translated by Arleen B. Dallery. In *The Primacy of Perception*, edited by James M. Edie, 3–11. Evanston, IL: Northwestern University Press.

Merleau-Ponty, Maurice. 2002. *Phenomenology of Perception*. Translated by Colin Smith. New York: Routledge.

Miller, Bruce, producer. 2017. *The Handmaid's Tale* (television broadcast). Hulu.

Nagel, Thomas. 1974. "What Is It Like To Be a Bat?" *Philosophical Review* 83 (October): 435–450.

Oelofsen, Rianna. 2015. "Decolonisation of the African Mind and Intellectual Landscape." *Phronimon* 16, no. 2: 130–146.

Nussbaum, Martha. 1999. *Sex and Social Justice*. Oxford: Oxford University Press.

Oyěwùmí, Oyèrónké. 1997. *The Invention of Women: Making an African Sense of Western Gender Discourses*. Minneapolis: University of Minnesota Press.

Spencer-Oatey, Helen. 2012. *What Is Culture? A Compilation of Quotations*. GlobalPAD Core Concepts. GlobalPAD Open House. https://warwick.ac.uk/fac/soc/al/globalpad-rip/openouse/interculturalskills_old/core-concept_compilations/global_pad_-_what_is_culture.pdf. Accessed January 23, 2023.

"Swart gevaar." 2022. *Dictionary of South African English*. https://dsae.co.za/entry/swart-gevaar/e07026.

Tortora, Suzi. 2005. *The Dancing Dialogue: Using the Communicative Power of Movement with Young Children*. St. Paul, MN: Redleaf Press.

Tsai, Addie. 2018. "(Straight) White Men Can't Dance: The Dancing Body as Racial and Gendered Ideology in American Popular Culture from 1980 to 2018." PhD dissertation, Texas Woman's University. Available at https://twu-ir.tdl.org/handle/11274/10750.

Verkuyten, Maykel, Jochem Thijs, and Hidde Bekhuis. 2010. "Intergroup Contact and Ingroup Reappraisal: Examining the Deprovincialization Thesis." *Social Psychology Quarterly* 73, no. 4: 398–416.

Vice, Samantha. 2010. "How Do I Live in This Strange Place?" *Journal of Social Philosophy* 41, no. 3 (Fall): 323–342.

Young, Iris Marion. 1980. "Throwing Like a Girl: A Phenomenology of Feminine Body Comportment Motility and Spatiality." *Human Studies* 3, no. 1: 137–156.

Zentner, Marcel, and Tuomas Eerola. 2010. "Rhythmic Engagement with Music in Infancy." *Proceedings of the National Academy of Sciences* 107, no. 13: 5768–5773.

10

The Experience of Community and the Meaningful Life

ADA AGADA

Introduction

In this chapter, I will discuss the traditional African conception of community and relate the experience of community with the idea of a meaningful life, with the ultimate goal of showing that a communal approach to human life helps combat pessimism. The pessimism, I will argue, arises from the knowledge of the fact of evil in the world, the certainty of death, uncertainty about the existence of an omniscient and omnipotent God, and the destabilizing impact these factors have on any illusion of coherence in the structure of a typical human life. The chapter is divided into three sections. The first section explores Afro-communitarianism. The second section teases out an African communitarian conception of a meaningful life in terms of fellowship and solidarity and critiques it against the backdrop of pessimism that is rooted in the reality of evil in the world as well as the human mind's inability to discern a clear purpose of human existence. The third section highlights the value of the communal experience through the exploration of the idea of the human being as a consolation-seeking entity in relation to Sartre's (1966) notion of the human being as a mere passion haunted by the spirit of seriousness.

On Afro-communitarianism

Communitarianism is a social theory of the relationship existing between the individual and larger groups that constitute a community of persons. It is often contrasted with individualism, the sociopolitical perspective dominant in today's liberal-capitalist Western society. Individualism upholds the notion of the individual as a rational, autonomous being with inalienable rights (Miller et al. 2016, 181). In the West, communitarianism is barely distinguishable from individualism; here, the main surviving communal features include dissemination of egalitarian ideals by governments, affirmation of the economic merit of immigration and multiculturalism, and a general recommendation of greater social inclusivity in the midst of ubiquitous narrow interest groups engaged in group struggles for relevance in a performance-driven world (Newman and de Zoysa 1997, 624–625). Indeed, Masolo (2010, 229) is of the view that Western communitarianism is not a developed communitarian theory but is rather a sociopolitical framework for safeguarding communal interest.

Discourse about African communitarianism, or Afro-communitarianism, revolves around discourse on radical communitarianism. In this strong sense, Afro-communitarianism supplies an ontological, epistemological, and ethical framework for thinking the person as a member of the community, which prescribes values that allow all law-abiding members to enjoy the benefits the community has to offer (Ikuenobe 2006, 53). The ideal model of Afro-communitarianism is traditional African village life considered as the closest approximation of what human existence looked like in precolonial times. However, the idealization of village life has posed a challenge for African philosophers and scholars. This challenge consists of reinventing the past in a contemporary theoretical formulation that takes into account the sophistication of postcolonial existence and the accompanying emphasis on individualism, with all the discontents of individualism that find their most concrete expression in the demand for inalienable human rights. Afro-communitarians have formulated theories like *négritude* (Senghor 1964), *ujamaa* (Nyerere 1968), consciencism (Nkrumah 1970), and ubuntu (Ramose 1999) that struggle to find a comfortable place for the individual in the community.

There are three broad variants of Afro-communitarianism in the literature, namely, radical, moderate, and limited communitarianism. Radical, or classical, communitarianism tends to diminish individualism while locating the highest value in communal solidarity. This gives the impression that it is the community that confers meaning on the individual. A life devoid of active fellowship with other lives will, then, count as an increasingly meaningless life. According to Mbiti (1989, 106), the pristine African communal ideal can be distilled into one dictum, namely: "I am, because we are; and since we are therefore I am." Mbiti expatiates thus:

> What then is the individual and where is his place in the community? In traditional life, the individual does not and cannot exist alone except corporately. He owes this existence to other people, including those of past generations and contemporaries. He is simply part of the whole. The community must therefore make, create, or produce the individual. . . . The individual can only say "I am, because we are; and since we are therefore I am." This is the cardinal point in the understanding of the African view of man. (Mbiti 1989, 106)

Pushing back against the seeming diminution of the individual, Gyekye formulates what has now come to be known as moderate communitarianism. According to Gyekye (2010, 114): "Moderate communitarianism . . . addresses the dual nature of the self, as a communal being and as an autonomous, self-determining, self-assertive being with a capacity for evaluation and choice. . . . Communitarianism . . . cannot disallow arguments about rights which may in fact form part of the activity of a self-determining, autonomous individual possessed of the capacity for evaluating or re-evaluating the entire practice of his community."

Against the backdrop of criticism that radical communitarianism diminishes the individual, some scholars have sought to go further than Gyekye on the path of reconciling the individual with the community by asserting their contemporaneity (see, for instance, Agada and Egbai 2018). The reconciliation effort births limited communitarianism, a version of moderate communitarianism that locates the criterion of personhood in the metaphysical reality of the individual and grounds the social self in the autonomous self, one existing in its own right as an absolute and discrete entity (Matolino 2018, 111–112). Limited communitarianism restricts the influence of the community to "how we conceive of social relations between, firstly, individual members' inter-relations and, secondly, each individual member and the collective that is known as the community" (Matolino 2018, 113). What Matolino does here is disagree with the thesis of the priority of the community over the individual in favor of a contemporaneity interpretation of individuality and community, such that the community merely functions as an incubator of values that improve the quality of life of the individual (Eze 2008, 388). Metz identifies these values as friendship, caring, and sharing, in the framework of his relationalist interpretation of the ubuntu ethical system. According to Metz (2007, 338), African communitarianism can be interpreted as advocating that "an action is right just insofar as it promotes shared identity among people grounded on good-will; an act is wrong to the extent that it fails to do so and tends to encourage the opposites of division and ill-will." On this reading of Afro-communitarianism, it is extant communal relations that confer meaning on a human life rather than the community as an entity, or even as a collection of individuals.

The so-called radical thesis is significant to the extent that it recognizes that the human being is not what I will call a *bare* existent (cf. Agada 2015, 180). A *bare* existent would be incapable of freedom and responsibility because it would exist independently of social structures and relations. Since the human being as a *bare* existent is an abstraction of culturally situated beings, the priority thesis of radical Afro-communitarianism is unimpeachable. Thus, for Ikuenobe (2006), the metaphysical interpretation of personhood suggested by Matolino does not weaken the plausibility of the radical thesis. A human being is human precisely because she is a moral or social self. Otherwise, she will be no different from a goat, for instance, or even a piece of rock.

Taiwo (2016) is not impressed by the passionate defense of Afro-communitarianism and urges African scholars to embrace individualism given that postcolonial urbanization and technological sophistication favor an individualistic social structure. However, Afro-communitarianism, as already noted, values the individual. A statement like *I am, because we are; and since we are therefore I am* can be interpreted as signifying the strength of the bond between the individual and other individuals in the society rather than the diminution of the individual and the elevation of the community to the status of an infallible and unmerciful god. The credo of togetherness in community is best understood in the light of Desmond Tutu's comment that "harmony, friendliness, community are great goods. Social harmony is for us the *summum bonum*—the greatest good. . . . Anger, resentment, lust for revenge, even success through aggressive competitiveness, are corrosive of this good" (Tutu 1999, 35). Friendliness and harmony thrive better where there is a reasonably high emphasis on communal relations, although it can also be argued that the emphasis is not essential in places like the West, where a high quality of life and security have been established on the basis of individualism and competitive industry.

Shorn of ideological posturing, which pitches a presumed African communalism against so-called Western individualism, Afro-communitarianism is compatible with modern ideals of an urbanized and technologically advanced society such as liberty, human rights, innovativeness, and democracy. The contribution of Afro-communitarianism to modern existence will then be emphasis on solidarity and fellow-feeling in a world where the individual increasingly feels alienated from a seemingly uncaring society that appears focused essentially on the maximization of the economic benefits of material existence while neglecting less material or emotional aspects of human well-being.

Afro-communitarianism and the Meaningful Life

A meaningful life can be understood in terms of a purposeful life or an eventful life. Purposeful and eventful lives are said to be meaningful to the extent that those who lead these lives see a coherent pattern at play at the practical level of everyday existence and believe this to be the case on the basis of rational conviction. A person with a high drive for success will consider her life largely meaningful at any point even though set goals remain unrealized. Hope functions as a marker of purpose and confers meaning on a life that will otherwise appear frustrated. Another person who has acquired so much property and wealth or who spends all her time traveling round the world in cruise ships and meeting new people will likely consider her life purposeful and meaningful. A hermit who renounces the world and goes to live in the forest where he spends his time meditating and walking among the trees may also consider his life purposeful. A similar report can be made about a mass murderer who enjoys the gory act of killing.

Obviously, self-report about the meaningfulness of a life is not adequate for concluding that a life is meaningful. The Nazi technocrats in Berlin who directed Holocaust operations and the death-camp commanders who executed orders from superiors might have believed they were leading meaningful lives in obeying orders that ensured their rise up the ladder of success in Nazi Germany, but most rational people would object to the attachment of the value of meaning to a life directly responsible for the murder of hundreds of thousands of people. Recognizing the inadequacy of the subjective criterion of "Alas, does my life like this have any meaning at all?" (Morioka 2015, 55), Metz identifies the objective criterion for determining meaningfulness. The objective criterion demands that activities self-reported as markers of meaning must be open to external scrutiny and validation (Metz 2002; cf. Bennett 1984). The objective criterion puts issues of morality on the front burner in the determination of the meaning-value of actions.

I use the term "meaning" positively in this work to encompass feelings and thoughts that are implicated in judgments about the worth of everyday living in relation to the totality of a life. Meaning thus indicates an emotional and intellectual appraisal of the value of human existence within the limits of human hopes and fears. A meaningful life is one that increasingly realizes goals that heighten the consolation of the individual and diminishes the terror of existence. More precisely, meaning is a marker of *consolation*. Terror flows from the singularity of the individual in a world where physical and moral evil abound and death is always nearby even as the individual is certain to disappear from the world stage without certain knowledge of why the world has to exist and herself in this selfsame world. A consolation is a state of mind, a tangible good, or an event that diminishes human fears and increases human hope (Agada 2015). Consolation is measured in terms of the pursuit of the moment-to-moment maximization of the state of joy, whether joy is realized eventually or not. The term consolation is particularly attractive in illuminating the idea of meaning in view of the impossibility of answering the question of what human life and universal existence are all about with epistemic certainty. The concept will be discussed in greater details in the third section in relation to the thought of Sartre.

In the Afro-communitarian literature, God, humans, spiritual entities, animals, vegetable, and mineral life all confer meaning. The case of animals, vegetable, and mineral life is straightforward. Animals provide both company as well as food (for nonvegetarians) and plants provide food. Trees, hills, and mountains have an aesthetic value that increases human satisfaction.

The transcendentalist dimension of Afro-communitarianism locates God as the being that confers meaning, such that a meaningful life is one lived in obedience to the will of God, or, better still, the gods who are closer to humans. While a transcendentalist account can claim that doing God's will within communal faith structures—for instance, church and mosque attendance and the ensuing positive feelings of belonging to a faith community—confers meaning on human life at a practical level, it is impossible to empirically demonstrate God's existence, making faith a conviction without a sure foundation and open to the constant threat of dissolution if a believer has sufficient grounds to doubt her belief. This situation applies to other spiritual entities. The pessimist will, then, be justified in declaring that if a believer is not sure of God's existence, the edifice of a coherent life that she has built around the conviction of doing God's will in the society collapses.

A subjective naturalistic account of meaningful existence puts a premium on self-reporting about the worth of a human life, while an objective naturalistic account emphasizes the importance of external, and moral, bases for determining meaningfulness (see Attoe 2020). Here, there is some tension between strong individualism that demands petulantly, "Alas, does my life like this have any meaning at all?" (Morioka 2015, 55) and the firm communalist voice that insists that "to be is to be in mutual complementary relationship . . . and its negation is to be alone" (Asouzu 2011, 103). Here one finds the communal idea that nihilism and pessimism can be overcome in the very experience of community, in the caring and sharing, the friendship and love, that banishes the sheer terror of the isolated human life. A communal conception of meaning, thus, affirms the higher value of an objective naturalistic approach to deciding what is meaningful over a subjective individualist approach.

Number becomes a significant factor in the creation of meaning, the addition of value to the lives of individuals. Not being alone indicates the power of the "we" to lift the "I" from the existential terror of isolation. Mbiti's dictum of *I am, because we are; and since we are therefore I am* captures the communal sense of a meaningful life so well. The individual who affirms her life as significant on the basis of shared bonds with other individuals can count on like-minded individuals collected in groups to vote in elections the way she does. Identity-based voting means higher chances of having favored political parties in power. Direct and indirect access to power increases the consolation of identity voters, the satisfaction of having their favored parties in power, and the hope of benefiting from favored policies.

In entering into relationships, the individual can get married and have children. Family life becomes a source of meaning, like work. For family and work involve participation in a broader social life, where individual anxieties and fears lose their intensity in the individual's knowledge that she can find someone who cares enough to listen to her and, perhaps, ameliorate her condition. Noting the value attached to numbers in African life, Senghor (1964, 148) writes that "procreation as the means of perpetuating the family and species occupies an important place in Negro-African society." The sphere of solidarity is extendable far beyond the family for friendship to thrive within narrow interest groups such as workers' unions and broader groups like clan formations and entire nations.

At this juncture, I introduce the notions of meaning in life and the meaning of life that rise to the fore in the debate about how a human life can be coherent and purposeful in the face of the seeming pointlessness of human existence in a world where there is a great amount of suffering (see, for instance, Camus 1975; Nagel 1979; Benatar 2013; Attoe 2020). On the one hand, meaning in life, in the positive sense mentioned earlier, involves separate and accumulated instances of good things and events in a single life or the total of all the moments of good things and events enjoyable in a life. On the other hand, the meaning of a life can only be decided after one must have answered the question "What does it all add up to?" in a larger cosmic context. To answer this question, one must ponder whether the universe has a purpose at all and whether human life holds any final significance in view of the moral evil (e.g., human wickedness) and physical evil (e.g., COVID-19 disease) that mar the enjoyable moments of meaning in a life. One must reflect on the absence of certain knowledge of the existence of a being like God who can perfect nature from the outside. One must also consider why the human mind is able to nurture hope and so successfully convince us that the concept of progress is on a sound footing and that we should pursue our goals with total commitment in order to enjoy the good life despite the futility that death signifies. The theist, atheist, deist, agnostic, or whatever, must be able to wonder alongside Sartre (1966, 792): "Everything happens as if the world, man, and man-in-the-world succeeded only in realizing a missing God," as if the semblance of order in the universe is a massive illusion.

While there can be no doubt that a life can be filled with many moments of meaning, this life as a whole fails to be meaningful because the evils of life that mingle with the goods of life pursue the individual in her day-to-day striving to the very end. This end is the cessation of being with the individual still not reaching any certain knowledge about the reason for her existence and why the universe itself has to exist. One may say that there is no evil in the world and that admitting it exists is mere anthropomorphism. A good response would be that the human being is nature, that this being shares so completely in nature's heritage that if it identifies evil in the world, there is, indeed, evil. The fact that this being thinks at a sophisticated level does not make it less natural.

The community makes a tempting claim about shielding the individual from the fundamental philosophical question of a purposeful existence by simply bringing her out of the solitary space that magnifies the question and urging her to be stoic. The communal experience fails to shield the individual from absolute solitude, a state in which the mind ponders the question of purpose, since the community is not all-powerful and all-knowing enough to answer the question of what the ultimate purpose of life and the universe can be. In the first place, the community can be a wicked judge that perpetrates injustice against the individual instead of dispensing fair justice. Second, the utter singularity of the individual is a burden the community cannot lift off the shoulder of the individual by immersing her in the family, in narrow and broad interests groups, and in the wider life of the nation. Death terminates the process of the day-to-day pursuit of the comforting emotion of joy. With the disappearance of the individual, it is as if she never existed. It may be true that the good deeds of the individual may live on for thousands of years in the memory of the community as represented in every generation. But very few individuals achieve this immortality by reputation. Additionally, such immortality can only endure for as long as the world itself endures. A cataclysmic event like a catastrophic nuclear conflict, a pandemic that wipes humans off the face of the earth, and the death of the solar system itself will finally destroy the resilient communal memory.

African phenomenologists like Serequeberhan (1994) and Hountondji (1996) have located the African's authentic and meaningful existence in a sociopolitical context where the pre-independence promise of freedom and even development are realized, leading to improvement in quality of life in a postindependence dispensation. While such improvement can indeed enrich the moments of meaning in a life, it is communally mediated and suffers from the ultimate meaninglessness that community cannot sufficiently compensate for. Authenticity and, therefore, meaningfulness emerge from a collective consciousness imposed by a responsible political leadership in cooperation with a responsive followership. Hountondji and Serequeberhan leave untouched the intimate aspect of the meaning of the individual's life beyond the communal framework.

Community, Consolation, and Meaning:
A Cross-cultural Conversation with Sartre

While the community fails to answer the question of the ultimate meaning of life that, in the first place, drives the individual to seek comfort in communal relations, the experience of community has a practical value in helping the individual to increase the moments of meaning that make life worth living while the individual is alive. I will employ the term "consolation" to convey a sense of the practical interest of living that the community sustains. After briefly discussing the term, I will engage Sartre's notion of the human being as useless passion in relation to the idea that the community supplies the framework for the actualization of consolation.

The twenty-first-century African philosophical orientation of consolationism (see Agada 2015, 2019; Agada and Egbai 2018) defines the human being as *homo melancholicus*, or melancholy being, the consolation-seeking being. The melancholy being is the thinking being whose rationality finds its bearing from the standpoint of this being's understanding of itself as an emotional entity. For the melancholy being, reason is at the service of emotion precisely because this being's life is bound up with the pursuit of the moment-to-moment maximization of the affect of joy. Actualizing joy is this being's consolation in the face of pessimism.

Consolationism submits that the human mind can reach the conclusion that there is an ultimate purpose motivating behavior at all levels of existence from the mere evidence of progress in the world, as in the endless circle of emergence, development, and disappearance of entities. Societies evolve, become more advanced, build empires, and reach higher heights of intellectual development even as individuals are born and they die. Nonliving matter appears to obey a logic inherent to it and that indicates internal purposiveness or organization. While the evidence of progress does not conclusively support the idea that there is a discoverable grand purpose of life and universal existence, the mind persists in its quest and reaches the intuition of perfection. As I have stated elsewhere:

> The kernel of consolation philosophy is that the universe may
> well have a purpose which the human mind can intuit as the
> realization of a perfect state of being for conscious beings and
> the perfection of nature in a way that makes all actualities and

outcomes complete and perfect. The intuition finds its practical expression in our faith in progress, towards which we strive politically, economically, existentially, without ever arriving at an ideal state and with death putting an end to the struggle towards the ideal state of perfection (which conditions every kind of striving as cause). But then it is the condition of whatever is defined by its essential status as a yearning existent to always fall short of this purpose. Striving anchors reality and the human mind assures us that there should not be purposeless striving even as the fundamental status of striving indicates a final purpose which we intuit as the realization of an ideal state. (Agada 2019, 4–5)

The idea of perfection as the grand purpose motivating the striving of the universe from outside is no more than an intuition. However, postulating perfection as the goal of the universe helps one understand why striving evidences itself everywhere as a promise of a best state that, tragically, cannot be realized for the reason that whatever persists as yearning must remain steadfast to its nature as constant seeking of the ideal of perfection.

An entity like the human being with an advanced consciousness, and immersed in a universe of striving, becomes a melancholy being. This being in its emotional dimension pursues the maximization of the emotion of joy and the diminution of the emotion of sadness and in its rational dimension recognizes optimism and pessimism as cognitive correlates of the emotional states of joy and sadness. Thus, I say that the human being is a consolation-seeking being. Consolation is measured as meaning, in terms indicating the intensity of the joy and sadness states. The greater the level of joy and its cognate states like satisfaction and contentment, the greater the meaning in a life even if this meaning must be cancelled in death. As an entity fit for consolation, the human being is not entirely useless passion as Sartre has noted. The melancholy being is passion indeed because it is nothing beyond yearning, but this passion is not useless because the singularity of the individual not only indicates the existential terror of solitude but also reveals the fear of this terror as a fundamental motivation to seek out community (Agada and Egbai 2018, 150). The experience of community, accordingly, involves a necessary relationship between melancholy beings.

The Conversation

Sartre rightly sees the human being as a passion, an interested entity continually in search of meaning in a better state of existence. In the framework of the dichotomy of being-in-itself and being-for-itself, this passion is a useless passion, making Sartre's theory of being an ontology of terror. I refer to Sartre's philosophy as an ontology of terror because he tirelessly hammers on the futility of the great project of the human being, which is the endeavor of the nonsufficient for-itself (conscious being) to finally constitute itself as an in-itself (nonconscious being), which is sufficient being. Such a synthesis will mark the attainment of perfection for the human being that then becomes God, the *ens causa sui*. As Sartre (1966, 784) notes:

> Each human reality is at the same time a direct project to metamorphose its own For-itself into an In-itself-For-itself and a project of the appropriation of the world as a totality of being-in-itself, in the form of a fundamental quality. Every human reality is a passion in that it projects losing itself so as to found being. . . . Thus the passion of man is the reverse of that of Christ, for man loses himself as man in order that God may be born. But the idea of God is contradictory and we lose ourselves in vain. Man is useless passion.

What Sartre calls uselessness I call futility. He considers the idea of God contradictory because what exists as consciousness is, in fact, a negation of what exists as itself (the in-itself), independent of abstraction. Thus, conscious being, which has no sufficiency beyond its existence as the negation of inert being, cannot transform into a conscious being that possesses the fullness of being. Hence, the lamentation: "Everything happens as if the world, man, and man-in-the-world succeeded only in realizing a missing God . . . as if the in-itself and the for-itself were presented in a state of disintegration in relation to an ideal synthesis" (Sartre 1966, 792). Perfection is always indicated as the logical terminus of yearning but is, paradoxically, always impossible (Agada 2015).

What remains for humans, then, is consolation. Finding consolation means that the for-itself, or the individual, will responsibly employ her basic freedom. What interests me at this juncture, and with particular reference to freedom and ethics, is Sartre's casting doubt on his idea of an absolute freedom and asking: "Will freedom by taking itself for an end escape all *situation*? Or on the contrary, will it remain situated?" (Sartre 1966, 798). A situated freedom is one restricted by the experience of community. The for-itself then becomes a for-others, a social being. The pursuit of meaning in community involves the rejection of what Sartre (1966, 796) calls the spirit of seriousness, which "considers values as transcendent givens independent of human subjectivity, and . . . transfers the quality of 'desirable' from the ontological structure of things to their simple material constitution." This spirit overstates human importance, intellectually and emotionally, since it deceives humans into thinking that the project of human transformation to God-hood is possible, whereas humans are so constituted that they will always be incomplete. Rejecting the spirit of seriousness implies recognizing our human limitations, the futility of our striving, and not exaggerating our importance, as the existential situation of the drunkard is no more pathetic than that of the president of a country. Willingness to enter into solidarity with other humans becomes a mark of humility, in the knowledge that the spirit of seriousness is unwarranted.

While the apotheosis of the anguished human can never be reached, this consolation-seeking being can find moments of meaning in her life in communion with other human beings. To be sure, conflict is bound to arise given the radical individuality of all melancholy beings and the imperfection of the community considered as a moral or legal court, but this eventuality is no cause for overindulging in pessimism. Such overindulgence will amount to exhibiting the spirit of seriousness. Humans are born to enjoy the moments of meanings that their lives offer even in full knowledge that their lives are ultimately meaningless.

The communal experience certainly does not eliminate the existential terror that magnifies the anguish of knowing that one yearns in vain ultimately, but this experience lowers the intensity of the terror and makes life valuable while one exists. An entirely pessimistic perspective will lead one to the conclusion that it is better not to have existed at all in view of the impossibility of perfection. This strong pessimistic perspective is, however, the spirit of seriousness in disguise. As Gordon (2000, 79) has noted while critiquing Sartre's existentialism, denying sociality, and the admittedly imperfect meanings that accompany it, is a kind of bad faith, a kind of lying to oneself, since such amounts to denying our humanity. An entirely pessimistic standpoint overlooks the moments of meaning that a life can enjoy and denies these moments a reality they possess while they last. The enduring value of community, as revealed in the Afro-communitarian literature, is the embrace of an *amor fati* stance that eschews the spirit of seriousness by calmly celebrating the *we* in *I am, because we are; and since we are therefore I am*. *Amor fati* is used here as the calm acceptance of events as eventualities that are neither free nor rigidly conditioned before their occurrence.

Conclusion

In this work, I presented the African conception of community in terms of the celebration of relationships that broaden human solidarity. I teased out a communal theory of meaning that identifies a meaningful life with one characterized by immersion in a social life of sharing. I showed that the communal conception of meaning is threatened by pessimism about human existence in view of the futility of a seemingly purposeless existence. I engaged in a cross-cultural conversation with Sartre and highlighted the relevance of the notion of the human being as passion haunted by the spirit of seriousness to the conception of the same human being as a consolation-seeking being. I noted that while pessimism about human existence is well founded, the experience of community enhances practical living by blunting the edge of pessimism through increasing the moments of meaning an individual can ever find in her solitary state. The communal experience takes into full account the impossibility of the human being attaining her apotheosis but affirms, nevertheless, that this being is fit for consolation and should legitimately enjoy the moments of meaning guaranteed to it as a passion useful to the community of human beings.

References

Agada, Ada. 2015. *Existence and Consolation: Reinventing Ontology, Gnosis, and Values in African Philosophy*. St. Paul, MN: Paragon House.

Agada, Ada. 2019. "Rethinking the Metaphysical Questions of Mind, Matter, Freedom, Determinism, Purpose, and the Mind-Body Problem within the Panpsychist Framework of Consolationism." *South African Journal of Philosophy* 38, no. 1: 1–16. doi:10.1080/02580136.2018.1560589.

Agada, Ada, and U. O. Egbai. 2018. "Language, Thought and Interpersonal Communication: A Cross-cultural Conversation on the Question of Individuality and Community." *Filosofia Theoretica: Journal of African Philosophy, Culture and Religions* 7, no. 2: 141–162. doi: 10.4314/ft.v7i2.9.

Asouzu, Innocent I. 2011. "Ibuanyidanda and the Philosophy of Essence." *Filosofia Theoretica: Journal of African Philosophy, Culture and Religions* 1, no. 1: 79–118.

Attoe, Aribiah D. 2020. "A Systematic Account of African Conceptions of the Meaning of/in Life." *South African Journal of Philosophy* 39, no. 2. doi:10.1080/02580136.2020.1771822.

Benatar, David. 2013. "Still Better Never to Have Been: A Reply to More of My Critics." *Journal of Ethics* 17: 121–151.

Bennett, James. 1984. " 'The Meaning of Life': A Qualitative Perspective." *Canadian Journal of Philosophy* 14: 581–592.

Camus, Albert. 1975. *The Myth of Sisyphus and Other Essays*. Translated by J. O'Brien. New York: Penguin.

Eze, Michael O. 2008. "What Is African Communitarianism? Against Consensus as a Regulative Deal." *South African Journal of Philosophy* 27, no. 4: 386–399. doi:10.4314/sajpem.v27i4.31526.

Gordon, Lewis R. 2000. *Existentia Africana: Understanding Africana Existential Thought*. New York: Routledge.

Gyekye, Kwame. 2010. "Person and Community in African Thought." In *Person and Community: Ghanaian Philosophical Studies, I*, edited by Kwasi Wiredu and Kwame Gyekye, 102–122. Washington, DC: Council for Research in Values and Philosophy.

Hountondji, Paulin. 1996. *African Philosophy: Myth and Reality*. 2nd ed. Translated by Henri Evans. Bloomington: Indiana University Press.

Ikuenobe, Polycarp. 2006. *Philosophical Perspectives on Communalism and Morality in African Traditions*. Lanham, MD: Lexington Books.

Masolo, D. A. 2010. *Self and Community in a Changing World*. Bloomington: Indiana University Press.

Matolino, Bernard. 2018. "The Politics of Limited Communitarianism." *Filosofia Theoretica: Journal of African Philosophy, Culture and Religions* 7, no. 2: 101–122. doi: 10.4314/ft.v7i2.7.

Mbiti, John S. 1989. *African Religions and Philosophy*. London: Heinemann.

Metz, Thaddeus. 2002. "Recent Work on the Meaning of Life." *Ethics* 112, no. 4: 781–814.

Metz, Thaddeus. 2007. "Toward an African Moral Theory." *Journal of Political Philosophy* 15, no. 3: 321–341. doi: 10.1086/340462.

Miller, Daniel, Elisabetta Costa, Nell Haynes, Tom McDonald, Razvan Nicolescu, Jolynna Sinanan, Juliano Spyer, Shriram Venkatraman, and Xinyuan Wang. 2016. *How the World Changed Social Media*. London: UCL Press.

Morioka, Masahiro. 2015. "Is Meaning in Life Comparable? From the Viewpoint of 'The Heart of Meaning in Life.'" *Journal of the Philosophy of Life* 5, no. 3: 50–65.

Nagel, Thomas. 1979. *Mortal Questions*. New York: Cambridge University Press.

Newman, Otto, and Richard de Zoysa. 1997. "Communitarianism: The New Panacea?" *Sociological Perspectives* 40, no. 4: 623–638.

Nkrumah, Kwame. 1970. *Consciencism: Philosophy and Ideology for De-colonization*. New York: Monthly Review Press.

Nyerere, Julius K. 1968. *Ujamaa: Essays on Socialism*. Nairobi: Oxford University Press.

Ramose, Mogobe B. 1999. *African Philosophy through Ubuntu*. Harare: Mond Books.

Sartre, Jean-Paul. 1966. *Being and Nothingness*. Translated by Hazel E. Barnes. New York: Pocket Books.

Senghor, Léopold Sédar. 1964. *On African Socialism*. Translated by Mercer Cook. New York: Praeger.

Serequeberhan, Tsenay. 1994. *The Hermeneutics of African Philosophy: Horizon and Discourse*. New York: Routledge.

Taiwo, Olufemi. 2016. "Against African Communalism." *Journal of French and Francophone Philosophy* 24, no. 1: 81–100. doi: 10.5195/jffp.2016.759.

Tutu, Desmond. 1999. *No Future without Forgiveness*. New York: Random House.

Part 3

Art, Culture, Language, Politics, and Liberation

11

Savage Objects

On the Restitution of Alienated Meaning

ACHILLE MBEMBE

Introduction

It is one thing to make a normative and outside judgment on African cultural artifacts without taking into account their history, their hetero-geneity, or the enigma of which they are the expression.[1] It is another to seek to grasp, through their distinctive properties, their substance, and their functions, the ways of being and seeing of Africans: or again, taking them as an intermediary, to want to learn the metaphysical kernel from which the world, whose authors the Africans were, made sense, and first of all, to their own eyes and for themselves.[2] Indeed, whether or not they were linked with the exercise of particular cults or rituals, whether or not they were taken as works of art, these objects, often viewed as disconcerting (in truth matters of traits and traces), have always aroused on the part of the West all sorts of sensations, ambiguous feelings, visceral and even contradictory reactions—obsessive fear, fascination and wonder, horror, frustration and repulsion, or even execration. Everywhere that they made their appearance, they tended to give rise to effects of blindness. Considered from the start as dirty, ugly, and monstrous objects, as signatures of the shadow resisting all translation, they shook up existing ocular frameworks and put back on the agenda the old question of understanding what an image is and how it differs from a simple silhouette; about what art is and what aesthetic experience in general is, and how it manifests itself in its pure truth.

Besides the foregoing, which could be identified as the "missionary gaze," this chapter focuses on the conceptual-ethnographical gaze. The phenomenological import of this, namely, how the social meaning of these objects has a deeper ontological effect on the European, is expounded. African art served to mediate a particular self-awareness of a Europe that was battling to understand its new subjecthood as the dominator of the world. Currently, the question being asked is whether Europe should restitute these objects to those entitled to them. However the meaning of their presence in Europe, what they signify in European consciousness, is not radically interrogated. The chapter contends for a critical turn to the essential issues within the context of the nature of aesthetic experience, and its political consequences. What is it that one is seeking to repatriate and why? Is the work that these objects were supposed to accomplish in the history of European consciousness finished?

The Historic-Epistemic Gazes of African Cultural Artifacts

Of all the gazes brought to bear on these manifestations of the cultural creativity of our peoples, three in particular merit our attention. These are: the Christian missionary gaze, the racial-othering gaze, and the ethnographic gaze with an ontologizing of aesthetics.

Animism, Paganism, and Idolatry

Let us start with the missionary gaze, to whose eyes these artifacts were essentially the effects of a satanic imagination. This theological-pastoral gaze began to take shape during the first evangelization, which occurred in the kingdoms of the Congo between 1495 and 1506, and again between the seventeenth and eighteenth centuries; then in that of Dahomey in the seventeenth century.[3] Evidently, the diabolization of African objects from the fifteenth century proceeded from an unreflected heritage that, with few exceptions, numerous missionary figures carried along.[4] Indeed, the devil long constituted the nocturnal part of Christian culture in the West.[5] Between the twelfth and thirteenth centuries, the diverse demons that had populated old imaginations were reduced to a single one, Satan, absolute master of Hell and God's rival on earth. Little by little, the figure of Satan invaded several domains of social and imaginary life.[6] Satan symbolized the war of worlds and the confrontation between good and evil, reason and madness. At the same time, he attested to the split character of the human figure that he surrounded and on the inside of which he hollowed out an almost insuperable void (Boureau 2004). Between 1480 and 1520, and again between 1560 and 1650, this demonic obsessive fear reached its culminating point—as is attested by the interminable trials, the great hunts, and the great number of witches burned at the stake—when a junction came about between the Satanic figure, on the one hand, and the body and the sexuality of women, on the other (Bechtel 1997). The first phase of missionary expansion into Africa bore in it the traces of this essential tension. As the "mission" came to be, the "devil's place" would thus move to Africa, a region of the world deeply ruled, it was thought at the time, by chaos, by a life requiring order to be put into it and in need of a salvation that could only come from outside (McCabe 2007).

Quite unsurprisingly, the first missionaries interpreted African objects through the paradigm of "diabolical witchcraft" that had prevailed in the West for many centuries. These objects were put on trials similar to the proceedings carried out, under Christianity, against dolls pierced with needles, against the curses thrown about here and there, against the potions one concocted, against the contact one sought with the dead, against the witches' Sabbaths, against broomsticks and black masses, against host desecrations, bestial copulations and all sorts of gory sacrifices, all of which were only made possible, it is argued, by belief in Satan and in his powers. Presented as material symbols of the Africans' proclivity for engaging in idolatry, worship of the dead, and the practice of gory sacrifices, cultural objects in particular were subject to the reprobation of missionaries.[7]

For the most part, the missionaries saw in them only a marker—yet another—of the essential difference between the savage mentality and that of civilized humanity.[8] Missionary campaigns were founded on two pillars: the refutation of the metaphysical foundations of the worship of the natives and, wherever it was necessary, religious repression with the aim of conversion. In the logic of Christianity, the converted must recognize that the path that they have been on leads straight to their ruin. Renouncing one's life and previous ways, one must repent and undertake an internal reversal at the end of which a new subjectivity is to be acquired, new ways of inhabiting the world, the body, and objects. In practice, conversion led to the invention of mixed cultures, made up of borrowings of all kinds, of games of mixtures, of risky reappropriations, of hybrid aesthetic practices (Formont 2017). Conversion originated manifold misunderstandings, multiple paradoxes, and a complex process of redefinition of each of the protagonists of the encounter.[9]

This context is the one in which the missionary antipagan discourse developed. This discourse influenced, more than has been recognized, the conceptions that the West formed of African objects, of their substance, of their status, and of their functions. It rested on the postulate according to which the Blacks lived in the night of the inmost animal. The African world, as for it, was a priori bereft of the idea of a sovereign God that would be the norm of every norm and the cause of every cause. There was, at least, no clear awareness of any such principle. By contrast, this world was peopled with a multitude of beings, of multiple divinities, ancestors, soothsayers, intercessors, all sorts of genies who ceaselessly vied for preeminence. With these forces and entities, primitive societies entertained relations of immediacy and immanence (Bouche 1874). Of this pile of beliefs, one could hardly speak about any sort of religion as such, for it was so difficult to sort out what pertained to ritual murders, to the worship of spirits, and what participated in the simple worship of matter. Alongside these figures, a panoply of forces (maleficent for the most part) structured the universe and presided over each person's life. These included all kinds of fetish objects, which the missionaries likened to idols (Brasseur 1997). These idols, in their roughness and their excessive features, constituted the objectal manifestation of the state of corruption in which the black race was plunged (Zerbini 2007). Through such objects, did primitive peoples not seek to constrain and control powers? Did these objects not simultaneously manifest the fear and dependency that such peoples experienced in their regard? Such dependency nevertheless had no divine aim. It implied nothing less than nothingness, the mere nothing of man in the face of an absolute supremacy, the presence of the horrifying (Descoqs 1928).

Accordingly, many of these objects were destroyed during the major religious feasts, while many others—as a result of collection, of theft, of pillage, of confiscation, and of gifts given—came to be found in museums of the West.[10] "Do not forget to send us, at the earliest opportunity, a collection of things from your new country," hastened to write Father Augustin Planque in 1861 to the missionaries sent to Africa. "We would like to have in our museum all your gods for a start, weapons, tools, household utensils; in a word, nothing should be left out" (Bonemaison 2007, 2).[11] Christianity indeed presented itself as the religion of truth and of salvation. Religion of the radical rupture, it sought to abolish ancient forms of worship. Hence vast campaigns were organized to extirpate idolatry.[12] Accordingly, temples were ransacked or literally desecrated. Manifold fetishes—figurines made of diverse materials (hair endings, fingernails, metal nails), shells of diverse forms and colors, dried bugs and insects, collections of roots, marmites and pitchers filled with vegetal preparations and ointments—were violated. In their place, crosses were planted. Amulets were confiscated and rosaries were handed out, as were effigies of saints. Demons and sorcerers were prosecuted through public punishments and punitive spectacles.[13] The endeavor was made to end all feasts and rites, to aggress musical instruments, and prohibit certain dances as well as the supposed worship of the dead and practices of contacts with the invisible.

DIFFERENCE AND APOCALYPSE

Backdropped by theories, in vogue at the time, of "universal history" and of differences between human races, a second type of gaze emerged in the nineteenth century. The language of race and of blood was on people's tongues. On the one hand, the idea according to which God revealed himself in the Christian religion, the only true religion, endured. On the other, the notion took hold according to which the history of the world was fundamentally the history of progress toward the consciousness of freedom.[14] This universal history, it was maintained, presented itself to us in the form of a rational process that ought to lead to the triumph of reason or, in any case, to the reconciliation between the rational and the real (Hegel 2013, 2005). But it was only held to have become concrete where reason was able to insert itself into the great human passions (including need, forces, and instincts), and even wherever it left passions to act in its stead. In other terms, universal history could only be envisaged on the condition that reason and truth consciously took on the form and structure of myth (Cassirer 2017).

As it happens, the great myth of the nineteenth century was that of race (Mbembe 2017). It is through race, it was thought, that the "Absolute Idea" is accomplished. Hegel, for example, considered that in each era of history, there was indeed one and only one nation, one and only one people that is the real representation of the world spirit and that "has the right to rule all the others" (Cassirer 2017, 273). Faced with this nation, with this people or with this race, "other nations are absolutely without rights." They "no longer count in universal history" (Hegel 2005, 343). In this system in which a given race grants itself the title of "sole bearer of the world-spirit," and where reason turns to myth, race was no longer the name of a supposed community substance. It was a structuring force, a fiction in possession of its own reality and able to produce reality (Voegelin 1997). The racial was a biological determination (that which is of the order of blood, of hereditary transmission) as much as that which is of the order of the body, the body of a people endowed with a will to power. But it was also an available affective disposition and able to be mobilized if necessary; it was the phantasmagorical representation of difference of an ontological nature.

The black race in particular was deemed an inferior variety of the human race. The things of which it was the author were, by principle, bereft of life. Its objects were the manifestation neither of some sovereign will of any sort, nor of its own proper energy whose ultimate aim would be freedom. In them, the very idea of the symbol found its end, yielding only to a hideous ugliness—the field in which a fundamental arbitrary force circulates. Because they were not made by moral subjects, the objects of blacks could only arouse scorn, terror, and disgust. Before them, one experienced now a sort of impotent horror, now the vertiginous feeling of danger. This is because, in this profane world of things and of bodies, humanity, as a living animal, had only ever been an always already alienated thing, ready to be cut up, cooked, and consumed during gory sacrifices. During these feasts of matter, during which violence exerted its ravages within, the body itself, similar to the object supposed to represent it, was no longer the substrate of any spirit (Coquery-Vidrovitch 1964). The maker and user of an object controlled the object the same way that this object controlled its maker. At bottom, a relationship of strict similarity connected the two. Neither one nor the other existed for their own end but instead for an end that was foreign to them. If there was bedazzlement, it could only be blind. And creation was not put in the service of any durable order. One created precisely with the aim of making the operation of sacrifice and destruction possible. And that is what these objects signified—the impossibility of escaping the limits of the thing, of returning from animal slumber, of rising up toward humanity (Bataille 1989). In these works, the exorbitant and the banal came together. They attested in any case to the tragic character of an arbitrary existence, destined for nothing. If, in fact, they fulfilled practical functions, they nevertheless had no substance. As the receptacles of the obscure passions of human existence, they above all fulfilled desires that were either turned away from reality or else nonsublimated. Moreover, they were linked to repugnant bodies. The feeling of shame and the strange measure of scorn with which these bodies were beset were displaced onto these artifacts, as objectal metaphors of substanceless function.

Finally, in their excessive crudeness, their sensual coarseness, and their barely veiled erotic stain, the objects of blacks were above all sexual objects. They testified to an uninhibited thrust toward the outside, to a nonsublimated life of organs typical of primitive sexuality. In keeping with the missionary gaze, the art of the pagans was considered to be driven by an unintegrable violence. This is because this art, in its very origins, was seized by torment of the sexual. Here, bodily functions and genital functions were demetaphorized. If, in some way, art is the enactment of the unconscious, this latter was, among primitives, dominated by archaic images of penetration, of savage and epileptic coitus, and of primordial bisexuality. The individual was in truth neither a man, nor a woman, but each time also animal and object, or all three, only one more than the other, as Freud might say (Freud 1991).

As a result, these objects spoke above all of the predispositions of the primitives' drives. When they concerned the body and the sexual, or when they presented them to be seen, it was hardly to open the way up to representation, less still to sublimation, but instead to sensation. They were therefore not about representation. They were about excitation. The drives that they triggered in those who saw them did not aim to throw any ray of light into the darkness. They aimed to reawaken and to reactivate a sort of link to originary destructiveness that shocked as much as they attracted, fascinated, but also deranged, ultimately generating a deep anxiety of castration. The affective intensity that they freed up was not of the order of rapture. They were capable of shocking the person who might encounter them, to fit the appearances of the real yet cut loose from them, but also to give free rein to fundamental passions of existence that the West had wanted to keep under the yoke, as condition of the passage from the world of the indistinct to that of culture.

THE ONTOLOGIZATION OF AESTHETICS

At the start of the twentieth century, a third type of gaze—at times ethnographic, at times conceptual—emerged (Einstein 1915).[15] The conceptual gaze asserted the plastic and purely formal qualities of "black objects," the sensation of depth evoked through African sculpture or again its way of engendering space, that is, its power of affective intensification of the image. This ethnographic gaze sought to anchor these objects in their context of birth with the aim of disclosing their social meanings. In the process, these objects were conferred a status as works of art, even if, once again, they were not really deciphered in their own terms.[16] For Carl Einstein, for example, the art of the Black is above all shaped by religion. Sculpted works are venerated, as they were by all the peoples of antiquity. The executant fashions his work as if it was divinity. Further still, the artist creates a god and his work is "independent, transcendent and free of all ties." This work is not commissioned to imitate nature, as in the European tradition. "The African work of art does not mean anything. It is not a symbol. It is the god" (Einstein 1915, 102). It brings to the point of collapse every distinction between signifier and signified.

For others, the strength of African works can be explained by their capacity to manipulate the world by way of magic (Bréton 1957). This is seen as interesting because they are held to be a platform on which one can rest in the hope of going beyond the limits of Western civilization. Europe, it was argued, had forgotten something fundamental, something that a return to the African sign might enable it to rediscover; something stemming from the memory of pure forms, freed from every origin and, in this respect, susceptible to opening the path to an ecstatic state—that ultimate degree of expressive intensity and the sublime point of sensation.

This freeing from all origin was at the same time a freeing from all perspective. In Black art, so the claim went, the psychic distance between spectator and image was reduced. Suddenly the invisible aspects inherent to the image appeared. What thus took shape was the possibility of an absolute perception. The object was no longer only contemplated by consciousness but also by the psyche. Not clear, what is the difference between consciousness and the psyche? If this is so, it is because Black art suggests other ways of representing space, whose character is at once symbolic and optic. What it gives to be seen is a mental equivalent of the image rather than the image itself. It gives rise therefore to another modality of seeing. To see does not require that the eye be immobilized. On the contrary, the point is to liberate the eye, to render it active and mobile, to set it in relation to manifold other psychic and physiological processes. Only on this condition can seeing actively reconstruct reality. The eye, in these conditions, is not a dead organ. Going on what it sees and what it recognizes, its work is to explore what is missing, that is, to reconstruct, on the basis of multiple traces and indications, the object staged in the image, in short to give rise to its appearing, to its coming alive.[17]

The Europe that rediscovered African objects at the start of the twentieth century was haunted by the two tales of (re)commencement and of the end. As the commencement is the point of departure of a mutation toward something else, its question is to know whether art can effectively serve as a point of departure toward a future that would not merely be a simple repetition of the past. As for the end, it may be inflected either in the mode of accomplishment (the spirited experience of meanings that would be unconditionally valid), or that of catastrophe. There are ends that render every recommencement impossible. And there are conflagrations that prevent the advent of the end, or that portray it only in the mode of catastrophe. At the start of the twentieth century, African objects contributed to rekindling this debate at the heart of a Europe searching for other ideas of time, the image and truth. This Europe was one of conquest, whose world domination was relatively established, but that was simultaneously beset with doubt, for, in the last instance, this dominion over the rest of the world—and colonialism in particular—rested, as Aimé Césaire would later suggest, on an apocalyptic structure (Césaire 2000 [1952]). This Europe wondered whether its dominion over the world was ultimately not purely spectral; and whether it were not possible to elaborate an idea of time, the image, and truth that was not a simple idea of nothingness but a veritable thought of being and of relation. African objects have thus fulfilled functions of an irreplaceable nature in the historical trajectory of Europe. They have not merely served as tokens of its chimerical (and often disastrous) quest for the unveiling and manifestation of truth in the world, or of its desperate search for a compromise between spirit, the sensible, and matter. In almost spectral fashion, they have also served to remind Europe of the extent to which the appearing of spirit in matter (which is the proper question of art) always requires a language, another language, the language of the other, the other's arrival in language.

The Question of Restitution

Presently, the question being asked is whether or not to restitute these objects to those entitled to them. Very few people, however, are concerned to understand what originally justified their presence in Europe and to know what they were the signifier of in European consciousness. In such conditions, it is important to return to the essential issues. What precisely does one want to divest themselves of? What is one seeking to repatriate and why? If the work that these objects were supposed to accomplish in the history of European consciousness was finished, what will it have produced in the end and who ought to bear the consequences of it? After so many years of these objects being present in its institutions, has Europe finally learned to come to terms with those who come from outside, and even from an extreme remoteness? Is Europe finally ready to embark on the path toward those destinations that are still to come, or is it no longer anything other than the pure event of a crack, a thing split in pure loss, without depth or perspective?

MILLSTONE OF DEBTS

Legalism and paternalism comprise the two sorts of response generally mobilized by those who stand opposed to this project of restitution. Some claim that, in the last instance, the law (as it happens, diverse variants of European property law) by no means authorizes the return or transfer of these artifacts to those rightfully entitled to them. One is careful not to call into question the external origin of these artifacts and their creators. Nevertheless, the response given to the question of knowing to whom they belong is presented as if it was absolutely independent of the—supposedly prejudicial—question of knowing where they come from and who their authors are. In other terms, a caesura is introduced between the law of property and use on the one hand and the act of creating and the creating subject on the other. It is notably asserted that having made something does not automatically make one the owner of that thing. To make an object is one matter. Having the right to use, enjoy, and dispose of that thing, exclusively and absolutely, is another matter altogether. And just as making is not the equivalent of possessing, a work's origin is not enough of a condition to lay claim to its possession or to a right of possession. One also acts as if, in truth, the conditions in which these objects were acquired is entirely unproblematic; as if, from start to finish, it involved transactions between equals on a free market, whereby the value of objects was determined by an objective pricing mechanism. The conclusion drawn is that, having endured the market test, these objects are no longer "vacant and without masters." They are alleged henceforth to be "inalienable," the exclusive property either of a public authority as such (which manages them through its museums) or of private individuals who, having bought them, are qualified, in the view of the law, to enjoy them fully, unhindered. From a legal viewpoint, the debate on the restitution of African objects is thus declared unfounded, as their presence in Western museums and other private institutions has nothing to do with confiscation and, in this respect, requires no judgment of a moral or political kind.

Some others—sometimes the same individuals—claim that Africa does not have the necessary institutions, infrastructures, technical or financial resources, or the qualified staff or know-how to ensure that the objects in question will be protected and conserved. Returning these collections to such environments would expose them to the serious risk of destruction, or of deterioration, vandalism, or despoliation. Keeping them in Western museums is thus deemed the best way to safeguard them, even if this requires loaning them out to Africans from time to time. Others, finally, certainly want to restitute the objects, including in the absence of any claim from the allegedly despoiled African communities. But there can be no question of recognizing a debt of any sort to anyone whomsoever. How can we prevent a conception of law as cynical as this one from masking the real nature of the disagreement thus obfuscated, that is, from reducing a cause as eminently political and moral as this one to a simple fight between solicitors and accountants, unless by turning our backs to it? To claim, as a pretext, that the law and right are autonomous, and have no need of supplement, indeed amounts to disentangling the law from every obligation to justice. The law's function is then no longer to serve justice but to sanctify existing force relations.

We need to leave behind an approach to restitution that is exclusively quantifiable, since restitution is then considered from the sole viewpoint of the institution of property and the law that ratifies it. So that the restitution of African objects is not the occasion for Europe to buy itself a good conscience at a cheap price, the debate must be recentered around the historical, philosophical, anthropological, and political stakes of the act of restitution. One then sees that every authentic politics of restitution is inseparable from a capacity for truth, such that honoring truth and acts of repairing the world become, by the same token, the essential foundation of a new link and a new relationship. Of all the regions of the Earth, ours—though this is certainly not the entirety of its history—is no doubt distinguished from others by the nature, the volume, and the density of what was removed and wrested from it and of which it was dispossessed. Is it because the continent never prevailed, from across the seas, over an indisputable empire? Or, as the poet Aimé Césaire recalled in other circles, because it invented neither gunpowder nor compass?[18] Or again because its name was never known and feared in faraway lands, except perhaps for the harshness of its climate—and according to Hegel, the ferociousness of its potentates and its cannibal festivities, which is the alpha and omega of every racist phantasmagoria? Anything they were unable to ransack the Europeans often burned down. Predation upon bodies would not be enough. During the colonial occupation properly speaking, they held countless inhabitants to ransom or destroyed what these latter held to be precious. With the granaries run dry, the livestock cleaned out, the harvests burned, many lands were depopulated, subjected as they were to illness and malnutrition, to forced labor, to the extracting of rubber and to other forms of corvée, not to mention exposed to the ecological disturbances brought about by colonization.[19]

Practically no domain was spared; not even ancestors and the gods. Europeans even went so far as to desecrate burial places. In the whirlwind, they carried off just about everything—objects of finery, others related to the basic necessities of life, fine fabrics; sumptuous necklaces, rings, artistically made jewelry inlaid with gold, copper, or bronze, belts, diverse gold-broached objects, including swords, shields used by warriors, doors, ornamental openwork seats and thrones with figures of men, women, and animals and elements of flora and fauna, magnificent fibula, bracelets and other spangles, and thousands and thousands of "medicaments" that they would identify with "fetishes." What to say of the sculpted wood pieces with their finely carved curved lines and knotwork? Or of the braiding and weaving of all sorts, the countless reliefs and bas-reliefs, the bronze or wooden human figures, combined with heads of quadrupeds, images of birds, snakes, plants like the marvelous landscapes of popular tales, sounds, and multicolored fabrics? How can we forget, in addition, the thousands of skulls and strings of human bones, most of which were stacked high in university basements, hospital laboratories, and the storage rooms of Western museums? When all is said and done, is there a single Western museum that does not rely, in its concept, on African bones?[20]

As several observers have noted, a good number of ethnographic missions began to resemble such predatory activities as abductions and pillages, hunts, and raids.[21] Indeed, the adjacency of natural objects, diverse artifacts, and stuffed wild animals in many Western (ethnographic and military) museums of the nineteenth century attests to these amalgams. The collection of material objects belonging to these "peoples of nature" often went hand in hand with that of hunting trophies, and therefore with the killing and dismembering of animals (MacKenzie 1988). A museological process then ordered the set of these items, transforming the totality of the spoils (animals included) into cultural products.[22] Projects of collection were therefore not limited to objects or to the dismemberment of human bodies.[23] The capture of wild animals was also part of it, including everything from "the smallest insects to the largest mammals."[24] Such was also the case with manifold zoological and entomological specimens. Little wonder, then, that during the collecting of masks, the heads of masks were, in a dramatic gesture of decapitation, separated from their costumes. As Julien Bondaz suggests, "The vocabulary used to designate the practices of collection well accounts for such overlaps" (Bondaz 2014). If we must recognize that all these objects did not become items of collection through exclusively violent means, the modes of their acquisition were nonetheless often in keeping with practices of predation.

LOSS OF WORLD

All these objects were part of a generative economy. Products of an open system of mutualization of knowledge, they expressed the marriage between the individual and singular genius (*génie*) and the common genius, as part of participatory ecosystems in which the world was not an object to be conquered but a reserve of potentials, and in which there was no pure and absolute power but that which was the source of life and of fecundity.

Concerning restitution, it is therefore necessary to come back to the essential issues. To explain the permanence of the removals we have suffered by the absence of scientific and technological prowess and of firepower is only a veil that hides what is most at stake. For starters, the history of African technical systems and of their operating frameworks remains to be written. Further, sight has probably been lost of the fact that science and technology do not exhaust the relationship that the human genus entertains with the world, matter, and all living beings. Science and modern technology are only mediations among many others of the human presence in nature and in existence. Science and religion are not necessarily opposed to magic, the profane is not the antithesis of the sacred, and the magical mode of existence is not necessarily pretechnological. There exists no single evolutive scale, extending along a linear trajectory, that would serve to provide an authoritative measure and judgment over all modes of existence.

That Africa did not originate thermobaric bombs does not mean that it created neither technical objects nor works of art, or that it was closed to borrowings or to innovation. It privileged other modes of existence within which technology stricto sensu constituted neither a force of rupture and diffraction, nor a force of divergence and separation, but a force of splitting and multiplication. At the heart of this dynamic, each concrete and distinct reality was always and by definition a symbol of something else, of another figure and structure. In this system of permanent reflections, of mutual relationships of correspondence and multiple schemes of mediation, each object ceaselessly enveloped, masked, disclosed, and exposed another object, extended its world and inserted into it. Being was not opposed to nonbeing. Within a tension as intense as it was interminable, the one would strive each time to incorporate the other. Becoming acted as identity, this reality that emerges only after the event—not qua that which completes and consecrates but that which always begins, announces, and prefigures; that which authorizes metamorphosis and transition (to other places, to other figures, to other moments). For this plastic humanity, it was more important to insert oneself into the world with the aim of participating in it and extending it than it was to mathematize, dominate, and subjugate it. If not all works of art were ritual objects, they were nonetheless made to come alive by way of ritual acts. For that matter, no object existed except in relation to a subject, as part of a reciprocal definition. The attribution of subjectivity to any inanimate object took place through rituals, ceremonies, and these relations of reciprocity. Such is the world that we lost, that African objects bore and whose epiphany they celebrated through the plurality of their forms. This world is one that no one will ever be able to restitute to us.

The objects were, for their part, vehicles of energy and movement. Living matters, they cooperated in life. Even when mere utensils and devices in themselves, they had a share in life, that is in physical life, in psychic life, and in energetic life, in the sort of life whose primary quality was circulation. Perhaps this is why, as powers of engendering, subversion, and masquerade, as much as privileged markers of paganism and animism, they were subject to such diabolization. How, today, can one intend to restitute them to us without de-diabolizing them beforehand—without one having oneself "renounced the devil"? We have therefore been, over a relatively long period, the warehouse of the world, at once its vital source of supplies and the abject subject of their extraction. Africa will have paid the world a heavy tribute, and it is far from being over. Incidentally, there is something colossal, uncountable, almost priceless that has been lost for good, and that is attested by the life of all our objects in captivity, just as that of all those of ours inside the carceral landscape of yesterday and of today. In certain circumstances, some of these objects played a properly philosophical role. They also served as mediators between humans and vital powers. For humans they served as a means to think their own shared existence.

Indeed, behind the technical gestures that went into making them, a particular horizon was hidden—the mutualization of resources that generated ways not susceptible to endangering the whole of the ecosystem; the unconditional refusal to turn everything into commodities; the duty to open the door and speech to the dynamics of partner relationships and the uninterrupted creation of commons. Losing them thus led to a real impoverishment of the symbolic world. Behind each one of these objects lay some métier, and behind each métier a font of knowledge and understandings that were incessantly acquired and transmitted, as well as technical and aesthetic modes of thinking, figurative sorts of information, a certain charge of magic, in short human effort to tame the very matter of life, the assortment of its substances. One of their functions included the putting of forms and forces in relation while symbolizing them, that is, the activating of powers making it possible to move the world.[25] All that is gone—and this is the heavy tribute that Africa will have paid Europe, that region of the world to which we are tied by an intrinsic relationship of extraction and removal. This is perhaps one of the reasons that many Africans attach to the memory of Europe a note at once of fascination and of infamy. There is perverse fascination of the brute force and power exerted, a power of deliberate untruth and of the practically permanent denial of responsibility. And infamy, because many Africans are convinced that Europe wants nothing concerning them; that what it wants is an essentially obedient and docile Africa; that it wants an Africa akin to a corpse stripped of its shroud, which, although basically lifeless, ceaselessly revives itself and rises up in its coffin; that the sort of African that Europe tolerates and accepts is the African whose energies it does not stop capturing and hijacking, one who obeys with the docile fidelity of the animal able to recognize its master once and for all.

The Capacity for Truth

The West long refused to acknowledge that it owed us any debt at all. It refused to acknowledge the millstone of debts that—accumulated over the course of its world conquest—it has dragged along ever since. Today, most of the West's defenders claim, by contrast, that we are indebted to it. As they put it, we owe it a debt of "civilization," insofar as some of us have, they point out, benefited from the wrongs that, sometimes with our own complicity, were done to us. Today, the West does not simply want to rid itself of the strangers that we are. It also wants for us to take back our objects. Without giving any account of itself, it finally wants to be able to declare: "Not having done you any wrong, I owe you all strictly nothing." By inviting us to take back our objects and to liberate the spaces that they occupied in its museums, what, then, does it seek? To weave new relationships? Or, in this era of closure, does it seek to reiterate something it has always suspected, namely that we were person-objects, disposable by definition? Will we facilitate its task by renouncing every right to remembrance? Will we dare to go further and decline the offer of repatriation? Thus transforming these objects into the eternal proof of the infamy that it committed, but that it wants to take no responsibility for, will we ask it to live forever with what it has taken and assume its Cain-like figure to the very end?

But suppose that we yield to the offer, and that instead of a verita-ble act of restitution, we satisfy ourselves with a simple recuperation of artifacts henceforth without substance. How are we to sort out objects and their use-value, on the one hand, from works of art sensu stricto on the other? Or objects of ritual and cult from ordinary objects, when very few people are sure of what each of these objects is in itself, of how they were made and how they "functioned," of what energies they served as repositories for and that they were able to release, of the circumstances in which they did so and of their effects on matter as well as on humans and the living in general? When it comes down to it, all this knowledge was lost. As Pol Pierre Gossiaux explains, African art replied to an aes-thetics that may be qualified as cumulative. Its objects resulted "from the assembling and accumulation of disparate elements" whose "sense and function came from the formal and semantic relations thus created by their accumulation" (Gossiaux 2007). The object assembled in this way was qualified as "beautiful" only to the extent that it fully assumed its ritual functions. Such accumulations, Gossiaux makes clear, did not come about by chance. They demanded lengthy apprenticeships and initiations into the handling of secular knowledges that have been lost.[26] Beyond the objects as such, who will restitute the acts of thought that were associated with them, the types of cognition at stake in them, the forms of memory and imagination that they mobilized and of which they were, in turn, the product?

In addition, between that which went and that which returns, the gap is great. Most of these objects have been deformed and become unrecognizable. The objects present in the collections and the museums were not only cut off from the cultural contexts in which they had been summoned to take part.[27] Some have endured numerous wounds and amputations, including physical, and now bear considerable scars.[28] Let's take, as an example, the masks and other objects previously used in the dance ceremonies. Most arrived in Europe coiffed, adorned with all sorts of finery (feathers of owls, eagles, vultures, quails or roosters, or porcupines quills, and even dresses made from the inner bark of pigmented papyrus). These distinctive styles and bits of finery, as well as the context in which they were invited to make their appearance, made them receptacles of meaning. And they were as important as the morphological qualities of the objects or, as Gossiaux points out, "the articulation of their geometry in space." Nevertheless, the Europeans would systematically strip them "of everything that seemed to conceal their apparent structures."[29]

Even if among most of the peoples that produce these objects the opposition between myth and technology, and between technology and ritual, was by definition weak, how are we also to identify all the diverse customs—from among the masks, statues, and reliquary-statuettes, flyswatters, the vegetal debris, the human bones and amulets, the animal skins, the kaolin, the seashells and the padouk powder, the assegais, drums, and other objects consecrated to rites of passages or initiation—that is, to set apart those that were intended to honor the dead or to chase away evil spirits, and others still that were required for therapeutic or divinatory practices?

By Way of Conclusion

Who can honestly deny that what was taken were not only objects but, along with them, enormous symbolic deposits, enormous reserves of potentials? Who does not see that the large-scale monopolizing of African treasures constituted a colossal and practically incalculable loss, and, consequently, is not liable to a purely financial compensation, since what it led to was the devitalization of our capacities to bring about worlds, to give rise to other figures of our common humanity?

So the issue cannot simply be to restitute materials, styles, decors, and functions. For how is the meaning to be restituted? Is it lost for good? Who will recompense the fact of having, forever, to live with this loss? Is it no more than compensable? A certain Europe does not want to trouble itself with these questions. For it, restitution is not an obligation. Faithful to a variant of legalism inherited from its long history, it considers that an obligation can arise only when a legal constraint exists. In its eyes, all restitution, whatever one says, is a modality among others of payment. There is nothing to be paid without the prior existence of a debt. All restitution consequently entails the existence, avowed or disavowed, of a debt. Now, Europe deems that it is not our debtors and that we are not its creditors. So no debt needs honoring. Were there any debt, we would be unable to oblige its payment. It is not obligable. Europe considers that, in the current state of affairs, there are no legal means obliging it to restitute our objects. What characterizes obligation, properly speaking, is the possibility of sanctioning a case of noncompliance.

And if, despite all this, Europe does end up returning these objects, it will be done voluntarily, in an act of generosity and liberality and not as an obligation to whomever it may be. In this case, as in others, at issue is not to do justice but to perform an act of gratuitousness and benevolence. The act of restitution does not stem from gratuitousness and kindness. The act of restitution stems from an obligation. And there are obligations from which one cannot be discharged in keeping with existing legal constraints. They continue to be obligations for all that. Indeed, other obligations arise from which one can discharge oneself voluntarily. Through a duty of conscience. But it is a long time since we have stopped believing in the use of making appeals to one's conscience. All restitution, if it is to be authentic, must be enacted on the basis of an equivalent recognition of the seriousness of the prejudice suffered and the wrongs inflicted. There is strictly nothing to be restituted (or to be returned), whenever one considers that one has caused no wrong, that one has taken nothing that demanded permission of any sort. This is how the act of restitution is inseparable from the act of making reparation. "To reestablish" or "to restore" (the other name for restitution) is not the same thing as "to repent." For that matter, one is not the condition of the other. Similarly, restitution without compensation (or restoration) is by definition partial. But there are irreparable loses that no compensation can ever undo—which does not mean it is not necessary to compensate. To have given compensation does not mean that one has erased the wrong. It does not result in any absolution. To compensate, as Kwame Anthony Appiah underlines, is about offering to repair the relationship (Appiah 2004). Further still, restitution is an obligation whenever a conscious, malicious, and deliberate act of destruction was undertaken on another's life. In precolonial systems of thought, the most damaging wrongs were considered those that caused harm to what Tempels called "vital force."

In contexts where life was fragile, or was liable to being diminished, every attack on the integrity of being and on the intensity of life, however slight, merited restoration. In its plenary meaning, restoration (or restitution) implied that the damages suffered could be valued. The calculation of damages could be expressed in economic terms. But, in the last instance, damages were established according to a measure of the value of life. It was ultimately the measure of violation of life suffered that served as a basis for the valuation of damages or restitution.[30] Wholly in keeping with this philosophy, veritable restitution is therefore one that participates in the restoration of life. The law subtending it is more person- than goods- and property-oriented. There is no restitution without reparation. Wherever material damages and interests come into play, the only sense they have is to perform that restoration of life.

Neither is there any real restitution in the absence of what we must indeed call the capacity for truth. From this viewpoint, "to render" pertains to an unconditional duty—to the infinitely irrecusable thing that is life, all life, that form of debt unable to be discharged as a matter of principle. For Europe, the restitution of our objects means that it stop approaching us with the attitude of one for whom only their own reality counts and is necessary. Europe cannot purport to return our objects to us while remaining convinced that one's being a subject lies in an insistence on one's own distinction and not in the sort of mutuality demanded by the reticular world that became ours. Each singular life counts. History is not only a matter of force; it is also a matter of truth. Authority and dignity are not merely a donation coming from strength and power. One is therefore called upon to honor truth, and not only strength and power.

The truth is that Europe took things from us that it will never be able to restitute. We will learn to live with this loss. Europe, for its part, will have to take responsibility for its acts, for that shady part of our shared history of which it has sought to relieve itself. The risk is that by failing to give an account of it while restituting our objects, it concludes that, with the restitution complete, our right to remind it of the truth is removed. But for new ties to be woven, it must honor the truth, as the truth is the teacher of responsibility. This debt of truth cannot be erased as a matter of principle. It will haunt us until the end of time. Honoring it goes by way of a commitment to repairing the fabric and the visage of the world.

Notes

1. The idea of African "objects" or "artifacts" is one of a general set, or again of an entire population of "things" or material productions, whether these latter take on an aesthetic function or call for an investment of the same kind. On these discussions in the European context, see Schaeffer (2004, 25–45).

2. See Mveng (1980); Senghor (1967); and Césaire (2009).

3. Lopes and Pigafetta (1965, 81–82); Cuvelier (1946); and Dapper (1989, 89–367); and on Dahomey in the seventeenth century, consult Bonfils (1986, 161–174).

4. In the register of exceptions, read for example Balard (2007, 74–93).

5. See Muchembled (2002).

6. Consult Ostorero and Anheim (2003).

7. By way of example, read Carroll (1967).

8. On these debates, see Lévy-Bruhl (2013 [1922]); Lévy-Bruhl (2019 [1927]); Lévy-Bruhl (2016 [1928]). On debates at the time, further consult Leroy (1927) and Allier (1927).

9. On this topic, Comaroff and Comaroff (1991); and Comaroff and Comaroff (1997). See also Mbembe (1988).

10. See the works of Zerbini (2007, 2011); as well as Pettinaroli (2013).

11. Cited in Bonemaison (2007, 2).

12. For a notorious case, consult Duviols (2008); and Boulaga (1981).

13. See, for example, Amade (2018).

14. See Schmidt and Oksenberg (2009).

15. In this work, Einstein (1915) endeavors to study the formal qualities of "black objects," whereas in *Afrikanische Plastik* (Einstein 1921), he is more interested in their functions and meaning within their societies of origin.

16. See Bidault (2013).

17. I draw here in part on Carlo Severi's analysis (2017).

18. "Those who invented neither gunpowder nor compass / those who could not ever tame steam or electricity / those who have not explored either seas or sky / but without whom the earth would not be the earth," from Césaire (2017, 47).

19. By way of illustration, read Martin (2014).

20. Arndt (2013).

21. See Bondaz (2013). See also Jacobs (2006).
22. See Dias (1999, 590).
23. Roberts (1998); Roque (2011); and Zimmerman (2001).
24. Consult Bondaz (2014).
25. On this topic, see the works of Pierre Bonnafé (1987, 1973, 1978).
26. Not only the making but also the conservation and restoration of objects required a host of technical knowledges about the botanical, vegetal, mineral, and organic worlds. The utilizing of wood, for example, demanded a minimum of knowledge about its components, notably about those concerning what made it moisture- and weather-resistant. Similarly for animal oils and fats, and the diverse pigments and elements such as fire, the function of which was to make objects nonputrescible. On this subject, read Pol Pierre Gossiaux (2007).
27. For Johannes Fabian, it is precisely this practice of "decontextualization" that is specific to ethnographic collection. See Fabian (2004).
28. See Speranza (2008).
29. See Gossiaux (2007).
30. See Temples (1969, 80).

References

Allier, Raoul. 1927. *Les non-civilisés et nous: différence irréductible ou identité foncière.* Paris: Payot.

Amade, José Sarzi. 2018. "Trois missionnaires capucins dans le Royaume de Congo de la fin du XVIIe siècle: Cavazzi, Merolla et Zucchelli—Force et prose dans les récits de spectacles punitifs et de châtiments exemplaires." *Veritas* 139: 137–160.

Appiah, Kwame Anthony. 2004. "Comprendre les reparations: Réflexion préliminaire." *Cahiers d'études africaines* 1, no. 173–174: 25–40.

Arndt, Lotte. 2013. "Vestiges of Oblivion: Sammy Baloji's Works on Skulls in European Museum Collections." *darkmatter*, November 18. www.darkmatter 101.org/site/2013/11/18.

Balard, Martine. 2007. "Les combats du père Aupiais (1877–1945), missionnaire et ethnographe du Dahomey pour la reconnaissance africaine." *Histoire et Missions Chrétiennes* 2, no. 2: 74–93.

Bataille, Georges. 1989. *Theory of Religion.* Translated by Robert Hurley. New York: Zone Books.

Bechtel, Guy. 1997. "La sorcière et l'Occident: La destruction de la sorcellerie en Europe des origines aux grands buchers." Paris: Plon.

Bidault, Coline. 2013. "La présentation des objets africains dans DOCUMENTS (1929/1930), magazine illustre." *Les Cahiers de l'Ecole du Louvre* 3, no. 3: 5–13.

Bondaz, Julien. 2011. "L'ethnograhie comme chasse: Michel leiris et le animaux de la mission Dakar-Djibouti." *Gradhiva*, no. 13: 162–181.

Bondaz, Julien. 2013. "L'ethnographie parasitée? Anthropologie et enthomologie en Afrique de l'Ouest (1928–1960)." *L'Homme*, no. 206: 121–150.

Bondaz, Julien. 2014. "Entrer en collection: Pour une ethnographie des gestes et des techniques de collecte." *Les Cahiers de l'Ecole du Louvre* 4, no. 4. http:// journals.openedition.org/cel/481. DOI: 10.4000/cel.481.

Bonemaison, Michel. 2007. "Le Musée Africain de Lyon d'hier à aujourd'hui." *Histoire et Missions Chrétiennes* 2, no. 2. https://www.cairn.info/revue-histoire-monde-et-cultures-religieuses1-2007-2-page-143.htm.

Bonfils, Jean. 1986. "La mission catholique en République populaire du Benin aux XVIIe et XVIIIe siècles." *Nouvelle Revue*: 161–174.

Bonnafé, Pierre. 1973. "Une grande fête de la vie et de la mort: le miyali des Kukuya." *L'Homme* (June): 97–166.

Bonnafé, Pierre. 1978. "Le lignage de la mort, in Nzo lipfu." Paris: Nanterre.

Bonnafé, Pierre. 1987. "Une force, un objet, un champ: le buti des Kukuya au Congo." *Systèmes de pensée en Afrique noire*, no. 8: 25–67.

Bouche, J. E. 1874. "La religion des nègres africains, en particulier des Djedjis et des Nagos's." In *Le Contemporain*, 2nd ed., 57–875. N.p.: n.p.

Boulaga, Fabien Eboussi. 1981. *Christianisme sans fétiches: Révélation et domination*. Paris: Présence Africaine.

Boureau, Alain. 2004. *Satan hérétique: Naissance de la démonologie dans l'Occident médiéval (1280–1330)*. Paris: Odile Jacob.

Brasseur, Paule. 1997. "Les missionnaires catholiques à la côte d'Afrique pendant la deuxième moitié du XIX siècle." *Mélanges d'Ecole française de Rome, in Italie et Méditerranée* 109, no. 2: 723–745.

Bréton, André. 1957. *L'Art magique*. Paris: Club français du livre.

Carroll, Kevin. 1967. *Yoruba Religious Carving: Pagan and Christian Sculpture in Nigeria and Dahomey*. London: Geoffrey Chapman.

Cassirer, Ernst. 2017. *The Myth of the State*. New Haven: Yale University Press.

Césaire, Aimé. 2000 [1952]. *Discourse on Colonialism*. New York: Monthly Review Press.

Césaire, Aimé. 2009. "Discours prononcé à Dakar le 6 avril 1966." *Gradhiva* 10: 1–7.

Césaire, Aimé. 2017 [1939]. *Journal of a Homecoming/Cahier d'un retour au pays natal*. Translated by N. Gregson Davis. Durham: Duke University Press.

Comaroff, Jean, and John Comaroff. 1997. *The Dialectics of Modernity on a South African Frontier*, vol. 2. Chicago: University of Chicago Press.

Comaroff, Jean, and John Comaroff. 1991. *Of Revelation and Revolution*, vol. 1. Chicago: University of Chicago Press.

Coquery-Vidrovitch, Catherine. 1964. "La fête des coutumes au Dahomey: historique et essai d'interprétation." *Annales*, no. 4: 696–716.

Cuvelier, Jean. 1946. *L'ancien royaume du Congo: Fondation, découverte et première évangélisation de l'ancien royaume du Congo*. Bruges: Desclée De Brouwer.

Dapper, Olfert. 1989. "Description de l'Afrique." In *Objets interdits*, edited by A. Van Dantzig, 89–367. Paris: Fondation Dapper.

Descoqs, Pedro. 1928. "Métaphysique et raison primitive." *Archives de philosophie* 5, no 3: 127–165.

Dias, Nelia. 1999. "L'Afrique naturalisée." *Cahiers d'études africaines* 39, nos. 155–156: 583–594.

Duviols, Pierre. 2008. *La lutte contre les religions autochtones dans le Perou colonial: L'extirpation de l'idolatrie entre 1532 et 1660*. Toulouse: Presses Universitaires du Mirail.

Einstein, Carl. 1915. *Negerplastik*. Leipzig: Verlag der Weissen Bucher.

Einstein, Carl. 1921. *Afrikanische Plastik*. Berlin: E. Wasmuth.

Fabian, Johannes. 2004. "On Recognizing Things: The 'Ethnic Artefact' and the 'Ethnographic Object.'" *L'Homme* 170: 47–60.

Freud, Sigmund. 1991. *On Sexuality: Three Essays on the Theory of Sexuality and Other Works*. Translated by James Strachey. London: Penguin.

Fromont, Cécile. 2017. *The Art of Conversion: Christian Visual Culture in the Kingdom of Kong*. Chapel Hill: University of North Carolina Press.

Gossiaux, Pol Pierre. 2007. "Conserver, restaurer: écrire le temps en Afrique. *CeROArt* 1. https://doi.org/10.4000/ceroart.253.

Hegel, G. W. F. 2005. *Philosophy of Right*. Translated by S. W. Dyde. Mineola, NY: Dover Philosophical Classics.

Hegel, G. W. F. 2013. *Lectures on the Philosophy of History*. Translated by Ruben Alvarado. Aalten, Netherlands: WordBridge.

Jacobs, Nancy J. 2006. "The Intimate Politics of Ornithology in Colonial Africa." *Comparative Studies in Society and History* 48, no. 3: 564–603.

Leroy, Olivier. 1927. *La raison primitive: Essai de réfutation de la théorie du prélogisme*. Paris: Guethner.

Lévy-Bruhl, Lucien. 2013 [1922]. *Primitive Mentality*. Los Angeles, CA: HardPress.

Lévy-Bruhl, Lucien. 2016 [1928]. *The "Soul" of the Primitive*. London: Routledge.

Lévy-Bruhl, Lucien. 2019 [1927]. *How Natives Think*. Translated by Lilian A. Claire. London: Routledge.

Lopes, Duarte, and Filippo Pigafetta. 1965. *Description du royaume de Congo et des contrées environnantes*. Translation and notes by Willy Bal. Louvain: Nauwelaerts.

MacKenzie, John. 1988. *The Empire of Nature: Hunting, Conservation and British Imperialism*. Manchester: Manchester University Press.

Martin, Jean. 2014. *Le rapport Brazza: Mission d'enquête du Congo—rapport et documents (1905-1907)*. Paris: Le passager clandestin.

Mbembe, Achille. 1988. *Afriques indociles: Christianisme, pouvoir et État en société postcoloniale*. Paris: Karthala.

Mbembe, Achille. 2017. *Critique of Black Reason*. Translated by Laurent Dubois. Durham, NC: Duke University Press.

McCabe, Michael. 2007. "L'évolution de la théologie de la mission dans la Société des Missions Africaines de Marion Bresillac à nos jours." *Histoire et Missions Chrétiennes* 2, no. 2: 1–22.

Muchembled, Robert. 2002. *Une histoire du diable: XIIe–XXe siècle*. Paris: Points.

Mveng, Engelbert. 1980. *L'art et l'artisanat africains*. Yaounde: CLE.

Ostorero, Martine, and Étienne Anheim. 2003. "Le diable en procès: Démonologie et sorcellerie à la fin du Moyen-Âge." Special issue of *Medievales*, no. 44.

Pettinaroli, Laura, ed. 2013. *Le gouvernement pontifical sous Pie XI: Pratiques romaines et gestion de l'universel (1922–1939)*. Rome: Collection EFR.

Roberts, Allen F. 1998. *A Dance of Assassins: Performing Early Colonial Hegemony in the Congo*. Bloomington: Indiana University Press.

Roque, Ricardo. 2011. *Headhunting and Colonialism: Anthropology and the Circulation of Human Skulls in the Portuguese Empire, 1870–1930*. Cambridge: Cambridge University Press.

Schaeffer, Jean-Marie. 2004. "Objets esthetiques?" *L'Homme*, no. 170: 25–45.

Schmidt, James, and Amélie Oksenberg Rorty, eds. 2009. *Kant's "Idea for a Universal History with a Cosmopolitan Aim": A Critical Guide*. Cambridge: Cambridge University Press.

Senghor, Léopold Sédar. 1967. "Standards critiques de l'art africaine." *African Arts* 1, no. 1: 6–9.

Severi, Carlo. 2017. *L'objet-personne: In Une anthropologie de la croyance visuelle*. Paris: Editions de la Rue d'Ulm.

Speranza, Gaetano. 2008. "Sculpture africaine: Blessures et altérité." *CeROArt* 2. https://doi.org/10.4000/ceroart.624.

Tempels, Placide. 1969. *Bantu Philosophy*. Translated by Colin King. Paris: Présence Africaine, HBC.

Voegelin, Eric. 1997. *Race and State*. Translated by Ruth Hein. Columbia, MO: University of Missouri Press.

Zerbini, Laurick. 2007. "La construction du discours patrimonial: les musées missionnaires à Lyon (1860–1960)." *Outre-Mers* 95, no. 356–357: 125–138.

Zerbini, Laurick. 2011. "Les collections africaines des Oeuvres Pontificales: L'objet africain sous le prisme du missionnaire catholique." *Objets des terres lointaines*, edited by Essertel Yannick, 31–51. Milan: Silvana Editoriale.

Zimmerman, Andrew. 2001. *Anthropology and Antihumanism in Imperial Germany*. Chicago: University of Chicago Press.

12

On the Phenomenology of a
Shared World in Achille Mbembe

Schalk Gerber

Introduction

Achille Mbembe, the Cameroonian philosopher and historian, is a self-described *penseur de la traversée* (thinker of the crossing) whose story is one of constant motion and of crossing borders, a thinker "for whom critique is a form of care, healing and reparation," and for whom "the idea of a common world, how to bring it into being, how to compose it, how to repair it and how to share it"—has ultimately been his main concern.[1] But, as I will illustrate in this chapter, this understanding of the in-common is not some form of cosmopolitanism that uncritically celebrates globalization by appropriating the modern idea of humanism. It does not suppose some universally shared quality like reason. It is indeed the opposite. By taking the critique of the entanglement of capitalism and race seriously during the early stages of the advance of globalization, that is, colonialization, Mbembe's understanding of the reparation in and of a shared world is based on the lived experiences in Africa. To understand why this distinction is so important, one may ask, as in the first section of this chapter: How does Mbembe's thinking relate to other attempts of formulating a phenomenology of African lived experience? This overview may be sketched by turning to Mbembe's commentators and critics. After establishing Mbembe's position beyond the binary Subject-Other of alterity that has dominated these debates, I will retrace the line of thinking within the phenomenological tradition that Mbembe follows to Nancy, which Mbembe furthers through the help of Fanon in formulating the notion of reparation in relation to a rethinking of our being-in-the-world *with* others according to our shared being (our being-in-common), which is not a common-being, concluding with a discussion on Mbembe's notion of Afropolitanism.

Situating Mbembe among His Commentators and Critics

When it comes to the commentary on and critique of Mbembe, it has mostly focused on his book *On the Postcolony*, which made him famous and that many regarded as a paradigm shift in postcolonial theory from India to Africa. A lot of this commentary and critique against him is, to my mind, the result of a misreading of his work based on what may be summarized in two main points: First, the fact that commentators and critics alike place Mbembe's thought within the already established schema of two camps that postcolonial theory has been divided into, namely, on the one side the Marxist-Sartrean-Fanonian camp that is considered to be materialistic, and on the other hand, the postcolonial ethics camp based in Levinas and Derrida that is also seen to be text focused.[2] Second, the fact that the books—which by themselves (thematically and content-wise) directly contradict most of the critique put against him—were first published in French and, in some instances, translated and published in English only at a much later stage.[3]

The combination of these two points is often coupled with the impulse to defend against—rather than critically engage with—Mbembe's critique of an *uncritical* Marxist moral-political-economic evangelism and national (nativist) discourses.[4] This impulse has led these efforts to paint Mbembe, for instance, as embracing neoliberal capitalistic ideas in the celebration of globalization. Or that he advocates a variation of a cosmopolitical idea based on the uncritical embracing of the humanism ideals of modernity without considering the existential-phenomenological condition of black people. Put differently, Mbembe's thought has often been forced to fit into the Levinasian ethics camp specifically and thereby the binary Subject-Other framework of alterity in general. Furthermore, this formulation of Mbembe requires thinkers to dismiss his thought as not taking the black condition seriously to formulate their position against him. I will not go into specific instances here. Instead, I will simply outline Mbembe's position, which will clarify that such a critique does not hold. What these critiques moreover neglect to acknowledge is how their positions actually share a lot more with that of Mbembe than what they readily admit in (1) taking as their departure point the black experience and its ontological degradation as nonbeing; (2) that they all strive, following Fanon, for a rehumanizing of the Black Man/Woman. When these two points are taken up, it reveals, perhaps more importantly, and more productively, how Mbembe's position differs from other attempts that directly oppose themselves to him in thinking this rehumanization.

Thus, to position Mbembe's thought, I will briefly discuss here two of the most relevant positions that oppose themselves directly to Mbembe, coming from Tendayi Sithole and John Lamola. Sithole opposes his position to Mbembe to make a case for the appropriation of decolonial thought over postcolonial theory, especially that of Nelson Maldonado-Torres, who rereads Fanon with Levinas.[5] For Sithole, the subjectivity of the oppressed Other, that is, the black subject or "infra-human," needs to take center stage for a new subjectivity (as fully human) to emerge. For this to happen, what is first required is the liberation of the world from its antiblack solidarity with the help of a decolonial critical analysis. Lamola, in turn, opposes Mbembe by applying Marx's framework of labor exploitation to that of the African slave to link this to the black existential condition with the help of a Sartrean-Fanonian position.[6] Moreover, both Lamola and Sithole argue for a *differed* rehumanization. The Subject or Other first needs to be established through an event of liberation, whereupon either ethics or reparation (or both) can follow. Mbembe's move to think rehumanization, given the ontological degradation of the African condition, differs from these maneuvers. In thinking Nancy with Fanon, Mbembe thinks ontology and ethics and, by extension, reparation as co-originary, which I will unpack in more detail later. To state it briefly, Nancy's position differs from both the Sartrean and Levinasian maneuvers as follows.

The Sartrean position takes the Subject as its ground for ethics, seen in the famous statement that "existence precedes essence" (Sartre 2007, 22). The ontology of the Self (in the Heideggerian sense) comes before and therefore grounds ethics. The Self stays at the center (as with the Subject of modernity), although not as essentialized, but condemned to freedom to create his or her own morals, which furthermore leads to the possibilities of authentication or alienation: "Thus *my* freedom is condemnation. . . . But since I am free, I am constrained by my freedom to make it mine, to make it *my* horizon, *my* view, my morality, etc." (Sartre 1992, 433). In the "Letter on Humanism," Heidegger, however, critiques Sartre's formulation as follows: "By way of contrast, Sartre expresses the basic tenet of existentialism in this way: Existence precedes essence. In this statement he is taking *existentia* and *essentia* according to their metaphysical meaning, which from Plato's time on has said that *essentia* precedes *existentia*. Sartre reverses this statement. But the reversal of a metaphysical statement remains a metaphysical statement" (Heidegger 1998, 250). This move, moreover, is not only the cause of tension in Sartre's formulation of the Self, but it also means that the relation of the Self to the Other is still problematic, and for the Sartre of *Being and Nothingness*, it meant the Other is related to the *stare* (*gaze*) that alienates the Self from itself: "I grasp the Other's look at the very center of my act as the solidification and alienation of my own possibilities. . . . But at the same time the look alienates them from me" (Sartre 1993, 47). The problem here becomes the limitation of possibilities in the encounter with the Other that the reintroduced metaphysical framework of the Self-Other brings. Ethics is a self-centered project, whereas the relation to the Other is one of *domination* that is constituted by the stare of the Other.

In turn, it was Levinas who seemed to "save us" from the alienating stare or gaze of the Other by redefining the relation to the Other as *liberating* instead of dominating. As Visker puts it: "For the gaze of the Other, we now discovered, did not just stare at us, it also concerned us. And henceforth, the French *regarder* lost its Sartrean overtones and the threat once contained in '*Autrui me regarde*' somehow was transfigured into the promise of an ethical deliverance" (Visker 1999, 326). But where one might think that Levinas provides us with a way out of metaphysics, one has to consider how Levinas makes a similar move to Sartre by staying within the Self-Other framework. Thus, let us then consider the Levinasian position in contrast to that of Sartre. Where Sartre places the Self at the center, or as the "foundation" of ethics, *Levinas simply reverses this and places the other as Other at its center*: "In my own analyses, the approach to others is not originally in my speaking out to the other, but in my responsibility for him or her. That is the original ethical relation" (Levinas 1997, 44). The Other serves as the foundation of ethics, insofar as the Other's face is a trace of God (the actual foundation of ethics). This means that the Self is always in an asymmetrical—as opposed to reciprocal and symmetrical—relation to the Other, who grounds the ethical relation and thereby pulls the center away from the Self toward the Other. Hence, Levinas famously claims that *ethics is more fundamental than ontology*, a reversal of the Sartrean position of the ontology of the Self that comes before and grounds ethics. As Levinas puts it: "Being before the existent . . . is freedom before justice. . . . The terms must be reversed" (Levinas 1969, 41). It is thus the Other that calls us to be ethical instead of human beings condemned to freedom. Therefore, Heidegger's statement on Sartre also holds true for Levinas, that is, "the reversal of a metaphysical statement remains a metaphysical statement." But in the case of Levinas he would perhaps embrace this point of critique, since it is exactly a return to a metaphysics of the Other against an ontology of the self or Same that he advocated. Ethics comes before ontology, or as Derrida puts it, for Levinas, "ethics is therefore metaphysis" (Derrida 2005, 122). Both the Sartrean and Levinasian maneuvers, however, stay in the metaphysical schema of alterity (that seeks to posit a foundation), which they aim to overcome.

Mbembe, in following Nancy's position to think ontology and ethics (and reparation) *co-originary*, shifts beyond the frame of alterity (Subject-Other). This shift is to think alterity in terms of the plurality of singularities (being singular plural), which are co-original. Thus, instead of the Self-Other framework, where ontology grounds the relation to the other (ethics), or ethics grounds ontology, Nancy suggests that "being is singularly plural and plurally singular" (Nancy 2000, 28). This is "because none of these three terms [being singular plural] precedes or grounds the other, each designates the co-essence of the others" (Nancy 2000, 37).

Put another way, alterity is thought differently according to our being-in-the-world that is *always already* being-in-the-world *with* others. Being-*with* accordingly becomes the "orientating point."[7] Mbembe develops this position most concretely in *Out of the Dark Night* (2021 [2010]) and extends it in subsequent works like *Critique of Black Reason* (2017 [2013]) but already indicated it as early as 2004 when he writes:

> How best to overturn these perpetual and predominant imaginings of Africa? One strategy is to constitute an argument that relies less on difference—or even originality—than on a fundamental connection to an elsewhere. Though the work of difference has performed important functions in the scholarly practice that sought to undercut imperial paradigms, it is clearly time, in the case of Africa, to revisit the frontiers of common-

ality and the potential of sameness-as-worldliness. This is a far
cry from a proposition that would aim at rehabilitating facile
assumptions about universality and particularity. After all, the
unity of the world is nothing but its diversity. As Jean-Luc Nancy
argues, "the world is a multiplicity of worlds, and its unity is
the mutual sharing and exposition of all its worlds—within this
world." As for the "sharing of the world," it is, fundamentally,
"the law of the world." If, as we believe, the world has nothing
other, if it is not subject to any authority, and if it does not have
a sovereign, then we must read Africa in the same terms as we
read everywhere else. This is not tantamount to diminishing
aspects of its supposed originality or even its distinctiveness or
the potency of its suffering. (Mbembe and Nuttall 2004, 351)[8]

If Mbembe is to be critiqued on this point in view of the current aim
and context of this essay, it is perhaps that he does not explicate this
position in the more familiar phenomenological terminology, which I
will attempt to do here.

A Brief Detour to Nancy

The previous section highlighted some of the criticisms against Mbembe
and argued why they miss the essential point of his thinking. To orient
ourselves toward what I think is that essential point, I find that it is valuable to review the ways in which Jean-Luc Nancy has influenced Mbembe.
In so doing, this section will briefly highlight Nancy's departure from a
Heideggerian *Mitsein* and how this works to reorient *Dasein* away from
a being-unto-death and toward thinking the most concrete ontological
structure of our existence. That is to say, our finite existence in the world
always already with others. To achieve this, I will outline three important markers in Nancy's thought that set the phenomenological scene for
Mbembe.[9]

First, in the 1980s, in a period where Nancy worked closely with
Lacoue-Labarthe at the Center for Philosophical Research on the Political
at the Ecole Normale Supérieure, Nancy made the case for an understanding of community that aims to avoid totalitarianism by rethinking the
ground of community traditionally thought as a common-being, a shared
characteristic like race, nationality, and so forth, as an unground. In *The*

Inoperative Community, this ungrounding of community Nancy named the being-in-common. The in-common refers to our being-in-the-world as always already being-*with* others. Simply put, we find ourselves existing not in a vacuum, isolated from the world, which is then overcome in a secondary and derived effort. We find ourselves always already existing *with* others. Here the *with* itself is no-thing (as in a substance that can serve as a ground). Instead, it refers to the exposure of our *Dasein* to the always already *Mitdasein*.[10] It concerns the finite existence we share instead of the construction of an infinite fixed identity that determines who belongs and who does not. The question of the political becomes the question of the *with*, of relation as such. Therefore, the existence of others is pregiven and needs no justification, categorization, or approval according to the appeal to a Subject, Other, or any otherworldly principle. A sense of community, hence, is the constant exposition between the plurality of beings who exists together, that is, the exposition of the existence they share. The question then becomes not of who is included, but rather how those who exist together can take part in creating a dignified shared existence together.

The second important marker concerns Nancy's progression from the idea of being-in-common to a full reappropriation of Heidegger's fundamental ontology. More specifically, Nancy rethinks Heidegger's *Mitsein* analysis. For Nancy, Heidegger's emphasis of creating meaning in *Dasein*'s being-toward-death means that the relation to the other—which is initially co-original in every aspect—becomes indifferent. In other words, the question of authenticity overshadows the question of being-*with*. For Nancy, meaning is created not in the question of death but *between* singular beings. This point becomes especially clear in Nancy's text on Heidegger's *Originary Ethics*, where Nancy takes up the question of the relation of ethics in the critical reading of the "Letter on Humanism."[11] In it, Heidegger first shifts the question away from the authenticity of *Dasein* to explicating the "essence" of being human as *ek-sistence* (LH, 247). Ek-sistence, however, "is not identical with the traditional concept of *existentia*, which means actuality in contrast to the meaning of *essentia* as possibility" (LH, 248).[12] It is instead thought of in terms of *ecstasis*. Ek-sistence, thought as *ecstasis*, means "standing out," which does not coincide with *existentia* in either form or content (LH, 249). Stated together, "the ecstatic essence of the human being consists in ek-sistence" (LH, 248). Nancy emphasizes that the difference between essence as ek-sistence in standing out and essence as fixed is that ecstatic ek-sistence designates a conduct: the conduct of making sense. Accordingly, sense is not given as fixed, but our being consists of the conduct of making sense, of being open to making sense (OE, 180). Nancy importantly adds that "this Being-outside-itself, or this 'ecstatic essence,' does not occur to an already given 'self.' It is, on the contrary, through it that something like a 'self' (a subject, and a responsible subject) can come about" (OE, 180). Thus, Nancy is further emphasizing the break with the Self-Other framework.

For Heidegger, furthermore, the *ek*-sisting is another way of formulating the *there* or *Da Dasein*, where existing there means a dwelling in the world (LH, 257). Ethics is then related to thinking this dwelling of the *Da*, our existing in the world. To make this point, Heidegger returns to the basic meaning of the word ethics from ethos (which means abode or dwelling place). Simply put, "ethics ponders the abode of the human being" (LH, 271). The abode of the human is of course its *Dasein*; the *Da* as dwelling; its being-in-the-world; its ek-sistence or as Heidegger likes to phrase it the "truth of being." Thus, ethics as the thinking of the abode of the human being, also means that "thinking which thinks the truth of being as the primordial element of the human being, as one who eksists, is in itself originary ethics" (LH, 271). Or as Nancy puts it: "Ethos needs to be thought of as 'abode.' . . . The abode is the 'there' in that it is open. The abode is thus much more a conduct than a residence (or rather, 'residing' is above all a conduct, the conduct of Being-the-there). The thinking of this conduct is thus the 'original ethics,' because it thinks of *ethos* as the conduct of/according to the truth of Being" (OE, 188). In short, ethics and ontology are co-originary.

Furthermore, thinking as the conduct of being is contrasted with thinking as the logic of the animal rationale of humanism of modernity. The conduct of being itself is the action of making sense (the opposite of fixing sense), which is also described as the *letting be* of Being: "So making sense is not of sense's making; it is making Being be, or *letting* it be (. . . *sein lassen* means to let be, to give, to entrust to the activity of being as such)" (OE, 177). For Nancy, moreover, this means that ethics as ethos is the letting be or conduct of making sense in the dwelling *with* others, the *ek* of *ek-sistence* as exposure to others, which Heidegger implies but does not develop (OE, 181). Ethics becomes the thinking as conduct of being, or the letting be of making sense between beings as opposed to being subjected to fixed sense from elsewhere. In the case of racism, this means that one is subjected to a fixed sense or including the fixing of moral principles, and the making sense with others of being is denied.

For if thinking as original ethics were to provide "maxims which could be reckoned up unequivocally," it "would deny to existence nothing less than the very *possibility of acting*" (OE, 181). One could say then that by assigning a fixed value to what it means to be human, to human value, then one is denying those assigned a fixed meaning the very *possibility of acting*. Ethics accordingly is doing justice to the making sense of being with others.[13]

The third important marker in Nancy's thought refers to Nancy developing the insight of the originarity of ethics as the dwelling or being-in-the-*world*-with-others to the question of the world in relation to globalization. Nancy does this by connecting the ethos as dwelling place with *habitus* as the inhabiting of the world with others: "It is a having with a sense of being: it is a manner of being there and of standing in it. A world is an ethos, a *habitus* and an inhabiting: it is what holds to itself and in itself, following to its proper mode. It is a network of the self-reference of this stance" (Nancy 2007, 42). This stance in the world means that the conduct of the letting be of making sense together is the creation of the world each time, rather than having a fixed sense imposed from the outside. Nancy contrasts this exposition of being-with with the exploitation of the very ontological structure of our existing together in the world. Nancy accordingly critiques the economic exploitation of humans where humans are à la Marx reduced to things, that is, valued in monetary terms under the enclosure of the capitalistic worldview. In the process of being fixed with value (*Wert*), human dignity (*Würde*)—which is not measurable (or as Nancy puts it, *incommensurable*)—is lost. Again, the world is divided into the creation of the world as the co-creation of meaning that constitutes human dignity. And the construction of a worldview that values, orders, and manages humans as things, where human dignity is lost. In turn, it is the creation of the world as the making sense of the inhabiting of the world with others that *liberates*, for Nancy, human dignity from exploitation.

Decolonization as the Dis-enclosure of Our Shared World

How does Mbembe think with Nancy? When it comes to Mbembe's engagement of Nancy's thought, it may be best formulated in Mbembe's reposing the question concerning the philosophical impetus of decolonization focusing on the Black experience at large and Africa in particular.

For Mbembe, this means a critical confrontation with Europe. It concerns, on the one side, the question of independence and self-determination. On the other side, it concerns rethinking the relation of Africa and the rest of the world according to the ontological structure of our shared existence within one world. Thus, in *Out of the Dark Night*, Mbembe takes up anew the philosophical reflection on the notion of decolonization, which "may have been reduced to a set of discontinuous 'happenings' and 'occurrences' at multiple and often unrelated geographical sites and loci. Its *eventfulness*, singularity, and intensities weakened, its phenomenality may have been diluted" (Mbembe 2021 [2010], 61).[14] It has been reduced to a weak understanding of a mere historical event of the transfer of power from the mother city to the colonial possessions at the time of independence, which was more economically viable once the structural conditions of coerced and unequal exchange between center and periphery were in place. Therefore, it has lost its rebellious content, Mbembe holds, in the hands of historians, political theorists, and economists. Although decolonization in Africa has since faded behind many different names, Mbembe reminds us that it still was a fully valid political, polemical, and cultural category that makes up the strong understanding thereof. It resembled a "liberation struggle" or, in the Bissau-Guinean poet Amilcar Cabral's suggestion, a "revolution" (Cabral 1979, n.p.). What concerns us here is this philosophical sense of decolonization, along with the lived experience of the destruction of the system of colonization while establishing new relationships between the subject and the world. Decolonization, for Mbembe, is then an abbreviation that stands for the difficult problem of restoring the subject, opening up the world—and following Fanon—the universal ascent to human existence.[15]

Accordingly, Mbembe states that the philosophical horizon of decolonization and the anticolonialist movement that made it possible within the lived experience in Africa can be summarized by the notion of the *dis-enclosure of the world* (*la déclosion du monde*) as formulated by Nancy.[16] That is the opening up of something closed, the lifting of an enclosure. The idea of dis-enclosure (*déclosion*) includes that of *éclosion*, meaning hatching or coming into being. Thus, it is an eruption, or advent of something new. It is an opening out or blossoming of that which has been enclosed. For Mbembe the question of the dis-enclosure of the world, which is at the same time the question "of belonging to the world, inhabitance of the world, creation of the world, or the conditions in which we make a world and constitute ourselves as inheritors of the world—is at the heart of anticolonial thought and the notion of decolonization. One could even say that this question is decolonization's fundamental object" (ODN, 80). At once, we have here the move to think ethics and ontology co-originary, as making sense in the inhabiting of the world with others at play.

Mbembe also employs Nancy's notion of being-in-common for the first time. He puts it as follows:

> If, as Jean-Luc Nancy maintains, *being-in-common* comes from sharing, then the democracy to come will be founded not only on an ethics of encounter, but also on the sharing of singularities. It will be built on the basis of a clear distinction between the *universal* and the *in-common*. The universal implies a relation of inclusion in some already constituted thing or entity. The essential feature of the *in-common* is communicability and shareability. It presupposes a relation of cobelonging between multiple singularities. It is thanks to this sharing and this communicability that we produce humanity. Humanity does not already exist premade. (ODN, 130)

In the *Critique of Black Reason* Mbembe further develops the ethico-political implication of the in-common of our shared world in terms of a sense of community in Africa as well as the relation between Africa and the rest of the world: "But there is only one world. We are all part of it, and we all have a right to it. The world belongs to all of us, equally, and we are all its coinheritors, even if our ways of living in it are not the same, hence the real pluralism of cultures and ways of being" (Mbembe 2017 [2014], 187). The ethical responsibility for thinking this in-common is thus a shared responsibility: "The project of a world in common founded on the principle of 'equal shares' and on the principle of the fundamental unity of human beings is a universal project" (Mbembe 2017 [2014], 176). Put differently, this universal project is guided by the critical engagement of a shared history of taking responsibility for a shared future. In Mbembe's words: "The path is clear: on the basis of a critique of the past, we must create a future that is inseparable from the notions of justice, dignity, and the in-common" (Mbembe 2017 [2014], 177). Restated, the "desire for the fullness of humanity is something we all share," but for this desire to be met, reparation is required as part of the dis-enclosure of the world we share, that is, "we must restore the humanity stolen from those who have historically been subjected to processes of abstraction and objectification"

(Mbembe 2017 [2014], 182). And it is the relation of our in-common and reparation that brings us to how Mbembe thinks beyond Nancy with the help of Fanon.

The Reparation of Human Dignity

Returning to the notion of decolonization as dis-enclosure, Mbembe writes:

> Fanon's thinking about the disenclosure of the world is a response to the colonial context of servitude, submission to foreign masters, and racial violence. In such conditions—as under slavery earlier—the concept of the human and the notion of humanity, which are *taken for granted by part of Western thought*, were not self-evident. In fact, faced with the black slave or colonial subject, Europe never stopped asking itself, "Is this another man? Is this something other than a man? Is he another copy of the same? Or is he something other than the same?" In anticolonial thinking, humanity does not exist a priori. (ODN, 81)[17]

This point is perhaps made most potently by Fanon in his critique of Sartre (and one can extend this to the Levinasian position and the European phenomenology at large) that the schema Sartre proposes *presupposes* that both the Self and the Other are *fully human*: "Though Sartre's speculations on the existence of The Other may be correct (to the extent, we must remember, to which *Being and Nothingness* describes an alienated consciousness), their application to a black consciousness proves fallacious. That is because the white man is not only The Other but also the master, whether real or imaginary" (Fanon 1986, 138). Where in order to be a master (fully human), the Black Man/Woman needed to be considered as *less than human*, as occupying the "zone of non-being" (Fanon 1986, 10). Put differently, since the Black Man/Woman is considered within the Western metaphysical worldview of modernity as not being able to reflect on the meaning of their own existence self-consciously and hence to be not fully human, no Self-Other relation as described by Sartre and Levinas can take place from the start.[18] It is excluded beforehand. The encounter with the Black Other cannot take place as a Self-Other relation. It is a *Self-Nothing* relation. And therefore, it can be avoided by keeping "it" *apart* from the Self. Stated in yet another way, recognition and misrecognition can only take place between humans. Hence for Mbembe, following Fanon, what is required to be "a human amongst other humans" is a *reparation* of the humanity of those from whom it has been stolen.[19] Furthermore, if thinkers like Sartre and Levinas help formulate the problematics of ethics, thinkers like Fanon address the limitations of their formulation while adding additional paths of inquiry based on, in this instance, the lived experience of the Black Man/Woman.[20]

To be sure, Mbembe phrases the degradation in ontological terms in *On the Postcolony*, with indirect reference to Hegel's thought, as follows: "In the colonial principle of rationality, however, there is a clear difference between being and existing. Only the human exists, since the human alone can represent the self as existent and have a consciousness of what is so represented. From the standpoint of colonialism, the colonized does not truly exist, as person or as subject" (Mbembe 2001, 187). Rather, as Mbembe discusses in Heideggerian terms, the black subject is reduced to a thing that is a nonbeing, an empty figure, *nothing*:

> The "thing" is, in Heideggerian terms, "a something and not nothing," but it is not at this level that colonialism defines the colonized as absolute void. For the *being-a-thing* of the colonized does not prevent their being, in some circumstances, "things of value." This "value" is to be usable, and that usefulness makes them objects, tools. Their *being-a-thing* of value lies precisely in this function as implements and in this usefulness. . . . From this instant, the native is only so far as he/she is a thing denied, is only in as *something deniable*. In short, from the standpoint of a "self" of one's own, he/she is nothing. In the colonial principle of rationality, the native is thus that *thing that is, but only insofar as it is nothing*. (Mbembe 2001, 187)[21]

It is thus this description of the ontological degradation to a nonbeing, to nothing, that Mbembe finds in Fanon and helps him to go beyond Nancy to describe the *enclosure of race* as "an extraordinarily sterile and arid region" (ODN, 81). The enclosure of race in general, and Blackness in particular, then is the zone of nonbeing. The denial of being human means the denial of making sense with others, the being-in-common itself, and hence to take part in this making sense with others in the world is denied. In other words, the very notion of humanism as describing the animal rationale during modernity was employed to dehumanize the "barbaric people" of Africa. This classification moreover allowed the justification and exploitation of black slaves during early colonialism, and the continued exploitation of the labor of black peoples during colonialism and apartheid.

Accordingly, Mbembe describes decolonization as the dis-enclosure of the world (Nancy) and the rise to humanity (Fanon) as follows: "Humanity is to be *made to rise [faire surgir]* through the process by which the colonized subject awakens to self-consciousness, subjectively appropriates his or her I, takes down the barrier, and authorizes him- or herself to speak in the first person. This awakening and appropriation aim not only at the realization of the self, but also, more significantly, at an *ascent into humanity*, a new beginning of creation, the disenclosure of the world" (ODN, 81).[22] The rise to humanity, moreover, does not merely entail liberation (as in the case of someone considered as fully human and discussed earlier in relation to Nancy) but the reparation of the humanity stolen, that is, the letting be of making sense that constitutes human dignity.

Reparation in this instance, however, should not be understood in economic terms where human dignity is reduced to monetary value (*Wert*) that is measurable and exchangeable. Rather reparation, in relation to human dignity, I would suggest, refers back to its root *reparare*, that is, *to make ready again.* Concerning the reparation of nonbeing to a human being, this means to be made ready again to create meaning with others. It means *to let be* of the conduct of making sense of one's dwelling in a shared world. As opposed to being subjected to fixed meaning imposed from somewhere else, that may be used to justify economic exploitation. Put differently, the implication of Mbembe's reading Nancy with Fanon designates that the co-originarity of ethics and ontology means the co-originary of ethics, ontology, and reparation. Where the letting be of the making meaning with others is at the same time the reparation of human dignity. Or as Mbembe puts it:

> *To repair is to be alive.* So that's the first sense of reparation—to be alive and to take care of something that matters because that thing is a very condition of my survival with others, my being with others, my moving on with others, my leaving something behind for others, something through which they might remember me. Reparation is the opposite of destruction. It is about building a liberating memory, not dwelling in a traumatic memory, the kind of toxic memory that opens up the door to envy, revenge and nihilism. (Goldberg 2018, 216)[23]

The African Lived Experience of Reparation

Thus, if the dis-enclosure of the world means a shift to thinking the inhabiting of the world as the creation of meaning with others over being subjected to fixed meaning that allows for the justification of exploitation, then this position emphasizes that the reparation of the self is always *with* others. One cannot achieve reparation as an isolated self or metaphysical Subject since one does not exist in the world in a solipsistic fashion. It contradicts the very dwelling in the world with others that make up the structure of our existence. As Mbembe puts it: "It is true that such a world is above all a form of relation to oneself. But there is no relation to oneself that does not also implicate the Other. The Other is at once difference and similarity, united" (Mbembe 2017 [2014], 178). This insight also reveals something of the limit of the *uncritical* employment of a Marxist framework that does not allow for the philosophical reflection on these lived experiences of reparation since the framework only allows for the formulation of a suppressed subject that needs revolution and liberation through destruction. This is not to say that the lived concrete experience of subjection is not taken into account and that the struggle against these oppressive structures should end. It rather means that the complex lived experience in Africa is divided into moments of subjection *and* reparation, which *both* call for philosophical reflection.

And it is this complex taking account of that Mbembe wants to convey with the notion of Afropolitanism. Mbembe explains that Afropolitanism as the struggle for the creation of the world in moments of reparation can historically be outlined in at least two instances. The first instance refers to, for example, the creative production of writers such as Ahmadou Kourouma, Yambo Ouologuem, and Sony Labou Tansi—situated on the African Atlantic Coast—whose new sensibilities are to be distinguished from the Negritude movement spearheaded by Léopold Sédar Senghor. The difference can be explored on at least three levels where the break is created: by (1) relativizing the fetishism of origin by showing that there is no such thing as pure origin; (2) making room for a new problem to take its place, that is, that of self-creation, self-generation, and self-explanation; and (3) an aesthetic of transgression in writing, shouting, music with the aim of forcing the world to come into the world (ODN, 232–235).

The second instance, for Mbembe, corresponds to Africa's entry into a new age of dispersion and circulation characterized by the intensification of African migration and new diaspora movements around the world. As Mbembe writes: "With the emergence of these new diasporas, Africa no longer constitutes a center in itself. It is now made up of poles between which there is constant passage, circulation, and trailblazing. These poles connect to and prolong each other. They form so many regions, layers, and cultural deposits from which African creation draws constantly" (ODN, 234–235). Reparation is experienced in the new forms of African creativity where the question of origin and movement, which has been kept separate for so long, are thought together. In Mbembe's words: "For a long time, African creation concerned itself with the question of origins, while dissociating it from the question of movement. Its central object was firstness [*priméité*]: a subject that refers only to itself, a subject in its pure possibility. In the age of dispersion and circulation, this same creation is more concerned with the relation to an interval than to oneself or an other" (ODN, 235). It means that Africa presents itself now not in reference to a unique being, but to a regained ability to branch: "Africa itself is now imagined as an immense interval, an inexhaustible citation open to many forms of combination and composition" (ODN, 235).

This creation through the "circulation of worlds" further manifests itself, of course, given not only the dispersion of people of African descent due to historical forced migration across the world, meaning that "today, millions of people of African origin are citizens of various countries of the globe" (ODN, 237). But it is also enacted in the dispersion of population groups within: "Historically, the dispersion of populations and cultures was not only a matter of foreigners coming to establish themselves in Africa. In fact, the precolonial history of African societies was entirely a history of people in constant movement across the whole continent" (ODN, 236). It is this "culture of mobility," Mbembe moreover notes, "that colonization in its time attempted to freeze via the modern institution of the border" (ODN, 237). Together with the *immersion* of various people into Africa, this dispersion of people makes up the circulating of worlds and the being-in-the-world with others that Mbembe calls Afropolitanism. It is a cultural, historical, and aesthetic sensitivity toward the interlocking of worlds in the inhabiting of a shared world: "So Afropolitanism is not the same as Pan-Africanism or Negritude. Afropolitanism is a style and a politics, an aesthetic and a certain poetics of the world. It is a way of being-in-the-world that in principle refuses any form of victim identity. That is not to say that they are ignorant of the injustices and violence that the law of the world has inflicted on this continent and its people" (Mbembe 2007, 29). It rather orients itself toward the dis-enclosure of the world, of the letting be of making sense in the inhabiting of the world with others. It allows for the experience of reparation—taking part in it—rather than wanting to impose a new fixed meaning on those who have been denied the freedom to make their own meaning with others.

Conclusion

In explicating Mbembe's notion of the in-common of a shared world, this chapter aims to do two things. First, it aims to show that Mbembe's contribution to African phenomenology does not fit into the Subject-Object, that is, the Marxian-Sartrean-Fanonian and postcolonial-Levinasian-ethics framework. It goes beyond this framework by thinking together Nancy and Fanon. Second, this chapter means to explore Mbembe's position to think the rehumanizing of the African subject. In taking seriously the ontological degradation to nonbeing that justified its economic exploitation as a thing, his position differs from other attempts in that (1) it designates the reparation of human dignity in the making meaning of being-in-the-world with others, which is the opposite of being subdued to a fixed meaning from elsewhere and the solipsistic attempt to create meaning by a Subject; and (2) it thinks both the lived experience of subjection *and* reparation that divide the African lived condition.

Notes

1. Mbembe (2020), interview with Malka Gouzer. For an overview of the question of the world in phenomenology, see Landgrebe (1940, 38–58).

2. For the schema, see the introduction of Hiddleston (2014, 6). For an overview of the main critique against *On the Postcolony*, see Mbembe (2006, 143–178).

3. For example, Mbembe's major works *On the Postcolony* originally published in 2000 and translated and published in English in 2001; *Out of the Dark: An Essay on Decolonization* (orig. 2010; trans. 2021); *Critique of Black Reason* (orig. 2014; trans. 2017); *Necropolitics* (orig. 2016; trans. 2019); and *Brutalism* (orig. 2020). This delay means that *Out of the Dark Night* is only published in English ten years after its French publication, although it was written three years before *Critique of Black Reason*.

4. For this critique, see especially, Mbembe (2002).

5. See Sithole (2014); Maldonado-Torres (2008); and Ndlovu-Gatsheni (2013), whom Sithole is following.

6. See Lamola (2018); and Lamola (2019, 48–60).

7. Regarding how Nancy's move to think ethics and ontology as co-originary differs from the binary schematic of the Subject-Other, see Watkin (2007).

8. See also Mbembe (2002).

9. To be sure, Nancy cannot be considered a phenomenological thinker in the traditional sense of taking the subject as a starting point. It is precisely this position that Nancy critiques and replaces with the thinking of being-with, which is still situated in the fundamental ontology of Heidegger (hence phenomenological) but thought differently. Christopher Watkin accordingly describes Nancy's philosophy as deconstructive phenomenology. See Watkin (2009).

10. See Heidegger (1996, 114); Nancy (1993). It is important to note here that Nancy does not simply take over Heidegger's notion of being-with uncritically but instead rethinks its implications and shortcomings in Heidegger's thought and employment, especially in his rectoral address of 1933. Nancy dedicated a whole book to this. See Nancy (2000).

11. Nancy (2003, 180), hereafter cited in the text as OE. This translation is based on an article first published in a heavily abridged form in as "L' éthique originaire de Heidegger." Heidegger (1998), hereafter cited in the text as LH.

12. Cf. section 3.5.

13. See Nancy (2003).

14. Mbembe (2021), hereafter cited in the text as ODN.

15. See Fanon (1986, 197).

16. See Nancy (2008, 158–162).

17. Emphasis mine.

18. See especially Hegel (1980).

19. See Fanon (1986, 112).

20. This point of critique, of course, accounts for the attempts to rethink Sartre and Levinas with Fanon. Nevertheless, they fail to account for the limitations of the Self-Other framework, which the Nancian-Mbembian move attempts to address.

21. Mbembe draws directly from Heidegger's text on *What Is a Thing?* See Heidegger (1967, 6).

22. See also Fanon (2004, 2).

23. Emphasis mine.

References

Cabral, Amilcar. 1979. *Unity and Struggle: Speeches and Writings of Amilcar Cabral.* New York: New York University Press.

Derrida, Jacques. 2005. "Violence and Metaphysics." In *Writing and Difference,* translated by A. Bass, 97–192. London: Routledge.

Fanon, Frantz. 1986. *Black Skin, White Masks*. Translated by C. L. Markmann. London: Pluto.

Fanon, Frantz. 2004. *The Wretched of the Earth*. Translated by R. Philcox. New York: Grove Press.

Goldberg, David Theo. 2018. "The Reason of Unreason: Achille Mbembe and David Theo Goldberg in Conversation about Critique of Black Reason." *Theory, Culture and Society* 35, nos. 7–8: 205–221.

Hegel, Georg Wilhelm Friedrich. 1980. *Lectures on the Philosophy of World History*. Cambridge: Cambridge University Press.

Heidegger, Martin. 1967. *What Is a Thing?* Translated by W. B. Barton Jr. and Vera Deutsch. Lanham: University Press of America.

Heidegger, Martin. 1996. *Being and Time: A Translation of* Sein und Zeit. Albany: State University of New York Press.

Heidegger, Martin. 1998. "Letter on Humanism." In *Pathmarks*, 239–276. Cambridge: Cambridge University Press.

Hiddleston, Jane. 2014. *Understanding Postcolonialism*. London: Routledge.

Johnson, Walter. 2004. "The Pedestal and the Veil: Rethinking the Capitalism/Slavery Question." *Journal of the Early Republic* 24, no. 2: 299–308.

Lamola, M. John. 2018. "Blackhood as a Category in Contemporary Discourses on Black Studies: An Existentialist Philosophical Defence." *Transformation in Higher Education* 3, no. 1: 1–9.

Lamola, M. John. 2019. "Breaking the Gridlock of the African Postcolonial Self-Imagination: Marx against Mbembe." *Angelaki* 24, no. 2: 48–60.

Landgrebe, Ludwig. 1940. "The World as a Phenomenological Problem." *Philosophy and Phenomenological Research* 1, no. 1: 38–58.

Levinas, Emmanuel. 1969. *Totality and Infinity: An Essay on Exteriority*. Translated by A. Lingis. The Hague: Martinus Nijhoff.

Levinas, Emmanuel. 1997. *Outside the Subject*. Translated by M. B. Smith. Stanford: Stanford University Press.

Maldonado-Torres, Nelson. 2008. *Against War: Views from the Underside of Modernity*. Durham, NC: Duke University Press.

Mbembe, Achille. 2001. *On the Postcolony*. Berkeley: University of California Press.

Mbembe, Achille. 2002. "African Modes of Self-Writing." *Public Culture* 14, no. 1: 239–273.

Mbembe, Achille. 2006. "On the Postcolony: A Brief Response to Critics." *African Identities* 4, no. 2: 143–178.

Mbembe, Achille. 2007. "Afropolitanism," translated by L. Chauvet. In *Africa Remix: Contemporary Art of a Continent*, edited by C. Kellner, 26–30. Johannesburg: Jacana.

Mbembe, Achille. 2019 [2016]. *Necropolitics*. Durham: Duke University Press.

Mbembe, Achille. 2020. *Brutalisme*. Paris: La Découverte.

Mbembe, Achille. 2020. "Ignorance Too, Is a Form of Power." Interview with Malka Gouzer. Available at https://www.chilperic.ch/interview/achille-mbembe-15.html.

Mbembe, Achille. 2017 [2014]. *Critique of Black Reason*. Johannesburg: Wits University Press.

Mbembe, Achille. 2021 [2017]. *Out of the Dark Night*. New York: Columbia University Press.

Mbembe, Achille, and Sarah Nuttall. 2004. "Writing the World from an African Metropolis." *Public Culture* 16, no. 3: 347–372.

Nancy, Jean-Luc. 1993. *The Inoperative Community*. Edited by Peter Connor. Minneapolis: University of Minnesota Press.

Nancy, Jean-Luc. 2000. *Being Singular Plural*. Translated by Anne E. O'Byrne and Robert D. Richardson. Stanford: Stanford University Press.

Nancy, Jean-Luc. 2003. "Originary Ethics." In *A Finite Thinking*, edited by Simon Sparks, 172–196. Stanford: Stanford University Press.

Nancy, Jean-Luc. 2007. *The Creation of the World or Globalization*. Translated by François Raffoul and David Pettigrew. Albany: State University of New York Press.

Nancy, Jean-Luc. 2008. "Dis-Enclosure." In *Dis-Enclosure: The Deconstruction of Christianity*, edited by Michael B. Smith and translated by Bettina Bargo and Gabriel Malenfant, 158–162. New York: Fordham University Press.

Ndlovu-Gatsheni, Sabelo J. 2013. "Why Decoloniality in the 21st Century." *The Thinker* 48, no. 10: 5–9.

Sartre, Jean-Paul. 1992. *Notebooks for an Ethics*. Chicago: University of Chicago Press.

Sartre, Jean-Paul. 1993. *Being and Nothingness: An Essay on Phenomenological Ontology*. New York: Washington Square Press.

Sartre, Jean-Paul. 2007. *Existentialism is a Humanism*. Yale: Yale University Press.

Sithole, Tendayi. 2014. "Achille Mbembe: Subject, Subjection, and Subjectivity." PhD dissertation, University of South Africa.

Visker, Rudi. 1999. "The Gaze of the Big Other: Levinas and Sartre on Racism." In *Truth and Singularity*, 326–356. Dordrecht: Springer.

Watkin, Christopher. 2007. "A Different Alterity: Jean-Luc Nancy's 'Singular Plural.'" *Paragraph*: 50–64.

Watkin, Christopher. 2009. Phenomenology or Deconstruction? The Question of Ontology in Maurice Merleau-Ponty, Paul Ricoeur and Jean-Luc Nancy. Edinburgh: Edinburgh University Press.

13

The Voice of African Philosophy

TSENAY SEREQUEBERHAN

Then one day the rumor spreads: a student has killed the English governor of the Indies, or: the Italians have been defeated at Dogali, or: the Boxers have exterminated the European missionaries; and then horror-stricken old Europe curses against the barbarians . . . and a new crusade is undertaken against those unfortunate people.

And notice: the Europeans have had their own oppressors and have fought bloody struggles to liberate themselves, and . . . they erect statues and marble memorials to their liberators. . . . But don't say to Italians that the Austrians came to bring us civilization: even the marble columns would protest. We, of course, have gone forth to extend civilization, and in fact now those people love us and thank heaven for their fortune.

—Antonio Gramsci, "Oppressed and Oppressors"[1]

All translations are mine unless otherwise indicated, and all emphases in the original unless otherwise indicated. An early version of this chapter was my presentation at the HBCUs and Philosophy IV: Race and Resistance Conference, organized by the Department of Philosophy and Religious Studies, Morgan State University, April 7, 2018. A substantially different and shorter version, under the same title, in a Turkish translation, was published in *Sabah ülkesi*, no. 55 (April 2018). And a still shorter and much earlier version was the keynote address I delivered at the Annual Bill of Rights TransAfrica Convocation Day, December 2, 2004, Morgan State University, Baltimore, Maryland, USA.

Section 1

We are today, at the end of the second decade of the twenty-first century, at a point in time when the *universe* of Eurocentric dominance is being engulfed by the *multiverse* of our shared humanity. From the fifteenth century to the middle of the twentieth century, Africa, and its diverse peoples, fell victim to the slave trade and colonial dismemberment. Relegated to nonexistence, the Continent was cloaked in darkness and was peopled in the sight of Europe—that is, the continent whose ruling classes were avidly engaged in the voracious plunder of the globe—by a strange "prelogical" humanity.[2]

On this side of the Atlantic, as James Baldwin tells us, reflecting on the experiences of his generation, the very name and image of Africa was associated with self-effacement and shame and was, in this manner, utilized to subdue the descendants of the "dark" Continent (Baldwin 1993a, 79–80).[3] On the other side of the Atlantic, on the other hand, before Pablo Picasso's creative genius transformed the very nature and character of modern art, many an African mask was piously consigned to the flames. Where the myopic, narcissistic, and self-flattering episteme of "la mission civilisatrice" and "The White Man's Burden" saw grotesqueries, there Picasso sighted a revealing artistic possibility.[4] And so, African "primitivism" had enabled him to discern the disclosive power of art.[5] In this, as in many other aspects of life, by the mid-twentieth century, Africa was steadily corroding and/or eroding and dissolving the pejorative assessments that had defined its subjection.

Today, in the words of Gianni Vattimo, expressed in the twilight years of the last century: "after the end of colonialism and the dissolution of Eurocentric prejudices" history cannot anymore pretend to have a "unitary sense," in view of the fact that it has been "fractured into a number of stories irreducible to a single guiding thread" (Vattimo 1996, 22). The singularity of European dominance has given way to a variegated humanity that sees its diversity as its most precious possession. This is an actualized possibility that, in an ongoing manner, is dependent—for its continued existence—on our openness to each Other.[6] This multiplicity is the originative source of our shared future, grounded as it is in our mutual and reciprocal stance of compassion and solidarity.

Now, all of this is a direct dialectical effect, or outcome, of the demise of colonial empires leaving behind a multiple diversity of hybridized cultures and histories. This global, intermixed, and self-emancipated humankind is presently in the process of forming a new worldwide community through struggles deriving their energy from the tremendous creativity set free by the collapse of direct colonial rule. As is well known, a central pillar in this bright dawning of mutual recognition and reciprocity was the dure and protracted African anticolonial struggle.[7] The richness of this struggle, in its hybrid history—constituted against the grain of colonial subjection—is a historicity of fusion, of indigenous and colonial elements, which constitutes its vibrant actuality.[8]

In this "fusion of horizons" (Gadamer 1982, 273–274) there is instituted an originary-originative history out of the self-understanding of the instituting historicity of those engaged in the anticolonial struggle.[9] For, as Cornelius Castoriadis has observed, "the great majority of men and women living in [a] society are the source of creation, the principle bearers of the instituting imaginary" (Castoriadis 1991, 6). This ontic creativity is grounded on the ontological character of our being-in-the-world that exists—always—out of a past and in openness to a possible future. In this in-between, which, as Hans-Georg Gadamer tells us, is "the true locus of hermeneutics" (Gadamer 1982, 263),[10] and out of it, what has-been, the past, sets the horizons of the possible, the yet-to-be, the future, projected in response to our present exigencies.

In this *image*, or interpretation, what is of vital importance is how those engaged in it (i.e., the anticolonial struggle) understand and see themselves in this in-between. For, as Gadamer puts it, the "effects of effective-history" our effectual past, "determines in advance" (Gadamer 1982, 267)[11] our overall precomprehension and orientation to the future. This enduring and enabling past in its effectuality, bestowed on the transient present, opens the future, in all its possibilities. In this regard, as Baldwin insightfully observes: "To accept one's past—one's history—is not the same as drowning in it; it is learning how to use it" (Baldwin 1993c, 81). But what exactly does "learning how to use it [i.e., one's history]" mean?

Section 2

In 1957—the first year in the calendar of Black African Independence, proclaiming the demise of the Gold Coast colony and the birth of an independent African state, named after the great Ghana civilization of medieval Africa—Dr. Kwame Nkrumah declared: "Our independence [i.e., the independence of Ghana] is meaningless unless it is linked up with the total liberation of the African continent" (Nkrumah 1980, 121). In the words of Nkrumah, Africa had found its voice. This was a *voice* singularly focused on reclaiming the humanity—and thus the freedom—negated by European colonialism.

In other words, and concretely, "our independence is meaningless" if it does not directly implicate us in the "the total liberation of the African continent." In this regard Nkrumah has in mind not merely physical geography but, more importantly, the spiritual cultural horizon—the geography of existence—in and through which life is to institute itself in postcolonial Africa. He is concerned with highlighting the importance of probing the grounding source of our freedom. Indeed, it needs to be emphasized that his one explicitly philosophic text, *Consciencism* (1964), is focused on precisely this point.

As Marcien Towa has observed: "*Consciencism* appears as the form—the ideological and philosophic form—of the consciousness that Africa has of itself in the process of its own self-creation" (Towa 1973, 148). In this "consciousness . . . of itself," for Nkrumah, as he points out in chapter 3, the central chapter of *Consciencism*, the essential focus of postcolonial Africa has to be to reinvent itself in freedom by tangibly synthesizing or fusing the differing aspects of its colonial and precolonial heritage and, in this way, instituting its self-standing autonomous postcolonial actuality. This "fusion of horizons" (Gadamer) is, for Nkrumah, the possibility of a future—in freedom—for Africa.

In this regard, for Nkrumah, what must be reclaimed and validated is the heritage of the formerly colonized in and out of the context of the struggle. What must be reclaimed, in other words, is the being-in-the-world of the colonized, in the act of freeing or liberating themselves. For, "the process" of Africa's act of "self-creation" is that in and through which, as Frantz Fanon points out, "the colonized 'thing' becomes human in the very process through which it liberates itself" (Fanon 2002, 40).[12] The telos, in other words—the end goal of the liberation struggle—is itself none other than the concrete self-institution of the efforts that tangibly constitute this very process of struggle.

This is so because the demise of colonialism necessitates a rethinking and reclaiming of our heritage as the site of our newly actuated freedom. Here it ought to be remembered that Europe colonized Africa in the name of "civilization" and the general betterment of humanity. And so, the reversal of this process—the project of decolonization—must necessarily involve a putting-into-question of the *ideas* and *beliefs* in and through which Europe felt justified in its imperious colonial undertakings.

This rethinking is then, effectively, a critical mulling over of our heritage:[13] the systematic interpretative exploring and "learning how to use" that which we have been, in view of what we can possibly become.[14] An interlinked, ongoing, interpretative process in and through which, in the words of Fanon, "the colonized 'thing' becomes human in the very process through which it liberates itself." This too, as Towa points out, is what Nkrumah has in mind in affirming that *Consciencism* is "the form" of the awareness that Africa has of itself, "in the process of its . . . self-creation." In all of this—what must be firmly grasped is that "the . . . process through which it liberates itself," as Fanon puts it, or "the process of its . . . self-creation," in Towa's reading of Nkrumah, the aimed for result is that in and through which "the colonized 'thing' becomes human."

And, as Fanon reminds us: "Without this struggle [of self-creation], without this knowledge of praxis, there is nothing more than a carnival and a lot of blaring music" (Fanon 2002, 141; 1968, 147). Or, as Amilcar Cabral puts it, "If that [i.e., self-creation] does not happen, then the efforts and sacrifices accepted during the struggle will have been made in vain" (Cabral 1973, 56). Sadly enough, as is well known, these prognostications have indeed come to pass. Africa, today, is ruled by yesterday's servile colonial understudies—the *replicant* African ruling strata.[15]

Section 3

In this regard then, the contemporary practice of African philosophy is focused, among other things, on the systematic destructuring of the symmetry of concepts that constituted, and still residually constitutes, the theoretic buttress of empire. It is necessary, in other words, to reflexively undermine the theoretic "fig leaf" of colonialism that *thingifies*[16] and dehumanizes in the guise, and in the name, of "civilization."[17]

And so, on one level, the contemporary practice of African philosophy involves itself in a systematic reading and rereading of the hegemonic European tradition in view of undermining or destructuring it in terms of its own flawed conceited claims and untenable presuppositions. This is "the critical-negative aspect"[18] of the discourse of contemporary African philosophy. In this undertaking, the discourse of contemporary

African philosophy effectively partakes of the tangible process of the self-reclaiming of the formerly colonized by the systematic undermining of the internalized symmetry of concepts that had justified the dehumanized subjugation of the subjected.

For the longest time, European philosophy saw the social-historical formations in which it was situated as synonymous with human existence per se, and itself as the enunciation of *Truth* unvarnished. As Gadamer tells us, Enlightenment-inspired modern European thinking was grounded on "the prejudice against prejudice" (Gadamer 1982, 242). The brazen belief, or bias, that one's thinking is scientifically[19] grounded and thus beyond the limitations of prejudice and/or bias. In this epistemically untenable claim, the "thinker" is ensnared by the belief that her or his own perspective, or bias, is the very measure of the *True*. Spellbound by this self-deluding and rather ostentatious affectation the "thinker," in effect, transcendentalizes the biases and/or prejudices of his or her own age and culture in the very act, ironically, of claiming to be beyond them.

This, *grosso modo*, is Gadamer's critique of the Enlightenment. In this, what he effectively does is to appropriate, for philosophical hermeneutics, what Nietzsche and Heidegger had thematized as the impossibility of a nonsituated perspective, that is, the impossibility of the grounding claim of the Enlightenment. We all exist within the bounds of our lived historicity and thus the touchstone and source of our thinking is our finite situatedness. Indeed, as Gadamer puts it, "a standpoint . . . beyond any standpoint [*überstandpunktliche Standpunkt*]" is, in effect, "a pure illusion [*eine reine Illusion*]" (Gadamer 1982, 399).[20] It is imperative to remember, at this point, that the West subjugated the globe at a time, in its history, when it was under the firm grip of this "pure illusion." Indeed, the colonial globalization of Europe was the effective actualization of this "illusion."

Now that the symmetry of this self-deluding metaphysical "illusion" has been irrevocably undermined, on the level of political existence—by the political and/or armed struggles of the formerly colonized—it is necessary to authenticate this actuality by supplying it with its own concrete de jure philosophic underpinning. In other words, it is necessary to explore and cultivate the ontological-existential structures conducive to human solidarity. To explore the hermeneutics-of-existence that will nurture the amiable cohabitation of our planet. This is, indeed, an urgent necessity conditioned by our lived situation of multiplicity, on a fragile and threatened singular planet.[21] As Vattimo puts it, emphatically: "The future will belong to hermeneutics—or it will not be at all" (Vattimo 2015, 727).[22]

In view of all the preceding, contemporary African philosophy is an engaged and systematic exploring of both the legacy of our precolonial past and the more recent intellectual treasures produced by the African anticolonial struggle. In this regard, it must be noted and emphasized that it is in and through the *determined* involvement of the *present* that what had value in the *past* shows itself. Or, as Heidegger puts it: "The past opens itself only according to the resoluteness and force of illumination that a present has available to it" (Heidegger 2009, 39). Indeed, as Gadamer reminds us, our heritage does not just endure by "inertia."[23] To sustain itself it needs to be sifted and evocatively explored—in an ongoing manner—out of the exigent concerns of the present.

In this way the character and substance of our past, which has been found to be of value, is appropriated in considering new developments and understandings that, in their turn, further critically sieve, fine-tune, and nuance our heritage—in view of a desirable future. It is important to note, at this point, that minus the hyperbolic otherworldly claims of Hegel's notion of Spirit, this pedagogy of "learning how to use" one's past—in view of a possible, or desirable future—is akin to the incessant self-unfolding of the dialectic that institutes itself by measuring-up-to and surpassing itself. This is what Hegel refers to as the "labour of the negative" (Hegel 1967, 81), the ongoing dialectic of a lived pedagogy in which the hermeneutics of African philosophy is steeped and out of which it, in an ongoing manner, emerges.[24] This, then, is what it means to "learn how to use" our "history."

Section 4

This ongoing husbanding of the past is a properly philosophic task. In this regard, as the seventeenth-century Abyssinian philosopher Zar'a Ya'aqob points out, "the human being aspires to know truth and the hidden things of nature, but this endeavor is difficult and can only be attained with great labor and patience. . . . Hence people hastily accept what they have heard from their fathers and shy [away] from any (critical) examination" (Sumner 1985, 235). This "(critical) examination," this husbanding of tradition(s), is the task of philosophy in its relation to the heritage in which it is invariably sited. Philosophy sifts through and preserves that which is deemed to be useful and discards as superfluous—in and out of the needs and concerns of the present—the residual and the passé. This is what the young Karl

Marx refers to as "the immediate task of [a] philosophy, which is in the service of history" (Marx 1975, 244). In this "service," philosophy—that is, reflection—maintains a very close bond between *the world* and the *lived awareness* (i.e., the *Dasein*) that inhabits it.

For, as Frederick Douglass tells us: "We have to do with the past only as we can make it useful to the present and the future" (Douglass 2003, 154). In this making "useful," philosophic reflection tacitly appropriates the interpretative stance (or hermeneutic orientation) in and through which a tradition, as such, or a heritage, de facto sustains itself. It is in this way that traditions or heritages are instituted, maintained, and over time, in an ongoing critical manner—that is, in a lived tacit process of reinterpretation and interpretations—sustain themselves. In recognizing this, and actively appropriating it, we "learn how to use" our "history." For, appearances to the contrary, what had value in the past does not just endure, it must be evocatively and actively solicited by the concerns of the present.

In view of these constantly changing concerns, "effective-history" (Gadamer 1982, 267–274)—in its effectiveness—energizes, sustains, and constitutes our lived actuality. In this it acts as the implicit criterion in and through which is critically sieved, and projected into the future, all that which makes life possible.[25] It is in and out of this temporal inter-connectedness that lived *ek-sistence* emerges in its varied historicities. As Gadamer tells us, this is what implicitly happens in the actuality of our *ek-sistence* and that is why "understanding" is not a subjective act but occurs in and out of our *openness* to that which shows itself (Gadamer 1982, 258).[26]

The voice of African philosophy is thus focused on listening to and "learning" from the past, by reflexively echoing back and elucidating the meaning of the *call* of our freedom. It is the voice of a politically and conceptually attuned philosophic purging of all that was forced on us: a negative critique of Eurocentrism, parallel with a husbanding appropriation of Africa's colonial, precolonial, and postcolonial heritage. In this *way*, "the voice of African philosophy" would be focused on interpretatively reclaiming "the notion of humanity" (Césaire 1972, 79) denied the "darker" portion of humankind, for so long.

This is what Towa refers to as "notre identité humaine générique" (Towa 1979b, 71), which has been mangled and markedly damaged by colonial subjection. For this "our generic human identity" is the "constitutive activity of all culture [and history]," it is that which makes "all particular cultures [and histories]" possible, that which "engenders them all" (Towa 1979a, 87). This is the originative-originary humanness that colonialism systematically undermined. That is why, as we noted earlier with Nkrumah and Fanon, the colonized "thing" becomes human in the very process of reclaiming itself, that is, reclaiming its originative-originary humanness—that is, its "generic human identity"—in and out of the context of the present and, in so doing, reconstitutes itself in freedom (Towa 2011, 337–346).[27] It is this worthwhile project—an interpretative undertaking if ever there was one—that the "voice of African philosophy" hopes to articulate, deepen, and constantly fine-tune.

Section 5

As Baldwin reminds us: "It is a terrible, an inexorable, law that one cannot deny the humanity of another without diminishing one's own: in the face of one's victims, one sees oneself" (Baldwin 1993b, 71). In this *seeing*, the voice of African philosophy must compel, force, the Occident to face itself. Like Dorian Gray—averting his face from the grotesque *image* of his own making—the Occident, Euro-America, must be made to face and own up to the horrors of its imperious past. For, indeed, as Chinua Achebe has pointedly observed, "Africa is to Europe as the picture is to Dorian Gray" (Achebe 1989, 17).

The desperate "third world" refugees—mostly Africans—recently characterized by a European journalist as "the Mediterranean boat people," presently flooding the shores of the Occident, are the most recent victims of Europe's colonial depredations:[28] wealth amassing plunder ventures that made it—at the expense of all the rest of us—the *center*, in contradistinction to an impoverished *periphery*. In all of this, the aim is not to reject the West—nor merely to embrace Africa—but, as Ousmane Sembene puts it, to help develop "a synthesis. . . . A new type of [global] society" (Sembene 1983, 135) that would tangibly *institute* a future inclusive of *us* all. In the insightful words of Aimé Césaire, this would be "a universal rich with all that is particular" (Césaire 1955, 15).[29]

The *voice of African philosophy* is thus the self-imposed vocalization of this responsibility. The philosophic *respondere*, that is, the *response* of our *being* to the call of our freedom: Our humanness.[30] It is the reflexive-reflective counterpart to the practical efforts—that is, political, cultural, economic—in the Diaspora and on the Continent, focused on compelling the Occident to see itself in the horrors of its own making. In this *seeing*, and the boomerang counterglance of all the rest of *us*, it is possible, as Fanon stated not too long ago, "to put afoot a new humanity" (Fanon 2002, 305).[31] This, indeed, would be an appropriate appreciation of Gramsci's apt irony—with which we opened this chapter.

Notes

1. A high school essay written in 1910, anthologized in *History, Philosophy, and Culture in the Young Gramsci* (1975, 156). It is a testament to Gramsci's humanity and insight that he could highlight this paradox, in the Occident's relation to the rest of the globe, at a time when he was merely a high school student and the Occident was still under the firm grip of its imperious and delusional conception of itself—that justified its violent subjugation of the globe in the belief that it was rendering a vital service to humanity. The name "Dogali," that Gramsci mentions in the cited text, refers to the battle of Dogali of 1887 in which the forces of Italian colonialism were defeated by Ras Alula (an Abyssinian duke). The battle was fought on the eastern escarpment of the highlands of present-day Eritrea, a region whose population was actively engaged in fending off the aggressive advances of Abyssinian expansionism and Italian colonialism.

2. As is well known, the work of Lucien Lévy-Bruhl (the philosophically trained anthropologist who was appointed to the Chair of the History of Modern Philosophy at the Sorbonne in 1904) centered on the notion of a primitive, or prelogical, mentality that was the basic idea that determined European conceptions of the non-European world into the late 1950s. To his credit, toward the end of his life—as documented in his posthumously published notebooks—Lévy-Bruhl rejected this myopic perspective.

3. As Baldwin puts it: "At the time that I was growing up, Negroes in this country were taught to be ashamed of Africa. They were taught it bluntly . . . by being told that Africa had never contributed 'anything' to civilization. Or one was taught the same lesson more obliquely, and even more effectively, by watching nearly naked, dancing, comic-opera, cannibalistic savages in the movies" (Baldwin 1993a, 79–80).

4. Having experienced the expressivity of African masks, in an exhibition of "primitive art" in Paris, Picasso—despite his denials—utilized this expressivity to bypass the merely naturalistic/representational character of the European art of his time, which was also characteristic of his work, as evinced by the period of his work known as the "early years" (1892–1906). On Africa's influence on Picasso, see "Picasso's African-Influenced Period—1907 to 1909" (n.d.). For a more in-depth exploration of the influence of Africa on Picasso, see Le Fur (2017). An interesting anecdote: In response to a question by Florent Fels, an art critique,

in 1920, regarding African art, Picasso is said to have answered: " 'African Negro Art? Don't know it' " (Le Fur 2017, 7). And yet, in 1907, thirteen years earlier, he had categorically affirmed: "When I became interested in Negro art. . . . at that moment I realized that this was what painting was all about. Painting isn't an aesthetic process; it's a form of magic designed as a mediator between this strange, hostile world and us, a way of seizing the power by giving a form to our terrors as to our desires. When I came to that realization, I knew I had found my way' " (Le Fur 2017, 32). As Yves Le Fur shows, in detail, by a comparative assessment of works by Picasso and African masks and art objects, Picasso was very much influenced by this "primitive art." On this point, see Bevan (2006).

5. This "disclosive power," disclosive of truth, *grosso modo*, is what Heidegger claims for art in *The Origin of the Work of Art* (1935). In this regard as Richard E. Palmer puts it: "For Gadamer, following Heidegger, this is not a disclosure of some eternal, changeless essence; rather, for Gadamer it yields an existential sense that 'this is the way things are' " (Palmer 2001, 11–12). On this point Gadamer says the following: "An artwork 'says something to someone.' In this assertion is contained the dismay of finding oneself directly affected by what was said by the work, and being forced . . . to make it understandable to oneself and to others. I therefore continue to maintain that the experience of art is an experience of meaning, and as such this experience is something that is brought about by understanding. To this extent, then, aesthetics is absorbed into hermeneutics" (Gadamer 2001, 70). I hope my reader sees, despite Picasso's talk of "magic" and "power," the parallel train of thought in what Picasso says in note 5 and what Gadamer affirms, in the preceding citation.

6. On this point, see the concluding chapter of Serequeberhan (2007).

7. For an exploration of the *promise* and *shortcomings* of this struggle, see Serequeberhan (2015, chap. 1).

8. I say "against the grain of colonial subjection" because, in all the colonies, "fraternizing" with the "natives" or the de facto utilization of "native" ways of doing things—be they private or public—was prohibited: "going native" was not something looked upon kindly. We should remember that apartheid was not an exclusively South African affair. To this day in all major African cities, one can locate, with precision, the boundary lines that separated, in colonial times, the city from the "native quarter."

9. On this point, see Castoriadis (1987, 369–373).

10. The original: "In diesem Zwischen ist der wahre Ort der Hermeneutik" (Gadamer 1965, 279).

11. This is how I understand the sense of Castoriadis's insightful affirmation, within the context of the anticolonial struggle.

12. The original reads: "la 'chose' colonisée deviant homme dans le processus même par lequel elle se libère" (Fanon 1968, 36–37). It should be noted that what is being explored, in our explication of Nkrumah, Towa, and Fanon, is the

self-transformative activity of revolutionary action. This is, within the African context, what Karl Marx points to in the second paragraph of the "Third Thesis on Feuerbach" when he states: "The coincidence of the changing of circumstance and of human activity or self-changing can be conceived and rationally understood only as *revolutionary practice*" (Marx 1973, 121).

13. On this point, see Serequeberhan (2000, chap. 1).

14. In his marvelous essay "History as a System" (1935) in Ortega y Gasset (1961), José Ortega y Gasset writes: "Man lives in view of the past" (217). But, in terms of his own conception of "historical reason" (Ortega y Gasset 1961, 183), it would be more appropriate to say: "The human being lives out of a past and in view of a possible future."

15. On this point, please see the first chapter of Serequeberhan (2015).

16. As Aimé Césaire puts it: "A mon tour de poser une équation: colonisation = chosification" (Césaire 1955, 19). See also Césaire (1972, 21).

17. Incidentally, it is interesting to note that the term "civilization," derived from the French *civilisation*, entered the English language in the mid-eighteenth century at a time when the Occident—the British Empire—was encountering, in its explorations or plunder ventures (it amounts to the same thing!), Other peoples it labeled "savage" and in need of being "civilized." (http://www.dictionary.com/browse/civilization).

18. I first made use of this formulation in "The Critique of Eurocentrism and the Practice of African Philosophy" (Serequeberhan 1997, 142).

19. As Anne Hugon points out: "The European elite—stirred by the discoveries of Sir Isaac Newton, the writings of René Descartes and Francis Bacon, and Denis Diderot's publication in 1751 of the first encyclopedia—was becoming increasingly fascinated by science. . . . Toward the end of the 18th century, it was believed to be the mission of human reason to achieve perfect mastery of the world by discovering the laws of the universe" (Hugon 1993, 19–20). This is the source of the "scientific" attitude critiqued by Gadamer. Overall, this kind of scientism has now been surpassed. On this point, see Vattimo (2005, 45).

20. The original reads: "Der überstandpunktliche Standpunkt, von dem aus seine wahre Identität gedacht würde, ist eine reine Illusion" (Gadamer 1965, 358).

21. I use the word "singular" to describe our planet because, to our knowledge, it is the only one of its kind. It is "threatened" or endangered, moreover, not only by our cantankerous history of warfare and the reckless utilization of nuclear weapons and weapons of mass destruction but also by our unthinking polluting that is destabilizing the natural environment and accelerating global warming. As I write these words, the West Coast of the USA, namely California, is burning. And the nightly TV news makes all of us helpless—and tacitly complicit—spectators of an immensely terrifying terrestrial inferno, sustained by our polluting negligence.

22. The COVID-19 pandemic—by which our globe has been totally engulfed—aptly highlights the urgency and danger signaled by Vattimo's affirmation.

23. As Gadamer tells us: "Even the most . . . solid tradition does not persist by nature because of the inertia of what once existed. It needs to be affirmed, embraced, [and] cultivated" (Gadamer 1982, 250).

24. On this point, see Serequeberhan (1994). For a recent assessment of African philosophical hermeneutics, see Komo (2017). See also Janz (2015, 480–484).

25. This is the basic insight of Nietzsche's second "untimely" meditation, *On the Advantage and Disadvantage of History for Life* (Nietzsche 1980). This also is the view that Ortega articulates in his 1935 essay "History as a System" (Ortega 1961).

26. On this point, see also the concluding chapter of *Existence and Heritage* titled "Frantz Fanon, Thinking as Openness" (Serequeberhan 2015).

27. The views expressed in these pages (i.e., 337–346) recapitulate—more or less *verbatim*—the ideas of Towa referred to in Towa (1979b) and Towa (1979a). And so these are, for Towa, views he firmly held since he repeats them—unchanged—after first expressing them thirty-two years ago in 1979. Now, *grosso modo*, these views refer to the inventive openness to *being* that constitutes the generic humanness of the human being. As is well known, this is what Heidegger in *Being and Time* refers to as our *Dasein*, the character of whose *ek-sistence* has been forgotten and covered over by the metaphysical tradition. This conceptual similitude regarding the *being* of the human being is a theme that, for obvious reasons, I cannot explore here but that will be properly engaged in the last chapter of my forthcoming book *Thinking the Present* (under contract, State University of New York Press).

28. On this point, see Saunders (2015). In this purportedly "investigative" piece of journalism, it does not occur to Mr. Saunders to *question*—in any way—the skewed economic relation of Africa to Europe (based on the violent colonial past and the equally violent neocolonial present) that makes the former dependent on the latter and is, ultimately, the source of what he refers to as "the Mediterranean boat people." For Mr. Saunders, the "flow of people back and forth . . . has been a part of both continents' economies for decades." Indeed! Is it then, a "natural" state of affairs?

29. In full Césaire writes: "Ma conception de l'universel est celle d'un universel riche de tout le particulier, riche de tous les particuliers, approfondissement et coexistence de tous les particuliers" (Césaire 1956, 15).

30. This refers to the last sentence in the first paragraph of section 2.

31. The original reads: "Pour l'Europe, pour nous-mêmes et pour l'humanité, camarades, il faut faire peau neuve, développer une pensée neuve, tenter de mettre sur pied un homme neuf" (Fanon 1968, 316).

References

"Picasso's African-Influenced Period—1907 to 1909." n.d. https://www.pablopicasso. org/africanperiod.jsp.

Achebe, Chinua. 1989. "An Image of Africa: Racism in Conrad's *Heart of Darkness*" (1975). In *Hopes and Impediments*. New York: Anchor Books.

Baldwin, James. 1993a. "East River, Downtown: Postscript to a Letter from Harlem" (1961). In *Nobody Knows My Name*. New York: Vintage Books.

Baldwin, James. 1993b. "Fifth Avenue, Uptown: A Letter from Harlem" (1960). In *Nobody Knows My Name*. New York: Vintage Books.

Baldwin, James. 1993c. *The Fire Next Time*. New York: Vintage Books.

Bevan, Stephen. 2006. "Picasso 'Stole the Work of African Artists.' " *The Telegraph*, March 12. http://africanartists.blogspot.com/2015/05/picasso-stole-work-of-african-artists.html.

Cabral, Amilcar. 1973. "National Liberation and Culture." In *Return to the Source: Selected Speeches of Amilcar Cabral*, edited by the Africa Information Service. New York: Monthly Review Press.

Césaire, Aimé. 1955. *Discours sur le colonialisme*. Paris: Présence Africaine.

Césaire, Aimé. 1956. "Lettre à Maurice Thorez." Paris: Présence Africaine.

Césaire, Aimé. 1967. "An Interview with Aimé Césaire." Conducted by the Haitian poet René Depestre in Havana, Cuba, at the Cultural Congress of Havana.

Césaire, Aimé. 1972. *Discourse on Colonialism*. New York: Monthly Review Press.

Castoriadis, Cornelius. 1987. *The Imaginary Institution of Society*. Cambridge, MA: MIT Press.

Castoriadis, Cornelius. 1991. *Philosophy, Politics, Autonomy: Essays in Political Philosophy*. Edited by David Ames Curtis. New York: Oxford University Press.

Douglass, Frederick. 2003. "What to the Slave Is the Fourth of July?" In *Narrative of the Life of Frederick Douglass, an American Slave, Written by Himself*, 2nd ed., with selected reviews, documents, and speeches, edited and introduced by David Blight. Boston: Bedford/St. Martin's.

Fanon, Frantz. 1968. *The Wretched of the Earth*. New York: Grove Press.

Fanon, Frantz. 2002. *Les damnés de la terre*. Paris: La Découverte.

Gadamer, Hans-Georg. 1965. *Wahrheit und Methode*. Tübingen: J. C. B. Mohr.

Gadamer, Hans-Georg. 1982. *Truth and Method*. New York: Crossroad.

Gadamer, Hans-Georg. 2001. *Gadamer in Conversation*. Edited, translated, and introduced by Richard E. Palmer. New Haven, CT: Yale University Press.

Gramsci, Antonio. 1975. "Oppressed and Oppressors." In *History, Philosophy, and Culture in the Young Gramsci*, edited by Pedro Cavalcanti and Paul Piccone. Saint Louis, MO: Telos Press.

Hegel, G. W. F. 1967. *The Phenomenology of Mind*. Translated by J. B. Baillie. New York: Harper & Row.

Heidegger, Martin. 1960. *The Origin of the Work of Art* (1935). Translator unknown. Stuttgart: Reclam.

Heidegger, Martin. 2009. "Indication of the Hermeneutical Situation." In *The Heidegger Reader*, edited and introduced by Günter Figal. Bloomington: Indiana University Press.

Hugon, Anne. 1993. *The Exploration of Africa: From Cairo to the Cape*. New York: Harry N. Abrams.

Janz, Bruce. 2015. "Hermeneutics and Intercultural Understanding." In *The Routledge Companion to Hermeneutics*, edited by Jeff Malpas and Hans-Helmuth Gander, 474–485. New York: Routledge.

Komo, Louis-Dominique Biakolo. 2017. "The Hermeneutical Paradigm in African Philosophy." *Nokoko*, no. 6, *African Studies Journal*. https://carleton.ca/africanstudies/wp-content/uploads/Nokoko-6-08-The-Hermeneutical-Paradigm-in-African-Philosophy-Genesis-Evolution-and-Issues.pdf.

Le Fur, Yves. 2017. *Through the Eyes of Picasso: Face to Face with African and Oceanic Art*. New York: Flammarion.

Marx, Karl. 1973. "Thesis on Feuerbach" (1845). In *The German Ideology*. New York: International.

Marx, Karl. 1975. "A Contribution to the Critique of Hegel's Philosophy of Right: Introduction (1843–4)." In *Karl Marx, Early Writings*, introduction by Lucio Colletti, translated by Rodney Livingstone and Gregor Benton. New York: Vintage Books.

Nietzsche, Friedrich. 1980. *On the Advantage and Disadvantage of History for Life*. Translated with an introduction by Peter Preuss. Indianapolis, IN: Hackett.

Nkrumah, Kwame. 1980. "Extract from the Midnight Pronouncement of Independence, 5–6 March 1957." In *Revolutionary Path*. London: PANAF Books.

Ortega, José y Gasset. 1961. *History as a System and Other Essays: Toward a Philosophy of History*. New York: W. W. Norton.

Palmer, Richard E. 2001. *Gadamer in Conversation*. New Haven, CT: Yale University Press.

Saunders, Doug. 2015. "The Real Reasons Why Migrants Risk Everything for a New Life Elsewhere." *Globe and Mail*, April 24, updated March 25. https://www.theglobeandmail.com/news/world/the-real-reasons-why-migrants-risk-everything-for-a-new-life-elsewhere/article24105000/.

Sembene, Ousmane. 1983. *The Last of the Empire*. London: Heinemann Educational Books.

Serequeberhan, Tsenay. 1994. *The Hermeneutics of African Philosophy: Horizon and Discourse*. New York: Routledge.

Serequeberhan, Tsenay. 1997. "The Critique of Eurocentrism and the Practice of African Philosophy." In *Postcolonial African Philosophy*, edited by E. C. Eze. Cambridge, MA: Blackwell.

Serequeberhan, Tsenay. 2000. *Our Heritage*. Lanham, MD: Rowman & Littlefield.

Serequeberhan, Tsenay. 2007. *Contested Memory: The Icons of the Occidental Tradition*. Trenton, NJ: Africa World Press.

Serequeberhan, Tsenay. 2015. *Existence and Heritage*. Albany: State University of New York Press.

Sumner, Claude. 1985. *Classical Ethiopian Philosophy*. Addis Ababa: Commercial Printing Press.

Towa, Marcien. 1973. "*Consciencisme*." *Présence africaine*, no. 85 (1st Quarter): 148–177.

Towa, Marcien. 1979a. "Propositions sur l'identité culturelle." *Présence africaine*, no. 109 (1st Quarter): 82–91.

Towa, Marcien. 1979b. *L'idée d'une philosophie négro-africaine*. Yaoundé, Cameroun: Editions CLE.

Towa, Marcien. 2011. *Identité et transcendence*. Yaoundé, Cameroon: L'Harmattan.

Vattimo, Gianni. 1996. *Credere di credere*. Milan: Garzanti.

Vattimo, Gianni. 2005. "The Age of Interpretation." In *The Future of Religion*, edited by S. Zabala. New York: Columbia University Press.

Vattimo, Gianni. 2015. "Conclusion: The Future of Hermeneutics." In *The Routledge Companion to Hermeneutics*, edited by Jeff Malpas and Hans-Helmuth Gander, 721–728. New York: Routledge.

14

Communal Space, Communal Temporality

Kwasi Wiredu and Henri Bergson in Dialogue

Justin Sands

Introduction

African and decolonial philosophy often draw upon the Continental tradition to build arguments, develop ideas, and critique established or otherwise entrenched concepts. This is particularly true for thinkers as varied as Frantz Fanon, Paulin Hountondji, Achille Mbembe, and Tsenay Serequeberhan who reference various branches of phenomenology to craft their own philosophical approach. Yet while one can find Continental philosophy as a resource for these disciplines, outside of Mbembe one sees extraordinarily little interchange in the other direction. That is, one rarely sees recent African or Africana thinkers influencing contemporary Continental philosophy that does not specifically designate itself as "African," "decolonial," or otherwise critical of Western traditions. I am pleased that one of the aims of this anthology is to address this lacuna and to provide an access point for future interchanges.

This chapter presents a dialogue between Kwasi Wiredu and Henri Bergson, and through this, it teases out the following contributions: First, Wiredu's notion that a self only becomes a person through community holds a sense of temporality that can be revealed through Bergsonian *duration*. Likewise, Bergson's understanding of the interpenetrability between time and space brings Wiredu's sense of personal becoming into a phenomenological register, giving it a sense of time-consciousness that engages the political and the hermeneutical. Finally, Wiredu's sense of Akan metaphysics brings Bergson's interrelation between memory, the world, and the self further into a cultural-political register.

When in dialogue, both show how one cannot become a person without community and that this becoming entails an interconnected worldhood. My argument is that we can better understand how the inter-subjective relationship between the self, other, and world is a becoming (i.e., temporality) that manifests itself (i.e., is spatial) in an enduring relationship (i.e., is interpenetrative). What I seek to improve upon is the dynamic nature of the interplay between personhood and worldhood through a qualitative understanding of temporality.

Wiredu: What Becomes of a Human Being?

FROM HUMAN TO PERSON

In *Cultural Universals and Particulars*, Wiredu situates his thinking as an investigation of universal metanarratives. Although not referencing Lyotard, one sees Wiredu working through a tradition that takes the mistrust of universal claims seriously, albeit not from a postmodern perspective (Lauer, 2002). However, while being sympathetic to these critiques, he still finds that there must be a foundational, universal construct that binds humanity, but which evades a metanarrative's totalization. "Human beings cannot live by particulars or universals alone," Wiredu (1996) argues, "but by some combination of both" (9).

For Wiredu, this combination begins with biology and thus any philosophical anthropology must accept that personhood is bound to human biology. Biologically speaking, communication is essential for human survival (where to get food, shelter, etc.) and thus communication is what binds biology to anthropology: in short, culture is ultimately born out of human communication, and communication is sine qua non for survival. Wiredu argues that "without communication, there is not even a human person," and he follows this by questioning how philosophy often presents meaning and thought as separate from the human condition (Wiredu 1996, 13).

However, this is not a mere attack on Kantianism(s); rather, Wiredu is presenting the conditions of possibility for a human to *become a person*. For this, he first needs to show how the foundation of meaning-making— and thus the creation of personhood—comes from the essential need to communicate. "The notion of different persons perceiving or apprehending the same entity," he argues, "presupposes a system of interpersonal correlation of inner experiences with external reality, which is inconceivable without communication" (Wiredu 1996, 19).

Unpacking how communication is bound to biology, Wiredu argues that cultural universals only exist because of humanity's shared biological makeup and that humanity only continues as a species because of its ability to communicate. Thus, cultural universals are *"vital* communications," by which he argues they are necessary for human existence, and "without communication there can be no human community" (Wiredu 1996, 21). What binds humanity is thus the shared biological necessity to communicate.

At this primitive stage communication is about survival and is not yet a cultural phenomenon. He finds that this is one of the reasons why there can be intercultural exchanges and how one even has the capacity to learn a foreign language: the universal and biological need for communication creates the capacity to share experience through said communication. The basic skills of reflective perception, abstraction, and inference are components of this fundamental exchange that allow human beings to structure their communication through an essential grammar. As Wiredu (1996) states, "A human being is a rule-following animal, and language is nothing but an arrangement of rules" (25). He then extrapolates that there is a connection between the universal need to communicate and epistemology since this communication requires a special arrangement—a grammar—to transfer information. Thus, whether it is where to go for shelter or a more complex symbolic reference, this transference of information is how it is possible to create meaning and proclaim possible truths. Wiredu (1996) thus calls language the "cultural universal *par excellence*" (28).

The human thus becomes a person through a community of communicants, which build and learn from each other and possibly learn from other communities. Customs, morals, and values are built through this communication. Society grows more complex as both the person and community grow, and as knowledge or truth claims pass on to future generations. This knowledge transference and the building of a culture is again a biological necessity, for Wiredu (1996), since "coexistence in society requires some adjustment or reconciliation of [conflicting] interests." In sum, coexistence requires a social order that can reconcile conflict and disagreement. This reconciliation can be found within the morals and values of each culture that attempts to "adopt a sympathetic impartiality" into its customs and mores to maintain order and/or peace (41).

Communicative language is therefore the foundation to the shared human experience. It is also necessary for keeping morality and values alive. This in turn sustains the community and, ultimately, means that communicative language is the foundation for culture. As Wiredu states: "The survival of human society is possible in the face of quite a lot of defaults and defections from the observance of the ethical principle, but unless it held a certain minimum of way in the thought and action of some individuals at least, there would be a collapse of human society" (Wiredu 1996, 41). Thus, morality is not just cultural but also biological: it is an *evolutionary force*. Therefore, Wiredu's sense of personhood moves from biology to anthropology, and then to the greater philosophical questions of morality, epistemology, among others. Personhood is a creative development that becomes individualized through the evolution of not just a people but the entire species. Moreover, by emphasizing the need to communicate and how it founds any possibility of an epistemology, Wiredu is also articulating a relational logic. This is a shared logic, not self-evident, and its rationality comes from its ability to transfer information of cultural significance. Often Wiredu has been criticized for being a relativist, particularly on this notion of relational logic. However, just as with the formation of a language—with its set of rules and grammar—or the formation of a religious belief system—with its set of symbolic-ritualistic references, creeds, doctrines—what Wiredu is arguing is that each community has a *shared* sense of rationality.[1]

Wiredu (1996) further argues that truth claims in and of themselves are only opinions to critique the false hierarchy between statements of fact and statements of opinion that mire the relativism debate (108–110). Rather than have capital "T" Truth claims versus relative truth claims, Wiredu (1995) argues that statements should be evaluated on their coherence to the rationality of their discourse or their shared, communal rationality. In effect, this opens our understanding of what counts as truth beyond a Western rationality but, for our purposes, it also shows how whatever counts as truth must be understood within a community.

Since rationalities can also overlap, many typical philosophical concerns—such as free will/determinism, or monism/dualism—are reframed from within a universal need to communicate. As Masolo (2010, 137) points out, this is a strong critique against Kantianism, which begins with metaphysical questions only to address anthropology afterward. Contrariwise, Wiredu argues that metaphysical claims are built *through* a social anthropology that is assembled from the basic biological need to communicate. This biological need builds the capacities required for abstract thought, which in turn build ideas, symbols, and other complex, meaning creating concepts. Thus, the mind is built from the body, only exists because of the body, and only develops (i.e., forms personhood) because of the body's need to socially communicate; recall that a human is not yet a person without communication.

In short, one's biological humanity is a given but one's personhood arises and is maintained through one's relationship with others. One's personhood becomes known through their communication, memory, and interaction with those around them. Consider how one is known through relationships: one cannot be a father without children, a husband without a partner. Moreover, one cannot be considered a "man" in a gendered sense without a shared network of references designating what a male is from a biological standpoint and what a "man" is from a sociocultural standpoint. Finally, consider how fluid these identifiers are where our concepts such as "father," "husband," and "manhood" are never static; their definitions are negotiated throughout a shared culture or network of referents and actants.

THE SPATIALITY OF EXISTENCE

Wiredu finds that the limitations of thinking are related to the limitations of language. His chief example is Christianity's misunderstanding of Akan thinking, where missionaries misappropriated Akan language as referents for Christianity's understanding of God, being, and so forth (Wiredu 1996, 46). Consequently, this created a misunderstanding of the Akan way of life whereby Westerners thought that their worldviews were overly supernatural, which is sadly a common result of mission work throughout Africa (Wiredu and Gyekye 1992). Contrariwise, Akan metaphysics makes no supernatural/natural distinction; even existence and nothingness are not definite concepts within the Akan way of thinking.

It is here where Wiredu articulates an important point regarding the Akan worldview and its metaphysics: the Akan hold no concept of existence outside of space; therefore there is no transcendence and, since God and other metaphorical concepts still maintain a *space* in Akan existence (even if it is within the realm of metaphor), there is no immanence. The terms do not adhere to nor can they describe Akan thinking:

> In radical contrast, the Akan Supreme Being is a kind of cosmic architect, a fashioner of the world order, who occupies the apex of the same hierarchy of being which accommodates, in its intermediate ranges, the ancestors and living mortals, and, in its lower reaches, animals, plants, and inanimate objects. Thus the universe of being is ontologically homogenous. In other words, everything that exists exists in exactly the same sense as everything else. And this sense is empirical, broadly speaking. In the Akan language to exist is *wo ho*, which, in literal translation, means "to be at some place." There is no equivalent, in Akan, of the existential "to be" or "is" of English, and there is no way of pretending in that medium to be speaking of the existence of something which is not in space. This locative connotation of the Akan concept of existence is irreducible except metaphorically. Thus you might speak of there existing an explanation of something . . . without incurring any obligation of special specification, because an explanation is not an object in any but a metaphorical sense, and to a metaphorical object corresponds only a metaphorical kind of space. The same applies to so-called abstract entities. In the Akan conceptual framework, then, existence is spatial. Now, since whatever transcendence means in this context, it implies existence beyond space, it follows that talk of any transcendent being is not just false but unintelligible from an Akan point of view. (Wiredu 1996, 49–50)

Existence is therefore entirely empirical and spatial. However, just because it holds no transcendence does not make it an immanent philosophy: since abstract thought holds a spatial concept, it maintains itself in a metaphorical or abstract space and thus cannot be rendered inherent or solely held "within" the mind.

In sum, what Wiredu's metaphysics reveals is a logic that stems from a shared community, through which its communicants become more than human beings, they become persons. Or, read simply, human beings become persons through a community that shares a language and logical framework. Finally, for Wiredu, this framework is entirely spatial and, since nothing can be spatial without a referent to judge space, spatiality is therefore communal.

PIVOTING TOWARD BERGSON

Though Wiredu articulates becoming a person and its relational/communalism, he rarely discusses the temporality of this becoming. He does, however, briefly discuss the issue when critiquing Kant's a priori rendering of time and space. The main thrust of his argument is that time is an "order of events" and that "time itself was conceived to be logically bound up with the notion of events" (Wiredu 2011, 28–29). While his argument is mainly presented to prove the empirical nature of temporality, it does not explore how memory and meaning-making arises through this ordering. Moreover, his metaphysics may question concepts like transcendence and immanence, but it does not question the temporal relationality of objects in existence. It seems as if time, for Wiredu, is left unexamined beyond it being an empirical experience, which may leave one asking, "How and when does this becoming happen?"

This is where I think Henri Bergson might be insightful, but with some qualifications. Bergson critiques how Western thought spatializes time and existence; indeed, his concept of *duration* is fashioned from critiques of spatialized constructs and their tendency to quantify temporal existence over and against any qualitative understanding. This being the case, how can one rightfully bring Wiredu's spatialized understanding of existence into dialogue with Bergson?

This impasse is breeched, I argue, through Wiredu's critique of immanence and transcendence: the fact that his reading of Akan metaphysics holds no transcendental categories does not imply that it is a purely immanent thought. Wiredu's critique of Western logic misconstruing Akan thought cuts both ways: just as transcendence and overt supernaturalism do not fit within Wiredu's reading of Akan metaphysics, neither does a pure immanence and overt materialism. We must remember that Wiredu's (1996) essential point regarding the Akan understanding of God and the supernatural is to show how incongruent they are to Western concepts.

Bergson critiques similar incongruencies within Western thought. He found that several philosophical debates misunderstand the underlying question of how a self relates to its world. For Bergson (2001, 96), the problem with these debates, and the reason why they are never resolved, lies within their conceptual framework.[2] Though he is known for his concept of temporality, addressing the problem with our conceptual approach to philosophy and thinking in general was essentially his ultimate concern. For him, the false character of these debates arises from how linguistic constructs immobilize thought, especially the spatialized metaphors that are woefully misemployed when discussing temporality.[3]

Bergson and Wiredu therefore share something in common: the problem of language superimposing itself on the ways in which we understand life and its creativity. Both thinkers, as I will argue later, eschew mechanistic paradigms by looking at the relationship between becoming and worldhood (i.e., community). However, they are different sides of the same coin: Wiredu emphasizes the relationship between *space* and sharing in this becoming, whereas Bergson emphasizes the relationship between *temporality* and sharing in this becoming.

Finally, while Bergson might lend a sense of temporality to Wiredu's thinking, Wiredu likewise can inform Bergson's muted understanding of space. As I will argue, Wiredu's understanding of the spatial field as a conceptualization of existence pushes against Bergson's quasi-totalized critique of spatialization. Bergson at times trips over himself when it comes to what are "good" and "bad" renderings of space and he has been criticized for sporadically misusing his own terminology.[4] Wiredu not only lends a dynamic sense of space where community happens, he also raises the concept of becoming into a political and moral philosophy. Perhaps this is where Wiredu might lend some clarity to Bergson and be an access point for future engagements.

Bergson: *Duration* and Its Creative Implications

DURATION AND THE MELODY OF TIME

Bergson first presents *duration* by wading into two philosophical debates: *Time and Free Will* (2001) concerns itself with determinism, whereas *Matter and Memory* (1991) concerns itself with monism and dualism debates. For Bergson, both debates render the relation between the body and consciousness into a mechanized process. Here, calculative reasoning frames consciousness—from its temporality to its contents—in terms of number or quantity. Yet what happens in the quantized version of consciousness is that spatial representations move beyond metaphor and become the perception of consciousness itself (Bergson 1991, 4–27; 2001, 4–7, 85–92).[5] The primary mistake Bergson sees within these mis-conceptualizations is the overdetermination of spatial metaphors to describe this relationship, which, in turn, become the ways in which we perceive the relationship between consciousness, the body, and the outside world. Here, one can think of how "clock time" dominates our conception of temporality and, thus, our access to temporality's potential.

Concerning free will, he finds that both determinists and liberationists confuse a spatialized construct of time for temporality itself: "by introducing space into our perception of duration, it corrupts at its very source our feeling of outer and inner change, of movement, and of freedom" (Bergson 1991, 74). In short, the problem of free will is not whether our decisions are determined *but how we perceive of our decisions* by cutting them into segments rather than as a flow of creative, successive events. "All of the difficulties of the problem and the problem itself," Bergson (2001) summarizes, "arise from the desire to endow duration with the same attributes as extensity [i.e., space], to interpret a succession by a simultaneity, and to express the idea of freedom in a language into which it is obviously unstranslatable" (221).

The untranslatable, here, is what lies at the heart of the problem. Bergson (2001) finds that philosophy and science seem "particularly concerned to prove that we perceive things through the medium of certain forms, borrowed from our own constitution" (222). That is, we use metaphor—which is derived from our experiences (i.e., constitution)—to describe not just what we perceive but how we perceive it. This causes a confusion regarding differences in *kind*, forsaking the notion that they are differences in *degree*. It is a perceptual confusion not just in rank and number or how we order our perceptions—where quantitative thinking resides—but also in how our faculties of perception work; the description of perception becomes confused with the means of perception itself.

Furthermore, quantification infects our perception of materiality where we attempt to sever the relationship between our perception of a thing from the thing itself (Bergson 1991, 23–28). And hence, the question of monism/dualism: our consciousness, separated from materiality, ignores how our perception of the thing is at play within the thing itself; how we draw our perception out of the thing and how perception and materiality are interpenetrative (Bergson 1991, 50, 68, 78–79). This confusion between perception and materiality misses how consciousness functions as a product of responding to stimuli or how outside interactions create emotions or ideas and, in turn, how these emotions or ideas effect outside stimuli (Bergson 1991, 139).

Recall Wiredu's notion of personhood as a corresponding relationship. Here, one can see how each person can be considered "outside stimuli" for the other person and how each's esteem of this relationship can and does affect the other. As I move on to the important role that memory plays in Bergson's analysis, keep this relationship in mind. Importantly, Bergson is discussing stimuli in general and not the problem of other selves, but one can see within it this the cogenerative nature of perception about which he is describing.

Continuing, for Bergson perception breaks phenomena down into images upon which consciousness projects meaning. Importantly, this "imaging" is necessary as a part of a consciousness seeking understanding of its world and, without it, one would be constantly overwhelmed. For example, hearing a foreign language for the first time sounds impermeable, but, as one becomes familiar with the language, it slows down and one can begin picking apart different words, recognizing their correlation to things/ideas. Eventually, as one learns the language, not only does it "slow down" but different contextual cues (such as sadness or sarcasm) become apparent. This is an illustration of consciousness breaking down phenomena to render it comprehensible. Barnard (2011) clarifies this, noting that "in order to not be overwhelmed, in order to function, it is crucial that our senses and our brain carve out certain clearly defined zones of stability in the flux of universal becoming. We are forced to create order by screening out vast amounts of sensory and mental information that pours into us" (10).

This will become important when I argue that Bergson is making a similar claim to Wiredu: that we do this not merely as an intellectual exercise, but do so to survive. Therefore, generating meaning (which eventually develops into personhood and culture) is a part of making survival sustainable. Where Wiredu sees vital communications as a biological necessity, our pattern-seeking behavior likewise creates images that we correlate to emotions/ideas for survival and to make survival meaningful.

Returning to Bergson, he finds that the distillation of *duration's* perception into images causes yet another problem of differences in kind rather than degree: we break images apart, categorize them, and, in doing so, we become reliant upon the object of perception (the image), forsaking its relation to other facets of our consciousness. Perception, here, is a matter of focus: focus is typically described as fixating upon a thing, but it also works in the opposite direction where other objects are negated (erased, discarded) to bring the thing in question into contrast with its surroundings. "My perception," Bergson (1991) argues, "contracts into a single moment of my *duration* that which, taken in itself, spreads over an incalculable number of moments" (208). Fell (2012) summarizes this: "[The] mind, able to contract in what is our present multitude of events and conceive them in their connection with each other, is [thus] able to join them in a meaningful unity" (37).

While this may be necessary for survival and even for individual and communal thriving, the consequence of the tyranny of the image is that it confuses distinction for reality. We yet again have a problem with emphasizing the separation of things through the image—the spatialization of our worldhood—at the cost of understanding that these entities stand in relation to other entities; that they are interconnected and interpenetrated through our perceiving of them.

Returning to monism/dualism, both sides confuse the relationship between the body, the space in which it inhabits and interacts with others, and how we perceive the temporality of its interactions. Bergson (1991, 65–69) dispels this confusion by untangling our understanding of time and space. The resulting clarity is how time, expressed as *duration*, is a qualitative multiplicity rather than a quantitative, mechanistic, successive progression.

His favorite illustration of this qualitative multiplicity is a melody: Recall a melody and think of how it forms in your mind. What makes a melody is the relation between tones and how they build off each other to create a cohesive, holistic "thing." Now, think of how meaning is created (e.g., sadness) as the melody changes; note how this is not just about tonality but also rhythm. Also, note that you are remembering this melody where you are recalling an auditory experience and, if you have heard this melody several times (a favorite song, perhaps), then the meaning of this melody is associated with other memories and those memories' meanings (perhaps it was played at a funeral). Finally, imagine this melody written on sheet music: sure, this representation could make the music identifiable and replicable; it could be used to explore the mathematical theory behind the melody and what makes it "work." While this may be valuable in some respects, it completely removes the meaning-making from the melody itself. It is as if the melody were a cadaver handed over for autopsy.[6]

Importantly, recall that Bergson's aim is not merely to describe temporality but to find a better description of consciousness. *Duration*, here, describes the interlacing of consciousness, stimulus, reception, influence, and action: that they are differences in degree and not in kind. As differences in degree, they can be parsed out for examination, but we must not forget that they are all multiplicities of conscious perception. Therefore, *duration* allows for the holistic understanding of living time rather than separating life and the world from time (as one sees in subject-object metaphysical constructs). Furthermore, *duration* shows the mobility of life through time and how we construe that mobility through a spatialized field. And finally, *duration* shows how time is not separated from the world—we do not access time, we live time—and thus it shows how time is a force: it is the mobility of consciousness through which it interpenetrates its world.

In summary:

- *Duration* is the mobility of consciousness's perception of its world;

- This makes it temporal while incorporating how consciousness construes its world;

- This entails how one perceives stimuli as an interpenetrative event;

- This event is coaffected through successive memory: one's consciousness and its stimuli imbues the other with meaning, endowing the other with ideas and emotions while imparting similar concepts and meanings;

- This establishes meaning-making as a cogenerative and interpenetrative process;

- *Duration* reveals that there is a constant movement between consciousness and stimuli to the point where they pierce each other;

- Thus, this interplay is ongoing, and, like a melody, it builds off prior events;

- Consciousness, through this movement of interplay, finds its freedom as it creates meaningful understandings that in turn influence further events or interactions with stimuli.

Being foundational to perception itself, our recognition of *duration* does not come easy. In fact, Bergson argues that *duration* is not something one can simply tap into; it is not a matter of flicking a switch. What follows will highlight its challenges and limitations.

PIVOTING TOWARD WIREDU

Bergson sought a reorientation of thinking about how consciousness operates. However, Bergson's operation is interior: Bergson's concerns against philosophy begin with introspection, how thought comes too easily for us, and how this can create mechanized notions of ourselves and our world. In this way, Lawler identifies Bergson as an immanent philosopher in contradistinction to so-called philosophers of transcendence who look externally beyond their limited faculties of understanding. Lawler, here, labels Derrida and Levinas as transcendent counterpoints, with the former looking externally through language and the latter through the other. Lawler (2003, 68–70) even mentions a "loneliness" in Bergson's *Matter and Memory* due to its introspective thrust. Although I think it is fair to place Bergson as an immanent philosopher, at least in a Western paradigm, I think that this comes with a disadvantage.

For one, it overshadows the possibility that Bergson should be read outside of an immanent/transcendent framework. I think Bergson's emphasis on interpenetration and cogenerative meaning-making places him within a relational framework that makes his thought excitingly comparative to African philosophy. Yet within this dialogue and its relational logic, one sees that Bergson needs a concept of politics or culture that Wiredu could possibly supplement.

Recall the illustration of the father and child where each influences the other's perception of the world and their own identity. I think that this paternal concept is best described relationally where the interpenetrative nature of engaging outside stimuli emphasizes a cogeneration; it is not merely one thing gaining meaning through memory and event—both entities cocreate meaning through their interplay and this grows as each new instance builds upon prior memories. Although Bergson himself may not wish to go in this direction, I do not see anything that prevents it. Furthermore, I think that it opens a space for a politics or culture within his work.

Recall Bergson's proclamation that we mistake differences of degree for differences of kind. Here, degree could emphasize the relationality and shared sense of all our perceptions; though we are perceiving one thing then another, we do not independently perceive them from each other. When we categorize by kind, we sever this relational comprehension. Sure, categorization has a purpose, but we must never mistake it as more than a mere picture of reality. We must be aware that it is dependent upon the interplay between memories of prior perceptions and the new experience of phenomena, of our consciousness's interplay between remembering and perceiving, of the mobility given to us through the novelty of each new perception as it interlaces with prior perceptions. If this is the case, then perhaps the entire immanent/transcendent debate has the same problematics as the free will/determinism and monism/dualism debates; it is a dispute that mischaracterizes differences in degree as differences in kind.

Wiredu and Bergson on Becoming in Time

Wiredu and Bergson each highlight a notion of becoming. Furthermore, both explore how we perceive and build relationships with our world. Both thinkers wish to clear away static concepts that render out the dynamism at play within being in the world. Through these insights I have presented a preliminary analysis to establish these connections.

The following aims to better understand how the interpenetrative relationship between the self, other, and world is a becoming (i.e., temporality) that manifests itself (i.e., is spatial) in an enduring relationship (i.e., is interpenetrative). In anticipation of future dialogues between Wiredu and Bergson, I will close by presenting a few key access points. This will be done in two brief entwining explorations. The first investigates the implications of *duration* opening a sense of temporality within Wiredu's personhood and his spatialized metaphysics. The second questions how Wiredu's sense of personhood might tease out a notion of culture latent within Bergson's thinking.

Experiencing Becoming

For Wiredu, space is social. This is inherent to his thought: if communications are vital, and the world becomes demarcated through this communication then the space of this world is socially imbued with meaning. More technically, Wiredu articulates the empirical nature of Akan metaphysics, noting how it is derived from experience and that anything like a Kantian a priori is a terminological contradiction:

> Yet, even if it is granted that the notion of space is *a priori*, it does not follow that what the notion refers to can so much as be spoken of as being *a priori* or otherwise. "*A priori*" applies to a mode of knowing, not a kind of entity or existent. If space is infinite, it may still be that the only way to conceive of it is through the notions of location or place and of infinite extendibility, both of which are empirical. This is certainly how space is conceived in the Akan language. (Wiredu 2011, 28)

Before I unpack this, let us quickly return to Bergson's so-called "loneliness" and how it speaks to Bergson's approach as well as to his results. On the one hand, if the world comes to us too easily then one must withdraw into a Cartesian-like meditation. It is not surprising, then, that such a hermetic withdrawal would render its findings for *a singular* consciousness; if one needs to turn within oneself to seek understanding then it is fair that one finds only oneself.

In contrast, let us look at Wiredu's approach. Here, Wiredu likewise seeks a foundational understanding but, instead of a singular self, what he finds is that one needs others to survive, a survival that happens only if there is interpersonal communication. Wiredu emphasizes the importance of a socially created world and, rather that withdrawing from it, he delves into it. It is as if Wiredu is responding to Bergson's critique, saying, "The world may come too easily for us, but that is why it must be our first exploration! We must begin with an anthropology."

Wiredu does an excellent job articulating this anthropology and how it expands outward to become a metaphysics of self and community. However, I find that the linkages between these notions could be explored further. In short, what I want to know is how this becoming happens and how it connects to a spatialized world. I think that Bergson, lonely as he may be, might provide this linkage.

Duration, for Bergson, is not just how a consciousness experiences phenomena and creates its world, it is also consciousness's mobile engagement with/in that world. In a sense, it describes the way in which we *are* time rather than describing us as living in or through "a time." Moreover, meaning-making happens when our memories of prior events interlace with each new and oncoming event, and our perception of phenomena is only rendered coherent when we break these perceptions down. Thus, we arrive at space: as an image of *duration*, it is also *a medium*. Space is where one interplays with phenomena while also being a phenomenon itself. Hence why we break it down into an image to make it intelligible in the first place. Here, in this medium, we not only experience the world; we build it as we create more and more memories and experiences.[7]

In this way, we create space. Or, as Wiredu puts it, from out of our concrete experiences and designation of places, a conceptualization of infinite space arises. From out of a "here," the designation of a "there" and other "theres" arise. Rather than space being an a priori, we derive the abstract notion of space through our experience/creation of places. For Wiredu, existence is empirically spatial and to abstract entities one correlates an abstract space; we first experience place in order to render reflections of its infinite possibilities. Out of these infinite possibilities comes the notion that space can be infinite. Note that it is infinite not just in the sense of "ever expanding" but also in the sense of possibility, where anything can happen within space. Once it happens, it becomes a place and is therefore meaningful and concrete.

Yet we must negotiate places with others, it must be communicated to others what these places are, or, more importantly, what they mean. Here, we begin to see not just the building of a particular culture, but also how one's personality (à la Wiredu) is built within and alongside that culture. *Duration*, where each instance is interlaced with memory and the novelty of the current experience, can help us uncover the interplay between the self, the cultural society, and the places that both have cogenerated.

Following Wiredu, this initially refers to vital communications, as in this is a place where you can find food, shelter, and so forth. Then these places build with meaning as they are experienced; places for shelter become villages, places for food become markets. When discussing the creation of the social, Wiredu (1996) comments upon knowledge being handed down and developed through the generations. When doing so, he notes how these memories and teachings develop cultures that in turn define individual personalities.

I think the same can be said for our places and this cultural development of space is not something that is static; it is a living phenomenon that we experience not just when we enter into these places but also when we recollect them, assimilate them, or bring them into contrast with others places. These places are cogenerated insofar as our social and personal memories of them are maintained every time we recollect them. In contrast and akin to *damnatio memoriae*, a place can cease to be if it is completely forgotten. Finally, a place can be recontextualized as we discover its previous history.

Regarding Bergson's notion of memory and its importance to meaning-making, this raises the question of social memory. It is here that I think Wiredu may have something to contribute to Bergson, namely a culture.

THE CULTURE OF *DURATION*

Bergsonian memory is dynamic and, if one had no prior recollections and every instance were new (literally every nanosecond), then one's consciousness would be constantly paralyzed—perhaps even in sheer terror and panic—since there would be no way to stop the onslaught of phenomena assaulting the senses. Hence why memory is crucial and thus his entry point to understanding.

However, one does not merely remember alone. Wiredu emphasizes that memories and traditions are handed down, that one is taught a culture, and, through living within that culture, one changes this culture while also passing it on to others. Through this, he articulates a culture as having social memory. This is why reading Wiredu and Bergson through a relational logic is important: for both there is a dynamic interplay between the self and its community (otherwise understood as phenomena) and through this play they cogenerate meaning by creating new memories. They also do this through reinterpreting prior memories as they redefine their relationships and as they pass these memories down through culture. Although Bergson begins with withdrawing from the world to better understand the *duration* of oneself within that world, he has not forgotten that the world exists. Rather, he has sought how one relates to this world by focusing on one's consciousness, which is the closest certainty one can have (again, very Cartesian).

What Bergson leaves underexplored is the other side of this equation. Although it is clear that we imbue phenomena with meaning, he does not go into detail regarding how this meaning changes the phenomena themselves. Rather, he sticks to describing how this interplay changes our understanding of the phenomena (again, sticking with the self). Though I cannot delve into this here, this where I find the cleavage between *duration* and his later work: Bergson needs a means to describe how the meaning placed upon the phenomenon (be it person or place) changes not just the self's understanding of the phenomenon but how it actually changes the phenomenon itself.

This is compounded by his muddy description of good and bad "space." As Addyman (2013) writes, "One would not obviously look to Bergson for an account of space; even if one did, one would not immediately find a clear elaboration of the issue. . . . Bergson's critics—and even his admirers—have tended to recognize only one form of space—the 'bad' space of 'spatialization' " (24–25). In short, Bergson stumbles when discussing good understandings of space, mainly because his focus transitions from critiquing mischaracterizations of space and temporality toward elaborating upon *duration*. Yet without a "good" rendering of space, it is difficult to move toward how two selves become a "we" (a society, or a politic) since there is no designation, or place, for this to happen.

Returning to Wiredu, his sense of becoming a person is predicated upon memory: one not only takes up the characteristics of their personhood but are even designated as a person through their culture. This culture requires an institutional, shared memory. Moreover, each self renders given places with meaning and history through this shared memory (Wiredu 1996, 159–167). That is, there is a *personal* (with all the implications of personhood) and *cultural* memory of places. And these need to be negotiated through a politics. Perhaps Wiredu's philosophy can point toward how Bergsonism can develop a good rendering of space, a social memory—a cultural *duration* of sorts—which might bridge the gap between Bergson's thinking on consciousness, politics, and the issue of other selves (the latter of which is where a culture not only happens but is preserved through memory).

For Future Dialogues: A Closing Note

My aim with this chapter was to bring two important thinkers into dialogue to reveal how their strengths might address lacunae within each's thinking. This entailed decisions regarding what to review and what to omit, and some may take issue with the aspects that I highlighted in crafting this dialogue. However, as an initial dialogue, what it shows is that Wiredu's concept of personhood and community has important contributions to phenomenology, while in turn Bergsonian *duration* (and perhaps in future dialogues, his élan vital) can be employed to adequately describe the temporal nature of Wiredu's sense of becoming. Far too often African phenomenologists are read in silos—as if their work only reveals something about their specific political context—and this trend needs to be broken.

What this dialogue revealed is how we can further understand the relational aspects of personhood and how it manifests and unfolds itself through time, space, and ultimately, community. As an initial dialogue, it may provoke more questions than it answered, but in so doing it furthers a larger phenomenological dialogue concerning the question: What, phenomenologically speaking, are we discussing when we speak of the political, the cultural, and the personal?

Notes

1. Wiredu (2009, 176; 1996, 191–210).
2. Cf. Lawler (2003, 64).
3. Cf. Guerlac (2006, 71).
4. Cf. Addyman (2013, 25).
5. See also Guerlac (2006, 50–60, 110–115).
6. Cf. Barnard (2011, 122).
7. Cf. Bergson (1991, 196–202).

References

Addyman, David. 2013. "Bergson's Matter and Memory: From Time to Space." In *Understanding Bergson, Understanding Modernism*, edited by Paul Ardoin, S. E. Gontarski, and Laci Mattison, 24–37. London: Bloomsbury.

Barnard, William G. 2011. *Living Consciousness: The Metaphysical Vision of Henri Bergson*. Albany: State University of New York Press.

Bergson, Henri. 1991. *Matter and Memory*. Translated by N. Paul and W. Scott Palmer. New York: Zone Books.

Bergson, Henri. 2001. *Time and Free Will*. Translated by F. L. Pogson. London: Dover.

Fell, Elena. 2012. *Duration, Temporality, Self: Prospects for the Future of Bergsonism*. Oxford: Peter Lang.

Guerlac, Suzanne. 2006. *Thinking in Time: An Introduction to Henri Bergson*. Ithaca: Cornell University Press.

Lauer, Helen. 2002. "Knowledge on the Cusp." In *The Third Way in African Philosophy: Essay in Honour of Kwasi Wiredu*, edited by Olusegun Oladipo, 171–214. Ibadan: Hope.

Lawler, Leonard. 2003. *The Challenge of Bergsonism: Phenomenology, Ontology, Ethics*. London: Continuum.

Masolo, D. A. 2010. *Self and Community in a Changing World*. Bloomington: Indiana University Press.

Wiredu, Kwasi. 1995. "Knowledge, Truth and Fallibility." In *The Concept of Knowledge: The Ankara Seminar*, edited by Robert Cohen, 127–148. New York: Springer.

Wiredu, Kwasi. 1996. *Cultural Universals and Particulars*. Bloomington: Indiana University Press.

Wiredu, Kwasi. 2009. *Philosophy and African Culture*. Cambridge: Cambridge University Press.

Wiredu, Kwasi. 2011. "Empiricalism: The Empirical Character of an African Philosophy." In *Identity Meets Nationality: Voices from the Humanities*, edited by H. Lauer, N. A. Appiah, and A. J. A. Anderson, 18–34. Legon-Accra: Sub-Saharan.

Wiredu, Kwasi, and Kwame Gyekye, eds. 1992. *Person and Community: Ghanaian Philosophical Studies, I*. Washington, DC: Council for Research in Values and Philosophy.

15

Artifacts of Emotion and Existence in Unjust Structures

UCHENNA OKEJA

Introduction

"Artifacts of emotion" refers to the creative expressions that dispossessed people at the fringes of society rely on to survive the harsh conditions they must live with daily. They are called artifacts of emotion because they refer to the tenacity of the hard-done-by to live normal lives despite cruel and unforgiving circumstances created by unjust social and political structures. My aim in this chapter is to show how artifacts of the emotion constitute a concept that enables us to grapple with questions about meaning in life for the people who live under unjust social and political structures. The meaning introduced by the concept is specifically suitable for this task because it captures a unique but shared circumstance of the dispossessed, humiliated, and marginalized who struggle with the effects of living daily under unjust conditions. Analyzing the experience of dispossessed people in light of this concept enables us to recapture the significance of their agency. The aim is therefore to engage in what could be regarded as a *phenomenology of everyday life*—a reflection on meaning and significance of everyday human experiences.

Virtually all African-descendant persons will wonder at some point why everything must be a struggle. What is the point of a life that is defined by unending struggles? Although it may be impossible to specify exactly the meaning of a life of unending struggle, it is possible to respond to the challenge it poses by exploring how the subjects of this experience tackle the uniqueness of their positionality. And, drawing from this response, one can explore whether it is useful to attempt to imagine how to live, in a meaningful sense, a life of unmitigated suffering and disadvantage. My goal in this chapter is to provide a metareflection that makes possible the imagination of how to live a life of unmitigated suffering and disadvantage. More precisely, I am interested in showing that this form of life is not devoid of meaning and a sense of purpose. I will pursue this goal by showing how "artifacts of emotion" is a concept that captures the creative expressions through which subjects of a life defined by unending struggle negotiate and triumph over their existential condition.

The core of my argument is that, when everyday life is reduced to an intense negotiation of reality that alone can guarantee survival, the result is that conceiving meaning in life becomes a task that is impossible to accomplish through a distanced reflection. In such a situation, surviving becomes the meaning of existence because such life is contingent upon how one negotiates extremely challenging circumstances. For one who must live daily with the disastrous effects of the intense negotiation of unmitigated suffering and disadvantage, the creative art of survival is a meaning-giving activity.

The conditions under which subjects of struggle exist make an abstract notion of "meaning in life" impossible. The reason is that a construction of meaning that is detached from concrete life is necessarily conditioned upon a "settled life," which is to say, a life that is a measure of value in the society. Thus, when the context for interrogating meaning in life is existence outside the normative order, or outside the realm of affirming sensibilities embedded in the social and political conditions of a society, the implication is that access to meaning in life will manifest differently. It will manifest as something that cannot be captured by conventional or prevailing norms and ordering concepts in the society. This is because being seen to be outside the normative order of a society implies being denied the possibility of meaning-making through the conventional concepts that structure imagination of what it means to be fully human. Thus, to account for the meaning of a life of unmitigated suffering and disadvantage considered to be outside the broadly shared normative order of a society, what we must do is to, like Ifeanyi Menkiti observed, "put ear to the singing rocks to hear, perhaps to know, what might be the source of it all, the tribulations, but also the grace" (Menkiti 2005, 22).

The chapter is divided into three parts. The introduction sets out the context of discussion. In what follows, I consider everyday experiences of subjects of unmitigated suffering and disadvantage. The goal is to show why artifacts of emotion is a conceptual approach that makes an understanding of this form of life possible. In the last section of the chapter, I show how artifacts of emotion is deployed to negotiate meaning in life under unjust structures. This means showing why the mobilization of artifacts of emotion is a viable response to a life of unmitigated suffering and disadvantage. I conclude with a reflection on the extent to which we can rely on the conceptual metaphor of artifacts of emotion as a means to access meaning in life.

The Nature of the Life of Unmitigated Suffering and Disadvantage

A good starting point of the discussion here is perhaps to consider a story that demonstrates how unjust social and political structures lead to a life of unmitigated suffering and disadvantage. My interest is neither to present proof of what constitutes structural injustice nor to show that certain patterns of institutional arrangements are susceptible to creating a life of unmitigated suffering and disadvantage. My aim is to show why it makes sense to imagine existential conditions that are mediated by deeply unjust social and political structures as a life of unmitigated suffering and disadvantage. This means that my aim is not so much to analyze the nature of structural injustice as it is to understand what this form of injustice means in light of the way it is experienced. To say it differently, the specific aim of this section is to understand what it means to experience a kind of despair that is caused by deeply unjust social and political structures. To this end, I will not aim to suggest what should be done to guarantee that social and political conditions do not cause the sort of suffering and disadvantage described. Such an exercise in ideal theorizing is no doubt interesting and useful, but it cannot replace the necessity of understanding the meaning and significance of the experience of living under unjust social and political structures. Besides, it seems that we can accomplish the task of spelling out what should be done to guarantee that social and political conditions do not produce lives of unmitigated suffering and disadvantage only when we have a full grasp of what this experience, this life, means.

To contextualize the experiences of the despairing individuals that make up the political category of "the people," J. Kisekka (2003, 67–68) recounted the story of a certain Kayo Nesmo as follows:

> Nesmo who was born in a village in Uganda. He spent most of his infancy in poverty. His mother did not have enough breast-milk to feed him; the family could not afford supplementary foods. Even the staple food that could be procured from the small shamba that Kayo's father had inherited from his grandfather was insufficient to feed the family of ten. So, they had to supplement it by working for food from neighbours. Oftentimes this meant trekking long distances to find one in need of their services. Kayo's father was a charcoal burner. No sooner had Kayo mastered the rudiments of reading, writing, and addition, than his father advised him to fend for himself as he, too, had done. Kayo Nesmo, who had by then been confirmed in his church, began his long journey of survival by burning charcoal. The owners, because of the trespass on private property or forest reserve, always harassed him. If they agreed on the mode of sharing, he always felt cheated. Whenever he took a sack of charcoal for sale, he hated to pay the market tax, so he resorted to traveling late at the night. Yet he had to pay the owner of the bicycle he used. Tired of this trade, he was attracted to the nearby town where he did a porter's job for a few coins per day. But as he could not afford to pay, as was needed, for each thing, Kayo went back to the village to resume his trade. He got a woman and rented a two-chambered grass thatched house. With one mouth more to feed, Kayo worked harder cultivating other people's gardens. Thus, he gained enough money to buy a piece of land and a radio. In due course, the woman gave birth to twins. He liked developmental ideas and was in a sense "development prostitute" in that he has tried almost whatever one government proposed through radio programmes. Despite all this, he has been unfortunate because any time he begins a new project, he is disappointed at the time of sales. The prices of

his products are set by forces beyond his control: they talk of the dollar effect, which he vaguely grasps. The prices of the necessities of life are always rising compared to his meager income. He is compelled to buy second-hand. Meanwhile his family grows, they talk to him of family planning, which he does not comprehend, but he entrusts these worries to God alone. Now in his forties he begins to question the name of Onesimo; he queries the so-called obligations to the church and the state. As I write, Kayo is on his deathbed surrounded by his six malnourished children of tender age. He is languishing longing to get Medicare which if found he could not afford.

One of the ways to deal with this sort of experience is to consider it an unfortunate situation. In the literature on injustice, a standard approach to the story of Kayo Nesmo would be to make the judgment that the problem he is confronted with is the injustice of poverty. Another way besides the narrative of injustice is to invoke the idea of intersectionality to argue that Kayo Nesmo and people like him do not just suffer because of one instance of injustice but due to interconnected structural arrangements that trap them in circles of oppression.

Certainly, there are things to learn about Kayo Nesmo's situation if we reflect on it from the angle of injustice or intersectionality. It seems, however, that the insights these approaches offer will not be sufficient to explain what it means to live as a subject of intersectionally embedded oppression. The quest for an understanding of the meaning of the sort of experience that defined the life of Kayo Nesmo is pertinent because it is the way to understand how meaning in life is negotiated in this kind of situation. Certainly, one's circumstances do not preclude the possibility of finding meaning in life. Thus, cut off as they are from conventional normative resources of the context in which their lives unfold, how do the Kayo Nesmos of our world give meaning to their lives? What tools do human beings create and deploy to accomplish the task of finding meaning in life under conditions such as the one in which the life of Kayo Nesmo unfolded? Answering these questions demands that we first articulate a meaningful understanding of the form of life in question. How, in other words, should we imagine the lives of the Kayo Nesmos of our world?

I propose to refer to the experience that defines Kayo Nesmo's life as *a life of unmitigated suffering and disadvantage*. I think this is an accurate view for three reasons. The first is that this form of life indicates a collective tragedy of the current historical moment. This form of life is not an outcome of a single circumstance or factor. Instead, it is the outcome of a series of long and interwoven historical encounters that have become so reified that it now manifests as a foretold misfortune that will surely come to pass. We see this in the reality that, being born in certain countries and positioned in certain ways in the world, means that one will inevitably have to contend with avoidable suffering and disadvantages, the end of which is unimaginable. The collective dimension of this tragedy—that is, the certainty that one will necessarily have to contend with avoidable sufferings and disadvantages—inheres in the fact that the very nature of the structures that mediate coexistence in the world reinforces the situation. Thus, so long as the world exists in its current form, people born or positioned in certain ways will have to contend with these avoidable sufferings and disadvantages. The point is therefore that our collective participation in the structures that govern the modern world reinforces the certainty that subjects of certain backgrounds and positionality will continue to contend with avoidable sufferings and disadvantages. This is nothing short of a collective tragedy of the modern world. Retorting that the issue here is the corrupt system of global governance does not take anything away from my point because the corruption invoked is itself the outcome of the reified historical encounters mentioned earlier.

The second reason I consider the experience of the Kayo Nesmos of the world as a situation of unmitigated suffering and disadvantage is that it is a disaster built on hopelessness. Socially and politically, hope is necessary because it enables us to continue to believe in the goodness and value of human beings. That is, hope inspires us to believe that, regardless of circumstances, the goodness of human beings will triumph. By this I mean hope shields us from the destruction of imagining the abyss of evil as our main orientation to reality. For the Kayo Nesmos of the world, however, life unfolds as an experience of powerlessness vis-à-vis the structures that mediate coexistence in society. This experience of powerlessness leads to hopelessness because it destroys a vital aspect of the belief in the goodness and value of human beings, namely, the understanding that all human beings have equal worth and could attain fulfillment of their purpose and find meaning in doing so.

Living in full realization that one cannot do anything to improve one's social and political conditions is a fundamental defeat that pushes one to the deepest abyss of despair. Such a situation leads to the loss of hope. A form of life characterized by this kind of hopelessness is certainly a human-made disaster and the suffering and disadvantage it embodies are unmitigated. And, they are unmitigated because the absoluteness of the experience is unparalleled. This is the reason the subjects of this experience live constantly with the pain of realizing that nothing worse than their present condition can be imagined.

The third reason I refer to the situation represented by Kayo Nesmo's experience as a life of unmitigated suffering and disadvantage is because of the damaging impact it has on agency. Living in a constant awareness of one's marginality over time leads to a blunting of one's self-perception as an agent, whether social, moral, or political. This is the case because the constitution of agency depends on certain prerequisites. We can see why this point is important when we consider the case of moral agency. Recently, Gillian Brock argued that certain needs must be satisfied for moral agency to be secured. These needs include (1) physical and psychological health, (2) security, (3) understanding, (4) autonomy, and (5) sufficiently decent social relations (Brock 2020, 22). These five basic needs must be met for us to function as moral agents. Not only do we need to be in good health to effectively carry out actions; we also need to be free from "psychological impediments and have adequate security to be able to act." I agree with Brock's argument because human beings are not the sort of beings that are born with a fully developed capacity to function as moral agents. Without nurture, it is impossible to grow and develop the full personhood we refer to when we talk about agency. One can argue that Kayo Nesmo's problem is that he has not shown readiness to confront the sources of his impoverishment. This would amount to saying that Kayo Nesmo and others like him are not acting in ways that will secure their moral agency through the satisfaction of their needs. It is surely reasonable to suggest that people should ensure the needs that guarantee their moral agency is secured. My argument that the situation represented by Kayo Nesmo's experience produces a life of unmitigated suffering and disadvantage is not a judgment about agency. It is an articulation of the meaning of a form of life that is characterized by deeply unjust social and political structures.

It will be reasonable to conclude based on this point that situations like the one Kayo Nesmo's life illustrates, where physical and psychological health, security, understanding, autonomy, and community are severely constrained, damages the capacity for agency. It is surely an absolute disadvantage and suffering to lose one's agential ability, hence the characterization of the situation of the Kayo Nesmos of the world as a life of unmitigated suffering and disadvantage. In a nutshell, the three reasons I have offered to explain why it makes sense to define a certain form of life as a life of unmitigated suffering and disadvantage demonstrate exactly the meaning attached to this form of life. The idea implies that a form of life described in this way represents a collective tragedy, a disaster built on hopelessness, and a form of life that operates to damage the agency of the subjects of the experience. The question to ask is how the subjects of this experience negotiate meaning in life. In the following section, I attempt to answer this question by considering first the nature of the tools that people whose situation is characterized as a life of unmitigated suffering and disadvantage employ to negotiate meaning in life. This will be complemented by a reflection on the ways in which these tools are deployed to accomplish this task.

Artifacts of Emotion and Negotiation of Meaning in Life

Reflecting on the blues, James Baldwin attempted to understand the circumstances of life that gave birth to this form of artistic expression. He used the blues as a metaphor to read the experiences of life that this creative expression embodies. He says that in his discussion of the blues, he wants "to speak about the blues not only because they speak of being, but because they contain the toughness that manages to make this experience articulate" (Baldwin 2011, 1). Baldwin speaks of the blues because he sees in them an "acceptance of anguish" and the expression of this acceptance that creates a kind of joy. His goal in reflecting on the blues is therefore to cut through the peripheral encounter with this creative response to life's stimuli to reveal the "true state" it articulates.

One might ask, why look to the blues to achieve this goal? Why not simply focus on those rational arguments that articulate in a careful and coherent manner, the sort of "true state" that the subjects of these experiences display in their responses to reality? Baldwin provides an answer by pointing to the fact that the blues are commentaries on events of which the singers are the principal witnesses. They are not songs that seek to imagine what is unreal or even merely possible. Instead, the blues mediate the experiences of disaster for a subject that is both a witness and a victim. In doing this, it provides the subject affected by the disaster a means to not just escape but, most importantly, to come to a point of acceptance. This acceptance, Baldwin argues, should not be seen as the creation of a fantasy out of the events that define a disaster one experiences as an affected subject and principal witness. He proposes that instead, we should see this acceptance as a form of triumph. That is, as a successful transformation of imagination that seeks to reveal to the subject of the experience of disaster the meaning of such a life. By achieving this, the subject is led to a new imagination that decouples a sense of meaning in life and the possibilities that will of necessity remain unrealized under the prevailing unjust social and political conditions.

To understand the importance of this explanation, we must understand the nature of the central concept at play. In other words, we must understand the sense in which the mobilization of the blues is an example of a broader perspective through which the knowledge of a life defined by unmitigated suffering or disaster is reflected. Framed as a direct question, the idea is this: What is the conceptual angle that enables the negotiation of meaning for one whose life is unmitigated suffering and disadvantage? Postulating a concept that captures how a life of unmitigated suffering under unjust conditions is negotiated certainly leads to a further question. This is a question about what it means to characterize a context as "existence under unjust structures." What does this way of describing the condition of existence mean and how does it lead to the idea that there is a form of life that is characterized by unmitigated suffering and disadvantage?

To answer these questions, I explain the notion of artifacts of emotion as a conceptual reference. This will be complemented by a discussion of the meaning of "existence under unjust structures," which constitutes the context in which the postulated concept functions. To this end, I shall proceed momentarily with an exploration of the two questions posed earlier to contextualize the way artifacts of emotion serve as a conceptual reference for the construction of a sense of meaning in life under unjust structures.

To analyze how artifacts of emotions functions as a concept and evaluate whether the concept provides an adequate orientation for finding meaning in life, it is pertinent to define the concept. Artifacts of emotion refers to creative accomplishments that give meaning to life under unjust social and political structures. They are manifest ways of accessing symbolic meaning for the people whose circumstances are primarily structured by constant humiliation and disorientation. The creative accomplishments the concept denotes include such signs and objects that are created to reflect the feelings and sensibility induced by the experience of life as a disaster. The creative accomplishments may be tangible or intangible, although sometimes there could be an overlap. Paradigmatic artifacts of emotion include poetry, dirges, lyrics of songs, drum texts, and symbols that codify deep feelings of powerlessness and anguish about the human condition.

The artifacts of emotion manifest in two primary forms we can describe as artifacts of positive emotions and artifacts of negative emotions. Artifacts of positive emotions manifest in the form of creative expressions that codify and give meaning to experiences that rejuvenate the belief in the goodness of human beings. They are creative expressions that are developed to celebrate the beauty of human life and its manifestations in different forms. The artifacts of negative emotions codify and give meaning to the experiences that challenge belief in humanity. They are manifest ways of recapturing the sense of humanity in extremely challenging circumstances where we face the nasty reality of the human condition. The positive arti-facts of emotion just described can be seen as a means through which we develop as sense of joie de vivre—that is, to be at peace with the world and live in full recognition of the beauty of human life and coexistence with others in society. The negative artifacts of emotion equip human beings with the means to survive despair and terrible conditions or experiences where it seems there is a total breakdown or a collapse of our sense of reality. The artifacts of negative emotions manifest in circumstances of extreme despair—in situations in which hope and belief in humanity is pushed to the most extreme limits imaginable. Examples of the negative artifacts of emotion include funeral poems, dirges, the blues, war music, and lamentations to fallen soldiers. In these different instances, the expe-rience of grief, loss, and impending tragedy are codified in specific forms of creative expression. These creative expressions provide a way to survive the extremely challenging circumstances of which they speak.

Although I refer in some parts of this chapter to the artifacts of positive emotion, my aim is primarily to consider how the artifacts of negative emotions enable the people at the fringes of society to negotiate and survive the nastiness and humiliations they must live with. My aim is to understand how the oppressed and marginalized negotiate meaning in life in circumstances in which structural injustice circumscribes every aspect of reality and, as a result, confines certain forms of life to perpetual marginal existence. The artifacts of emotion provide in such situations a viable means to understand social and political reality because they focus on experiences of the subjects as the life of real people. In doing so, the artifacts of emotion demonstrate that a reasonable response to suffering and disadvantage that result from unjust social and political structures of the society is to mobilize the possibilities that exist at the fringes—that is, outside the normative orders of the society. Thus, artifacts of emotion are tools that people at the margins of the society mobilize to negotiate meaning in a life that must be lived under conditions of extreme injustice.

With this understanding of the nature of the artifacts of emotion, we can now consider the ways it is deployed to negotiate meaning under unjust social and political structures. Returning to Baldwin's discussion of the blues is essential because he provides a description of how we ought to understand the existential condition that necessitates deployment of artifacts of emotion. To enable us to imagine the existential condition in question, Baldwin notes about the blues that they are "about work, love, death, floods, lynchings; in fact, a series of disasters which can be summed up under the arbitrary heading 'Facts of Life'" (Baldwin 2011, 132).

To characterize the existential condition that produced the blues, Baldwin refers to Bessie Smith, "a great blues singer" who died "in Mississippi after a very long, hard—not *very* long, but very *hard*—life: pigs' feet and gin, many disastrous lovers, and a career that first went down; died on the road on the way from one hospital to another. She was in an automobile accident and one of her arms was wrenched out of its socket; and because the hospital attendants argued whether or not they could let her in because she was colored, she died" (Baldwin 2011, 139). By means of his description of the use of blues by Bessie Smith, Billie Holiday, and others, Baldwin underscored that the lives of these individuals reveal more than their circumstances. They are witnesses to the "facts of life" that challenge them in the most extreme way.

Referring to another context, namely, that of Leah recounted by Jonathan Wolff and Avner de-Shalit in their book *Disadvantage*, we can understand further the point I am trying to make about the concept of artifacts of emotion. Leah's life is a tale of a socially conditioned shame. The child of an immigrant couple from North Africa who moved to Israel with her family, her life became an endless precarity at the fringes of society, due to a combination of social conditions. Wolff and de-Shalit pointed out exactly what it means to live under unjust structures by noting that Leah's life "is a harsh and miserable mess; she must struggle with poverty; she cannot afford anything beyond the basics; she cannot spoil herself; she cannot take care of her child because she is moody and gloomy all day and because is very, very poor; and she cannot reciprocate her parents' support and love. She is humiliated by the community, by the men who have power over her, and by her indigence. She had no proper education. She cannot be autonomous. . . . She has never had genuine opportunities to achieve what she had good reason to want to be or have. She says she had potential and is probably never likely to fulfill it" (Wolff and de-Shalit 2007, 2).

The point to note is that existence under unjust structures is still a form of living. By this I mean that subjects of this form of existence should not be understood squarely from the perspective of what they do not experience—that is, from the angle of what must be done for society to ensure that their experience is eradicated. Taking this form of life seriously, in addition to inciting in us a desire to produce theories that will lead to a more desirable state of affairs, should also mean that we do not erase the experience as one unpleasant inconvenience for the theorizing mind. We should attempt, as Baldwin suggested, to see it as a form of life that unfolds in its own circumstances. We must see it as a life that is lived courageously and given meaning by engaging the human capacity for creativity.

One of the ways artifacts of emotion are deployed to negotiate meaning under unjust social and political structures is through songs. When people situated in this way appropriate songs as a way of dealing with reality, they are "not making a fantasy out it," instead, they are "accepting it" (Baldwin 2011, 164). This is true even when this approach to negotiating extremely disastrous situations appears to be undergirded by some levity. The jest reflected in their response to reality indicates a full recognition that "there's something funny—there's always something a little funny in all our disasters, if one can face the disaster." They in this way demonstrate an "ability to know that, all right, it's a mess, and you can't do anything about it" and recognize that "you can't stay there, you can't drop dead, you can't give up, but all right, okay, as Bessie said, 'picked up my bag, baby, and I tried it again.' This made life, however horrible that life was, bearable for her" (Baldwin 2011, 164–165).

Considering this, the specific ways that artifacts of emotion are deployed to negotiate existence under unjust structures is not merely to process negative feelings or even to "laugh at the world." They are instead the means by which the hard-done-by bear witness to the "fact of life" that the conventional normative order in the society fails to account for. They are used as a way to codify the meaning and fact of this experience in the interest of the survival of the subject of the experience in human memory. To this end, there are at least two ways the deployment of the artifacts of emotion help the subjects of life under deeply ingrained unjust social and political structures to negotiate meaning in life. On the one hand, they are deployed as a way to survive a disaster that is impossible to name or subsume under the rubric of "reason," as represented in the core ordering concepts and normative order of society. On the other hand, artifacts of emotion serve to codify the witness that subjects of a life of unmitigated suffering and disadvantage bear about their own dehumanization and struggle to survive. In doing this, a sort of memory that is capable of teaching posterity about the triumph over experiences of extreme injustice is created. The sense of the point I am making here is similar to what John Dewey alluded to when he observed that "memory is vicarious experience in which there is all the emotional values of actual experience without its strains, vicissitudes and troubles. The triumph of battle is even more poignant in the memorial war dance than at the moment of victory" (Dewey 1920, 3).

As the means to survive a disastrous life, artifacts of emotion constitute the response to the situation eloquently described by Baldwin as "what happens to you if, having barely escaped suicide, or death, or madness, or yourself, you watch your children growing up and no matter what you do, no matter what you do, you are powerless, you are really powerless, against the force of the world that is out to tell your child that he has no right to be alive. And no amount of liberal jargon, and no amount of talk about how well and how far we have progressed, does anything to soften or to point out any solution to this dilemma" (Baldwin 2011, 166). The iconic folk songs, the blues, poetry, dirges, and myriad forms of creative expressions born out of the struggle with absolute despair are indeed the defiant response to a life of unmitigated suffering and disadvantage. They are the ways the subjects of the experiences Baldwin described respond courageously to life in their humiliating circumstances. They are the ways to show that triumph in these circumstances inheres in the acceptance of anguish, and not in the turning away from one's reality because of its ugliness and disastrousness. By negotiating reality through the artifacts of emotions, people who live under conditions of injustice show that, although nothing worse than what has happened to them can be imagined, the human spirit is able to look deep into the abyss and still affirm life.

As codification of the witness subjects of a life of unmitigated suffering and disadvantage bear about their dehumanization, the artifacts of emotion constitute a past that enables future generations to know where they are coming from and appreciate the imperative to care that this history is kept alive as a story of human triumph. In this sense, artifacts of emotion are a representation of the image of people that are embedded in specific social and political circumstance. They tell the story of the experience of struggle and triumph—in Baldwin's sense of acceptance of anguish. The past so constructed is a mirror for future generations to interrogate the cruelty and evil that unjust social and political structures met out on human beings in the name of difference—race, gender, color, religion, or class. This is the sort of thing Baldwin alluded to when he said: "I know what the world has done to my brother and how narrowly he has survived it. And I know, which is much worse, and this is the crime of which I accuse my country and my countrymen, and for which neither I nor time nor history will ever forgive them, that they have destroyed and are destroying hundreds of thousands of lives and do not know it and do not want to know it" (Baldwin 1993, 11).

Conclusion

A question one might ask is whether the attempt here to consider how people at the fringes of the society negotiate meaning in their circumstance applies to them alone. Put differently, what about the existence under unjust structures makes the recourse to the artifacts of emotion the specific way of negotiating reality by those who live a life of unmitigated suffering and disadvantage? Why is it not an approach to attaining meaning in life that is shared by all of humanity—for do we not all occasionally contend with situations that extremely challenge our belief in the goodness of humanity? I indicated earlier that the condition of unmitigated suffering and disadvantage is unique for three reasons. Living under unjust structures means to live a life of unmitigated suffering and disadvantage because it is a collective tragedy, a disaster built on hopelessness, and a situation that damages agency. It is a kind of humiliation that challenges human beings in the most extreme way.

The uniqueness of the artifacts of emotions, which makes it the most suitable way for people living a life of unmitigated suffering and disadvantage to negotiate reality and find meaning in life, is the humiliation that is at its core. To dehumanize someone or a people is certainly terrible, but the experience of dehumanization becomes uniquely cruel when social and political reality operate to generate constant humiliations that will serve as the foundation of such dehumanization. This is what happens to people whose lives manifest as unmitigated suffering and disadvantage.

In such a situation, unjust social and political structures define certain subjects outside the normative order and by so doing generate constant humiliations that form the basis of practices of dehumanization of the subjects of this experience. Because the hard-done-by are constructed to be outside the normative order of society, the artifacts of emotion provide them a reliable means to negotiate reality and find meaning in life.

Besides the foregoing, even if we were to assume hypothetically that people positioned differently than those whose experience I have discussed can negotiate reality and find meaning in life through mobilization of the artifacts of emotion, nothing about the experience of the subjects of unmitigated suffering and disadvantage will change. Neither the uniqueness of their experience nor the reliability of their means of negotiating reality and finding meaning in life will change just because others have been shown to be capable of utilizing this approach. My goal in this chapter has been to show that to live at the fringes is not to live without a striving for meaning in life. Through the act of surviving, the dispossessed at the fringes of society triumph over despair and create a sense of meaning.

References

Baldwin, James. 1993. *The Fire Next Time*. New York: Vintage Books.

Baldwin, James. 2011. *The Cross of Redemption: Uncollected Writings*. Edited by Randall Kenan. New York: Vintage Books.

Brock, Gillian. 2020. *Justice for People on the Move*. Cambridge: Cambridge University Press.

Dewey, John. 1920. *Reconstruction in Philosophy*. New York: Henry Holt.

Kisekka, J. 2002. "The Destiny of the Individual in Contemporary Africa." In *Ethics, Human Rights and Development in Africa*, edited by A. T. Dalfovo et al., 67–76. Washington DC: CRVP.

Menkiti, Ifeanyi. 2005. *Of Altair the Bright Light*. Chelsea, MA: Earthwinds Edition.

Wolff, Jonathan, and Avner de-Shalit. 2007. *Disadvantage*. Oxford: Oxford University Press.

16

Experience and Text

Toward an African-Language Phenomenology

ALENA RETTOVÁ

Introduction: Texts and Experience

In *African Philosophy: Myth and Reality* (Hountondji 1996 [1983]), Paulin Hountondji presents a definition of African philosophy that has since then become one of the most quoted—but also much criticized—definitions of the field. To Hountondji, African philosophy is "a set of texts, specifically the set of texts written by Africans and described as philosophical by the authors themselves" (Hountondji 1996 [1983], 33). This definition became the foundational statement of Hountondji's critique of ethnophilosophy, a trend of African philosophy that interprets as philosophy practically any manifestation of culture: life practices, artifacts, and so forth. In *The Struggle for Meaning: Reflections on Philosophy, Culture, and Democracy in Africa* (2002, French 1997), Hountondji pursues his philosophical formation in phenomenology and states that there is a hiatus between his work on phenomenology and his critique of ethnophilosophy. He sees the connection of these two areas in the idea of "philosophy as a strict science" and he also mentions that experience is voiced in language ("phenomenology of language"). Both Hountondji and Husserl work with the assumption that language per se is a neutral system of signs, free of any cultural or historical determinants. Transcendental, but presumably also psychological (i.e., individually embodied), experience is expressed in this abstractly understood language as the human capacity of signification.

This chapter argues that there is no such general language. Experience is voiced each time in a *specific* language. The specific qualities of this language deeply impact both the way such experience is *expressed* and even how lived reality is *experienced*. I further argue that African philosophy, and especially African phenomenology, must consider these specific qualities of experience, experienced by an embodied subject and voiced in a specific language. The first part of the chapter interrogates the impact of language on thought and perception. While this part rehearses well-known facts and, inevitably, addresses these in a somewhat superficial, even semi-academic manner, this section is key because these linguistic insights have been insufficiently understood in the discourse on African philosophy, which is where this chapter situates its target readers. African philosophy has been based on very limited linguistic scholarship for decades, and some of these faulty insights continue being circulated and seriously debated, even today. A proper consideration of language and its link to thought and experience paves the way for the second half of the chapter, which charters the vast terrain of African-language philosophical texts.

The argument for considering language specificity is the foundation to introduce the concept of genre as the way language is assembled in text. I argue that genre is a key parameter in philosophy. It is through genre that language is anchored in a cultural and historical context. I note the glaring absence of African-language texts in contemporary African philosophy, understood here as a discourse or a field where thinkers engage in debates about philosophical thought in Africa, and conclude that proper consideration of genre unfolds a variety of Afrophone texts for a philosophical understanding. Insisting on the importance of an African-language phenomenology, I signal toward existing texts that formulate such phenomenological observations in African languages.

Voicing Experience: Does (the) Language Matter?

Tanzanian writer and philosopher Euphrase Kezilahabi voices his conviction of the importance of using African languages in very strong words: "Language is more than a signifying system. Language is the 'house of

Being.' By writing in foreign languages we allow the Western world to be the center of value of our Being." Critical of the practice of African writers to employ languages of European origin, he states that such foreign languages "objectify [Africans'] views within [their] signifying systems" and "push [them] to orchestrate peculiarities of [their] own cultures." As a result of this, African literature becomes "a literature of *odes to the exotica* and vulgar anthropologism" and "a phenomenology of prostitution" (Kezilahabi 1985, 359, emphasis original).

What leads Kezilahabi to such strong words? The discourse of postcolonial theory and criticism is itself a good example of how African theory is compromised for its reliance on (predominantly) English. Karin Barber suggests postcolonial theory presents "a binarized, generalized model of the world which . . . has produced an impoverished and distorted picture of 'the colonial experience' and the place of language in that experience" (Barber 1995, 3). The "postcolonial Other," Barber further suggests, is "defiant yet accessible, conveniently articulate in English and consolingly preoccupied with his or her relations to the center" (Barber 1995, 3).

Why is language so important? To answer this question, we need to interrogate the relationship between language and thought: How does thought reflect language? How does language affect thought? The linguistic relativity hypothesis, also known as the Sapir-Whorf hypothesis, postulates that thought is affected by the structuring function of language, and thus speakers' perceptions of the world are relative to their specific languages (Gumperz and Levinson 1996; Deutscher 2011). Hountondji himself refers to linguistic relativity in his 1982 article, where he demonstrates how both Aristotle and Kagame derive an ontology from language. After this article, Hountondji moves closer and closer toward acknowledging the validity of these arguments: "The reflection on human languages led . . . [us] to recognise that any individual thought, however personal and original, is based on a collective, pre-personal, anonymous way of viewing and classifying things around us" (Dübgen and Skupien 2019, 167). This consideration even makes him adopt a more charitable perspective on ethnophilosophy.

The linguistic relativity hypothesis is generally accepted by linguists and where opinions differ is the extent of this relativity: What exactly does this "affectedness" of knowledge by language mean? In African philosophy, the linguistic relativity hypothesis has been hugely influential, most notably in the work of Alexis Kagame, who derives ontology from the grammatical structure of Bantu languages (Kagame 1955, 1976), or John S. Mbiti, who linked the (lack of the) capacity of Africans to envisage and project the future to the presumed lack of grammatical categories referring to the distant future in African languages (Mbiti 1970 [1969]). Both philosophers, arguably, took linguistic relativity too far in assuming a direct, one-to-one correspondence between grammatical categories of specific languages and the concepts used by the speakers of these languages to think about reality. Yet, I suggest that a more moderate version of linguistic relativity is valid. The rest of this section is a detour from the general argument of this chapter, one that is nevertheless necessary in order to show the dramatic effects of language on thought and to facilitate a more nuanced understanding of the concept of linguistic relativity.

Language affects thought on multiple levels: affective and aesthetic; semantic and connotative, tying languages to cultures, and cognitive. It has been demonstrated by psycholinguistic science (more later) that, depending on the specific language, which is currently active in our minds, we literally *see the world differently*. The language-specific qualities of the multiple different ways of seeing the same world concern a whole range of aspects of languages; from sounds or cultural connotations down to grammar or the metaphorical coding of experience. I will consider language as matter here: the way language affects us physically through bodily sensations; language as meaning: the way language creates and communicates meanings; and language as knowledge: the way language structures our cognitive apparatus and, through that, shapes and even generates knowledge of the world.

In his groundbreaking *Decolonising the Mind*, Ngũgĩ wa Thiong'o gives language a pivotal role in the project of epistemic decolonization. He develops his argument through his childhood experience. He states, "Language was not a mere string of words. It had a suggestive power well beyond the immediate and lexical meaning" (Ngũgĩ 1986, 11). This "suggestive power" refers to the aesthetic and affective workings of language, and these depend on the materiality of language: on the sounds and texture of language, on "the feel" of morphemes or grammatical qualities. It is related to the nonconceptual level of language, or what Kristeva calls "the semiotic" (Kristeva 1980). The play between "the symbolic" (the meaning, the message, the conceptual and communicative content of a text with at least a gist that constitutes a common understanding among all speakers competent in a language) and "the semiotic" (the unique feels and sounds, textures and tastes that a text evokes in specific speakers) (Kristeva 1980) can be experienced in accessing texts in an unknown language that is closely related to one's mother tongue. In reading the same text in English and Russian, for instance, as a native speaker of Czech, I "get" the semiotic in Russian while I read the text for the symbolic in English. I understand the English perfectly—grammar and vocabulary—yet the text does not stimulate my imagination; I follow the text at the conceptual and communicative level, in a rational and distanced way. In spite of my not understanding many things about the Russian text, it still engages my imagination and I can "see" the signifieds behind the signifiers. I have thus a sensitivity to Russian, on account of my native competence in Czech, which I lack in English, despite an advanced competence acquired over three decades of my life.

Through its material qualities, language has a direct physical impact on the speakers. Indeed, language learning, and handling language in general, gives us pleasure, and a very specific kind of pleasure: "Researchers found that the process of learning a language and acquiring a wider vocabulary has the effect of stimulating the same part of the brain as having sex or eating chocolate" (Joshi 2014).

Kezilahabi's evocation of the Heideggerian "language is a house of being" and of the Gadamerian "hermeneutical horizon," or in Kezilahabi's words "horizon of the unsaid" (Kezilahabi 1985, 224), is directly linked to the semantic level of language: to language as meaning. Language is a system and we never learn isolated words: we always acquire words in semantic fields and endowed with connotative meanings (emotional and imaginative associations). To give one example, a "cow" in most Western cultures is seen as a stupid beast, one utilized for food. By contrast, for the Maasai or the Hindu, cows are embodiments of deities. If even such a simple concrete noun can have such vastly different cultural meanings, what is the case with abstract nouns such as "the good," "humanity," "ubuntu," "utu," or "uzuri"? Language is embedded in culture and every word has a hermeneutical "horizon of the unsaid," or "a circle of understanding which cannot simply be entered into by means of arbitrary chosen theories of knowledge" (Kezilahabi 1985, 226), thus an inexhaustible reservoir of additional meanings. There is no simple way to express these along with translating a word or a phrase.

Acquiring another language means adopting another culture and, quite literally, becoming another human being. Indeed, psychologically speaking, multilingual people have multiple personalities (although, of course, not every instance of acquiring a language will have such a powerful effect, especially if the acquisition is limited). In her account of language acquisition, Ekaterina Matveeva says, "In 2011 I learnt Italian and went to Italy discovering a new world . . . If you want to unwind your personality and get slightly more optimistic, you should go to Italy" (Matveeva 2015). While the tone of this quotation is playful, the article presents a serious "phenomenology of language acquisition," so to say, and demonstrates convincingly how acquiring a language affects the learner's personality—an observation that is likely to resonate with most multilingual individuals. Interestingly, one reader of Matveeva's article asked: "Any theories about what happens when one speaks Esperanto?"

The last and arguably the most interesting level of the ways in which language impacts thought is the cognitive level: language as knowledge. It tells how experience is encoded in language, how language "formats" experience. These effects derive, on the one hand, from the structure of language, such as its grammatical properties. As I will show later, grammar affects ethics, in encoding human relationships (politeness registers; expression of self, of group identity, etc.); it affects epistemology, in encoding knowledge about the world and its conceptualizations. On the other hand, language affects thought through its quality of being metaphorical. Metaphors are the true building blocks of thought, in providing the images through which we approach the realities we encounter, and metaphors are vastly different across different cultures. I will discuss these two aspects, starting with metaphors.

As cognitive linguists Lakoff and Johnson argue, language is metaphorical. Metaphor is a kind of experience by proxy: "The essence of metaphor is understanding and experiencing one kind of thing in terms of another" (Lakoff and Johnson 2003, 5). Metaphors are omnipresent in the way we conceptualize the world: "Our concepts structure what we perceive, how we get around the world, and how we relate to other people. . . . Our conceptual system is largely metaphorical . . . metaphors . . . structure how we perceive, how we think, and what we do" (Lakoff and Johnson 2003, 3). Lakoff and Johnson have exposed the far-reaching influence of metaphors on our thinking and demonstrate that "metaphor plays a very significant role in determining what is real for us" (2003, 146) and "truth is always relative to a conceptual system that is defined in large part by metaphor" (2003, 159).

Even our basic concepts of time, for instance, are derived from metaphors (mostly metaphors of spatial relations), and metaphors are dramatically different in different languages. To give one salient example, most languages conceptualize the future as lying "ahead" while the past is "behind" the speaking subject. In contrast, speakers of the Bolivian language of Aymara conceptualize the future as being "behind them," while the past lies in front (Núñez and Sweetser 2006). The explanation of this seemingly counterintuitive conceptualization of time is explained by cognitive linguists Núñez and Sweetser:

> Cognitive research on metaphoric concepts of time has focused on differences between moving ego and moving time models, but even more basic is the contrast between ego- and temporal-reference-point models. Dynamic models appear to be quasi-universal cross-culturally, as does the generalization that in ego-reference-point models, FUTURE IS IN FRONT OF EGO and PAST IS IN BACK OF EGO. The Aymara language instead has a major static model of time wherein FUTURE IS BEHIND EGO and PAST IS IN FRONT OF EGO; linguistic and gestural data give strong confirmation of this unusual culture-specific cognitive pattern. (Núñez and Sweetser 2003, 401)

Culturally different metaphors are easy to pinpoint. The effects of phonetics or of grammar are perhaps finer and more elusive, but they also have substantial impact on how we see and understand the world (Athanasopoulos et al. 2015). So, for instance, the system of tenses and aspects in a language affects how we perceive actions:

> English has a grammatical toolkit for situating actions in time: "I was sailing to Bermuda and I saw Elvis" is different from "I sailed to Bermuda and I saw Elvis." German doesn't [sic] have this feature. As a result, German speakers tend to specify the beginnings, middles, and ends of events, but English speakers often leave out the endpoints and focus in on the action. Looking at the same scene, for example, German speakers might say, "A man leaves the house and walks to the store," whereas an English speaker would just say, "A man is walking." . . .
> Bilingual speakers . . . switch between these perspectives based on the language most active in their minds. (Athanasopoulos, quoted in Weiler 2015)

Athanasopoulos concludes, on the basis of his psycholinguistic experiments with bilingual people: "By having another language, you have an alternative vision of the world. . . . You can listen to music from only one speaker, or you can listen in stereo. . . . It's the same with language" (quoted in Weiler 2015). Bilingual speakers "listen to the world" in stereo.

Next to actions, grammar also encodes how we conceptualize objects. In languages with grammatical gender, gender marking affects the qualities we associate with objects that are inanimate. The Bantu noun class system is a classification of reality involving up to twenty-three categories, defined not by gender but by other semantic qualities (animate/inanimate, prolonged objects, liquids, etc.) and expressed in the morphology and syntax of these languages. In his pioneering studies (Kagame 1955, 1976), Alexis Kagame has developed an ontological projection characterized by four dominant categories, derived from the fine-grained system of Bantu noun classes.

Finally, grammar expresses politeness registers as well as other human relationships. Take for instance this passage from Jan Karafiát's book *Broučci* (Fireflies; 2004 [1876]):

Maminka Broučka pěkně umyla, Brouček přistavěl ke stolu židle, a maminka už nesla polívčičku na stůl. Sedli si, sepjali nožičky a tatínek se modlil . . . Na to říkal Brouček svou modlitbičku. (Karafiát 2004 [1876], 6)

(Mother washed Beetle nicely, Beetle placed chairs to the table, and Mother was already carrying soup to the table. They sat down, clasped their legs and Father prayed. . . . Then Beetle said his prayer.) (My translation)

All the underlined words in Czech are diminutives—something sheerly impossible to translate into English, because the two languages work differently with diminutives.[1] Yet, the use of diminutives plays a key role in the book. On the one hand, it is a frequent component of children's language, and *Broučci* is a book for children. Diminutives also express the smallness of the beetles and their objects and environment. But diminutives also reflect the beetles' humility and a loving relationship with others. Karafiát was a Catholic priest and many influences of his Christian convictions can be observed in his writing, such as the humble acceptance of life, its difficulties and joys, and of death, as manifested by the beetles. Diminutives thus encode a certain register of human relationships and even a certain life philosophy—one that was later interestingly recontextualized by Karel Čapek through his concept of "človíček" (diminutive of "human").[2]

Linguistic relativity significantly affects the capacity of translation: a perfect translation does not exist. Translation is not a philosophical panacea to cultural plurality, and we are thus left with the need to account for the specificities of languages and for how they affect experience: experience is always rooted in culture and language—in a *specific* language. The only way to do justice to the experience of *specific* cultures is to operate in these cultures' languages. How can this be achieved? Ngũgĩ has advocated for the adoption of African languages by African writers (1986). How applicable is this requirement for philosophers (Kresse 1999)? Wiredu advises against the use of African languages in African philosophy, on account of two reasons. One is the sheer multiplicity of African languages (the continent is home to two to three thousand languages), which would make it impossible for philosophers across Africa to understand one another; philosophers are also "not as important as Ngũgĩ to be translated quickly and often enough" (Kresse and Wiredu 2000). The other reason concerns the limited possibilities of expression of philosophical concepts in African languages, which is the foundation of Wiredu's own take on translation as a method to distinguish universals from particulars.[3]

While this latter argument about African languages' limited capacity of expression can easily be refuted, the first argument is valid: there is no satisfactory way to select a philosophical lingua franca for the whole continent, and translation is a costly and cumbersome insertion into the philosophical business. Established philosophers are unlikely to switch to writing philosophy in African languages and translation is helpful but not a solution.[4] A solution, then, consists in identifying already *existing* corpuses of texts (Rettová 2007). These texts are descriptions of experience as well as theorizations, their authors are located already *within specific languages*, and their work is relevant within specific language communities. I maintain that an insistence on *specific* language is key for phenomenology; an African-language phenomenology, then, could in fact depart from these existing discourses, which record and code experience in African languages.

"To the Texts Themselves": Language, Genre, Literature

Insisting on the specificity of language, of course, dramatically changes the perspective on African philosophy. "Mainstream" African philosophy, a discourse established in the second half of the twentieth century, has by now produced a long list of monographs, histories, and anthologies, and is represented in surveys and encyclopedias of world philosophies. Yet, we would, in this body of writing and thinking, look in vain for texts on African philosophy in African languages. This discourse solely uses European languages, most prominently English, French, and Portuguese but also German, Italian, Czech, or other European languages. It is thus an entirely Europhone and, one would be tempted to add, Eurocentric discourse, "writing back" to colonial stereotypes about Africans, Africa, and philosophy. If one were to look for books in Swahili, Yorùbá, isiXhosa, or isiZulu, one would struggle. Does this mean that the texts that Hountondji is speaking about are absent—or are yet to be produced? Where are African-language texts?

The "mainstream" tradition of African philosophy in fact eclipses the presence of an immensity of philosophical texts and traditions of philosophy conveyed by African languages. First of all, such texts are invisible to it because of the factor of language; but even for people who do understand, speak, or write African languages, there is an additional factor that occludes the existence of African-language philosophy: genre. "Mainstream" African philosophy operates on the assumption that the genre of philosophy is nonfictional prose, a conviction it draws from Western traditions of philosophy that have privileged this genre for centuries now.[5] This genre has by now been elevated to a superior position as *the* genre for philosophy, on the assumption it is the genre of simple and transparent linguistic expression that truthfully mirrors and communicates thought and experience. This is of course a false assumption, as has been demonstrated by twentieth-century linguistics and literary theory: there is no pure linguistic expression of truth, even less linguistic access to the real. On the contrary, the linguistic medium is shaped by a number of conventions and determinants, one of them being genre. Yet, this belief in language and nonfictional prose as a transparent medium of thought is a pervasive conviction that has maintained its grip on philosophical discourse, especially in the Anglo-American traditions of philosophy—which have had a strong impact on African philosophy and its understandings of philosophy. The prevalence of nonfictional prose in Western philosophy is, however, a historical contingency and should not be imposed on other cultures that have different genres to express their philosophies.

Because of this bias, mainstream African philosophy fails to see Afrophone texts of philosophical expression and retrieves from African languages at best isolated words or short texts of "traditional" culture, such as divination poetry or (typically) proverbs. Such a tokenistic approach to African languages still prevails and results in a largely impressionistic engagement of African cultures in philosophy, even after decades of valid critiques of "ethnophilosophy": that is, philosophers develop philosophical conclusions about African thought based on their impressions of African cultures, often even without support in, say, anthropological sources (where one can expect some methodological rigor). African philosophy thus lacks a clear and reliable methodology when it comes to how it draws on African cultures and African-language cultural givens.

A text-based approach in African philosophy, like the one Hountondji is proposing in *The Struggle for Meaning*, provides that methodology: it works with African texts and engages in textual analysis. In order to successfully integrate texts in African languages, however, it is especially key to reconsider the issue of the genre(s) of these texts. Genre is the way language is conventionally assembled in a text. Genres are always specific to cultures and languages, and just like there are no universal languages, there are also no universal genres. Genres have a decisive impact on the meaning communicated by the text (Barber 2007). Taking genre seriously is the magic "Open Sesame" formula to unlock a vast field of texts for philosophical analysis. This is a generally valid observation, but a consideration of genre is key especially for African philosophy, because these various "other" genres are in fact the preferred ones for philosophical expression in African cultures and being receptive to these expressions is a simple yet powerful act of undeniably refuting the doubts about the existence of "African philosophy," however they may be motivated or formulated. It is thus not only philosophically but also politically important to redress this condition of genre blindness.

Hountondji provides helpful ideas toward a text-based understanding of African philosophy. In his second book, *The Struggle for Meaning*, he further develops his definition of philosophy as "a set of texts" in *African Philosophy* (Hountondji 1996 [1983], 33). He responds to the critiques leveled against his definition since the publication of his first book and clarifies, for instance, the issue of writing that was an often-criticized element of his definition. He readily accommodates oral texts under the umbrella of "texts": "Oral texts . . . are still explicit discourses. . . . The only possible site of emergence of philosophy, its most general genre [is] human speech" (Hountondji 2002, 98). Where he does, however, stand firmly on his position, is in reiterating his insistence on the textual, that is, verbally articulated, nature of the philosophical discourse: "African philosophy was first of all that: the set of texts devoted to the definition of an African worldview" (Hountondji 2002, 95). And then he makes one additional step and asserts: "I refused, as a matter of principle, all confusion of genres, all conceptual slippage. African philosophy, if the expression was to mean anything at all, had to exist historically on the same mode as all the philosophies in the world: as a literature. Now it so happens that such a literature does exist" (Hountondji 2002, 93–94).

This identification of philosophy with "a literature" insists on a firm rooting of African philosophy in traditions of textuality. Additionally, the fact that Hountondji says he refuses "all confusion of genres" before relegating the role of philosophical discourse to "literature" is significant. It means that literature *is* the genre of philosophy. Hountondji is not excluding here any tradition of textuality from the prerogative of being philosophy. On the contrary, he is introducing the concept "literature" to advocate for a broad and inclusive understanding of textuality as the defining feature of the discourse that carries, produces, or perhaps *is* philosophy.

Hountondji makes one more very important assertion in *The Struggle for Meaning.* He himself focuses on one specific textual tradition of African philosophy, that borne by European languages, and he emphasizes "the urgent need to put an end to the extraverted nature of all European-language African discourse" (Hountondji 2002, 73). How does European-language discourse steer clear of this quality of extraversion? Is it even possible, given the fact that it derives and departs from "Eurocentric" or "Western" discursive contexts? Attempting to avoid this extraversion appears as squaring the circle for Europhone African philosophy. The accusation of extraversion reveals the urgency of accessing a more inclusive range of texts as the foundation of African philosophy, in particular texts in African languages.

Paraphrasing Edmund Husserl's famous proclamation, we can say African philosophy needs to go "to the texts themselves"! The "texts of African philosophy" must include texts in languages of African origin. In unfolding these discourses, African philosophy stands before a true paradigmatic shift. What are such African-language texts, possibly in genres different from nonfictional prose, that communicate philosophy? A wealth of philosophical thought is present in texts in such "other" genres in African languages (Rettová 2021). Texts in African languages talk about ethics and morality, life and death, humanity, the world, the nature of reality or of truth (Rettová 2007).

For instance, two texts in Swahili, a nineteenth-century poem, Sayyid Abdallah bin Ali bin Nasir's *Al-Inkishafi* (the poem has appeared in many editions and translations; see for instance Mulokozi 1999), and a twentieth-century novel, Euphrase Kezilahabi's *Kichwamaji* (1974), elaborate a "phenomenology of death." They describe, interrogate, and reflect the phenomena of death, dying, and being dead. Three main approaches to death can be isolated in the two texts: *Al-Inkishafi*'s main approach is the imagination of being dead, projecting the sensations of decay into an intact, sentient body. *Kichwamaji* also introduces this imagination of an intact body being subject to decay but departs from it to develop a philosophical, detached reflection about the fact of death and the meaning of death. Where *Kichwamaji*, however, ventures on the phenomenological terrain is in its depiction of animal deaths. Both humans and animals empathize with dying animals, and dying itself is explored here in the process, not as the completed state of being dead. The same poem, *Al-Inkishafi*, also established the subjective foundation of experience and constitutes the inner sphere ("soul," "subjectivity," "interiority") (cf. Rettová 2020). *Al-Inkishafi* and *Kichwamaji* contain a phenomenological view and description of lived reality. These two texts, connected through a web of intertextual references, are in two distinct genres, both of which have been richly used in Swahili culture to speak about philosophical topics. A far wider set of Afrophone texts, of various genres, deals with philosophical topics in argumentative or reflective ways.

These texts would rarely be classified as "philosophy"; often they would be called "poetry" or "literature." Yet, it is in these waters that African-language phenomenologists need to fish; a proper consideration of language and genre opens these texts to philosophical readings.

Conclusion: Toward an Afrophone Phenomenology

Phenomenology insists on experience being the only access we have to reality. Human perception is a filter through which every piece of information about reality passes. Experience is only ever recorded in texts, and as this article has argued, it is also only ever made and articulated through language and within the confines of language. Language is always assembled conventionally in textual genres. This consideration constitutes a link between the world of texts (language, linguistics, [post]structuralist understanding of language and genre) and the material grounding of experience in historical, cultural, and physical, bodily conditions of the speakers. The disciplines and methods needed to understand the expression of experience in text range from phenomenology as a way of accessing reality, via linguistics and literary studies as ways to analyze the textual expression, to history, hermeneutics, anthropology, or cultural studies as ways to understand the contexts that impact the body that experiences, expresses, and records its experience.

This chapter has argued that the "literature," which Hountondji calls for African philosophy to be, exists, has long existed, and also exists in African languages. Language and culture dramatically change the kind of philosophy that grows out of them, and the field of African philosophy has so far only insufficiently addressed the wealth of thought and ideas present in African cultures and communicated in African languages. The chapter thus urges philosophers to go back "to the texts themselves" and to examine these texts as authentic expressions of philosophical thought in Africa. To access this body of texts, it is first necessary to reflect on the nature of philosophical discourse, on its linguistic expression, and on its genres. Insisting on the word "literature," African literature and more specifically African-language literature is a record of African experience, and thus a foundation of an African and African-language phenomenology.

Notes

1. Both existing translations (Karafiát 1942, Karafiát 2001 [1994]) of the book avoid tackling the issue of the diminutives.

2. See Čapek (1988–1991), Opelík (2013), and Senft (2018).

3. Wiredu introduces translation as a method in African philosophy. He suggests that African philosophers can employ the specificities of languages to filter out cultural specificities (i.e., nonuniversal issues) (1980, 1998a and b). Translation shows whether a statement translated from one language to another is meaningful or not, and that shows whether the philosophical issue being translated is a universal one—meaningful also to the speakers of the target language—or one only relevant to the community speaking the source language. Wiredu sees translation as a way to avoid what he calls "ontological fantasies" (1980, 35), that is, considering seriously philosophical concepts derived from the setup of specific languages, concepts that lose their meaning through translation, and he elaborates three examples, the concept of existential being (see below in this chapter, also in Wiredu 1996); the concept of the mind (1987); and the correspondence theory of truth (1998b).

However, translation does not work in such a binary fashion; anything can be translated, and the field of translation studies has identified and theorized the strategies of translation depending on the nature of the text, the target audience, the ideology of the translator, and a number of other linguistic, social, economic, or political factors. Yet, nothing can be translated perfectly. Quine speaks of the "indeterminacy of translation" (1960, 1969; in African philosophy, Quine's findings have been applied to Yorùbá expressions of belief and knowledge by Hallen and Sodipo [1997]) while Barbara Cassin (2004) and Emily Apter (2008) use the term "intraduisibles" or "untranslatables," respectively in French and in English, to refer to key concepts of theory. While these thinkers mainly interrogate the ability to translate statements of science and theory, untranslatability has been theorized with general validity.

4. Cf. Chike Jeffers's anthology (2013): Jeffers asked renowned African philosophers to write short texts in their native languages and then published these texts along with their English translations; while the book is a fascinating project, it has remained an exercise in translation, sterile in that it has had no repercussion in the language communities of these languages and fails to stimulate or influence philosophical discussions in these languages.

5. Western philosophy, too, has employed genres other than nonfictional prose: dialogues, aphorisms, multiple genres of poetry. In his history of Western philosophy "from Homer to Descartes," Kratochvíl states: "Surprisingly diverse literary genres have been used in the service to philosophical expression, chronologically, for instance, Ionic prose, the poem, the anecdote, the speech, the dialogue, the letter, the learned inquiry, the discourse, the treatise, the essay, the novel, the scientific inquiry. . . . The literary genre always corresponds in some way to what the philosophical nature of philosophy consists in, with specific authors; partly it is due to the historical period and the nature of the work" (Kratochvíl 2010, 24; my translation from Czech). Specific political conditions also prompted philosophers to use specific channels of expression. Under repressive regimes, philosophy hid from censorship in "other" genres and mostly far from academia. For instance, in the Eastern Bloc between 1945 and 1989, it was the protest song or theater that were key genres of philosophical expression. Some philosophical orientations had their preferred genres, for instance, existentialism has heavily relied on theater and the novel. Kratochvíl also mentions that a specific genre is preferred in a specific environment, "and with it also the style of thinking adequate to it" (Kratochvíl 2010, 25), giving the example of academic philosophy favoring "scientific inquiry." This style, he adds, "tends to be complemented or compensated by philosophical texts we would place in fictional literature, that is, art, with respect to their genre; sententiae and aphorisms are in between, while personal or mystical texts are the other extreme" (Kratochvíl 2010, 25). He also adds that "the philosophical quality of the text . . . is not determined by its literary genre" (Kratochvíl 2010, 25).

References

Apter, Emily. 2008. "Untranslatables: A World System." *New Literary History* 39, no. 3: 581–598.

Athanasopoulos, Panos, Emanuel Bylund, Guillermo Montero-Melis, Ljubica Damjanovic, Alina Schartner, Alexandra Kibbe, Nick Riches, and Guillaume Thierry. 2015. "Two Languages, Two Minds: Flexible Cognitive Processing

Driven by Language of Operation." *Psychological Science* 26, no. 4: 518–526. http://journals.sagepub.com/doi/10.1177/0956797614567509.

Barber, Karin. 2007. *The Anthropology of Texts, Persons and Publics: Oral and Written Culture in Africa and Beyond*. Cambridge: Cambridge University Press.

Bearth, Thomas. 1995. "Sein und Nichtsein—kuwa na kutokuwa." In *Swahili-Handbuch*, edited by Gudrun Miehe and Wilhelm J. G. Möhlig, 207–237. Cologne: Rüdiger Köppe.

Cassin, Barbara. 2004. *Vocabulaire européen des philosophies: Dictionnaire des intraduisibles*. Paris: Éditions du Seuil.

Čapek, Karel. 1988–1991. *Od člověka k člověku I–III*. Prague: Československý spisovatel. Available online at https://www.mlp.cz/.

Deutscher, Guy. 2011. *Through the Language Glass: Why the World Looks Different in Other Languages*. London: Arrow Books.

Dübgen, Franziska, and Stefan Skupien. 2019. *Paulin Hountondji: African Philosophy as Critical Universalism*. Cham: Palgrave Pivot.

Gumperz, John J., and Stephen C. Levinson, eds. 1996. *Rethinking Linguistic Relativity*. Cambridge: Cambridge University Press.

Hallen, Barry, and J. Olubi Sodipo. 1997. *Knowledge, Belief, and Witchcraft: Analytic Experiments in African Philosophy*. Stanford: Stanford University Press.

Hountondji, Paulin J. 1982. "Langues africaines et philosophie: l'hypothèse relativiste." *Les Études philosophiques* 4: 393–406.

Hountondji, Paulin J. 1996 [1983]. *African Philosophy: Myth and Reality*, 2nd ed. Translated by H. Evans with the collaboration of J. Rée, introduction by Abiola Irele. Bloomington: Indiana University Press. (Translation of *Sur la "philosophie africaine": Critique de l'ethnophilosophie*. Paris: François Maspero, 1976.)

Hountondji, Paulin J. 2002. *The Struggle for Meaning: Reflections on Philosophy, Culture, and Democracy in Africa*. Translated by J. Conteh-Morgan, foreword by K. A. Appiah. Athens: Ohio University Press.

Jeffers, Chike, ed. 2013. *Listening to Ourselves: A Multilingual Anthology of African Philosophy*. Foreword by Ngũgĩ wa Thiong'o. Albany: State University of New York Press.

Joshi, Priya. 2014. "Learning a New Language Stimulates Same Pleasure Centres in the Brain as Sex and Chocolate." *International Business Times*. http://www.ibtimes.co.uk/learning-new-language-stimulates-same-pleasure-centres-brain-sex-chocolate-1471766.

Kagame, Alexis. 1955. *La philosophie bantu-rwandaise de l'Être*. Mémoires in-8° de l'Académie royale des Sciences coloniales. Brussels: Pontificia Universitas Gregoriana.

Kagame, Alexis. 1976. *La philosophie Bantu comparée*. Paris: Présence Africaine.

Karafiát, Jan. 1942. *Fireflies*. Translated by Rose Fyleman. Leighton Buzzard, UK: Faith Press.

Karafiát, Jan. 2001 [1994]. *Fireflies.* Translated by Daniela Bísková. Prague: Albatros.

Karafiát, Jan. 2004 [1876]. *Broučci.* Prague: Albatros.

Kezilahabi, Euphrase. 1974. *Kichwamaji.* Dar es Salaam: East African.

Kezilahabi, Euphrase. 1985. "African Philosophy and the Problem of Literary Interpretation." Unpublished PhD dissertation, University of Wisconsin, Madison.

Knappert, Jan. 1971. "Swahili Metre." *African Language Studies* 12: 108–129.

Knappert, Jan. 1979. *Four Centuries of Swahili Verse: A Literary History and Anthology.* London: Heinemann; rpt. London: Darf, 1988.

Kratochvíl, Zdeněk. 2010. *Filosofie mezi mýtem a vědou: Od Homéra po Descarta.* Prague: Academia.

Kresse, Kai. 1999. "The Problem of How to Use African Language for African Thought: On a Multilingual Perspective in African Philosophy." *African Philosophy* 12, no. 1: 27–36.

Kresse, Kai, and Kwasi Wiredu. 2000. "Language Matters! Decolonization, Multilingualism, and African Languages in the Making of African Philosophy: Kwasi Wiredu in Dialogue with Kai Kresse." (Dialogue originally from 1996.) *Polylog: Forum for Intercultural Philosophizing* 1, no. 2: 1–50. http://www.polylog.org/them/1.2/dlg1-en.htm.

Kristeva, Julia. 1980. *Desire in Language: A Semiotic Approach to Literature and Art.* Edited by Leon S. Roudiez, trans. by T. Gora and A. A. Jardine. New York: Columbia University Press.

Lakoff, George, and Mark Johnson. 2003. *Metaphors We Live By.* Chicago: University of Chicago Press.

Matveeva, Ekaterina. 2015. "Does Your Personality Change When You Speak Another Language?" Fluent in 3 Months. https://www.fluentin3months.com/personality/.

Mbiti, John S. 1970 [1969]. *African Religions and Philosophy.* Garden City, NY: Anchor Books, Doubleday.

Mulokozi, M. M. 1999. *Tenzi tatu za kale (Fumo Liyongo, Al-Inkishafi, Mwanakupona).* Dar es Salaam: TUKI.

Ngũgĩ wa Thiong'o. 1986. *Decolonising the Mind: The Politics of Language in African Literature.* London: James Currey; Nairobi: Heinemann Kenya; Portsmouth, NH: Heinemann; Harare: Zimbabwe.

Núñez, Rafael E., and Eve Sweetser. 2006. "With the Future Behind Them: Convergent Evidence from Aymara Language and Gesture in the Crosslinguistic Comparison of Spatial Construals of Time." *Cognitive Science* 30: 401–450.

Opelík, Jiří. 2013. "Chudák Karel." Insitut pro stadium literatury. http://www.ipsl.cz/index.php?id=313&menu=echa&sub=echa&str=aktualita.php.

Quine, Willard v. O. 1960. *Word and Object.* Cambridge: MIT Press.

Quine, Willard v. O. 1969. *Ontological Relativity and Other Essays.* New York: Columbia University Press.

Rettová, Alena. 2007. *Afrophone Philosophies: Reality and Challenge*. Středokluky: Zdeněk Susa.

Rettová, Alena. 2020. "'Moyo wangu, nini huzundukani?' Self and Attention in Sayyid Abdallah bin Ali bin Nasir's *Al-Inkishafi*." *Journal of World Philosophies* 5, no. 2: 28–42.

Rettová, Alena. 2021. "Philosophy and Genre: African Philosophy in Texts." In *Africa in a Multilateral World: Afropolitan Dilemmas*, edited by Albert Kasanda and Marek Hrubec, 203–228. London: Routledge.

Řehák, Vilém. 2007. "Kazimoto and Meursault: 'Brothers' in Despair and Loneliness—Comparing Kezilahabi's *Kichwamaji* and Camus' *L'Etranger*." *Swahili Forum* 14: 135–151.

Senft, Lukáš. 2018. "Věříš prostě v člověka (Karel Čapek jako politický myslitel)." *Tvar*. https://itvar.cz/veris-proste-v-cloveka-karel-capek-jako-politicky-myslitel.

Weiler, Nicholas. 2015. "Speaking a Second Language May Change How You See the World." *Science*, March 17. http://www.sciencemag.org/news/2015/03/speaking-second-language-may-change-how-you-see-world.

Wiredu, Kwasi. 1980. *Philosophy and an African Culture*. Cambridge: Cambridge University Press.

Wiredu, Kwasi. 1987. "The Concept of Mind with Particular Reference to the Language and Thought of the Akans." In *Contemporary Philosophy: A New Survey*, vol. 5: *African Philosophy*, edited by Guttorm Fløistad, 153–180. Dordrecht: Martinus Nijhoff.

Wiredu, Kwasi. 1996. *Cultural Universals and Particulars: An African Perspective*. Bloomington: Indiana University Press.

Wiredu, Kwasi. 1998a. "Toward Decolonizing African Philosophy and Religion." *African Studies Quarterly* 1, no. 4: 17–46.

Wiredu, Kwasi. 1998b. "The Concept of Truth in the Akan Language." In *African Philosophy: An Anthology*, edited by E. C. Eze, 176–180. Malden, MA: Blackwell.

Contributors

Ada Agada is a researcher at the Centre for Leadership Ethics in Africa (CLEA), University of Fort Hare, with specialist interest in African philosophy, metaphysics, philosophy of religion, and intercultural philosophy. He is the author of *Choice*'s Outstanding Academic Title winner *Existence and Consolation: Reinventing Ontology, Gnosis, and Values in African Philosophy* (2015). His latest work is *Consolationism and Comparative African Philosophy: Beyond Universalism and Particularism* (2022).

Carmen De Schryver is an assistant professor of philosophy at Trinity College, Hartford, Connecticut. She specializes in phenomenology, Africana philosophy, and decolonial theory with an emphasis on questions of comparative methodology and canon formation. Her work has appeared in the *Southern Journal of Philosophy* and in *Husserl Studies*.

Patrick Eldridge joined the Department of Humanities and Languages at the University of New Brunswick (Saint John) as an assistant professor of philosophy after completing his PhD at the Higher Institute of Philosophy of KU Leuven. He regularly teaches courses on the history of philosophy and his research primarily concerns phenomenological approaches to memory and time as well as images and aesthetics.

Thabang Dladla was born and raised in Soweto and is a founding member of the Azanian Philosophical Society (APS), a multidisciplinary social sciences and humanities association. A PhD candidate in philosophy at the University of South Africa, he teaches philosophy at the University of Limpopo. His research interests are African philosophy, social and political philosophy, critical race theory, and Black radical historiography.

His published works include "Archie Mafeje and the Question of African Philosophy: A Liberatory Discourse," published in the *South African Journal of Philosophy* in 2017.

Schalk Gerber studied philosophy and theology in South Africa at the Universities of Pretoria and Stellenbosch, in the Netherlands at VU Amsterdam, and in Germany at the Universities of Konstanz and Münster. His PhD thesis is on rethinking the ethical demand in dialogue with Achille Mbembe and Jean-Luc Nancy. His current research focuses on the intersection of philosophy of religion and decolonial thought, including the recent publication "From Dis-Enclosure to Decolonization: In Dialogue with Nancy and Mbembe on Self-Determination and the Other."

Lewis R. Gordon is an American philosopher at the University of Connecticut who works in the areas of Africana philosophy, existentialism, phenomenology, social and political theory, postcolonial thought, theories of race and racism, philosophy of religion, philosophy of education, and philosophies of liberation and aesthetics. He has written particularly extensively on Africana and black existentialism, postcolonial phenomenology, race and racism, and on the works and thought of W. E. B. Du Bois and Frantz Fanon. His most recent book is titled *Fear of Black Consciousness*.

Paulin J. Hountondji is a Beninese French philosopher, politician, and academic considered one of the most important figures in the history of African philosophy. Since the 1970s he has taught at the Université Nationale du Bénin in Cotonou, where he is a professor of philosophy. In the early 1990s he briefly served as minister of education and minister for culture and communications in the government of Benin. His publications include the classics *African Philosophy: Myth and Reality* (1976) and *The Struggle for Meaning: Reflections on Philosophy, Culture and Democracy in Africa* (2002).

M. John Lamola obtained his PhD degree from Edinburgh University and a professional MBA degree from Embry-Riddle Aeronautical University. He is an associate professor in philosophy of technology at the University of Johannesburg. He publishes on Marxian epistemology, Sartre's existential anticolonial philosophy, and on the representation of Africans and their participation in the technologies of the Fourth Industrial Revolution. Professor Lamola's work is published in premier international journals, including the *International Journal of Social Robotics* and *AI and Society*.

His recent book is *Sowing in Tears: A Documentary History of the Church's Struggle against Apartheid, 1960–1990.*

Keolebogile Mbebe is a lecturer in the Department of Philosophy at the University of Pretoria. Her doctoral studies and other areas of research revolve around issues concerning the coloniality of transitional justice jurisprudence, social and political justice, race, the philosophy of emotions, moral philosophy, philosophy of law, and philosophy of history. Mbebe is a founding member of the Azanian Philosophical Society (APS), a multidisciplinary academic association created for the promotion of African philosophy and autonomous African scholarship in the academy.

Achille Mbembe, born in Cameroon, obtained his PhD in history at the Sorbonne in Paris in 1989 and a DEA in political science at the Institut d'études politiques (Paris). He is currently a professor at the University of Witwatersrand and has taught extensively as a visiting professor across the USA. A cofounder of Les Ateliers de la pensée de Dakar and a major figure in the emergence of a new wave of French critical theory, he has written extensively on contemporary politics and philosophy, including *On the Postcolony* (2001), *Critique of Black Reason* (2016), *Necropolitics* (2019), and *Out of the Dark Night: Essays on Decolonization* (2020).

Mabogo Percy More is a former professor of philosophy at the University of the North, University of Durban-Westville, and University of KwaZulu-Natal. He is the 2015 winner of the Frantz Fanon Lifetime Achievement Award and has published widely on Fanon, Sartre, Biko, and Black Consciousness. His latest book publication is *Sartre on Contingency: Anti-Black Racism and Embodiment.*

Rianna Oelofsen is a senior lecturer at the University of Fort Hare, South Africa. She has published a number of articles and book chapters, and coedited a book collection entitled *An African Path to a Global Future.* Areas of specialization and publication include African philosophy, education and decolonization, race and gender theory, phenomenology, and feminism.

Uchenna Okeja is a professor of philosophy at Rhodes University and a research associate at Nelson Mandela University, South Africa. His background is in political philosophy, ethics, and critical theory. His current research focuses on migration, global justice, and deliberative democracy.

His most recent publication is *Deliberative Agency: A Study in Modern African Political Philosophy* (2022).

Abraham Olivier is a professor of philosophy at the University of Fort Hare, visiting professor at the University of Bayreuth, and cofounder and cochair of the Centre for Phenomenology in South Africa. He is the author of *Being in Pain* and editor/coeditor of several special journal issues, for example, *Southern Journal of Philosophy*, *International Journal of Philosophical Studies*, *Journal of the British Society for Phenomenology*, and *Angelaki*. He has published numerous peer-reviewed articles and book chapters on topics relating phenomenology, philosophy of mind, and African philosophy.

Alena Rettová is a professor of African and Afrophone philosophies at the University of Bayreuth, Germany, where she leads an ERC-funded project on Philosophy and Genre: Creating a Textual Basis for African Philosophy. Her books include *African Philosophy: History, Trends, Problems* (2001), *Afrophone Philosophies: Reality and Challenge* (2007), and *Chanter l'existence: La poésie de Sando Marteau et ses horizons philosophiques* (2013).

Justin Sands is a research fellow at the University of the Free State, an extraordinary fellow at North-West University, and deputy head of department and senior lecturer in theology at St. Augustine College of South Africa. Born in the USA, educated at KU Leuven in Belgium, Sands is currently finishing his second PhD in philosophy at the University of Fort Hare. He has published widely across the disciplines of theology, philosophy, and religious studies, as seen in his book, *Reasoning from Faith: Fundamental Theology in Merold Westphal's Philosophy of Religions*. His primary research focus is in hermeneutic phenomenology, where he explores the relationship between theory and praxis, and how this relationship manifests itself within the world.

Tsenay Serequeberhan, born in Eritrea, is a professor at Morgan State University in the USA, and his major publications thus far are *The Hermeneutics of African Philosophy* (1994) and *Existence and Heritage* (2015). His work has a double focus (Continental and Africana philosophy) and is centered on social-political questions and concerns, broadly conceived. He is presently working on a book-length manuscript exploring our postcolonial "effective-history" (Gadamer), to be titled *Thinking the Present*.

Index

www.ingramcontent.com/pod-product-compliance
Lightning Source LLC
Chambersburg PA
CBHW030637270326
41929CB00007B/111